Kaplan
Civil Service
Exams

PUBLISHING

New York

This publication is designed to provide accurate and authoritative information in regard to the subject matter covered. It is sold with the understanding that the publisher is not engaged in rendering legal, accounting, or other professional service. If legal advice or other expert assistance is required, the services of a competent professional should be sought.

Executive Editor: Jennifer Farthing
Editor: Megan Gilbert
Production Editor: Leah Strauss
Interior Design: Michael Warrell, Design Solutions
Typesetter: Virginia Byrne
Cover Designer: Carly Schnur

Published by Kaplan Publishing, a division of Kaplan, Inc.
888 Seventh Ave.
New York, NY 10106

Printed in the United States of America

September 2006
06 07 08   10 9 8 7 6 5 4 3 2

ISBN-13: 978-1-4195-4211-4

Kaplan Publishing books are available at special quantity discounts to use for sales promotions, employee premiums, or educational purposes. Please email our Special Sales Department to order or for more information at kaplanpublishing@kaplan.com, or write to Kaplan Publishing, 1 Liberty Plaza, 24th Floor, New York, NY 10006.

C O N T E N T S

KAPLAN

PART THREE: RESOURCES

HOW TO USE THIS BOOK

No matter which type of civil service exam you plan on taking, this book provides you with up-to-date information, targeted lessons, and plenty of practice questions to hone your skills to do your best on test day. First, this section offers information on the different types of exams—federal, state, municipal—as well as the most common entry-level exams you might encounter when applying for a civil service job. The rest of this book includes the following information:

Part One: The Tests and Test Strategies offers detailed information on how to find civil service jobs. Chapter 1 covers general schedule information, which tells you about the different pay scales for different levels of federal jobs. In this chapter you will also learn about the application process for many civil service jobs. Finally, general trends in federal, state, and municipal employment are reviewed so you can learn more about your future career. Chapter 2 provides a jump-start to earning a top score on any civil service exam by providing you with Kaplan's top score-raising strategies for both paper-based exams and computer-based exams.

Part Two: The Question Types is where you should turn when you need to prepare for your upcoming exam. As the title implies, all the most-tested skills—clerical ability, reading, vocabulary, writing, math, following directions and memory, decision making and reasoning—are covered in detail here. You will not only review lessons in each of these skills, but also learn about the different question types found on most civil service exams. Tips and more score-raising strategies, along with practice questions to test your knowledge and improvement are also found in this section. Altogether, the content in this part of this book will prepare you to get the score you need for the job you want.

Part Three: Resources will be especially helpful in researching your options for employment within the government. A list of jobs and job categories as well as details about benefits and veterans' preference will help you make more informed decisions about your civil service career.

Which Civil Service Test Should I Take?

As you would expect, the civil service test you take depends entirely on what job you are applying for. It also depends on whether you are applying for a federal, state, or municipal job. The following section covers important information about all the different types of exams, as well as details about the most common entry-level exams for those applicants who have not worked in civil service before. Finally, terminology related to applications and testing will be explained throughout.

Federal, State, Municipal Jobs— Federal, State, Municipal Exams

Perhaps you are looking for a job with the federal government. As you will read in Chapter 1, there is a staggering number of job categories and positions. Except for salespeople, the federal government employs a large share of every profession, from janitors, to administrative assistants, to lawyers and accountants. Obviously, the exams for entry into these positions are very different. The only thing that federal civil service exams have in common is that they are generally the same for different job categories. This means that if you are applying to be a clerk with the federal government, you will be taking the same clerical exam whether you are applying for a job in California or New York.

State civil service exams, on the other hand, are different in every state. Typically the state department that is offering the job creates the civil service exams. For example, if you want to be a health administrator for the state, the Department of Health Services (or your state's equivalent) will develop and administer the exam. So, if you are applying for a position in Texas, you are likely to take an exam that is different from someone applying for the same position in Florida. Bear in mind though, that your ranking based on a state exam may not qualify you for employment throughout the entire state. When applying for an exam, make certain that the results will make you eligible to work in the geographical location you want within your state.

On the municipal or local level, the variety of exams is even greater. Depending on whether you are applying to work for the county, city, or other local government, you will face different exams. At this level, exams are developed and administered by the level of government to which you are applying. For example, a county administrative assistant will sit for a different exam than a city administrative assistant. Don't worry about exam content being drastically different—you will soon learn that there are some similarities.

After reading this, you might be wondering how any book can help you prepare for the specific exam you are taking. The good news is that even though every exam varies to some degree, the general skills that are tested remain the same. Variety is expected, but taking a cue from the standards set by federal exams, most state and local governments try to maintain similar exams that test the same basic skills required to succeed in different positions.

Test Content

As we have said, even through the great variety of civil service exams, there are still many skills that are tested regardless of where you take your exam or where you are applying for work. On almost any civil service exam you can expect to be tested on at least a few of the following skills:

- Reading Comprehension
- Writing Ability
- Math
- Decision Making/Reasoning
- Clerical Ability
- Following Directions/Coding/Memory

You should note that the names for some of these skills may vary. For example, reading and writing may be called Verbal Ability—but regardless of the name, the skills tested are more or less the same. Question types within each section will also vary. For example, a math section may test just straight calculations—such as $413 + 766 = ?$—or it may include word problems or questions with graphs or other data. Don't worry, each of these topics as well as explanations of different question types will be discussed in detail in each of the review chapters in Part Two of this book.

Test Format

Almost without exception, civil service exams are in a multiple-choice format. This means that each question will be followed by a set of answer choices. Generally, there is only one correct answer, but you may encounter questions where you are asked to "check all that apply." By far the most common questions will ask you to choose the

Other Test Formats

The multiple-choice civil service test is just one kind of test you may have to take to gain employment with the government. Other types of tests include written tests (such as submitting a writing sample), physical tests (such as those required for most safety and labor positions), practical tests (such as those required for emergency medical technicians) as well as personal surveys (such as the Personal Characteristics and Experience Inventory).

one best, correct answer to each question. Multiple-choice questions typically have either four or five answer choices. This varies depending on the exact exam you take, but to prepare you for either of these situations this book includes questions with four and with five answer choices.

Difficulty Level

Civil service exams, particularly entry-level ones, may have questions at varying levels of difficulty. For example, a lower-level exam may only test mathematic skills up to arithmetic and word problems; a higher level exam may test algebra and even geometry. The same can occur with other skills such as reading (longer, more difficult reading passages on higher-level exams) or reasoning (more complex situations for higher-level exams). These skill levels will be addressed in each of the review chapters so that you have comprehensive preparation for nearly any entry-level civil service exam offered.

Competitive Exams

Competitive exams are exactly what they sound like. When you take your exam, your score will be ranked along with the scores of everyone else who took the same exam. Generally, your score earns you a spot on an eligibility list. Here is how this works. Say 100 people take the same civil service exam. Everyone reaches the minimum passing score, but those who score higher are placed higher on the list. When a job vacancy needs to be filled, only those at the top of the list are hired or make it to the next step. There are cases where the exam is just the first step in the application process. Your score on the exam may only qualify you for the next round of the application process. Interviews, personal histories, and additional exams are often part of the hiring process and you will need to complete those successfully to eventually be hired. Although a top score does not guarantee you will be hired, it is very important that you score as high as you can on any competitive exam to increase your chances of getting the job you want. (To learn more about the eligibility list and exam scoring, see Chapter 2.)

Open Competitive Exams

For this type of exam, the terminology varies—they may also be called **general or public competitive exams**—but you should know that **open competitive exams** are those that are open to the public. In other words, you do not have to have any previous civil service experience to take these exams. However, if you do have civil service experience and this exam is for an altogether different job from the one you have now, you are usually still eligible to take it. You might even get preference for having previous government employment experience.

Noncompetitive Exams

There are cases where the exam you take will not place you on an eligibility list. Instead, anyone receiving a passing score will be eligible for the job, hence the name **noncompetitive exams**. Test-takers who pass may simply be listed alphabetically (not ranked by score) and each person will be one step further along in the application process.

Noncompetitive Employment

Noncompetitive employment, in general, works most like the private sector. Applicants meeting the basic application requirements earn the job without ever having to take an exam. Situations where no civil service exam is required to earn a job occur most when the nature or level of the job does not require testing. In these cases a certain level of education or other particular qualifications are enough to be considered for a job. For example, a lawyer applying for a job opening is not required to take a civil service test as he or she has already earned a specific degree making him or her eligible for employment.

Noncompetitive Appointment

Noncompetitive appointment occurs when applicants with special preference are appointed to a certain job. This includes former government employees, veterans, and applicants with disabilities. The considerations vary on the federal, state, and municipal level, but these conditions could exempt you from taking a civil service exam if you meet the other qualifications or requirements for the job. If you have any questions about noncompetitive appointment, contact the department to which you are applying.

Continuous Recruitment

Some states and local governments use what they call **continuous recruitment**. Regardless of whether there are actual job vacancies, exams are given on a regular basis to establish an up-to-date list of eligible applicants. Exams may be given as often as once a month or as little as twice per year. When you are researching jobs and exams, be aware that you can take these exams knowing that positions are likely to become available more often even if one is not available at the moment.

Promotional Exams

Only those employees who already work for the government are eligible for **promotional exams**. If you have never worked for the government before, you do not need to know any more about these right now. However, once you are employed with the government, and after you have worked for some time on your job, you may be eligible to earn a higher position in your field. Keep an eye out for upcoming promotional exams that may become available to you.

The Most Common Entry-Level Competitive Tests

You already read about the most commonly tested skills. Here is how each of those skills finds its way into entry-level civil service exams. Pay close attention as these entry-level exams are the focus of this book.

Administrative

At entry level, administrative positions are usually limited to administrative assistants and other office support positions. As you would expect, strong communication skills are critical to succeed in these types of jobs. Civil service exams for these positions may or may not test basic math, but you can definitely expect to see questions that test your knowledge of clear written expression, vocabulary, grammar, spelling, and reading comprehension. In addition, other skills such as decision making and reasoning may be tested. To be in top form to answer any questions that test these skills, pay particular attention to Chapters 4, 5, and 8, although other chapters will also be of use before test day.

Investigative

The word *investigative* may conjure up thoughts of private investigators or police detectives. Although some law enforcement positions are considered investigative, the kinds of investigative positions discussed here are not. Data collectors, compliance officers, and claims investigators are just a few job descriptions that fit into this category. A broad range of skills are required for these jobs so you will need to focus on most of the review chapters in this book in order to succeed on exams for investigative jobs. In addition to basic reading, writing, and math skills, you can expect to be tested on decision making and reasoning, following directions, and memory.

Clerical

Clerical jobs are especially detail oriented. Clerical positions include clerks, stenographers, typists, telephone/switchboard operators, and other data support positions. Regardless of the job title, clerical employees must be able to recognize, file, organize, and retrieve data and other records quickly and accurately. As a result there is a heavy focus on these skills on any civil service exam for clerical positions. Typing tests are usually given separately, but the civil service exam will usually test memory and coding, alphabetization, filing, records management, and other administrative practices. The way in which these skills are tested almost always measure your speed and accuracy. Expect several sections with strict time limits. You may not be expected to answer every question and guessing penalties (see Chapter 2) will often be applied to these sections. Keeping your focus and maintaining accuracy and speed will be crucial for success on these sections. A detailed discussion of these skills and question types appears in Chapter 3.

Personal Characteristics and Experience Inventory Questions

There is an increasing trend in civil service testing that includes a sort of personal survey. Imagine multiple-choice questions that do not have correct answers. These questions, which cover your work personality (do you work best on your own?), work preferences (do you prefer a flexible schedule?), and experience (do you have experience with managing other employees?), do not have "correct" answers. You should not try to study for this section or to guess what your employer wants you to say—honesty in your answers is the only way to go when answering these questions. If you want to learn more about how this section works, refer to Chapter 9.

Other Common Tests

Knowing that there are as many exams as there are jobs, you are probably not surprised that there are other civil service exams besides administrative, investigative, and clerical exams. This section covers the basics of these jobs and job categories.

Labor/Mechanical

Although these types of jobs do not require any administrative skills (reading comprehension, writing, clerical ability), they do require a certain level of mechanical aptitude, basic reasoning, and basic arithmetic. Chapters 6 and 8 of this book are a good introduction to some of these skills. It is important to note that some labor positions may not require an exam at all. Read the job announcements carefully to know exactly what the basic requirements for employment are.

Law Enforcement

When you consider that every police officer, corrections officer, highway patrol officer, detective, sergeant, inspector, and warden (to name just a few) in the United States must pass an exam for employment or promotion, you realize these are very common exams. Exams do vary depending on whether you are applying for a federal, state, or local position, but you can expect to be tested on reading comprehension, written expression, judgment and reasoning, memory and observation, and visualization.

Emergency Medical Technicians (EMT)

EMTs and paramedics are definitely in high demand in the realm of civil service. Although many state and local governments use the National Registry of Emergency Medical Technicians written and practical exams for certification, some opt to use their own civil service exams. When applying you should find out what exam you will be taking when applying to become an EMT or paramedic. If you are taking the NREMT, subjects will include such medical topics as: cardiology, breathing, trauma, pediatrics, and operations.

Firefighter

You may not automatically think "civil service" when you think of firefighters, but you would be wrong. There is no national (federal) firefighter exam, but many different cities and counties use a similar exam that tests reading, writing, basic math, memorization, visualization/orientation, mechanical aptitude, and reasoning.

Summary

Hopefully you have learned some useful information about taking civil service exams and about what you are likely to face on test day. For now, you have made a great start in learning about the types of jobs and exams that are available.

The Resources section at the end of this book offers even more information about the different types of jobs and job categories in federal, state, and local government. If you have not decided on a career path yet, this is a good place to browse for the wide variety of options available. The Resources section also includes something important to any job seeker: salary and benefits. Veterans should be especially interested in this section as it includes information about the unique opportunities and advantages when applying for a civil service job.

For now, your next step is to learn even more about the application process in Chapter 1. There you will also learn about some of today's fastest-growing government job markets. For the best skills review, start with Chapter 3: Clerical Ability. If your exam does not test these skills you can move straight to Chapter 4: Verbal Ability—Reading and Vocabulary. Remember, not every skill covered in this book is found on every civil service exam. It's best to review what you will be tested on and to focus on skills you feel you need help with.

Remember, reading this book is a great beginning to your future. Good luck with your new career in civil service!

PART ONE

The Tests
and
Test Strategies

1

Qualifications, Requirements, and Applications

In addition to preparing for your civil service exams, finding job announcements, deciding which ones are right for you, and assembling the necessary application materials requires a good deal of time and attention to detail. This chapter will help you navigate through the application process and provide information on some of the forms you will have to complete to be considered for certain jobs.

How to Look for Job Announcements

The federal government maintains a website called USAJOBS that lists all federal job openings. Check out www.usajobs.gov for listing, applications, and other vital information about civil service employment. If you are specifically looking for jobs within the U.S. Postal Service, you will find job announcements in the following locations:

1. On public and employee bulletin boards in your local post office
2. On public bulletin boards in post office buildings accepting applications
3. At federal job information centers
4. In state employment offices
5. On public bulletin boards in local, federal, state, and municipal buildings

You will also find job announcements on public bulletin boards or newsletters provided by:

1. Colleges and universities
2. Veterans' organizations
3. Community service organizations
4. Community newspapers
5. Women's and minority associations

Announcements will vary from job to job, but what follows is a sample announcement so you can get familiarized with the kind of information they contain. Unlike this sample, each job opening will contain an announcement number that will play an important role in your application process.

Administrative Assistant

Department(s): Agriculture, Forest Service, Homeland Security, Federal Emergency Management Agency (FEMA), Agriculture, Animal and Plant Health Inspection Service, Justice, US Marshals Service, Army Materiel Command, Headquarters

Agency: Social Security Administration

Description/Duties: The Administrative Assistant serves as the District Manager's confidential assistant for labor relations and personnel matters as well as aspects of budget execution, personnel administration, procurement and supply, contract administration, travel, payroll services, payroll services, reports management, facility management, etc. Provides administrative support for the staff and routinely trains other employees and subordinate office employees in administrative and other assigned (e.g. LAN) systems. Provides technical, operational or systems administration support to the office.

The Application Process

You may apply for most civil service jobs with a resume or an Optional Application for Federal Employment (OF-612), or any other written format you choose, as long as it contains the information required by the job announcement. It is essential that you follow the application instructions in the vacancy announcement to which you are applying. If your resume or application does not provide all the information requested in the job vacancy announcement, you may lose consideration for a job. Help speed the selection process by keeping your resume or application brief and by sending only the requested material.

You can obtain the OF-612 from www.usajobs.gov. When filling out your application materials, type or print clearly in dark ink. You must have an original signature and current date on any application form. Don't leave any lines blank.

Entire applications may be thrown out if any questions are left unanswered. If you don't know how to answer, respond by writing "N/A" or "not applicable."

KSAs

KSA is an acronym for "Knowledge, Skills, Ability"—three criteria that government agencies use to determine whether job applicants will be competent employees. Generally, there are four to six standard KSAs per vacancy announcement, many of which repeat from one announcement to the next. For instance, if you're applying to seven different positions as a financial consultant, it's likely that the vacancy announcements will be very similar. You'll be able to save time by copying your KSAs almost verbatim from one application to the next.

Agencies Requiring Special Forms

Some agencies require forms other than a resume or OF-612, some of which are listed below. You can find these forms on the same website you found the OF-612.

- Department of Homeland Security I-9, Employment Eligibility Verification Form.
- Department of Veterans Affairs, Application for Associated Health Occupations (VA Form 10-2850c).
- Department of Veterans Affairs, Application for Physicians, Dentists, Podiatrists, Optometrists and Chiropractors.
- Department of Veterans Affairs, Application for Nurses and Nurse Anesthetists.
- Defense Logistics Agency and the Defense Contract Management Agency's Automated Staffing Program (ASP). This automated process interfaces with a commercial package called Resumix that is deployed throughout the Department of Defense. Resumix produces a computer-scannable resume analyzed by a computer. When entering your resume, be sure to echo the language used in the job announcement.
- Human Resource Services Center, Civilian Job Kit. Servicing the Office of the Secretary of Defense, Defense Agencies, and Department of Defense Field Activities, this job kit contains all the information needed to successfully complete a resume and apply for employment with the Department of Defense.
- Citizenship and Immigration Services Applicant Survey (G-942). This form is required when applying for jobs at the Department of Homeland Security and US Citizenship and Immigration Services.
- Department of the Interior Applicant Background Survey form (DI-1935 B). This form is required when applying for jobs at the Department of the Interior, including the National Park Service, Bureau of Indian Affairs, Bureau of Land Management, and Bureau of Reclamation.

Figuring out what forms to include for your application packet and filling them out correctly and completely takes a bit of organization and time. Once you are finished, check the job announcement for specific information about where to send your application materials.

Be careful not to pin all your hopes on one job; remember, the more jobs you apply for, the greater your chances are to gain employment in civil service. Federal jobs are highly competitive, and, chances are, you will not get the first job you are interested in, even though you may be qualified and have filled out your application materials correctly. Keep trying! Stay on top of your application process, and keep up with the job announcements. Now that we've reviewed the application process, let's look at some general trends in the civil service arena.

General Trends in Civil Service Employment

You may be wondering why civil service jobs are in such high demand. One word: stability. Although fluctuations in government spending can affect the civil service job market, a higher level of job security is available, especially if you work for the federal government. In fact, the federal government is the largest employer in the United States.

Federal Government Employment

Of the three branches of government—legislative, judicial, and executive—the executive branch employs nearly all of the 2 million civil servants working for the federal government.

The executive branch has a total of 15 departments. These departments, along with a simplified description of their responsibilities, follow:

1. Agriculture, which oversees antihunger programs and works to improve agriculture and its interests.
2. Commerce, which handles patents and the census, and helps to increase economic growth.
3. Defense, which manages the armed forces.
4. Education, which supports schools and other educational institutions.
5. Energy, which manages energy resources.
6. Health and Human Services, which conducts research and manages social service.
7. Homeland Security, which aims to protect the country and handles immigration.
8. Housing and Urban Development, which oversees issues relating to public housing and housing laws.
9. Interior, which runs national parks and manages conservation programs.
10. Justice, which promotes public safety by preventing crime.
11. Labor, which oversees issues relating to the workplace and gathers data for the Bureau of Labor Statistics.

12. State, which runs consulates and embassies and issues passports.

13. Transportation, which plans and constructs roads and other infrastructure.

14. Treasury, which collects taxes, prints money, and oversees banks.

15. Veterans Affairs, which is designed to assist veterans and their families.

Working for the U.S. Postal Service

Postal Workers are a special type of civil service employee with a special exam required for all applicants. The Postal Worker Exam, also known as Exam 473, tests memory, accuracy, speed, and attention to detail.

Before you sign up to take this exam, you should know that even though the USPS has over 600,000 employees, job opportunities within the USPS are actually expected to decline overall as a result of increased automation. However, employees leaving the workforce will need to be replaced, so you can still expect job openings with the postal service. All of these factors make getting a job with the USPS extremely competitive so be prepared when you take your exam. If you would like to know more about this exam, take a look at Kaplan's Postal Worker Exam.

According to the Bureau of Labor Statistics (BLS), the departments of Defense, Veterans Affairs, and Homeland Security are the three largest employers among all executive branch departments. The BLS also reports that the three largest occupational groups are from the following job categories:

- Professional and related (including scientists, engineers, lawyers, and computer scientists)
- Management, business, and financial (including managers, legislators, and accountants)
- Office and administrative support (including clerks and administrative assistants)

The smallest occupational group is farming, fishing, and forestry, with just 0.2 percent of all jobs.

Although growth is expected overall for federal jobs, growth is limited to certain types of jobs. Security, management, and computer jobs are all expected to increase. However, several job categories are expected to decline over the next few years, specifically office and administrative support positions. That is not to say there are no jobs available, but with increased automation, some jobs are being eliminated.

State and Municipal Employment

Perhaps you are more interested in working for your state or local government. It might surprise you to know that local government has twice the number of employees as the state government. And together, state and local governments employ nearly 8 million people. You might want to check openings in your local government first as you will find many of the same jobs.

According to the BLS, by far the largest occupational group is service. This group includes correctional officers, firefighters, home health aides, police, janitorial staff, and recreation and landscaping workers. Specifically, the largest growth through 2014 in state and local government is expected to be for lawyers, emergency medical technicians (EMTs), firefighters, and computer specialists. That said, growth is also expected in several other occupations, including social work, clerical, and law enforcement (see sidebar on the following page).

Summary

In the beginning of this chapter you learned about how to look for a job and most important, how the job application process works. As you are looking for a job, you should refer back to this chapter often to ensure that you understand each of the steps that will lead you closer to being hired. You can also consult the General Schedule Information provided so you know the pay range of the job you are applying for.

Knowing the general trends of government employment will also help you determine a career path that will offer you success and stability. This information hopefully allows you to make an informed decision about which level—federal, state, or local—you want to work in.

All of this knowledge puts you closer to starting your new government career, but you cannot forget about the exam. In the next chapter, Kaplan provides the best score-raising strategies for any civil service exam.

Working in Law Enforcement

Corrections officer, police officer, inspector, highway patrol…what do they all have in common? They are all civil service jobs and they are all expected by the BLS to have a large growth through 2014. Although a large number of these jobs are available on a state and municipal level, the federal government also employs a significant amount of "protective service" employees. With job growth remaining steady for these types of jobs, competition will be keen. To learn more about the specific tests required to apply for law enforcement jobs, go to ***www.kaptest.com.***

KAPLAN

CHAPTER TWO

Kaplan's Score-Raising Strategies

General Test Information and Strategies

As you know, there are as many different civil service tests as there are jobs. However, regardless of which test you take there are always some strategies you can apply to earn a higher score. This chapter not only provides general information about civil service exams, but also Kaplan's top general test-taking strategies.

Know How the Test Is Scored

When you receive your exam handbook, assuming one is provided, be sure to read about how the exam is scored. For example: Is each question worth one point? Is your score calculated on a scale? What is a passing score? How are your scores used? Will points be deducted for incorrect answers? What follows are some of the major scoring issues you should be aware of before you take any exam.

Raw vs. Scaled Scores. Generally speaking, the total number of questions you answer correctly is your raw score. So, if you take a test with 100 questions worth one point each and answer 70 of them correctly, you receive a raw score of 70. Coincidentally, you have also received a 70 percent, since you answered 70 out of 100 questions correctly.

But what if you take a test with 37 questions worth one point each—how will your score be converted to a percentage? In these cases, a scaled score is calculated. Test developers create a mathematical formula for calculating a scaled score so that every test taker's score can be more easily compared. You are not likely to be told the exact way in which your scaled score is calculated, but it is always found using your raw score. And of course, the higher your raw score, the higher your scaled score.

Eligibility List Ranking.   If you read "How to Use this Book" you know that your score on an exam can affect your position or rank on an eligibility list. Typically, your scaled score will be used to rank you against everyone else who took that particular exam and only those who scored highest will have the first opportunity to continue the application process and possibly get the job. Clearly, every single point matters so take the exam scoring process very seriously when preparing for and taking any civil service exam.

Passing Scores.   Whether your exam results earn you a spot on an eligibility list or whether they automatically earn you a job, generally a passing score is set by the department offering the exam. A general standard for passing scores is 70 percent, but you should always read your test information carefully for specific information on what is considered a passing score or what scores are needed to achieve a ranking that is likely to increase your chances of getting off the list and into a job. Although earning a passing score puts you in contention, it is always better to achieve as high a score as you can.

Guessing Penalty.   Before you take your civil service test, find out if any part of the test you take has a guessing penalty. A guessing penalty, usually a fraction of a point deducted for every incorrect answer, is designed to discourage random guessing to complete an exam, especially when speed and accuracy are being tested. If no points are deducted for incorrect answers, ALWAYS GUESS if you do not know the answer. On multiple-choice questions there is a chance that you could guess the correct answer and that could mean more points toward your final score.

If any part of your test does have a guessing penalty, you should still guess… carefully. Begin by eliminating choices that are absolutely wrong. Using the process of elimination, continue to eliminate choices that don't seem to be correct. If you can narrow the possible choices down to two, your chances of guessing the correct answer increase dramatically. That said, if you are being tested on speed and accuracy, do not spend much time eliminating possible incorrect answers. Pace yourself so that you can answer as many questions as you can without losing valuable points for incorrect answers.

Pencil and Paper Strategies

Believe it or not, written tests provide their own opportunities for scoring more points. Here are the two best strategies for increasing your score on a paper-and-pencil exam.

Answer Easy Questions First.   This strategy may seem obvious, but it is often underused. On paper tests you usually have the freedom to skip around to different questions (be careful not to skip to a different section of the exam if you are instructed not to do so!). Rather than answer all the questions in order, find those that seem easy to you and answer them first. Not only will your confidence increase, but you will have earned another point toward your final score. On most exams, every question is worth the same point value. Do not spend time trying to answer a difficult question if there is an easier one worth the same amount. Remember, you are trying to earn as many points as you can to bring you one step closer to the civil service job you want.

Answer Sheet Strategies.   This may sound simple, but it is extremely important: Do not make mistakes filling out your answer sheet. When time is short, it is easy to get confused going back and forth between your test book and your answer sheet. If you know the answer but fill in the wrong bubble, you won't get the point. To avoid mistakes on the answer sheet, try some of these methods:

- **Circle the Questions You Skip:** Perhaps the most common exam disaster is filling in all of the right answers—in all the wrong places. If you are allowed to write in the test booklet, put a big circle around any question numbers you skip to help you locate these questions when you are ready to go back to them. Also, if you accidentally skip a line on the answer sheet, you can always check it against your test booklet to see where you went wrong.
- **Circle Your Answers in Your Test Booklet:** If you are permitted to write in the test booklet, circling your answers makes it easier to check your answer sheet against your booklet. It also makes the next strategy possible.
- **Fill in Five or More Answers at Once:** Time is of the essence on any exam. To save time and ensure accuracy when marking your answers on the answer sheet, transfer your answers after every five questions rather than after every question. That way, you won't keep breaking your concentration to mark the answer sheet. You will end up with more time and less chances to make a mistake.

Find the Right Pace

Throughout the exam, you should keep track of time. You need to work quickly, but not so fast that you are making careless errors and losing valuable points. Ideally, having a few minutes at the end of the exam to look over your answers is helpful. However, it is more important that you answer as many questions correctly as possible. The exam proctor will usually announce how much time is remaining. If not, wear a watch so you know that when half the time has passed you should have completed roughly half the exam.

You also need to be careful at the end of a section when time may be running out. You don't want to have your answers in the test booklet and not be able to transfer them to the answer sheet because you have run out of time. If there are just two minutes left, and you still have a few questions to answer, you should start transferring your answers one by one to ensure that every question you answered earns credit.

Computer-Adaptive Strategies

Although the majority of civil service tests are paper-and-pencil, you may face a civil service exam that is a computer-adaptive test (CAT). Your job announcement will provide all the details about this type of exam and how it works, but for your convenience here is a brief description of a CAT test.

Here is how a CAT test works. There is a large pool of potential questions ranging from moderately easy to very difficult. To start, you are given a question of moderate difficulty. If you get it right, the computer will give you a harder question next. If you get it wrong, the computer will give you an easier question next. In other words, the computer scores each question and then uses that information—along with your previous responses and the requirements of the test design—to determine which question to present next. The process continues throughout, and the computer will be able to accurately assess your ability level.

If you keep getting questions right, the test will get harder and harder; if you make some mistakes, it will adjust and start giving you easier problems. But if you begin to answer the easier problems correctly, the test will go back to the difficult ones.

Ideally, you are given enough questions to ensure that scores are not based on luck. If you get one hard question right, you might just have been lucky, but if you get ten hard questions right, then luck has little to do with it. So the test is self-adjusting and self-correcting.

You will see only one question at a time. Because the computer must score a question before providing you a new one, you will be required to answer every question. For this reason, too, once you have confirmed your response and moved on to the next question, you will not be able to return to a question. The computer has already scored your response and has selected a new question for you.

On a CAT, random guessing can significantly lower your scores. So if you don't know the answer to a question, just eliminate whatever answer choices you can and then select the answer you think is best.

Another major consequence of the CAT format is that hard questions are worth more than easy ones. It has to be this way, because the very purpose of this adaptive format is to find out at what level you reliably get about half the questions right; that is your scoring level.

Imagine two students—one who answers 10 basic questions, half of which she gets right and half of which she gets wrong, and one who answers 10 very hard questions, half of which she gets right and half of which she gets wrong. The same number of questions have been answered correctly in each case, but this does not reflect an equal ability on the part of the two students.

In fact, the student who got 5 out of 10 hard questions wrong could still get a very high score. But in order to get to these tough questions, she first had to get medium-difficulty questions right. So, you definitely want to get to the hard questions if you can, because that means your score will be higher.

Finally, and perhaps most importantly, you do not need to have a lot of computer experience to take this kind of test. Even basic computer skills will allow you to complete the exam with no problem. Additionally, tutorials are offered before the exam so that you can familiarize yourself with exactly how to use the computer to take the test.

Skill-Specific Strategies

Now that you have mastered the general test strategies, you are ready for some more specific score-raising strategies. The following strategies will help you earn crucial points when answering reading and math questions. Remember though, each of the review chapters in this book has even more strategies that are specific to the different question types you may encounter on test day. Start by reviewing these first.

Answer What Is Being Asked

You might wonder what is so strategic about answering a question. This strategy relies on details. Often, under the stress of test conditions, what you think you are being asked and what you are actually being asked are two different things. Consider the following question:

A certain pump can drain a full 375-gallon tank in 15 minutes. At this rate, how many more minutes would it take to drain a full 600-gallon tank?

    (A) 9
    (B) 15
    (C) 18
    (D) 24
    (E) 25

If you read the question too quickly and found the answer was (D), you would have just missed out on a valuable point. The correct answer is actually (A). Here is how you might have missed it.

You are given that a pump can drain a 375-gallon tank in 15 minutes. Therefore, the rate of the pump is 375 gallons\15 minutes, or 25 gallons per minute. At this rate, the pump will drain a 600-gallon tank in 600\25, or 24 minutes.

To get the correct answer, you have to know exactly what the question is asking. It is not asking how many minutes it would take to drain a full 600-gallon tank. The question asks, how many *more* minutes would it take to drain a full 600-gallon tank. This question requires you to take one more step with your calculations by subtracting 15 from 24. It will take 24 − 15, or *9 more minutes* to drain the 600-gallon tank, making (A) the correct answer.

It can be very easy to gloss over the details of a question when you have a limited amount of time. You will not earn extra points for how quickly you find the correct answer; the only way to earn points is to answer exactly what is being asked. Take a little extra time to review a question or your answer before you move on to the next. Do not sacrifice accuracy for speed when completing your civil service exam.

Prediction/Prephrasing

Prediction and prephrasing essentially mean the same thing: to guess what the answer to a question might be. But if the answer choices are right there for you to read, you might be wondering how this strategy will help you. Sometimes, and most often with reading comprehension questions, the answer choices may be very similar. In fact, there may be more than one answer choice that works, but the correct one is the one that *best* answers the question. Reading through the answer choices, you could easily become confused as to which one really is the best answer. You can avoid this by covering up the answer choices as you read the question. Then, you can predict or prephrase what you think the answer is. Now your task becomes finding the answer choice that most closely matches your prediction.

If you are asked to make an inference about a reading passage, it is best not to use this strategy. You will learn even more about this strategy in other chapters, but for now, understand it can be an important way to earn extra points on test day.

Math: Picking Numbers and Backsolving

Sometimes you get stuck on a math question just because it is too general or abstract. A good solution to this problem is to substitute particular numbers for the equation variables; this strategy is called **picking numbers**.

A good scenario for picking numbers is when the answer choices to percent problems are all percents. Look at the following example.

From 1985 to 1990, the document production of office x increased by 20 percent. From 1990 to 1995, the document production increased by 30 percent. What was the percent increase in the document production in the office over the entire ten-year period from 1985–1995?

    (A) 10%
    (B) 25%
    (C) 50%
    (D) 56%
    (E) 60%

Rather than attempting to solve this problem in the abstract, choose a number for the document production in 1985 and see what happens. There is no need to pick a realistic number. You are better off picking a number that is easy to work with. In percent problems, the number that is easiest to work with is almost always 100.

Now that you have a number, plug it into the problem. The document production from this office in 1985 was 100. What would the 1990 document production be? Twenty percent more than 100 is 120. Now, if 1990's document production was 120, what would the number of documents in 1995 be? What is 30 percent more than 120?

Be careful. Do not just add 30 to 120. You need to find 30 percent of 120 and add that number on.

Thirty percent of 120 is $(0.30)(120) = 36$. Add 36 to 120, and you get 156 documents in 1995. What percent greater is 156 than 100? It is a 56 percent increase. The answer is (D).

Another ideal scenario for picking numbers is when the answer choices to a word problem are algebraic expressions.

If n computers cost p dollars, then how many dollars would q computers cost?

(A) $\dfrac{np}{q}$

(B) $\dfrac{nq}{p}$

(C) $\dfrac{pq}{n}$

(D) $\dfrac{n}{pq}$

(E) $\dfrac{p}{nq}$

The difficult thing about this question is it uses variables instead of numbers. Picking numbers will help make it more real. First, pick numbers that are easy to work with. For example, $n = 2$, $p = 4$, and $q = 3$. The question then becomes: "If two computers cost \$4.00, how many dollars would three computers cost?" The answer is \$6.00. When $n = 2$, $p = 4$, and $q = 3$, the correct answer should equal 6. Plug those values into the answer choices and see which ones yield 6:

(A) $\dfrac{np}{q} = \dfrac{(2)(4)}{3} = \dfrac{8}{3}$

(B) $\dfrac{nq}{p} = \dfrac{(2)(3)}{4} = \dfrac{6}{4} = \dfrac{3}{2} = 1\dfrac{1}{2}$

(C) $\dfrac{pq}{n} = \dfrac{(4)(3)}{2} = \dfrac{12}{2} = 6$

(D) $\dfrac{n}{pq} = \dfrac{2}{(4)(3)} = \dfrac{2}{12} = \dfrac{1}{6}$

(E) $\dfrac{p}{nq} = \dfrac{4}{(2)(3)} = \dfrac{4}{6} = \dfrac{2}{3}$

Choice (C) is the only one that yields 6, so it must be the correct answer.

When picking numbers for an abstract word problem like this one, try all the answer choices. Sometimes more than one choice will yield the correct result. When that happens, pick another set of numbers to eliminate the coincidences. *Avoid picking 0 and 1*. These often give several *possibly correct* answers.

Sometimes it is not possible simply to pick numbers and solve the problem. In these cases, the answer choices become your tools, and you can work backward to find the right choice. This is **backsolving**, which essentially means plugging the choices back into the question until you find the one that fits.

Backsolving works best when:

■ The question is a complex word problem, and the answer choices are numbers

■ The alternative is setting up multiple algebraic equations

Backsolving is not ideal:

■ If the answer choices include variables

■ On algebra questions or word problems that have complex answer choices, such as radicals and fractions (plugging them in takes too much time)

Here is one example where backsolving works well.

A social welfare program draws 27 members. If there are seven more males than females in the program, how many members are male?

    (A) 8

    (B) 10

    (C) 14

    (D) 17

    (E) 20

The five answer choices represent the possible number of males in the program, so try them in the question stem. The choice that gives a total of 27 members, with seven more males than females, will be the correct answer.

Often, answer choices are arranged in ascending (least to greatest) or descending (greatest to least) order. If this is the case, start with choice (C) when backsolving. For example, plugging in (C) gives you 14 males in the program. Because there are seven more males than females, there are seven females in the club. But $14 + 7 < 27$. The sum is too small, so there must be more than 14 males; thus, you can eliminate answer choices (A), (B), and (C) just like that.

Either (D) or (E) will be correct. Plugging in (D) gives you 17 males in the program; 17 − 7 equals 10 singers, and 17 + 10 = 27 members total. Choice (D) is correct.

Calculators

When math questions are found on your civil service exam, you should find out if you are able to use a calculator during the exam. If calculators are permitted, here is some of the information you should know before and during the test.

Know What Kind of Calculator You Can Use

The department that administers your civil service exam should inform applicants if they are allowed to use calculators and if so, exactly which kind of calculators are allowed. For most civil service exams, you only need a basic function calculator. Scientific calculators and graphing calculators have more functions than you will need for the exam, but if you are comfortable using them, you can feel free to use them on test day. In short, bring a calculator you are already familiar with on test day.

What Is Not Allowed

As a rule, laptops, minicomputers, or machines that print, make noise, need to be plugged in, or calculators with a typewriter keypad or an angled readout screen are not permitted. There is a chance that scientific and graphing calculators may also be forbidden. To avoid any problems on test day, find out specifically what you are allowed to bring or if calculators are provided when you take your civil service exam.

Using Your Calculator during the Test

Here are some tips for using your calculator strategically during the test.

Don't Forget PEMDAS.   It won't help to start punching numbers into your calculator as soon as you read a problem. You will learn about the all-important Order of Operations in Chapter 6, but know that even when using a calculator, you must first solve the math in parenthesis (P), then exponents (E), then multiplication (M) and division (D), and finally addition (A) and subtraction (S). Before you turn to your calculator, know what you are doing, and what you are looking for.

Don't Use Your Calculator Too Often.   You will not need your calculator for every question. Remember, you are being tested on your math skills, not your calculator skills. The calculator is just a tool. Use it wisely and sparingly.

Don't Forget to Check Your Work.   You cannot assume the number the calculator says is absolutely correct. Test stress can cause careless mistakes so even though you meant to enter "+20" you may have only entered "+2." Making brief notes of what you enter into the calculator can help you spot places where you may have made an error. Don't lose time solving everything twice, but if there are any answers you are unsure about, go back and test them again.

Managing Stress

The countdown has begun. Your test date is looming. Anxiety is on the rise. Maybe you think you won't be ready. Maybe you already know what you need to, but you are going into panic mode anyway.

Remain calm. It is possible to minimize anxiety and stress—before and during the test. Remember, some stress is normal and good. Anxiety is a motivation to study. The adrenaline that gets pumped into your bloodstream when you are stressed helps you stay alert and think more clearly. But if you feel that the tension is so great that it's preventing you from using your study time effectively, here are some things you can do to get it under control.

Take Control

Lack of control is a prime cause of stress. Research shows that if you don't have a sense of control over what is happening in your life, you can easily end up feeling helpless and hopeless. Try to identify the sources of the stress you feel. Which ones of these can you do something about? Can you find ways to reduce the stress you are feeling about any of these sources?

Focus on Your Strengths

Make a list of areas of strength you have that will help you do well on the test. We all have strengths and recognizing your own will help build and maintain your confidence. You will be able to draw on your confidence as you need it, helping you solve difficult questions and keep test stress and anxiety at a distance. And every time you recognize a new area of strength, solve a challenging problem, or score well on a practice test, you will increase your confidence.

Imagine Yourself Succeeding

Close your eyes and imagine yourself in a relaxing situation. Breathe easily and naturally. Now, think of a real-life situation in which you did well on an assignment or other task. Focus on this success. Now turn your thoughts to your exam and keep your thoughts and feelings in line with that successful experience. Do not make comparisons between them; just imagine yourself taking the upcoming test with the same feelings of confidence and relaxed control.

Set Realistic Goals

Facing your problem areas gives you some distinct advantages. What do you want to accomplish in the time remaining? Make a list of realistic goals. You can't help feeling more confident when you know you are actively improving your chances of earning a higher test score.

Exercise Your Frustrations Away

Whether it's jogging, biking, pushups, or a pickup basketball game, physical exercise will stimulate your mind and body, and improve your ability to think and concentrate. A surprising number of students fall out of the habit of regular exercise, ironically because they are spending so much time prepping for exams. A little physical exertion will help you to keep your mind and body in sync and sleep better at night.

Eat Well

Good nutrition will help you focus and think clearly. Eat plenty of fruits and vegetables, low-fat protein such as fish, skinless poultry, beans, and legumes, and whole grains such as brown rice, whole wheat bread, and pastas. Don't eat a lot of sugar and high-fat snacks, or salty foods.

Keep Breathing

Conscious attention to breathing is an excellent way to manage stress while you are taking the test. Most of the people who get into trouble during tests take shallow breaths. They breathe using only their upper chests and shoulder muscles, and may even hold their breath for long periods of time. Conversely, those test takers who breathe deeply in a slow, relaxed manner are likely to be in better control during the session.

Stretch

If you find yourself getting spaced out or burned out as you are studying or taking the test, stop for a brief moment and stretch. Even though you will be pausing for a moment, it is a moment well spent. Stretching will help to refresh you and refocus your thoughts.

Preparing for Test Day

Is it starting to feel like your career is dependent on this civil service exam? You have known about it since the job announcement and have completed a lot of solid test preparation. As test day gets closer, you may find your anxiety is on the rise. Don't worry—after using this book to prepare, you will be in good shape. To calm any additional fears you may have, here are a few strategies for the couple of days before and after the test.

The Week before Test Day

In the week or so leading up to the test, you should do the following:

- Visit the testing center if you can. Sometimes seeing the actual room where your test will be administered and taking notice of little things—such as the kind of desk you will be working on, whether the room is likely to be hot or cold, etcetera—may help to calm your nerves. And if you have never been to the test center, visiting beforehand is a good way to ensure that you don't get lost on your way there the day of the test. Remember, you must be on time—if you are late you may not be able to take the exam.
- Practice working on test material at the same time of day that your test is scheduled for, as if it were the actual test day.
- Time yourself accurately. If you have two hours to complete the actual exam, don't allow yourself extra time as you are working through practice questions. Remember to find the right pace where you are able to work quickly without sacrificing accuracy.
- Evaluate thoroughly what your strengths and weaknesses are. If math is no problem for you, focus your remaining study time on subjects that still need improvement. Do not completely neglect your strong areas, though; after all, this is where you will rack up most of your points.

The Day before the Test

Try to avoid doing intensive studying the day before the test. There is little you can do to help yourself at this point, and you are more likely to exhaust yourself and burn out completely. Instead, review a few key concepts, get together everything you will need on the test day, and then take the night off entirely. Have a relaxing meal or watch some TV. Try not to think too much about the test.

The Day of the Test

- Leave early, giving yourself plenty of time.
- Read something to warm up your brain; you don't want your civil service test to be the first written material your brain processes that day.
- Dress in layers for maximum comfort. That way, you will be able to adjust to the testing room's temperature.
- In traveling to the test center, leave yourself enough time for traffic or mass transit delays.
- Be ready for a long day. Some exams may take up to three hours to complete—and that does not include registration or break times.

Last-Minute Reminders

Here are some other last-minute reminders to help you do your absolute best on test day:

- Read each question carefully, and reread it before choosing the answer.
- Do not let difficult questions slow you down. If you can, skip around until you find questions that you are more comfortable answering. If you can't skip a question, use the process of elimination on each of the answer choices, then guess and move on.
- Confidence is key. Your attitude and outlook are crucial to your performance on test day. Stay positive and don't spend your energy focusing on negativity.
- During the exam, try not to think about how you are scoring. Instead, focus on the question-by-question task of picking an answer choice. The correct answer is there. You don't have to come up with it; it's sitting right there in front of you!

Summary

Although each of the review chapters includes several skill-specific strategies, you should continue to use this chapter as a resource when you take the practice tests in this book. With any strategy, you need to practice using it so that when it really counts it will be second nature to you. Go back often to review the math strategies of backsolving and picking numbers when you work through the mathematics chapter. Or, if you know you are taking a computer-based exam, refer back to the section reviewing the CAT.

Now it's time to get started on your first skill-specific review chapter, complete with sample questions, strategies, and a practice test. If the exam you are planning to take tests clerical ability, begin with Chapter 3. If not, proceed to Chapter 4, Verbal Ability—Vocabulary and Reading.

PART TWO

The Question Types

CHAPTER THREE

Clerical Ability

Introduction

The term *clerical ability* might seem rather vague. Really, it is just another way of naming the skills of alphabetizing and filing, and comparing and checking. So what does this mean to you? Well, if the civil service job you seek is as a clerk, data entry person, or other office information specialist, then it means you can expect a large part of your civil service exam to test these aforementioned skills. This chapter begins with a detailed lesson about alphabetizing and filing, and comparing and checking. The lesson is then followed by samples of different question types that may be included on the civil service exam. Finally, if you still feel you need extra help to hone these skills, Kaplan provides tips for success to do your best. At the end of this chapter, test how much you have learned by completing the first practice test in this book. You can check the results of this 50-question test with the detailed answer explanations that follow.

Clerical Ability Lesson

Your clerical skills may not be what they should be in order for you to do your best on the civil service exam. Spend some time in this lesson so that you will be prepared to do your best on Practice Test 1 and on your actual exam on test day.

Alphabetizing Review

You may think that because you know the alphabet that alphabetization is a breeze. However, consider the following names: J. T. Thomas, Siobhan O'reilly, Chuck A. Genter, Chuck Allen Genter, S. Orenthal. How would you alphabetize these names by last name? The answer is: Chuck A. Genter, Chuck Allen Genter, Siobhan O'reilly, S. Orenthal, J. T. Thomas. To learn why this is the correct order, let's review some of the main rules of alphabetization for people's names.

Rule 1: Last Name; First Name/Initial; Middle Name/Initial; Title.   When alphabetizing, always begin with the last name first. Put names in alphabetical order by last name first.

Example: Nancy Fine before Allen Zundt

If 2 or more people have the same last name, proceed to alphabetize by the first name or initial.

Example: Nancy Fine before Stephen Fine

If the last name is the same, and the first letter of a name and initial are the same, the initial name comes first.

Example: N. Fine before Nancy Fine

When first and last names are identical, names without a middle initial or name come first.

Example: Nancy Fine before Nancy L. Fine

When first and last names are identical, names with a middle initial come before names with a spelled out middle name when both the initial and name begin with the same letter.

Example: Nancy L. Fine before Nancy Louise Fine

When alphabetizing, always consider titles or other naming conventions such as Dr., Mrs., Mr., Prof., Junior, Jr., or III last. They are the least important way to determine how to alphabetize names.

Rule 2: Ignore Apostrophes.   There are several examples of last names with apostrophes. When alphabetizing these names, you should ignore the apostrophes and continue to follow the order of the alphabet as if the apostrophe were not there.

Examples:
Siobhan O'reilly before S. Orenthal
Ian Daclan before Joe D'agostino

Rule 3: Prefixes Are Not Considered Separately.   Many last names also have prefixes such as Mc, Mac, La, Da, Di, Van, and El to name a few. Whether these prefixes are attached (McDonnell) or separate (Di Napoli), they should be considered as part of a single last name.

Examples:
Tony Masters before Tonya McMann
Edward Denison before Rich Di Napoli

Rule 4: Ignore Hyphens.   When a last name contains a hyphen, pretend it is not there and consider both names as one and alphabetize accordingly.

Example: Hilary Hirsch-Cottrell before John Hirschel

Now that you have reviewed these important rules for alphabetizing the names of individuals, it's time to review the rules for alphabetizing the names of businesses, clubs, organizations, structures, and other institutions. Throughout this section, these will be simplified by the term *business*.

Rule 1: Consider the Name of the Business.   Names of businesses are alphabetized according to standard alphabetization rules.

Example: Art Supply Unlimited before Cash on the Go before Speedy Photo

When the business name contains the name of a person, you must revert back to the rules for alphabetizing individual names.

Example: Jerry Thompson and Co. becomes Thompson, Jerry and Co.

Rule 2: Ignore Apostrophes, Small Words, Hyphens, and Spaces.   Like when alphabetizing people's names, you should ignore any apostrophes and proceed accordingly.

Example: Andirson Roofing before Andi's Deli

Many business names contain small words such as *the, of,* and *&.* These are not considered when alphabetizing. With the initial "the," the "the" should follow. For example, The Golf Shop becomes Golf Shop, The.

Example: Golf Shop, The before Henry's Market

As with people's names, hyphens should be ignored when alphabetizing business names.

Example: Quick-i-Auto Repair before Quickly Completed Temp Agency

Business names that contain a space between two words representing a location should be considered as one word and alphabetized accordingly.

Example: South Bay Auto Parts before Southwestern Designs

Rule 3: Spell Out Numerals.   If a business name contains numerals, consider those spelled out in words when alphabetizing.

> Example: 2nd Avenue Deli becomes Second Avenue Deli

Rule 4: Consider the Location of the Business.   It often happens that businesses across the country have the same name. When alphabetizing these, first consider the city. Only if there are two or more in the same city or in a city of the same name should the state become a factor.

> Examples:
> Acme Tires, Alta Dena, CA before Acme Tires, San Diego, CA
> Acme Tires, Lexington, KY before Acme Tires, Lexington, MA

Rule 5: Simplifying Government Departments.   When alphabetizing government names, name and alphabetize by its purpose.

> Example: Department of Education becomes Education, Department of and would be listed before the Finance, Department of.

Not all of these rules are probably second nature to you. Believe it or not, quick and accurate alphabetization takes practice. Review these rules often and test yourself by gathering a list of people's names or business names to practice with. If you think you need more help, refer to the Tips for Clerical Ability Success section found later in this chapter.

Filing Review

Although you won't find any questions on the civil service exam related to the methods and procedures of filing, it is helpful to understand something about them. This part of the review covers some basic information about how things are filed, the best ways to file, and other rules for maintaining an up-to-date system.

Files are organized using a filing system. An office may use any variety of filing systems but the records must be in some sort of sequential order. One common filing system is the alphabetic system, which is when files are arranged in alphabetic order—something you now know all about. A numeric filing system organizes files by sequential numbers instead of by names.

Color-coding is used when there is a need to distinguish files within a filing system. An example would be using a certain color to distinguish different types of records. Color-coding like this means you can find a file quickly and easily. If the file is misfiled it will stand out by the color.

Using a tickler file (also called a reminder file) is a way to keep track of important dates. A tickler file should be easily accessible. You should routinely check the tickler, on a daily basis is best, to keep yourself updated.

Pulling and filing records might be a big responsibility of your civil service job. There will be times when you can return the file as soon as it is no longer needed. Other times the files will be put in a holding place until the file can be returned to the file cabinet.

In filing, these five steps should be used: inspecting, indexing, coding, sorting, and storing. Inspecting means making sure that the files are ready to file. No papers should be sticking out. Remove any paper clips or rubber bands. Removing paper clips and rubber bands will make the folder less bulky. Indexing is another word for naming a file. Names (of people, businesses, items) are most commonly used. The coding method is using an identifying mark on the document to ensure that the file is placed in the correct file. Sorting means arranging the files in the order or the filing system (for example, alphabetically). Files should always be stored in appropriate filing equipment such as fire-proof cabinets.

Filing Guidelines.   There are specific guidelines that are used to file more efficiently. When you pull a file or return a file, glance at it. Make sure that the papers are in proper order. Always keep the files neat. It will be easier to locate the paperwork. Files have to be able to fit in the drawer easily and should never be overstuffed.

Now that you have completed a review of both alphabetizing and filing, you are ready to review comparing and checking.

Comparing and Checking Review

Although you haven't yet learned exactly how these questions are set up, there are some lessons to be learned about the topics of comparing and checking.

Comparing, both in literal terms and in terms of the civil service exam, means seeing if and how two or more things are similar. Almost anything can be compared: letters, numbers, addresses, words, shapes, colors—the list is endless. The main thing to remember when comparing two things is to look at the details. Just as an example, 0.00005 and 0.000005 look similar, but they are in fact two completely different numbers. Only by comparing every element of every item being compared can you say whether they are exactly the same or not. If you remember only one thing from this review, it's that just because something appears to be the same, does not mean it is. Keep focused and examine the details.

If you think comparing is not important, think of the consequences on the job. If you're asked to compare a guest list and mailing list and fail to notice that some addresses are missing, it could result in serious complications. It should be no surprise that employers want to hire people who have a keen eye and are detail-oriented.

Checking is a more broad term that is much more difficult to define or explain. Think of some of the things you often check (and even double-check) in your daily life: that you set your alarm clock, the amount of gas left in the tank of your car, the time, that you've dialed the correct phone number. Or maybe you are the type of person who tends to assume things are settled and taken care of. If so, you need to train yourself to check details and to hone your skills so that nothing gets by you.

When it comes to civil service jobs, being detail-oriented (checking and double-checking the accuracy of information) is invaluable. That is precisely why some civil service exams test to see how detail-oriented you are. To start practicing this skill in your own life, try to be more careful and thoughtful in each and every one of your actions. For example, before you send an email, check your message for spelling and grammar; when you are relating your phone number, be sure you include all ten digits; as you are typing a report, make sure that you have the correct name and address required. This is a start to improving your checking skills.

Speed and Accuracy

If you think that spending time comparing and checking your work and being completely detail-oriented is time consuming, you would be partially correct. Indeed, it takes more time to be accurate and correct than it is to just do your work and hope for the best. However, with practice—hourly, daily, weekly—you will find that your ability to compare and check your own work will take less and less time.

Because being fast and accurate is so important, it's not surprising that comparing and checking questions on the civil service exam also test your speed and accuracy. Typically, there will be many more questions to answer than you will be able to complete (correctly or not) in the given amount of time. In fact, clerical ability sections on civil service exams tend to be the most closely timed sections of the entire exam. Additionally, there is often a guessing penalty. To discourage test takers from just answering as many questions as they can by randomly filling in bubbles on the answer sheet, there is usually a fraction of a point deducted for every incorrect answer. Because of this, it's more important to attempt to answer 20 questions correctly than to answer 50 questions by guessing.

Unfortunately, there's no good way to teach you to be fast and accurate at the same time. Although it's not something that can be taught, it is something that can be improved with practice—lots of it. If you want to learn some basic strategies for increasing your speed and accuracy, refer to Tips for Clerical Ability Success found later in this chapter.

Sample Clerical Ability Questions

When you are answering clerical ability questions, you need to be aware that there are several different formats these questions can take. This part of the chapter will review the five question types (two for alphabetizing and filing and two for comparing and one for checking—although comparing and checking is generally considered a single question type), but you should know that Practice Test 1 as well as any civil service exam may present these questions in a slightly different format. Let's get started.

Alphabetizing and Filing Questions

The two main types of alphabetizing and filing questions are:

1. questions with 4 words
2. questions about the letters of the alphabet

We will review each of these types now.

Type 1: Four Words.   This type of question is relatively self-explanatory. The question will list four words in random order. The words may be nouns, proper names, or even business names. You are asked which word would be first, second, third, or fourth. The number can vary, so you should focus on alphabetizing the words and then answering exactly the question being asked.

Here's an example:

When alphabetized, which of the following would be third?

horse

flower

tape

source

(A) horse
(B) flower
(C) tape
(D) source

In this example, the correct answer is (D). The correct alphabetical order of the words is: flower, horse, source, tape. Although this sample question is relatively easy, you can expect to find words and names that are much more challenging to alphabetize quickly and accurately.

Type 2: Alphabet Questions.   This question type doesn't bother with alphabetization. Instead, you have to know the alphabet itself and how each letter relates to the others. Sound confusing? Here is how these questions are set up.

Which one of the following letters is as far after G as U is after M in the alphabet?

(A) M
(B) P
(C) O
(D) L

In this case, the correct answer is (C). The letter U is the eighth letter after M. To find out which letter is after G, count eight letters: H (1), I (2), J (3), K (4), L (5), M (6), N (7), O (8).

Timing and Scoring on Alphabetizing and Filing Questions

As we already stated, clerical ability questions often include an element of speed. Let's face it, given enough time, it would be easy to alphabetize names and answer several questions about the positions of letters in the alphabet. As you practice and on test day especially, you should keep in mind that the time limits for answering these questions are likely to be very tight. In fact, you might not even be expected to answer every single question within the given amount of time. Additionally, you may be facing a fraction of a point deduction for each incorrect answer—just one way you are discouraged from guessing randomly. When you know all the details about the specific civil service exam you will be taking, keep these factors in mind. Knowing exactly what you will be up against on test day will help you prepare and hopefully earn a top score.

Now you're ready to move on to comparing and checking questions.

Comparing and Checking Questions

Although comparing and checking questions are usually considered a single question type, we thought it would help to separate them so as to present a greater variety of sample questions. On an exam, no distinction would be made between the two, but for study purposes we've broken the questions into three types:

1. address comparison questions
2. list comparison questions
3. checking questions

Comparison Questions

As the question name implies, these questions ask you to compare information. The type of information may vary, but your task is always to compare what you are given.

Type 1: Address Comparison.   Although this question type is specific to the Postal Worker Exam, you may find a similar question type if you are going to be working in an office that deals a lot with correspondence.

When answering these questions, you are comparing two lists—the correct list and the list to be checked. Each list contains an address. You must look at both the street address and the ZIP code in each list to determine if they are identical (choice A), if there is a difference in the street address only (choice B), a difference in the ZIP code only (choice C), or if there are differences in both the street address and the ZIP code (choice D).

Here is one example.

Correct List		**List to be Checked**	
Address	**ZIP Code**	**Address**	**ZIP Code**
1841 Chestnut Drive Memphis, TN	38111	1841 Chestnut Drive Memphis, TN	38111

(A) No errors
(B) Address only
(C) ZIP code only
(D) Both

In this question, the correct answer is (A) since the information in each column is exactly identical. Remember, although the information in the lists change, the answer choices are always the same.

It's important to know that for these questions you are usually penalized for answering incorrectly. For each correct answer, you receive one point. However, if you answer any question incorrectly, a fraction, usually one-third, of a point is subtracted from your total score.

Type 2: Lists.   This is a more common and general question type than that found on the Postal Worker Exam or other exams. For these questions you are presented with a two-column list, six rows long. Each list will contain similar information (usually six letters or six numbers) but rather than identifying specifically which element is different, you will be asked the number of items that are similar.

Here is an example.

How many pairs of the following sets of letters are exactly alike?

ghildsk	ghildsk
jiyurew	jyiurew
nfdsyeh	ndfsyeh
mseihq	mseihq
jdsyoeh	jsdyoeh
ieytheg	ieyhteg

(A) 0
(B) 1
(C) 2
(D) 3

If you looked carefully, you would have seen that only 2 pairs are alike and therefore (C) is the correct answer. This question type especially will require some practice, so be sure to focus on these in Practice Test 1.

Again, there is a high likelihood that a fraction of a point will be deducted from your score when you answer these questions. Because of this, strive to improve your speed and accuracy when answering lists questions.

Checking Questions

Because the idea behind checking questions is to test your attention to detail, there isn't just one question format. If there were, you could master just that specific type and ace the exam. Therefore, the distinguishing feature of checking questions is variety. Some questions will even involve numbers, but they are NOT math questions. It's important to keep in mind that you won't know exactly what you will be asked, so on test day you will really have to apply your skills of speed and accuracy.

Below is just one example of a checking question. You will find others on the practice test, but you should be prepared for anything when you take your civil service exam.

How many words in this sentence contain letters that appear only once in that word?

"Although it was already June in Amsterdam, the weather remained cool, rainy, and dreary."

(A) 4

(B) 5

(C) 6

(D) 7

This question is tricky, as most checking questions are. If you remember from Comparing and Checking Review, you have to consider each element separately and carefully. In this example, you need to identify how many words contain letters that appear only once in that word. It sounds tricky, but you are essentially looking for words that don't have any double or triple letters.

To answer this question, let's look at each of the words individually:

Although—the letter "h" appears twice

it—no repeated letters

was—no repeated letters

already—the letter "a" appears twice

June—no repeated letters

in—no repeated letters

Amsterdam—the letters "a" and "m" each appear twice

the—no repeated letters

weather—the letter "e" appears twice

remained—the letter "e" appears twice

cool—the letter "o" appears twice

rainy—no repeated letters

and—no repeated letters

dreary—the letter "r" appears twice

Now you can see that 7 words do not have repeated letters. Therefore, the answer is choice (D).

If this question type has you a little concerned, don't worry. These questions are designed to see how detail-oriented you are and how you can find a balance between being fast and being correct. As with other clerical ability questions, you will also need to avoid having fractions of points deducted from your score but answering as many questions as you can correctly. If you want to learn some techniques for answering these questions, refer to the Tips for Clerical Ability Success and make an extra effort when you complete Practice Test 1.

Tips for Clerical Ability Success

You may have noticed that these question types are quite specific and are really meant to challenge you. To help you do your best, we have Kaplan Target Strategies for each question type. Review these strategies and be sure to use them when answering the questions on Practice Test 1.

Kaplan's Target Strategy for Four-Words Questions

Here is Kaplan's Target Strategy for four-words questions.

Step 1. Start by alphabetizing by letter first. If all letters are the same, remember the alphabetization rules.
Step 2. Write a 1, 2, 3, 4 next to each word to indicate the alphabetical order.
Step 3. Check the question to find out which word you are looking for.
Step 4. Mark your answer and move on.

Let's review each of these steps in detail while we apply them to the following question.

When alphabetized correctly, which of the following would be third?
- (A) Helen Dickens
- (B) H. Dickens
- (C) Martin Dikenson
- (D) Robert Cilbert

Step 1. Start by Alphabetizing by Letter First. If All Letters Are the Same, Remember the Alphabetization Rules. It is important to note that the first step is NOT to read the question. For alphabetization questions like these, the question is always more or less the same. Don't start by reading the question, start right away by alphabetizing.

When alphabetizing by letter, Robert Cilbert would be first because C comes before D. That was easy. What comes next? Two last names are the same so you can't just alphabetize them by letter, you have to remember the rules. In this case, the name with just an initial comes before the spelled out name, so H. Dickens, then Helen Dickens. Finally, Dikenson is alphabetically last here, regardless of first name.

Step 2. Write a 1, 2, 3, 4 Next to Each Word to Indicate the Alphabetical Order.   You now know the correct order so rather than trying to keep it all straight in your head, write numbers next to each name to indicate the order.

(A) Helen Dickens   3
(B) H. Dickens   2
(C) Martin Dikenson   4
(D) Robert Cilbert   1

Step 3. Check the Question to Find Out Which Word You Are Looking For.   Now is when you refer back to the question to find out whether you are looking for the first, second, third, or fourth alphabetized word. In this question, you are asked to find the third, so Helen Dickens (A) is the answer.

Step 4. Mark Your Answer and Move On.   Mark choice (A) and move on. You won't have a lot of time to go back and double check your work or worry about whether you are correct. Don't second-guess yourself. Be confident with your answer and start the next question.

Kaplan's Target Strategy for Alphabet Questions

This strategy has four steps. These are:

Step 1. Right away, write out the alphabet clearly and neatly.
Step 2. For now, ignore the first letter in the question. Start by reading the relationship between the last two letters in the question.
Step 3. Count out the letters and be careful of direction!
Step 4. Mark your answer and move on.

To make sure you know how to put these steps into practice, let's apply them to this question found earlier in the chapter.

Which one of the following letters is as far after G as U is after M in the alphabet?

(A) M
(B) P
(C) O
(D) L

Step 1. Right Away, Write Out the Alphabet Clearly and Neatly.   Before you even start these questions on your civil service exam, take the time to write out the entire alphabet as neatly as you can somewhere on your test materials. (Don't write on anything you are instructed not to!) You only have to write it out once, so make sure it's legible and clear.

No matter how well you think you know the alphabet, and we're sure you do, you won't be able to answer these questions without writing them out first. Don't skip this important step for any reason.

Step 2. For Now, Ignore the First Letter in the Question. Start by Reading the Relationship Between the Last Two Letters in the Question.   The first letter written in the question is irrelevant until you know the relationship between the other two letters in the question. Skip immediately to the second half of the question. In this case, you should focus on "U after M."

Step 3. Count Out the Letters and Be Careful of Direction!   Here is where your written out alphabet comes in especially handy.

$$1\ 2\ 3\ 4\ 5\ 6\ 7\ 8$$
$$A\ B\ C\ D\ E\ F\ G\ H\ I\ J\ K\ L\ \textbf{M}\ N\ O\ P\ Q\ R\ S\ T\ \textbf{U}\ V\ W\ X\ Y\ Z$$

This allows you to see that U is the eighth letter after M. Now you can go back to the first part of the question that asks you to find the letter the same "distance" after G. Again, use the alphabet you wrote out.

$$1\ 2\ 3\ 4\ 5\ 6\ 7\ 8$$
$$A\ B\ C\ D\ E\ F\ \textbf{G}\ H\ I\ J\ K\ L\ M\ N\ \textbf{O}\ P\ Q\ R\ S\ T\ U\ V\ W\ X\ Y\ Z$$

When you are going back to read the first part of the question, pay careful attention to the "direction" mentioned in the question. Is it BEFORE or AFTER the letter? Obviously, this will have a great impact on your answer, so read carefully.

Step 4. Mark Your Answer and Move On.   When you know that O is the correct answer, mark it and move on. By having a visual record of how you answered the question using the alphabet, you are less likely to make careless errors. Fill in your answer sheet with confidence and move on to the next question.

Helpful Hint: Think about the following question. Which one of the following letters is as far after H as J is after G in the alphabet? There is a short cut with a question like this where two letters in the question (G and H) are right next to each other. If you think about it, you don't even have to count how many letters after G that J is. Because H is one after G, then the answer is one after J—the answer is K.

Kaplan's Target Strategy for Address Comparison Questions

Address comparison questions have their own strategy.

Step 1. Memorize the answer choices.
Step 2. Focus only on the item you are working on.
Step 3. Break up the addresses into smaller, more manageable pieces.
Step 4. When you find an error, stop checking that section of the item.
Step 5. Mark your answer and move on.

*Step 1. Memorize the Answer Choice*s.   For this question type, the answer choices never change. Memorizing them will save you time on test day. The choices are:

(A) No errors
(B) Address only
(C) ZIP code only
(D) Both

Commit them to memory so you don't waste time reviewing them repeatedly on test day.

Step 2. Focus Only on the Item You Are Working On.   This sounds like a simple strategy; but it can be surprisingly difficult when there are distractions in the exam room—and there are always distractions in the exam room. Test anxiety itself can make it difficult for you to focus. Use a sheet of paper or even your hand to keep you looking at only one item at a time.

Step 3. Break Up the Addresses into Smaller, More Manageable Pieces.   Remember that there are two sections to each address: the street address and the ZIP code. The street address has at least two lines: the number and street, and the city and state. That means there are three distinct parts to each address. You will be more successful at finding the errors if you don't try to look at too much information at once. Instead, try breaking each address into its three parts and then comparing each separate part with the List to be Checked.

As you work, use your pencil (always in your hand, ready to mark your answers) to mark your place on either the Correct List or the List to be Checked. Use your index finger on the other hand to mark the corresponding place on the other list. This is also a further example of a technique that helps you focus only on the information that is important at any given moment.

Step 4. When You Find an Error, Stop Checking That Section of the Item.   As you check, for example, the street address, you may notice right away that the street name is spelled differently on the List to be Checked. Stop right there. Don't check the street number; don't look at the city or state. You now know that the correct answer is either (B) or (D). Move on to the ZIP code and look for an error in it, so that you will know which answer is the right one. Remember, you are working as quickly as possible; when any part of an address is different, the address is different; and you should move on.

You may decide that it is worth it to make a mark in your test booklet any time you answer (A) No Errors to a question. That way, if you finish early, you can go back and check those items again, to make sure you didn't miss an error. It's more likely that you could miss seeing an error than it is that you would notice an error where there is none.

KAPLAN

Step 5. Mark Your Answer and Move On.   Don't waste time second-guessing yourself or stopping to check your answer yet again. To earn points you need to answer as many questions correctly as you can. Be confident that you answered correctly and move on to the next question. Remember, your time to answer these questions will be limited.

Kaplan's Target Strategy for Two-Lists Questions

Here are the steps you should take the answer two-lists questions.

Step 1. Focus on one pair at a time.
Step 2. As soon as you see an error, mark that pair.
Step 3. Don't look for errors that aren't there.
Step 4. Mark your answer and move on.

Now let's apply these four steps to the two-lists question found earlier in the chapter.

How many pairs of the following sets of letters are exactly alike?

ghildsk	ghildsk
jiyurew	jyiurew
nfdsyeh	ndfsyeh
mseihq	mseihq
jdsyoeh	jsdyoeh
ieytheg	ieyhteg

(A) 0
(B) 1
(C) 2
(D) 3

Step 1. Focus on One Pair at a Time.   If you try to consider all the letters at once, they will end up in a jumble in your head. The solution is to look at one pair at a time. If possible, use something to cover the pairs so you can consider each row separately. Looking down the column is useless, your task is to make sure that the items in the left column match exactly the items in the right column. Do not worry about the rows.

Step 2. As Soon as You See an Error, Mark That Pair.   When you are scanning each pair, as soon as you see an error, stop. You don't have to identify what the error is, you just have to note it. Even though the question asks for how many pairs are exactly alike, it might more helpful for you to mark pairs with errors. Whether you mark pairs that contain errors or pairs that are free of errors, be consistent. When you're done comparing, you need to be able to answer how many are exactly alike. It's up to you to keep track of which you are marking.

Step 3. Don't Look for Errors That Aren't There.   It's a common mistake to assume that you are seeing errors where there aren't really any. Don't start looking at pairs assuming anything. You won't earn points for your assumptions, only for completing the questions quickly and accurately. If you do not find an error, don't second-guess yourself.

Step 4. Mark Your Answer and Move On.   Speed is always a factor with clerical ability questions, so don't linger over the two lists. When you know how many pairs are error free, mark your answer sheet and move on to the next question.

Now you can review the final Kaplan Target Strategy.

Kaplan's Target Strategy for Checking Questions
Here is Kaplan's Target Strategy for checking questions.

Step 1. Read the question carefully.
Step 2. Mark your test booklet.
Step 3. Check and then double check.
Step 4. Mark your answer and move on.

Here is how to apply each of these steps to the sample question found earlier in the chapter.

How many words in this sentence contain letters that appear only once in that word?

"Although it was already June in Amsterdam, the weather remained cool, rainy, and dreary."

(A) 4
(B) 5
(C) 6
(D) 7

Step 1. Read the Question Carefully.   This step may seem obvious to you. Of course you are going to read the question. However, because the entire concept of checking questions is to test your attention to detail, you really have to read carefully. For example, what if you skimmed over the word "only" in the question. Maybe you would start looking for words that contain letters that appear more than once in that word. If you did this, you would be wrong. This means you not only miss out on one point, but also you might even lose a fraction of a point for answering incorrectly.

Step 2. Mark Your Test Booklet.   If you are permitted to write in your test booklet, mark up each question. Circle words, letters, or numbers that are relevant to the question. Don't try to solve or count everything out in your head. By writing things down, you are less likely to make careless errors.

Step 3. Check and Then Double Check.   Because these are checking questions, it shouldn't surprise you that you really need to check and recheck your answer. Set limits, but you should make sure you have answered exactly what you were asked and that you've paid close attention to the many details given.

Step 4. Mark Your Answer and Move On.   As important as it is to be accurate, you also need to be fast to complete as many questions as you can in the given amount of time. Don't spend more than 30 seconds on any question. When you think you have the correct answer, mark your answer sheet and move on.

Avoiding Errors on Your Answer Sheet

One commonly made mistake is a simple transposition error. In other words, when you look at question number 33 in your test booklet, determine the correct answer, then mark your answer on line number 34 of your answer sheet, you are likely to miss both of those questions. Furthermore, you may keep right on marking answers on the wrong line! That would have disastrous consequences.

Here is a simple technique that will help you avoid the wrong-line scenario. As you determine the correct answer for item number one and prepare to mark your answer sheet, say silently to yourself, "Number one is D," then look at your answer sheet, find the line for number one, and mark D. After marking the answer, look again at the number you just marked. Say to yourself silently, "D for number one," and then look back at your test booklet to double check that number one was the question you meant to answer "D." Continue with number two, and so on. This crosschecking becomes second nature after you practice it, and the extra fraction of a second you spend on each question will be well worth it, as you insure the accuracy of your answers.

Another technique for avoiding transposition errors is to keep the point of your pencil beside the number of the item you are answering. After you mark each answer, simply move the pencil down one line. It is best, however, to supplement this technique with the silent repetition of the numbers and letters previously described.

Difficulty Level

Please note that the difficulty of questions on the civil service exam you take will depend on the type of job you are applying for. The practice test includes clerical ability questions at intermediate and more challenging levels so that you are prepared for whatever civil service exam you face on test day.

Summary

In this chapter you have learned about a unique skill set required for the civil service exam. You know the kinds of clerical abilities that are expected of you as well as the different question types you may be facing on test day. The numerous Kaplan Target Strategies should help you do your best, even if you still need to improve your speed and accuracy. To accomplish this, here is a 50-question practice test. Using all the tips and strategies you have just learned, answer these questions. As you work, remember that speed and accuracy are what you are striving for. You must work quickly without making errors. In order to do that, you must focus intently on each item as it comes. Don't let your attention wander. Also, be sure to review the detailed answer explanations for any questions you miss.

Practice Test 1

50 Questions
17 Minutes

1 (A) (B) (C) (D)   14 (A) (B) (C) (D)   27 (A) (B) (C) (D)   40 (A) (B) (C) (D)
2 (A) (B) (C) (D)   15 (A) (B) (C) (D)   28 (A) (B) (C) (D)   41 (A) (B) (C) (D)
3 (A) (B) (C) (D)   16 (A) (B) (C) (D)   29 (A) (B) (C) (D)   42 (A) (B) (C) (D)
4 (A) (B) (C) (D)   17 (A) (B) (C) (D)   30 (A) (B) (C) (D)   43 (A) (B) (C) (D)
5 (A) (B) (C) (D)   18 (A) (B) (C) (D)   31 (A) (B) (C) (D)   44 (A) (B) (C) (D)
6 (A) (B) (C) (D)   19 (A) (B) (C) (D)   32 (A) (B) (C) (D)   45 (A) (B) (C) (D)
7 (A) (B) (C) (D)   20 (A) (B) (C) (D)   33 (A) (B) (C) (D)   46 (A) (B) (C) (D)
8 (A) (B) (C) (D)   21 (A) (B) (C) (D)   34 (A) (B) (C) (D)   47 (A) (B) (C) (D)
9 (A) (B) (C) (D)   22 (A) (B) (C) (D)   35 (A) (B) (C) (D)   48 (A) (B) (C) (D)
10 (A) (B) (C) (D)   23 (A) (B) (C) (D)   36 (A) (B) (C) (D)   49 (A) (B) (C) (D)
11 (A) (B) (C) (D)   24 (A) (B) (C) (D)   37 (A) (B) (C) (D)   50 (A) (B) (C) (D)
12 (A) (B) (C) (D)   25 (A) (B) (C) (D)   38 (A) (B) (C) (D)
13 (A) (B) (C) (D)   26 (A) (B) (C) (D)   39 (A) (B) (C) (D)

Note: In order to mimic the time constraints you will face on test day, you should spend approximately 17 minutes answering all 50 questions. If there are any questions you cannot complete within this time limit, do not guess. Leave them blank so that you can answer them at a later time.

1. When alphabetized correctly, which of the following would be second?
   (A) flag
   (B) house
   (C) decade
   (D) emotion

2. When alphabetized correctly, which of the following would be fourth?
   (A) microphone
   (B) neutral
   (C) lithograph
   (D) neutron

3. When alphabetized correctly, which of the following would be third?
   (A) excitement
   (B) earnest
   (C) early
   (D) earn

4. When alphabetized correctly, which of the following would be second?
   (A) catalog
   (B) catch
   (C) carbon
   (D) curb

5. When alphabetized correctly, which of the following would be third?
   (A) element
   (B) elephant
   (C) box
   (D) department

6. When alphabetized correctly, which of the following would be third?
   (A) carton
   (B) cartographer
   (C) cart
   (D) cartoon

7. When alphabetized correctly, which of the following would be second?
   (A) polarize
   (B) omnipotent
   (C) polygraph
   (D) omniscient

8. When alphabetized correctly, which of the following would be fourth?
   (A) Walsh, Carol C.
   (B) Walter, Henry Delano
   (C) Walsh, Joseph C.
   (D) Walsheim, Joe

9. When alphabetized correctly, which of the following would be third?
   (A) McDonough, Kevin
   (B) McDonohugh, K.
   (C) Da Costa, Hector
   (D) Costa, Hector David

10. When alphabetized correctly, which of the following would be fourth?
    (A) Albers, J. A.
    (B) Albers, John Anthony
    (C) Sorensen, Edward J.
    (D) Sorensen, Ed Joseph

11. When alphabetized correctly, which of the following would be second?
    (A) Smith, Joan
    (B) Smith, Joan J.
    (C) Smith, J.
    (D) Smithers, J.

12. When alphabetized correctly, which of the following would be third?
    (A) Read-i-mart
    (B) Ready Steady Office Supplies
    (C) Read for Life Program
    (D) Red Robin Trucking

13. When alphabetized correctly, which of the following would be fourth?
    (A) Henry Miller and Sons
    (B) Millerton Quarry
    (C) The Mill on the Hill
    (D) Haven Salon

14. When alphabetized correctly, which of the following would be second?
    (A) 11th Street Gym
    (B) Rayson Railroad Company
    (C) Ray's Diner
    (D) Evanston Auto Parts

15. When alphabetized correctly, which of the following would be fourth?
    (A) East Bay Records
    (B) Garrett Van Buren, Ltd
    (C) Eastern Construction
    (D) Van-B-Mine Auto Rentals

16. Which one of the following letters is as far after E as Q is after H in the alphabet?
    (A) M
    (B) N
    (C) O
    (D) P

17. Which one of the following letters is as far after C as T is after A in the alphabet?
    (A) R
    (B) U
    (C) V
    (D) X

18. Which one of the following letters is as far before L as O is before Z in the alphabet?
    (A) A
    (B) B
    (C) W
    (D) X

19. Which one of the following letters is as far before V as X is after P in the alphabet?
    (A) L
    (B) M
    (C) N
    (D) O

20. Which one of the following letters is as far after I as R is after G in the alphabet?
    (A) T
    (B) U
    (C) V
    (D) X

21. Which one of the following letters is as far before J as K is after B in the alphabet?
    (A) C
    (B) B
    (C) A
    (D) U

22. Which one of the following letters is as far before U as T is after J in the alphabet?
    (A) J
    (B) K
    (C) L
    (D) M

23. Which one of the following letters is as far after Q as J is after E in the alphabet?
    (A) V
    (B) W
    (C) X
    (D) Y

24. Which one of the following letters is as far before N as X is after S in the alphabet?
    (A) R
    (B) S
    (C) I
    (D) J

25. Which one of the following letters is as far after E as K is before R in the alphabet?
    (A) H
    (B) I
    (C) J
    (D) K

A. No Errors	B. Address Only	C. ZIP Code Only	D. Both

	Correct List		**List to Be Checked**	
	Address	**ZIP Code**	**Address**	**ZIP Code**
26.	21-C Southern Lane Baltimore, MD	62571	21-C Southern Lane Baltimore, MD	65271
27.	123 Lyric Way Conyers, MS	18282	123 Lyric Way Conners, MS	18282
28.	200 W. Jannine Dr. Missoula, MT	30707	200 W. Jannine Dr. Missoula, MT	30307
29.	18 Champlaine Way Rustic, NV	42101	18 Champaine Way Rustic, NV	24101
30.	62159 Rodaja Parsimony, KS	33489-6215	62159 Rodaja Parsimony, KS	33489-6215

31. How many pairs of the following sets of letters are exactly alike?

HIFGDA	HIFGDA
PEWHEI	PEWHEI
UENGSO	UEGNSO
MBDHEK	MBDHEK
PQNGGD	PQNGGD
OIEMGH	OIEMGH

(A) 3
(B) 4
(C) 5
(D) 6

32. How many pairs of the following sets of letters are exactly alike?

ehgsoe	ehgsoe
ththet	ththet
lmqbts	lmbqts
kehgng	kehgng
Imqyeo	lmqyeo
jqzdue	jqdzue

(A) 2
(B) 4
(C) 5
(D) 6

33. How many pairs of the following sets of numbers are exactly alike?

836459	834659
916533	916353
264821	268421
163943	169343
012039	021039
936129	936129

(A) 0
(B) 1
(C) 2
(D) 3

34. How many pairs of the following sets of letters are exactly alike?

JHEISH	JHEISH
KEIWNE	KEIWNE
OENMZN	OENMZN
MKENSH	MKENSH
BEVWE	BEWVE
JIHNEM	JIHNEM

(A) 2
(B) 3
(C) 4
(D) 6

35. How many pairs of the following sets of numbers are exactly alike?

821421	821241
726191	726191
827015	820715
287651	287651
009824	008924
721182	721182

(A) 0
(B) 2
(C) 3
(D) 4

36. How many pairs of the following sets of letters are exactly alike?

aebjhg	aebjhg
amanej	amanej
kejqez	keqjez
ikeplo	ikpelo
nmesda	mnesda
wierew	wierew

(A) 0
(B) 1
(C) 2
(D) 3

37. How many pairs of the following sets of numbers are exactly alike?

902711	902711
764201	764201
434309	434309
189361	189361
547789	547789
882718	882718

(A) 3
(B) 4
(C) 5
(D) 6

38. How many pairs of the following sets of letters are exactly alike?

GIHEKE	GIHEKE
KIWNEB	KWINEB
PQMZJI	PQMZIJ
MENTWN	METNWN
OPZIBS	OPZIBS
PONEHE	POENHE

(A) 0
(B) 1
(C) 2
(D) 3

39. How many pairs of the following sets of letters are exactly alike?

jehowe	jehowe
nwkebt	nwekbt
okejji	okejii
nleotn	nelotn
lnwezb	lnewzb
nqwerj	nwqeri

(A) 0
(B) 1
(C) 2
(D) 3

40. How many pairs of the following sets of numbers are exactly alike?

278126	278126
901272	902172
826482	824682
004657	004657
128532	125832
278917	278971

(A) 0
(B) 1
(C) 2
(D) 3

41. In the word INVOLUNTARILY, how many letters are used more than once?
(A) 0
(B) 1
(C) 2
(D) 3

42. In the following sentence, how many words contain letters that do not appear more than once in that word?

"It was difficult for me to comprehend how I could have gotten so lost on the narrow highway."

(A) 11
(B) 12
(C) 13
(D) 14

43. In the following number how many numbers are used more than twice?

1875327862190162846214123

(A) 3
(B) 4
(C) 5
(D) 6

44. In the word IMMEASURABLE, how many letters are used more than once?

(A) 1
(B) 2
(C) 3
(D) 4

45. In the following sentence, how many words contain letters that appear more than once in that word?

"It is strongly recommended that you make a reservation prior to arriving at the restaurant."

(A) 4
(B) 5
(C) 6
(D) 7

46. How many times does 2 come immediately after 3 when 3 comes immediately after an even number?

13268321605189323164532104232187

(A) 0
(B) 1
(C) 2
(D) 3

47. In the word LUMBERING, how many letters are used more than once?

(A) 0
(B) 1
(C) 2
(D) 3

48. How many times does 6 come immediately before 5 when 5 comes immediately before an odd number?

213656570652658965326932165976

(A) 0
(B) 1
(C) 2
(D) 3

49. In the following number how many numbers are used more than three times?

012782167432186491237289167298

(A) 0
(B) 3
(C) 4
(D) 6

50. In the following sentence, how many words contain letters that appear more than once in that word?

"Attempting to renovate a historical building can be challenging both physically and financially."

(A) 4
(B) 5
(C) 6
(D) 7

Answers and Explanations

1. D

The correct alphabetical order is: decade, emotion, flag, house. *Emotion* is second.

2. D

The correct alphabetical order is: lithograph, microphone, neutral, neutron. *Neutron* is fourth.

3. B

The correct alphabetical order is: early, earn, earnest, excitement. *Earnest* is third.

4. A

The correct alphabetical order is: carbon, catalog, catch, curb. *Catalog* is second.

5. A

The correct alphabetical order is: box, department, element, elephant. *Element* is third.

6. A

The correct alphabetical order is: cart, cartographer, carton, cartoon. *Carton* is third.

7. D

The correct alphabetical order is: omnipotent, omniscient, polarize, polygraph. *Omniscient* is second.

8. B

The correct alphabetical order is: Walsh, Carol C.; Walsh, Joseph C.; Walsheim, Joe; Walter, Henry Delano. Walter, Henry Delano is fourth.

9. B

The correct alphabetical order is: Costa, Hector David; Da Costa, Hector; McDonohugh, K.; McDonough, Kevin. McDonohugh, K. is third.

Be careful when alphabetizing last names with a space. Remember to ignore the space. In this case, Da Costa would be considered Dacosta so it would appear AFTER someone with the last name Costa.

10. C

The correct alphabetical order is: Albers, J. A.; Albers, John Anthony; Sorensen, Ed Joseph; Sorensen, Edward J. Sorensen, Edward J. is fourth.

If both men's names were Edward, the order of these last two names would be reversed. However, first names take alphabetical precedence over middle names and initials and Ed is before Edward.

11. A

The correct alphabetical order is: Smith, J.; Smith, Joan; Smith, Joan J.; Smithers, J. Smith, Joan is second.

This is tricky but you have to keep the rules of alphabetization straight. An initialed first name comes before a spelled out first name and a name with no middle initial comes before a name with a middle initial.

12. B

The correct alphabetical order is: Read for Life, Read-i-mart, Ready Steady Office Supplies, Red Robin Trucking. Ready Steady Office Supplies is third. Remember: when alphabetizing business names, you should ignore hyphens and spaces.

13. B

The correct alphabetical order is: Haven Salon, The Mill on the Hill, Henry Miller and Sons, Millerton Quarry. Millerton Quarry is fourth.

Remember that businesses with a person's name them are alphabetized as an individual would be. In this case, Henry Miller and Sons would be Miller, Henry and Sons. Also, the word "the" in choice (C) should be disregarded when alphabetizing.

14. D
The correct alphabetical order is: 11th Street Gym, Evanston Auto Parts, Ray's Diner, Rayson Railroad. Evanston Auto parts is second.

Don't forget that numerals should be alphabetized according to the spelled out number. In this question, 11th Street Gym would be Eleventh Street Gym. Also, you should have ignored the apostrophe in Ray's Diner when alphabetizing.

15. D
The correct alphabetical order is: East Bay Records, Eastern Construction, Garrett Van Buren, Ltd, Van-B-Mine Auto Rentals. Van-B-Mine Rentals is third.

Again, you have to be careful with business names that are also the names of individuals. In this case, Garrett Van Buren, Ltd would be alphabetized as Van Buren, Garrett, Ltd. You also have to ignore the hyphens in choice (D), which makes it the third name when all four choices are alphabetized.

16. B
Q is 9 letters after H and N is 9 letters after E.

17. C
T is 19 letters after A and V is 19 letters after C.

18. A
Z is 11 letters after O and A is 11 letters before L.

19. C
X is 8 letters after P and N is 8 letters before V.

20. A
R is 11 letters after G and T is 11 letters after I.

21. C
K is 9 letters after B and A is 9 letters before J.

22. B
T is 10 letters after J and K is 10 letters before U.

23. A
J is 5 letters after E and V is 5 letters after Q.

24. C
X is 5 letters after S and I is 5 letters before N.

25. D
K is 7 letters before R and L is 7 letters after E.

26. C

27. B

28. C

29. D

30. A

31. C
The third pair of letters are different. Therefore, 5 pairs are the same.

32. B
The third and sixth pair of letters are different. Therefore, 4 pairs are the same.

33. B

Only the last pair of numbers is the same. Therefore, choice (B) is correct.

34. C

The third and fifth pairs of letters are different. Therefore, 4 pairs are the same.

35. C

The first, third, and fifth pairs of numbers are different. Therefore, 3 pairs are the same.

36. D

The third, fourth, and fifth pairs of letters are different. Therefore, 3 pairs are the same.

37. D

All of the pairs of numbers are exactly alike. Therefore, choice (D) is correct.

38. C

The second, third, fourth, and sixth pairs of letters are different. Therefore, only 2 pairs are the same.

39. B

Only the first pair of letters is the same. Therefore, choice (B) is correct.

40. C

The second, third, fifth, and sixth pairs of numbers are different. Therefore, 2 pairs are the same.

41. D

The letters I, L, and N are each used twice in the word INVOLUNTARILY.

42. C

Remember, you are looking for words that do NOT have double letters. This rules out: *difficult*, *comprehend*, *gotten*, *narrow*, *highway*. Thirteen words do not have double letters.

43. B

The numbers 1, 2, 6, and 8 all appear more than twice.

44. C

The letters M, E, and A are each used twice in the word IMMEASURABLE.

45. C

The words *recommended, that, reservation, prior, arriving,* and *restaurant* each contain letters that appear more than once within the word.

46. C

You are looking for the following combination: (even number)32. This appears only twice.

47. A

Each letter is only used once.

48. D

You are looking for the following combination: 65(odd number). This appears three times.

49. C

The numbers 1, 2, 7, and 8 all appear more than three times.

50. D

The words *attempting, renovate, historical, building, challenging, physically,* and *financially* each contain letters that appear more than once within the word.

CHAPTER FOUR

Verbal Ability— Vocabulary and Reading

Introduction

For almost any job you are going to need to be able to understand what you read and communicate exactly what you mean. For this reason, you can expect to see vocabulary and reading comprehension questions on most civil service exams. Because these skills are critical to your continued success on the job, you can always improve them. This chapter includes separate lessons on vocabulary and reading comprehension as well as details about the types of questions you will face on test day. If these skills are not part of your strengths, focus your attention on Kaplan's tips for success, which offer the best strategies to earn maximum points. If these skills are a strength of yours, you should still commit to completing the chapter because there could be some information you haven't already mastered. Finally, test your knowledge and abilities by taking Practice Test 2, complete with detailed answer explanations for all 50 questions.

Vocabulary Lesson

To get a sense of the strength of your vocabulary, take a few minutes to go through the following list of words and see how many you know. Write your definition to the right of each word. To see how many words you defined correctly, check the definitions listed immediately following the exercise.

*Resolute*_____

Vanquish _____

Cautious _____

*Sullen*_____

*Legible*_____

Fawn (v.) _____

Adrift _____

Query _____

Impure _____

Disinterested _____

Here are the definitions:

Resolute: Determined

Vanquish: To defeat or conquer in battle

Cautious: Careful in actions and behaviors

Sullen: Depressed, gloomy

Legible: Possible to read or decipher

Fawn (v.): To act in a servile manner

Adrift: Wandering aimlessly; afloat without direction

Query: A question; to call into question

Impure: Lacking in purity; containing something unclean

Disinterested: Impartial; unbiased

If you got four or fewer definitions correct, you should start working to build your vocabulary as soon as possible. The techniques and tools in this chapter will teach you ways to improve your vocabulary and help you to make the most out of words you already know. If you got between five and eight definitions right, your vocabulary is about average. We recommend using the techniques and tools discussed below to further improve your skills. If you got more than eight definitions right, your vocabulary is above average, but you can always polish it further by reviewing the vocabulary-building plan below.

A Vocabulary-Building Plan

A great vocabulary cannot be built overnight, but you can begin building a good vocabulary with a little bit of time and effort. Here is our best advice on how to do just that.

Look It Up.   Challenge yourself to find at least five words a day that are unfamiliar to you. You could find these words listening to a news broadcast, or reading a newspaper, magazine, or novel. In fact, books that you choose to read for enjoyment normally contain three to five words per page that are unfamiliar to you. Write down these words, look them up in the dictionary, and record their definitions in a notebook. But don't only write a word's definition. Below your definition, use the word in a sentence. This will help you to remember the word and anticipate possible context questions.

Study Word Roots and Prefixes.   Many tricky vocabulary words are made up of prefixes and suffixes that can help you figure out at least part of the definition–which, thankfully, is often enough to help you get the right answer. For instance, if you know that the prefix *bio-* means "life," you might be able to decode the definition of *biodegradable*, which means *able to be broken down by living things*. Fortunately, many word roots may already be familiar if you speak or have studied a foreign language, particularly a Romance language such as French, Spanish, or Italian.

Think Like a Thesaurus.   On any test it is better to know a little bit about a lot of words than to know a lot about a few words. So, try to think like a thesaurus rather than a dictionary. For instance, instead of studying the dictionary definition of *lackluster*, you can study *lackluster* in a thesaurus along with words like the following: *drab, dull, flat, lifeless, lethargic, listless, sluggard, somnolent*. Instead of just learning one word, learn them together and you will get 12 words for one definition.

Personalize the Way You Study Vocabulary

It's important to figure out a study method that works for you and stick to it. But realize that most students don't learn best by reading passively from lists. The following techniques are proven ways to improve your study habits.

Use Flashcards.   Write down new words or word groups and run through them whenever you have some spare time. Write the word or word group on one side of an index card and a short definition or synonym on the other side.

Make a Vocabulary Notebook.   In a notebook, list difficult vocabulary words in the left-hand column and their meanings in the right-hand column. Cover up or fold over the page to test yourself. See how many words you can define from memory. You can continually update your notebook as you come across unfamiliar words.

Create Memory Devices.   Try to come up with hooks to lodge new words into your head. Create visual images, silly sentences, rhymes, whatever, to build associations between words and their definitions. For example, for the word *gregarious*, you could think of your friend "Gary" who is really outgoing and sociable.

Trust Your Hunches

Vocabulary knowledge is not an all-or-nothing proposition. When you are reading in your daily life, or even on the test, do not skip over a word you see just because you can't recite its definition. Take the time to get to know its meaning.

There are many levels of vocabulary knowledge:

- Some words you know so well you can rattle off their dictionary definitions.
- Some words you "sort of " know. You can't define them precisely and you probably wouldn't use them yourself, but you understand them when you see them in context.
- Some words you barely recognize. You know you have heard them before, but you are not sure what they mean.
- Some words you have never, ever seen before and you have no idea what they mean.

If a word falls in the second or third category, try some of the following techniques to help you to get a better fix on the word.

Try to Recall Where You Have Heard the Word Before

If you can recall a phrase in which the word appears, that may help you choose the correct answer. Let's say you come across the word *plight*. You don't know what it means, but you remember reading an article in the newspaper about New Orleans that detailed the *plight of the citizens* displaced by the hurricane. This can help you remember that this word means an unfortunate situation.

Think in Positives and Negatives

Sometimes just knowing the "charge" of a word—that is, whether a word has a positive or negative sense—will be enough to earn you points on a test. Take the word *auspicious*. Let's assume you don't know its dictionary definition. Ask yourself: Does *auspicious* sound positive or negative? How about *callow*? Negative words often just sound negative. Positive words, on the other hand, tend to sound more friendly. If you said that *auspicious* is positive, you are right. It means "favorable or hopeful." And if you thought that *callow* is negative, you are also right. It means "immature or unsophisticated." Although in most cases this strategy will help, there are some exceptions. For example, the word *mirth,* which means gladness, has a positive charge but seems negative.

You can also use prefixes to help determine a word's charge. *Mal-, de-, dis-, dys-, un-, in-, im-,* and *mis-* often indicate a negative, while *pro-, ben-, magn-,* and *eu-* are often positives. Some words are neutral and don't have a charge. But if you can get a sense of the word's charge, you can probably answer some questions on that basis alone.

Words Commonly Confused for One Another

Accept or *except? Alter* or *altar? Discrete* or *discreet?* Even if you know the difference between these words, when you are under pressure and short on time, it's easy to get confused. So, here's a quick review of some of the most common troublemakers.

Accept (v.): To take or receive. The CEO accepted the treasurer's resignation.

Except (prep.): Leave out. The Town Council approved all elements of the proposal except the tax increase.

Adverse (adj.): Unfavorable. This plan would have an adverse impact on the environment.

Averse (adj.): Opposed or reluctant. I am averse to doing business with companies that don't treat their employees fairly.

Advice (n.): Recommendation as to what should be done. I would like your advice about how to handle this situation.

Advise (v.): To recommend what should be done. I will be happy to advise you on your decision to attend business school.

Affect (v.): To have an impact or influence on. The expansion of Pyramid Shopping Mall will certainly affect traffic on the access roads.

Effect (n.): Result, impact. The proposal will have a deleterious effect on everyone's quality of life. (v.): To cause, implement. The engineers were able to effect a change in the train's performance at high speeds.

Altar (n.): An elevated structure, typically intended for the performance of religious rituals. The court refused to allow the construction of an altar on public property.

Alter (v.): To change. It should be a simple matter to alter one's will.

Among (prep.): Used to compare three or more items or entities. We can choose from among dozens of styles.

Between (prep.): Used to compare two items or entities. We can choose between these two styles.

Assent (n.): Agreement; (v.): to agree. Peter has given his assent to the plan.

Ascent (n.): Movement upward. The ascent to the summit was steep and difficult.

Assure (v.): To convince or guarantee. He has assured me that this is a safe investment.

Ensure (v.): To make certain. Please ensure that this is a safe investment.

Insure (v.): To guard against loss. There is no way to insure this investment.

Bazaar (n.): A market. I found these fantastic trinkets at the bazaar.

Bizarre (adj.): Very strange, weird. No one knew how to respond to such a bizarre question.

Cite (v.): To quote, to refer. The article cited our annual report.

Sight (n.): Something seen or visible; the faculty of seeing. What an amazing sight!

Site (n.): Location; (v.): to place or locate. This is the perfect site for a new office.

Complement (n.): Something that completes; (v.): to go with or complete. This item really complements our product line.

Compliment (v.): To flatter; (n.): a flattering remark. That was a sincere compliment.

Continual (adj.): Repeated regularly and frequently. Alan's continual telephone calls finally wore Rosa down and she agreed to a meeting.

Continuous (adj.): Extended or prolonged without interruption. The continuous banging from the construction site gave me a severe headache.

Decent (adj.): Proper, acceptable. You can trust Lena to do what is decent.

Descent (n.): Downward movement. The rapid descent of the balloon frightened its riders.

Discrete (adj.): Separate, not connected. These are two discrete issues.

Discreet (adj.): Prudent, modest, having discretion; not allowing others to notice. I must be very discreet about looking for a new job while I am still employed here.

Disinterested (adj.): Impartial, objective. We need a disinterested person to act as an arbitrator in this dispute.

Uninterested (adj.): Not interested. Charles is uninterested, but he will come along anyway.

Eminent (adj.): Outstanding, distinguished. The eminent Dr. Blackwell will teach a special seminar in medical ethics this fall.

Imminent (adj.): About to happen, impending. Warned of imminent layoffs, Loretta began looking for another job.

Incidence (uncountable noun: occurrence): Frequency. The incidence of multiple births is on the rise.

Incident (pl.: incidents) (countable noun: events, cases): An occurrence of an event or situation. She preferred to forget the whole incident.

Personal (adj.): Private or pertaining to the individual. Please mark the envelope "personal and confidential."

Personnel (n.): Employees. This year we had a 5 percent increase in personnel.

Precede (v.): To come before. The list of resources should precede the financial worksheet.

Proceed (v.): To go forward. Although Jules will be absent, we will proceed with the meeting as planned.

Principal (n.): Head of a school or organization, primary participant, main sum of money; (adj.): main, foremost, most important. Joshua is one of the principals of the company.

Principle (n.): A basic truth or law. I have always run my business based on the principle that honesty is the best policy.

Reign (v.): To exercise power; (n.): period in which a ruler exercised power or a condition prevailed. Under the reign of King Richard, order was restored.

Rein (n.): A means of restraint or guidance; (v.): to restrain, control. You need to rein in your intern, Carol—she's taking on much too much responsibility and doesn't seem to know what she is doing.

Than (conj.): Used to compare. I will be more successful this time because I am more experienced than before.

Then (adv.): I was very naïve back then.

Weather (n.): Climatic conditions, state of the atmosphere. The bad weather is going to keep people away from our grand opening.

Whether (conj.): Used to refer to a choice between alternatives. I am not sure whether I will attend the grand opening or not.

Now that you have completed the vocabulary lesson, the next step is to learn about the different question types you may face on a test day. Even if the civil service exam you take has a different format for vocabulary questions, the samples found here will still help you prepare for nearly any standardized vocabulary test.

Sample Vocabulary Questions

Although there are several vocabulary question types, the most common ones are found here. Before you review these question types, let's discuss difficulty level. Because some jobs require more education or experience, the questions on some civil service exams will be more difficult than others. The practice test in this chapter includes questions ranging from basic to intermediate so you can prepare for any level you may face. For questions that you find more difficult, be sure to use the tips and strategies found later in this chapter to understand how to deal with these questions on test day.

Question Type 1: Synonyms

A synonym is a word that is similar in meaning to another word. *Fast* is a synonym for *quick*. *Garrulous* is a synonym for *talkative*. On some civil service exams, a synonym question will read: "*Fast* most nearly means…." It will typically be followed by four or five answer choices.

Here is an example of a synonym question.

Genuine most nearly means:
- (A) Authentic
- (B) Valuable
- (C) Ancient
- (D) Damaged

Question Type 2: Antonyms

Antonyms are words that have the opposite meaning of one another. *Slow* is the antonym of *fast*; *taciturn* is the antonym of *garrulous*. An antonym question will usually read: "*Generous* means the opposite of…." Again, the question may be followed by either four or five answer choices, depending on the test.

Here is an example of an antonym question.

Generous is the opposite of
- (A) Altruistic
- (B) Vindictive
- (C) Allotted
- (D) Lucrative
- (E) Miserly

Question Type 3: Analogies

Analogy questions ask you to compare two words and then extend the relationship to another set of words. Simply put, an analogy is a comparison. When you say, "She is as slow as molasses," or "He eats like a horse," you are making an analogy. In the first example, you are comparing the person in question with molasses, and in the second example, you are comparing the person with a horse. Analogies look like this:

Talkative : Loquacious :: Thrifty : Miserly

The ":" and "::" are translated as:

Talkative IS TO Loquacious AS Thrifty IS TO Miserly

The symbols are used to show the relationship of the words to each other. Remember, on your civil service exam, analogies may use the symbol or may be written out in words. Here's a sample analogy question.

Edifice : Building ::
   (A) Shack : Bungalow
   (B) Tome : Book
   (C) Magazine : Newspaper
   (D) Couch : Bench

One set of words—*edifice* and *building*—is given. The second set is missing. Your job is to find the second set of words among the answer choices with the same corollary relationship that exists in the first set. In this case, the answer is (B). An *edifice* is another word for a *building* and a *tome* is another word for a *book*.

Analogies may seem challenging at first glance. However, once you become familiar with the format, you will find that they are pretty straightforward and very predictable. With practice, you can learn to get analogy questions right even when you don't know all of the vocabulary words involved. Here are some other helpful things to know about analogies.

The Classic Bridges.   Relationships between items in analogy questions need to be strong and definite, so there are some bridges that appear again and again. We call these classic bridges. Get to know these bridges; you will be able to identify them quickly and save yourself a lot of time getting to the correct answer choice on analogy questions. As you read through each one, use the space provided to come up with an example of your own.

Bridge 1: Character
One word characterizes the other.
Quarrelsome : Argue… Someone quarrelsome is characterized by a tendency to argue.
Vivacious : Energy… Someone vivacious is characterized by a lot of energy.
Your example: _____

Bridge 2: Lack
One word describes what someone or something lacks (or does not have).
Coward : Bravery… A coward lacks bravery.
Braggart : Modesty… A braggart lacks modesty.
Your example: _____

Bridge 3: Function
One word names an object; the other word defines its function or what it is used for.
Scissors : Cut… Scissors are used to cut.
Pen : Write… A pen is used to write.
Your example: _____

Bridge 4: Degree

One word is a greater or lesser degree of the other word.

Loud : *Deafening*… Something that is extremely loud is deafening.

Apartment : *Mansion*… An apartment provides housing on a lesser degree than a mansion. (Including the specific "lesser degree" might help you hone in on the right answer choice.)

Your example: _____

Bridge 5: Example

One word is an example of, or type of, the other word.

Measles : *Disease*… Measles is a type of disease.

Baseball : *Sport*… Baseball is a type of sport.

Your example: _____

Bridge 6: Group

One word is the group form of the other word.

Forest : *Trees*… A forest is made up of many trees.

Bouquet : *Flowers*… A bouquet is made up of many flowers.

Your example: _____

Everything you have learned so far will help you on test day. However, if you want to get a top score, review the following Tips for Vocabulary Success before you complete the practice test at the end of this chapter.

Tips for Vocabulary Success

Here are some strategies that will help you on test day. Be sure to review them often so that these strategies will be second nature to you when you take the practice test at the end of this chapter and most importantly when you take your civil service exam.

Kaplan's Target Strategy for Synonyms

Step 1. Define the stem word.

Step 2. Find the answer choice that best fits your definition.

Step 3. If no choice fits, think of other definitions for the stem word and go through the choices again.

Let's use Kaplan's Target Strategy for the sample synonym question found earlier in the chapter.

Genuine most nearly means:

    (A) Authentic

    (B) Valuable

    (C) Ancient

    (D) Damaged

Step 1. Define the Stem Word.   What does *genuine* mean? Something genuine is something real, such as a real Picasso painting, rather than a forgery. Your definition might be something like this: *Something genuine can be proven to be what it claims to be.*

Step 2. Find the Answer Choice That Best Fits Your Definition.   Go through the answer choices one by one to see which one fits best. Your options are: *authentic*, *valuable*, *ancient*, and *damaged*. Something genuine could be worth a lot or not much at all, old or new, or in good shape or bad. The only word that really means the same thing as *genuine* is (A) *authentic*.

Step 3. If No Choice Fits, Think of Other Definitions for the Stem Word and Go Through the Choices Again.   In the example above, one choice fits. Now, take a look at the following example:

Grave most nearly means:
    (A) Regrettable
    (B) Unpleasant
    (C) Serious
    (D) Careful

When you applied Step 1 to this example, maybe you defined *grave* as a burial location. You looked at the choices, and didn't see any words like *tomb* or *coffin*. What to do? Use the idea presented in Step 3; go back to the stem word, and think about other definitions. Have you ever heard the word *grave* used any other way? If someone were in a "grave situation" what would that mean? *Grave* can also mean *serious* or *solemn*, so (C) *serious* fits perfectly. If none of the answer choices seems to work with your definition, there may be a second definition you haven't considered yet.

Avoiding a Pitfall

Kaplan's Target Strategy for Synonyms should be the basis for tackling every question, but there are a few other things you need to know to perform your best on synonym questions. Fortunately, there is only one pitfall to watch out for.

Choosing Tempting Wrong Answers

Test makers choose wrong answer choices very carefully. Sometimes that means throwing in answer traps that will tempt you, but aren't correct. Be a savvy test taker; don't fall for these distracters. What kinds of wrong answers are we talking about here? In synonym questions, there are two types of answer traps to watch out for: answers that are almost right, and answers that sound like the stem word. Let's illustrate both types to make the concept clear.

Delegate most nearly means:
    (A) Delight
    (B) Assign
    (C) Decide
    (D) Manage

Favor most nearly means:
    (A) Award
    (B) Prefer
    (C) Respect
    (D) Improve

In the first example, choices (A) and (C) might be tempting, because they all start with the prefix *de-*, just like the stem word, *delegate*. It is important that you examine all the answer choices, because otherwise you might choose (A) and never get to the correct answer, which is (B). In the second example, you might look at the word *favor* and think, oh, that's something positive. It's something you do for someone else. It sounds a lot like choice (A), *award*. Maybe you pick (A) and move on. If you do that, you would be falling for a trap. The correct answer is (B) *prefer,* because *favor* is being used as a verb, and *to favor* someone or something is to like it better than something else—in other words, to prefer it.

If you don't read through all of the choices, you might be tricked into choosing a wrong answer. At this point, you have a great set of tools for answering most synonym questions. You know how to approach them and you know some traps to avoid. But what happens if you don't know the word in the question? Here are some techniques to help you figure out the meaning of a tough vocabulary word and answer a difficult synonym question.

What to Do if You Don't Know the Word

- Look for familiar roots and prefixes.
- Use your knowledge of foreign languages.
- Remember the word used in a particular context.
- Figure out the word's charge.

Let's examine each technique more closely.

Look for Familiar Roots and Prefixes.   Having a good grasp of how words are put together will help you tremendously on synonym questions, particularly when you don't know a vocabulary word. If you can break a word into pieces you do understand, you will be able to answer questions you might have thought too difficult to tackle. The prefix is the beginning of a word. In *biology*, the prefix is *bio,* which means life. The root of a word is an example of its basis. For example, the word *indigestible* has the word *digest* at its core. Look at the words below. Circle any prefixes or roots you know.

Benevolence
Insomnia
Inscribe
Conspire
Verify

Bene- means good; *somn-* has to do with sleep; *scribe* has to do with writing; *con-* means doing something together; and *ver-* has to do with truth. So, if you were looking for a synonym for *benevolence*, you would definitely want to choose a positive, or "good" word.

Use Your Knowledge of Foreign Languages.   Remember, any knowledge of a foreign language, particularly if it's one of the Romance languages (French, Spanish, Italian), can help you decode lots of vocabulary words. Look at the example words below. Do you recognize any foreign language words in them?

Facilitate
Dormant
Explicate

In Italian, *facile* means easy; in Spanish, *dormir* means to sleep; and in French, *expliquer* means to explain. A synonym for each of these words would have something to do with what they mean in their respective language.

Remember the Word Used in a Particular Context.   Sometimes a word might look strange to you when it is sitting on the page by itself, but if you think about it, you realize you have heard it before in a phrase. If you can put the word into context, even if that context is cliché, you are on your way to deciphering its meaning.

Illegible most nearly means:
    (A) Illegal
    (B) Twisted
    (C) Unreadable
    (D) Eligible

Have you heard this word in context? Maybe someone you know has had his or her handwriting described as illegible. What is illegible handwriting? The correct answer is (C). Remember to try to think of a definition first, before you look at the answer choices. Some of the answer choices in this example are tricks. Test writers know that it is can be easy to mistake eligible for illegible if you are under stress and working quickly. Don't fall for these tricks.

Here's another example:

Laurels most nearly means:
- (A) Vine
- (B) Honor
- (C) Lavender
- (D) Cushion

Is "don't rest on your laurels" a phrase you have ever heard or used? What do you think it might mean? The phrase "don't rest on your laurels" originated in ancient Greece, where heroes were given wreaths of laurel branches to signify their accomplishments. Telling people not to rest on their laurels is the same thing as telling them not to get too smug; rather than living off the success of one accomplishment, they should strive for improvement. The correct answer is (B). In this case, a cliché helped you deduce the answer.

Figure Out the Word's Charge.   Even if you know nothing about a word, have never seen it before, don't recognize any prefixes or roots, and can't think of any word in any language that it sounds like, you can still take an educated guess by trying to define the word's charge. Remember the discussion found earlier in the chapter about deciding if a word has a positive or negative charge? Well, on all synonym questions, the correct answer will have the same charge as the stem word, so use your instincts about word charge to help you when you are stuck on a tough word.

If it helps, mark each answer choice with a "+" for positive words and a "–" for negative words. If you are unsure of the answer, you can at least eliminate words with opposite charges. Word charge is a great technique to use when answering antonym questions, too.

Kaplan's Target Strategy for Antonyms

Step 1. Define the word. Then, think of a word that means the opposite.
Step 2. Find the answer choice that best fits your definition.
Step 3. If no choice fits, think of other definitions for the stem word and go through the choices again.

Let's practice with an example:

Dear means the opposite of:
- (A) Beloved
- (B) Close
- (C) Cheap
- (D) Family

Step 1. Define the Word. Then, Think of a Word That Means the Opposite. *Dear* is a pretty familiar word. You know it from the beginning of a letter as in "Dear Aunt Sue." So, you might define *dear* as *a term for someone you love*. The opposite might be *a term for someone you hate or dislike*. Use roots, context, or word charge to help you if you don't know the definition of the question word.

Step 2. Find the Answer Choice That Best Fits Your Definition. When we look at the answer choices—*beloved, close, cheap, family*—none of them fits our definition of the opposite of *dear*, which is *someone disliked* or *hated*. Since *dear* is an "easy" word, we have to figure that perhaps our definition is a little off. We have to refocus it.

Step 3. If No Choice Fits, Think of Other Definitions for the Stem Word and Go Through the Choices Again. When we use the term "Dear Aunt Sue," or "Dear Sir," what are we saying about that person? We say that we care about them and think that they are valuable—they are worth a lot to us. When people pay a lot of money for something, it is often expressed as, "they paid dearly." In other words, the purchase was worth a lot, and had a lot of value. Okay, so let's use valuable as our new definition of *dear*. Our antonym would then be the opposite of *valuable—worthless*, perhaps. Which of the answer choices comes closest to worthless? Choice (C), *cheap* is closest to *worthless*. That's the correct answer.

The rules that applied for attempting to find a synonym for a word applies to antonyms as well—the difference is that once you have defined the word, you are going to look for its opposite. When you don't find an obvious answer choice for a word you know, you can suspect that there is an alternate meaning for that word. Use your knowledge of the word's primary meaning and see if you can expand on it to arrive at the correct answer.

You can also use your knowledge of word roots, familiarity with the word in context, and the word's charge to help you select the answer to antonym questions. When looking at a word's charge on antonym questions, don't forget you are looking for words with the opposite charge. If the question word has a positive charge, your answer choice should have a negative one, and vice versa.

Kaplan's Target Strategy for Analogies

Step 1. Build a bridge.
Step 2. Predict your answer choice and select an answer.
Step 3. Adjust your bridge if necessary.

You might remember from earlier in the chapter that a bridge is a sentence you create to express the relationship between the words in an analogy. Building a bridge helps you zone in on the correct answer and prevents you from falling for traps that will lead you to the wrong answer. Let's use Kaplan's Target Strategy to examine a sample analogy question found earlier in the chapter.

Edifice : Building ::
    (A) Shack : Bungalow
    (B) Tome : Book
    (C) Magazine : Newspaper
    (D) Couch : Bench

Step 1. Build a Bridge.   In every analogy question, there is a strong, definite connection between the two stem words. Your first task is to figure out this relationship. A bridge is a short sentence that relates the two words in the question, and every pair of words will have a strong bridge that links them.

Step 2. Predict Your Answer Choice and Select an Answer.   You know that an edifice is another word for a building. Now you need to determine which answer choice relates two items in the same way. Use your bridge to do that. The bridge was: An edifice is another word for a building. Apply the same bridge to the incomplete pair:

A _____ is another word for _____.

So, when we predict the answer choice, we come up with two words that mean the same thing. A tome is a type of book. Take a moment to look at the incorrect answer choices:

(A) Shack : Bungalow
(B) Tome : Book
(C) Magazine : Newspaper
(D) Couch : Bench

The choices are all related in some way, but not in the way the bridge is defined. Building a strong bridge is essential to predicting an answer, selecting a correct answer choice, and avoiding traps. What if your bridge doesn't work? Sometimes you may find that even though you came up with a bridge, none of the answer choices fit. In this case, your bridge is either too broad or too narrow. You will need to refocus it. That's where Step 3 comes in.

Step 3. Adjust Your Bridge if Necessary.   Using the previous example, let's see how you can adjust a weak bridge.

Edifice : Building ::
    (A) Shack : Bungalow
    (B) Tome : Book
    (C) Magazine : Newspaper
    (D) Couch : Bench

Let's say you created this bridge: "An edifice and a building *can both be* lived in." Then you went to the answer choices and plugged in the bridge:

KAPLAN

(A) A shack and a bungalow *can both be* lived in.
(B) A tome and a book *can both be* read.
(C) A magazine and a newspaper *can both be* read.
(D) A couch and a bench *can both be* sat on.

You could say that nearly every choice fits. In this case, the bridge was too general, so you will need to adjust your bridge. What would a good adjustment be? Try to create a relationship between the words that is as specific as possible; the more specific your bridge is, the fewer choices will match it. A good bridge for this pair might be: "An edifice is another word for a building." Now try plugging that bridge into the answer choices.

(A) A shack is another word for a bungalow. **No.**
(B) A tome is another word for a book. **Yes.**
(C) A magazine is another word for a newspaper. **No.**
(D) A couch is another word for a bench. **No.**

It should now be easier to see the correct answer: edifice : building :: tome : book, which is choice (B).

Equally important as a good vocabulary is strong reading comprehension skills. The following lessons and strategies will help you improve these skills as you prepare for test day.

Reading Comprehension Lesson

As you can imagine, understanding what you read is a critical skill for success at any job, civil service or not. For this reason, many if not most civil service exams will include a section to test your reading comprehension skills. You will find both short (1 paragraph) and long (4–7 paragraphs) passages on the test. Shorter passages will generally be followed by a single question, while longer passages will be followed by as many as six questions. However, contrary to what you might expect, to answer each reading comprehension question correctly, you don't need to read the passage word-for-word. Instead, your best bet is to carefully *skim* the passage.

Serious Skimming

Each reading comprehension passage is written for a purpose: The author wants to make a point, describe a situation, or convince you of his or her ideas. As you are reading, ask yourself the following questions:

- What is this passage about?
- What is the point of this passage?
- What is the author trying to say?
- Why did the author write this?
- What are the two or three most important ideas or details in this passage?

Asking yourself questions as you read is known as active reading, and it's the key to staying focused and grasping quickly the point of a passage. Active reading means reading lightly but with a focus—in other words, *serious skimming*. This way, you can quickly find the main ideas and identify the tone of the passage. The questions themselves will help you fill in the details by directing you back to important information and specific details in the passage. Getting hung up on details while reading is a major reading comprehension pitfall. You need to grasp the outline, but you don't need to get all the fine features.

Components of Serious Skimming.

- Skim the passage to get the writer's drift. Don't read the passage thoroughly. It's a waste of time.
- As you skim, search for important points. Mark them in your test booklet. Don't wait for important information to jump out at you.
- Don't get caught up in details. The questions will often supply them for you or tell you exactly where to find them.

Organization

Before you practice serious skimming on a passage, it helps to know how they are typically organized so you can easily recognize some of the main features of a paragraph and of a passage as a whole.

Paragraph Organization.   A paragraph begins with an introductory sentence. This sentence, often called the topic sentence, tells you what the paragraph is about. For example, a paragraph about the importance of computers may begin: *It is almost impossible to calculate how much time and effort computers save employees in today's workplace.* By reading this sentence, you know what the passage is about (computers) and how the author feels (that computers are effective). You would expect the rest of the paragraph to give specific examples of how computers save time and make an office more efficient. At the end of the paragraph, the author will likely give a brief summary or opinion on what the paragraph covered. This is how most paragraphs are organized: introduction, supporting details, summary/conclusion. Even when skimming you should always read the first and last sentence of every paragraph closely, as they will tell you the most important or main ideas of a paragraph.

Passage Organization.   Luckily, passages such as essays, articles, and other nonfiction writing are organized in a similar way to the paragraphs that are found within them. A passage begins with an introductory paragraph. The entire paragraph introduces the topics and ideas that the author wants to convey. The introduction is followed by a number of body paragraphs, each of which goes into greater detail. Rather than the main idea, these paragraphs contain the specifics of the topic. Finally, the conclusion summarizes the ideas and details presented and offers a final thought about the entire passage.

On test day, knowing how a passage is organized can help you locate the correct answer to a question. If you are asked about a main idea, you know that the first and last paragraphs (or sentences) will be most helpful. If you are asked a detail question, know that you should be looking in the body of the passage. Skimming is a great way to get the gist of any passage and to help you answer any related questions.

Civil Service Reading Passages

On most civil service tests, the reading comprehension passages are divided into two types—short passages and long passages. However, depending on the exam you take, the topics of the passages can vary widely. In general, passage will *not* be works of fiction such as short stories, poems, narratives, or excerpts from novels. Instead, passages are nonfiction and the topics will be based on social sciences, natural sciences, and current events. On some exams, you may also be presented with descriptions of office procedures or office documents (memos, business letters, etc.). If the job you are applying for is very specific, such as a police officer, the subject matter of the reading comprehension passage may be law enforcement-related, such as a report from a crime scene. This book focuses on general works of nonfiction.

Four or Five Answer Choices?

Depending on which civil service test you take, each multiple-choice question will be followed by either four or five answer choices. Throughout this book, the number of answer choices varies between four and five to give you practice with both formats.

In order to succeed on reading comprehension questions, you must do some serious skimming and analyze information. You will not, however, need to have any previous knowledge about a topic to answer the questions. Everything you need to know will be right there in front of you. Reading comprehension instructions tell you to answer questions based on what is stated or implied in the accompanying passage or passages. Typically, short passages are usually followed by one to two questions, while longer passages are followed by five or more questions. To familiarize yourself with the types of questions, review the sample reading comprehension questions that follow.

Sample Reading Comprehension Questions

When you read passages on a civil service exam, you are reading for a specific purpose: to be able to correctly answer as many questions as possible. Fortunately, most reading comprehension questions, regardless of which civil service test you take, belong to one of four basic question categories. They are:

- Main Idea
- Detail
- Inference
- Vocabulary-in-Context

Main Idea Questions

Main idea questions test how well you understand the passage as a whole. They ask about:

- The main point or purpose of a passage or individual paragraphs
- The author's overall attitude or tone
- The logic underlying the author's argument
- How ideas relate to each other in the passage

Main idea questions often begin like this:

- Which one of following best expresses the main idea of the passage?
- The author's primary purpose is to…
- Which of the following would be an appropriate title for this passage?

If you are stuck on a main idea question, even after reading the passage, do the detail questions first. You can often use the detail questions to help you get a deeper understanding of the whole passage. Here are two sample main idea questions.

Based on the passage, the author believes that extraterrestrial life
- (A) exists only in science fiction
- (B) is abundant throughout the universe
- (C) will not be discovered in our lifetime
- (D) is physically impossible
- (E) may never be discovered because life may take vastly different forms in other galaxies

The article describes the experience of working as a grocery store clerk and waiter in order to
- (A) show that you should always treat others as you want to be treated
- (B) explain why people became waiters
- (C) suggest that believing in yourself is the key to success
- (D) demonstrate the value of hard work

Detail Questions

Detail questions ask about localized bits of information—usually specific facts or details from the passage. These questions sometimes give you a line or paragraph reference—a clue to where in the passage you will find your answer. Beware of answer choices that seem to reasonably answer the question in the stem but that don't make sense in the context of the passage or that are true but refer to a different section of the text.

Detail questions test:

- Whether you understand significant information that is stated in the passage
- Your ability to locate information within a text
- Your ability to differentiate between main ideas and specific details

Detail questions often begin like this:

- According to the passage/author…
- The author states that…
- The author mentions which one of the following as…
- Which of the following statements is true?

Sometimes the answer to a detail question will be directly in the line or lines that are referenced. Other times, you might need to read a few sentences before or after the referenced line(s) to find the correct answer. When in doubt, use the context (surrounding sentences) to confirm the right choice. If the passage is short, there may not be line references and you will have to locate the relevant information on your own. This is when passage mapping (see Tips for Reading Comprehension Success later in this chapter) is especially helpful.

Here are some sample detail questions.

According to the passage, the inspiration for firefighters' "Fill the Boot" fundraiser (paragraph 1) came from
  (A) a shoe store owner
  (B) performers who "pass the hat"
  (C) the National Firefighter's Association
  (D) a creative fire squad

In the phrase "lively progeny" (line 9), the author is referring to
  (A) her daughter
  (B) her students
  (C) herself
  (D) the reader

Inference Questions

To *infer* is to draw a conclusion based on reasoning or evidence. Often, writers will use suggestion or inference rather than stating ideas directly. But they will also leave you plenty of clues so you can figure out just what they are trying to convey. Inference clues include word choice (diction), tone, and specific details. For example, say a passage states that a particular idea *was perceived as revolutionary*. You might infer from the use of the word *perceived* that the author believes the idea was not truly revolutionary but only *perceived* (or seen) that way.

Inference questions test your ability to use the information in the passage to come to a logical conclusion. This question type often begins like this:

- It can be inferred from the passage that…
- The passage/author suggests that…
- The passage/author implies that…

The key to inference questions is to stick to the evidence in the text. Most inference questions have pretty strong clues, so avoid any answer choices that seem far-fetched. If you can't find any evidence in the passage, then it probably isn't the right answer.

Here are two sample inference questions.

The author suggests that Henry Ford's experience working on his father's farm
- (A) was traumatic
- (B) inspired Ford to become an engineer
- (C) turned Ford away from his desire to be a farmer
- (D) was uneventful
- (E) gave him the courage to try out some of his inventions

It can be inferred from the passage that the author
- (A) agrees with Ford that the present is the only thing that matters
- (B) believes that Ford placed too much emphasis on success
- (C) thinks Ford's industrial revolution undermined basic human values
- (D) believes we should be less dependent upon automobiles

Make sure you read inference questions carefully. Some answer choices may be true, but if they can't be inferred from the passage, then they can't be the correct answer.

Vocabulary-in-Context Questions

Vocabulary-in-context questions ask about the usage of a single word. These questions do not test your ability to define words; you are not being tested on your specific vocabulary knowledge. Instead, these questions test your ability to infer the meaning of a word from context.

Sometimes, the words tested on civil service exams are fairly common words with more than one definition. Many of the answer choices will be definitions of the tested word, but only one will work in context. If a vocabulary-in-context question has a line reference you should always use it.

Remember that the most common meaning of the word in question is RARELY right. You can think of this as the *obvious* choice. Say *curious* is the word being tested. The obvious choice is *inquisitive*. But curious also means *odd*, and that is more likely to be the answer. Using context to find the answer will help keep you from falling for this kind of trap. But you can also use these obvious choices to your advantage. If you get stuck on a vocabulary-in-context question, you can eliminate the obvious choice and guess from the remaining answers.

Here's a sample vocabulary-in-context question.

The word "abandon" as used in line 32 most nearly means
- (A) without restraint or control
- (B) to leave alone
- (C) to surrender
- (D) to move on
- (E) unusual or abnormal

Knowing about the question types is only half of your preparation. Keep reading to learn the best strategies for tackling passages and answering each question type quickly and accurately.

Tips for Reading Comprehension Success

If you are not confident in your reading comprehension skills, pay close attention to the following strategies. Here you will find general reading comprehension strategies, as well as specific strategies for longer passages and for vocabulary-in-context questions. Remember to use this section as a resource before you take the practice test found at the end of this chapter.

Kaplan's Target Strategy for Reading Comprehension Questions

Serious skimming is a vital component of Kaplan's Target Strategy for attacking reading comprehension questions. Once you have seriously skimmed the passage, here's how to approach the questions:

Step 1. Read the question stem.
Step 2. Locate the material you need.
Step 3. Predict the answer.
Step 4. Select the best answer choice.

Step 1. Read the Question Stem.   This is the place to really read carefully. Make sure you understand exactly what the question is asking. Is it a main idea question? Detail? Inference? Vocabulary? Are you looking for an overall main idea or a specific piece of information? Are you trying to determine the author's attitude or the meaning of a particular word?

Step 2. Locate the Material You Need.   If you are given a line reference, read the line mentioned and the material surrounding it. This will help clarify exactly what the question is asking and provide you with the context you need to answer the question correctly.

If you are not given a line reference, scan the text for keywords from the question and quickly reread those few sentences.

Step 3. Predict the Answer.   Don't spend time making up a precise answer. You need only a general sense of what you are after so you can recognize the correct answer quickly when you read the choices.

Step 4. Select the Best Answer Choice.   Scan the choices, looking for one that fits your idea of the right answer. If you don't find an ideal answer, quickly eliminate wrong choices by checking the passage. Rule out choices that are too extreme or go against common sense. Get rid of answers that sound reasonable but don't make sense in the context of the passage or the question.

Always make sure there is evidence for your inference in the passage; if it is not strongly implied, it is probably incorrect.

Try Kaplan's Target Strategy on the passage and question that follow.

Question 1 refers to the following passage.

Many mammals instinctively raise their fur when they are cold—a reaction produced by tiny muscles just under the skin that surround hair follicles. When the muscles contract, the hairs stand up, creating an increased air space under the fur. The air space provides more effective insulation for the mammal's body, thus allowing it to retain more heat for longer periods of time. Some animals also raise their fur when they are challenged by predators or even other members of their own species. The raised fur makes the animal appear slightly bigger, and, ideally, more powerful. Interestingly, though devoid of fur, humans still retain this instinct. So, the next time a horror movie gives you "goose bumps," remember that your skin is following a deep-seated mammalian impulse now rendered obsolete.

1. The "increased air space under the fur" mentioned serves primarily to
    (A) combat cold
    (B) intimidate other animals
    (C) render goose bumps obsolete
    (D) cool overheated predators

Step 1. Read the Question Stem.   In this case, the question is straightforward: what purpose does the increased air space under the fur serve? It asks you to find a detail in the passage.

Step 2. Locate the Material You Need.   You are not given a line reference, but because the passage is not very long, you should be able to quickly locate the quoted phrase and read that specific line as well as a line or two before and after. By doing this, you see that the author says that mammals raise their fur when they are cold.

Step 3. Predict the Answer.   Just by reading those lines around the reference, you can predict that the air space relates to staying warm.

Step 4. Select the Best Answer Choice.   Choice (A) is correct, but you should review the other answer choices quickly, just in case there is a detail you missed.

Choice (B) is mentioned later in the passage, but it explains that animals raise their fur to appear larger, not the function of the air space under the fur.

Choice (C) refers to a detail at the very end of the passage, but it does not relate specifically to the air space.

Choice (D) is not true. The passage mentions that the reaction provides insulation against the cold; it is not a way for animals to cool down.

Passage Introductions

Some of the longer passages you may encounter on a civil service exam could begin with a brief introduction that tells you what the passage is about. This is an important part of the question set and should not be skipped. The introduction helps you focus your reading by preparing you for the kind of information and ideas to come; don't ignore it. If there is no introduction, pay close attention to the introductory paragraph for information on the passage's topic.

Kaplan's Target Strategy for Reading Comprehension Questions can be used for both short and long passages. However, other strategies are useful only on longer passages. The following section outlines some of these strategies.

Long Passage Strategies

Aside from the obvious—that they are longer than short ones—long passages offer additional opportunities to increase your score. When you encounter a long passage remember the strategy of serious skimming. You should not attempt to carefully read every word of a long passage. Consider these strategies as well as the following tips while you take the practice test in this chapter and as you prepare for the official civil service exam.

Question Order. Reading comprehension questions often have a specific order for longer passages. In general, the questions correspond to the passage, so the first few questions ask about the beginning of the passage, the middle questions about the middle, and the last few questions about the end. The last couple of questions are likely to be main idea questions that ask you about the overall main idea of the passage. Use this to your advantage as you are answering several questions based on one passage.

Map It. Longer passages cover many aspects of a topic. For example, the first paragraph might introduce the subject, the second paragraph might present one viewpoint, and the third paragraph might argue for a different viewpoint. Within each of these paragraphs, there are several details that help the author convey a message. Because there is a lot to keep track of, you need to mark up long passages as follows:

- Write simple notes in the margin as you read.
- Write down the purpose of each paragraph.
- Underline key points.
- Concentrate on places where the author expresses an opinion.

These notes are your *passage map*. Your passage map helps you find the part of the passage that contains the information you need. The process of creating your passage map also forces you to read actively. Because you are constantly trying to identify the author's viewpoint and the purpose of each sentence and paragraph, you will be working hard to understand what is happening in the passage. This translates into points on the test.

What a marvelous and celestial creature was Leonardo
da Vinci. As a scientist and engineer, his gifts were unparalleled.
But his accomplishments in these capacities were hindered
by the fact that he was, before all else, an artist. As

(5)   one conversant with the perfection of art, and knowing the
futility of trying to bring such perfection to the realm of
practical application, Leonardo tended toward variability
and inconstancy in his endeavors. His practice of moving
compulsively from one project to the next, never bringing

(10)   any of them to completion, stood in the way of his making
any truly useful technical advances.

> *OP—L is great*
>
> *MainPoint—L is genius, but never stuck w/1 thing long enuf 2B a "scientist"*
>
> *OP—L under-achieved*

When Leonardo was asked to create a memorial for one
of his patrons, he designed a bronze horse of such vast proportions
that it proved utterly impractical—even impossible—

(15)   to produce. Some historians maintain that Leonardo
never had any intention of finishing this work in the first
place. But it is more likely that he simply became so intoxicated
by his grand artistic conception that he lost sight of
the fact that the monument actually had to be cast.

(20)   Similarly, when Leonardo was commissioned to paint
the *Last Supper*, he left the head of Christ unfinished, feeling
incapable of investing it with a sufficiently divine
demeanor. Yet, as a work of art rather than science or engineering,
it is still worthy of our greatest veneration, for

(25)   Leonardo succeeded brilliantly in capturing the acute anxiety
of the Apostles at the most dramatic moment of the
Passion narrative.

> *Ex #1—horse*
>
> *alt. opinion*
>
> *OP—L is a genius but impractical*
>
> *Ex #2—last Sup*
>
> *MainPoint L gets caught up in idea, forgets actual work*

Such mental restlessness, however, proved more problematic
when applied to scientific matters. When he turned

(30)   his mind to the natural world, Leonardo would begin by
inquiring into the properties of herbs and end up observing
the motions of the heavens. In his technical studies and
scientific experiments, he would generate an endless stream
of models and drawings, designing complex and unbuildable

(35)   machines to raise great weights, bore through mountains,
or even empty harbors.

> *OP—switching from art to science here*
>
> *Ex #1—Natural Ex#2—technical*
>
> *MainPoint: L's short attention span bad for science*

It is this enormous intellectual fertility that has suggested
to many that Leonardo can and should be regarded as one
of the originators of modern science. But Leonardo was not

(40)   himself a true scientist. "Science" is not the hundred-odd
principles or *pensieri* that have been pulled out of his
Codici. Science is comprehensive and methodical thought.
Granted, Leonardo always became fascinated by the
intricacies of specific technical challenges. He possessed the

(45)   artist's interest in detail, which explains his compulsion
with observation and problem solving. But such things
alone do not constitute science, which requires the working
out of a systematic body of knowledge—something
Leonardo displayed little interest in doing.

> *alt. opinion*
>
> *OP*
>
> *back?*
>
> *MainPoint—L is genius and a compulsive problem solver, but no scientist*
>
> *L no good at*

KEY:

OP = opinion
Ex = example
L - Leonardo

When Time Is Running Out on Long Passages.   If you work on short passages first and save long passages for last, you may find yourself racing against the clock. Remember, it is always best to skim the passage before you hit the questions. But if you only have a few minutes left, here's how to score fast points.

You can answer vocabulary-in-context questions and many detail questions without reading the passage. If the question has a line reference, locate the material you need to find your answer and follow the Target Strategy as usual. You won't have the overall picture to guide you, but you might be able to reach the correct answer just by focusing on the details and using the context around a particular word or line.

Also, remember to skip around within the section if you need to. You can usually tackle the passages in any order you like within the same section. So if you can see that one passage will be much easier for you than the others, work through that one first. But don't skip around after you have already read most or all of a passage. You have already invested your time reading, so try all the questions that go with it before you move to another passage.

Avoiding Tempting Wrong Answers

As we mentioned before, test writers are skilled at including answer choices that seem to be right, but are actually incorrect. Here is how to spot distracters for main idea, detail, and inference questions.

Incorrect answers to main idea questions are usually those that:

- Are too specific, dealing with just one small detail of the passage
- Are too general, going beyond the scope of the passage
- Contradict the passage
- Are too extreme

You can almost always eliminate wrong answer choices to detail questions for one of the following reasons:

- They don't answer the question that's been asked
- They use similar wording to the passage, but distort what was said
- They contradict the passage
- They go outside the scope of the passage, stating things that weren't said
- They use extreme wording

Wrong answer choices on inference questions are those that:

- Contradict the passage
- May or may not be true based on the passage
- Are too strongly worded
- Go beyond the scope of the passage, suggesting things that aren't discussed

Keep these in mind as you review the answer choices to questions; they could prevent you from losing points on test day.

Vocabulary-in-Context Strategy

Here's our strategy for vocabulary-in-context questions: Once you find the tested word in the passage, treat the question like you are completing a fill-in-the-blank. Pretend the word is a blank in the sentence. Read a line or two around the imaginary blank if you need to, then predict a word for that blank. Check the answer choices for a word that comes close to your prediction. If your prediction does not come close, substitute each of the answer choices for the word in the question. Choose the one that makes the best sense in the context of the sentence.

Summary

In this chapter you have learned what your vocabulary skills are like as well as several ways to improve them. You know three of the most common vocabulary question types and more importantly, you have reviewed Kaplan's Target Strategy for each. Your reading comprehension skills have also been boosted with a review of Kaplan's best strategies for understanding the passage and knowing how to find the answer to any of the four question types. To reinforce the lessons in this chapter, here is a 50-question practice test. Using all the tips and strategies you have just learned, answer these question and be sure to review the detailed answer explanations for any questions you miss.

Practice Test 2

50 Questions
50 Minutes

1 (A)(B)(C)(D) 14 (A)(B)(C)(D) 27 (A)(B)(C)(D) 40 (A)(B)(C)(D)
2 (A)(B)(C)(D) 15 (A)(B)(C)(D) 28 (A)(B)(C)(D) 41 (A)(B)(C)(D)(E)
3 (A)(B)(C)(D) 16 (A)(B)(C)(D) 29 (A)(B)(C)(D) 42 (A)(B)(C)(D)(E)
4 (A)(B)(C)(D) 17 (A)(B)(C)(D) 30 (A)(B)(C)(D) 43 (A)(B)(C)(D)(E)
5 (A)(B)(C)(D) 18 (A)(B)(C)(D) 31 (A)(B)(C)(D) 44 (A)(B)(C)(D)(E)
6 (A)(B)(C)(D) 19 (A)(B)(C)(D) 32 (A)(B)(C)(D) 45 (A)(B)(C)(D)(E)
7 (A)(B)(C)(D) 20 (A)(B)(C)(D) 33 (A)(B)(C)(D) 46 (A)(B)(C)(D)(E)
8 (A)(B)(C)(D) 21 (A)(B)(C)(D) 34 (A)(B)(C)(D) 47 (A)(B)(C)(D)(E)
9 (A)(B)(C)(D) 22 (A)(B)(C)(D) 35 (A)(B)(C)(D) 48 (A)(B)(C)(D)(E)
10 (A)(B)(C)(D) 23 (A)(B)(C)(D) 36 (A)(B)(C)(D) 49 (A)(B)(C)(D)(E)
11 (A)(B)(C)(D) 24 (A)(B)(C)(D) 37 (A)(B)(C)(D) 50 (A)(B)(C)(D)(E)
12 (A)(B)(C)(D) 25 (A)(B)(C)(D) 38 (A)(B)(C)(D)
13 (A)(B)(C)(D) 26 (A)(B)(C)(D) 39 (A)(B)(C)(D)

Choose the word that is most similar in meaning to the word in italics.

1. *Benefactor* most nearly means:
   (A) Critic
   (B) Recipient
   (C) Supporter
   (D) Mediator

2. *Seclude* most nearly means:
   (A) Isolate
   (B) Tempt
   (C) Acquire
   (D) Emit

3. *Initiative* most nearly means:
   (A) Satisfaction
   (B) Irritation
   (C) Money
   (D) Ambition

4. *Acquit* most nearly means:
   (A) Surrender
   (B) Obtain
   (C) Appraise
   (D) Clear

5. *Ultimate* most nearly means:
   (A) First
   (B) Secondary
   (C) Legitimate
   (D) Final

6. *Truncate* most nearly means:
   (A) Widen
   (B) Shorten
   (C) Pack
   (D) Join

7. *Erroneous* most nearly means:
   (A) Approximate
   (B) Unplanned
   (C) Mistaken
   (D) Sensual

8. *Imperative* most nearly means:
(A) Sad
(B) Timely
(C) Open
(D) Crucial

9. *Feasible* most nearly means:
(A) Workable
(B) Breakable
(C) Imperfect
(D) Evident

10. *Reparations* most nearly means:
(A) Compensation
(B) Sadness
(C) Thanks
(D) Antipathy

Choose the word that has the opposite meaning of the word in italics.

11. *Aptitude* means the opposite of:
(A) Inability
(B) Height
(C) Peak
(D) Talent

12. *Replenish* is the opposite of:
(A) Reward
(B) Supply
(C) Increase
(D) Deplete

13. *Disperse* means the opposite of:
(A) Gather
(B) Display
(C) Reverse
(D) Handle

14. *Abundant* is the opposite of:
(A) Scarce
(B) Lush
(C) Collect
(D) Loyal

15. *Polarize* is the opposite of:
(A) Delay
(B) Welcome
(C) Cancel
(D) Unite

16. *Mar* is the opposite of:
(A) Deaden
(B) Flatter
(C) Praise
(D) Enhance

17. *License* is the opposite of:
(A) Curb
(B) Tie
(C) Rule
(D) Impress

18. *Interminable* is the opposite of:
(A) Brief
(B) Constant
(C) External
(D) Physical

19. *Rudimentary* is the opposite of:
(A) Advanced
(B) Polite
(C) Regulated
(D) Essential

20. *Cede* is the opposite of:
(A) Make sense of
(B) Fail
(C) Get ahead of
(D) Retain

Choose the pair of words that show the same relationship to the pair of words given.

21. Impeccable : Flaw ::
(A) Impeachable : Crime
(B) Obstreperous : Permission
(C) Impetuous : Warning
(D) Absurd : Sense

22. Enunciate : Pronounce ::
    (A) Recite : Impress
    (B) Reiterate : Bother
    (C) Inquire : Ask
    (D) Elaborate : Explain

23. Vegetate : Active ::
    (A) Resist : Beaten
    (B) Mope : Gloomy
    (C) Grow : Small
    (D) Accept : Questioning

24. Debilitate : Weak ::
    (A) Empower : Strong
    (B) Countermand : Illegal
    (C) Abominate : Absent
    (D) Instigate : Guilty

25. Exculpate : Blame ::
    (A) Abash : Shame
    (B) Forswear : Violence
    (C) Decipher : Code
    (D) Forgive : Debt

26. Intransigent : Flexibility ::
    (A) Transient : Mobility
    (B) Disinterested : Partisanship
    (C) Dissimilar : Variation
    (D) Progressive : Transition

27. Realist : Quixotic ::
    (A) Scholar : Pedantic
    (B) Fool : Idiotic
    (C) Idler : Lethargic
    (D) Tormentor : Sympathetic

28. Scrutinize : Observe ::
    (A) Excite : Pique
    (B) Beseech : Request
    (C) Search : Discover
    (D) Smile : Grin

29. Paraphrase : Verbatim ::
    (A) Approximation : Precise
    (B) Description : Vivid
    (C) Quotation : Apt
    (D) Interpretation : Valid

30. Castigate : Wrongdoing ::
    (A) Congratulate : Success
    (B) Amputate : Crime
    (C) Annotate : Consultation
    (D) Deface : Falsehood

Read these passages and choose the best answer to each of the questions that follow each passage.

Diamond is the hardest known material and has long been used in various industrial shaping processes, such as cutting, grinding, and polishing. Diamond, sapphire, ruby (sapphire with chromium "impurities"), and garnet are increasingly important in various applications. For example, diamond is used in sensors, diaphragms for audio speakers, and coatings for optical materials. Sapphire is used in gallium nitride-based LEDs, ruby is used in check valves, and synthetic garnet is used in lasers intended in applications in medical products.

31. An appropriate title for this passage would be
    (A) The Timeless Allure of Precious Stones
    (B) Nontraditional Uses of Diamonds
    (C) Industrial Uses for Precious Stones
    (D) Gem Hardness and Utility

32. It can be inferred from this passage that
    (A) diamonds are more precious than sapphires
    (B) rubies come from the same type of stone as do sapphires
    (C) garnets are used in various industrial shaping processes
    (D) precious stones are more costly than ever

It is without question a travesty that our children are no longer given healthy, nutritious food options for lunch in our public schools. Hamburgers, pizza, and chocolate are not only giving our kids a bigger waistline, but these junk foods are also helping teach them poor eating habits. It is imperative that we change the mindset that any food is good food and start offering students better meals at the same prices. Otherwise, a new generation of obese Americans is a given.

33. According to the passage, over the past few years, school lunches have gotten
    (A) more expensive
    (B) more exotic
    (C) healthier
    (D) less nutritious

The Taj Mahal was built by the Mughal emperor Shah Jahan as a burial place for his favorite consort, Arjumand Banu Bagam. She was known as Mumtaz Mahal, "the Elect of the Palace." Construction began soon after her death in 1631. The Taj Mahal and the surrounding complex of buildings and gardens was completed by about 1653. The Taj Mahal is much more than an expression of love and loss, though. It's a breathtakingly symmetrical representation of heaven.

34. Which of the following best describes the main idea of the passage?
    (A) the Taj Mahal as an expression of love and loss
    (B) the history of the building of the Taj Mahal
    (C) the Taj Mahal as an architectural representation of heaven
    (D) the balance between the building and the gardens in the Taj Mahal complex

Consistently propped up by the press since its inception, Biosphere 2 came to be regarded during the late 1980s as an indicator of the possibility of human habitation in space. Even as many scientists worked to quench such lofty goals, the press was dubbing Biosphere 2 the most exciting scientific project undertaken since the moon landing. Then, as the project's first crew emerged from a supposed two-year isolation to be greeted by a swirl of negative attention and controversy, the publications that had trumpeted the project quickly reversed direction. Frustrated with their conception's failures, the project's financiers fired their management team and, in a reversal of their own, lashed out at the same press they had once courted.

35. In the second sentence, the author implies that
    (A) the media's expectations for the project were probably unrealistic
    (B) many scientists thought that aeronautical projects should not have ambitious goals
    (C) some scientists found the Biosphere 2 project more exciting than the moon landing
    (D) the project's management team should have heeded the advice of scientists

36. What is best meaning of the word *inception* in the first sentence?
    (A) commencement
    (B) announcement
    (C) review
    (D) invention

Leaders are not born strong. They grow that way based on events early on in their lives. Taking a look at the early life of any great leader shows moments where great strength was required. These moments of greatness brought out extraordinary grace and courage. It was only later that such qualities were on display for everyone to see.

37. Based on the information given, one can say that
    (A) leaders are larger in stature than normal people
    (B) nonleaders are incapable of grace and courage
    (C) great leaders emerge from great circumstances
    (D) leaders are required for great moments

Four years ago, the governor came into office seeking to change the way politics were run in this state. Now, it appears he has been the victim of his own ambitious political philosophy. Trying to do too much has given him a reputation as being pushy, and the backlash in the state has let him accomplish little. He may very well lose in his reelection bid.

38. Which of the following is the best definition of *backlash* as it is used in the passage?
    (A) primitive opinion
    (B) adverse proposal
    (C) reverse decision
    (D) negative reaction

Bear Mountain State Park opened in 1916 and rapidly became a popular weekend destination for many New Yorkers looking for an escape from the city grind. The ensuing unnaturally high volume of visitors to the area caused an upsurge in traffic, and it was soon apparent that the ferry services used to cross the Hudson were insufficient. In 1922, the New York State Legislature introduced a bill that authorized a group of private investors led by Mary Harriman to build a bridge across the river. The group, known as the Bear Mountain Hudson Bridge Company, was allotted thirty years to construct and maintain the bridge, after which the span would be handed over to New York State.

39. In context, "volume," most closely means
    (A) pollution
    (B) resentment
    (C) capacity
    (D) quantity

40. According to the passage, which is true about the bridge?
    (A) It was originally constructed by New York State.
    (B) It opened to the public in 1916.
    (C) It was necessitated by inadequate ferry services.
    (D) It took thirty years to build.

(1)   There are approximately 90 different elements that occur naturally, but most of the things we encounter are made up of combinations of only about one third of them. Like most things in life, elements are each unique and, yet, can be grouped into classifications with other elements because of similarities. Thus, elements can be grouped according to whether they are highly reactive, somewhat reactive, or inert.

(2)   Each element is made up of atoms. Within each atom is a certain number of protons and a matching number of electrons. This balance is necessary to keep each atom electrically neutral. An atom contains a nucleus with shells around it. The inner shell contains a maximum of two electrons. The next shell contains a maximum of eight electrons. Large atoms have a third shell that can contain a maximum of 32 electrons. As a general rule, if the outer shell is complete, it will seldom react with anything. If the outer shell still has room for several electrons, it is considered somewhat reactive. However, an atom that only needs one or two electrons to fill its outer shell will grab an electron or two from another atom. It is then considered highly reactive.

(3)   Table salt, which is the combination of sodium and chlorine, is an example of two highly reactive elements coming together. Sodium loses an electron from its outer shell, and chlorine gains that electron. This makes an ionic bond.

One is negatively charged, the other is positively charged. This "opposites attract" bond is very strong.

(4)   Another kind of bond is a covalent bond. This is a bond in which elements come together and share electrons. Oxygen has six electrons in its outer shell. It thus needs two more. Hydrogen has one in its outer shell. So, when two hydrogens meet one oxygen, the one electron in the outer shell of each hydrogen fills in the two missing in oxygen to complete it to eight. However, they simply share the electrons. It is a nice sharing bond.

(5)   There are six elements that usually do not combine with others. These are called inert gases. They have the maximum number of electrons in their outer shells so they are not looking to find another element to bond with. Four of these elements are helium, argon, neon, and krypton.

41. What is the main idea of this passage?
   (A) one third of the elements are common
   (B) the ninety elements
   (C) the classification of elements according to bonding preference
   (D) bonds versus elements
   (E) the periodic table

42. According to the passage, most common items are composed of
(A) approximately thirty separate elements
(B) combinations of approximately thirty separate elements
(C) approximately ninety different elements
(D) combinations of approximately ninety different elements
(E) the passage does not address this

43. The author of this passage uses the phrase *As a general rule* (paragraph 2) to indicate
(A) that most elements will combine with other elements given the right environment
(B) that most elements have two missing electrons in their outer shell
(C) that elements with full outer shells are not reactive
(D) how table salt is made
(E) the reactivity of hydrogen

44. Based on the passage, which of the following is a good definition of *inert*?
(A) inoperable
(B) slow
(C) inactive
(D) reactive
(E) powerless

45. According to the passage, which of the following is true?
(A) there are only four inert gases
(B) inert gases are elements that do not combine with other elements easily
(C) the six inert gases are helium, argon, neon, and krypton

(D) verification of inert gases has never been done
(E) inert gases are more readily able to combine with other elements than are sodium and chlorine

(1) At last count in the year 2004, it was estimated that there were over 800 million mobile phone users worldwide, almost one-eighth of the global population. Underscoring this dramatic number is a growing suspicion that the radiation emitted by these mobile phones may be dangerous to humans. There is no doubt that the body absorbs varying levels of radiation emitted by cell phones, but the question is, do these levels pose a health risk?

(2) Mobile phones employ radio waves, more specifically, radiofrequency (RF) energy, to wirelessly transmit voice data and other information between handsets and base stations. The Food and Drug Administration (FDA) and the Federal Communications Commission (FCC), share the responsibility of making sure every cell phone sold in the United States complies with certain safety guidelines that limit a person's exposure to RF energy. The amount of RF energy absorbed by a human body when in contact with a cell phone is measured by a unit known as the Specific Absorption Rate (SAR). A phone deemed "safe" by the FCC must not have a SAR level higher than 1.6 watts per kilogram (1.6 W/kg). Deeming a phone "safe," however, is misleading. The FDA states that though there is "no hard evidence of adverse health effects [of cell phone use] on the general public," they urge further research into the subject. This state-

ment is vague at best, and rather than answering our question, it brings up a number of others.

(3)   This vague stance by the FDA and FCC derives from the fact that most of the research findings on the possible negative affects of cell phone radiation have been controversial. An example of this was a study conducted on rats in 1995 at the University of Washington in Seattle by a research team headed by Henry Lai. Lai's team concluded that the exposure of rats to RF energy within the FCC cell phone SAR limits resulted in DNA breaks in the rats' brain cells. Such breaks could be linked to cancer and brain tumors. With good reason, these findings garnered much media attention; but they could never be clinically replicated, which cast serious doubt upon them. It is worth nothing, however, that one of the studies that tried to confirm Lai's findings was conducted by a group funded by the cell phone manufacturer Motorola.

(4)   The use of cell phones has only recently become widespread. Regardless of what research may indicate, time will offer the true answer as to whether cell phones are indeed dangerous. Let's hope, unlike the smoking of cigarettes 50 years ago, the outcome does not reach us too late.

46. The author's primary purpose in the passage is to
(A) dispel rumors about the negative side effects of cell phone use
(B) illustrate how the risks associated with using a cell phone outweigh the phone's positive uses
(C) describe how cell phones transmit voice data and other information
(D) discuss her personal views on the subject of cell phone radiation
(E) address the question of whether or not cell phone use is unhealthy

47. According to the passage, which of the following is true?
(A) Cell phone batteries utilize the power of RF energy.
(B) The FCC would consider a cell phone with a SAR level of 1.5 W/kg as unsafe.
(C) Henry Lai concluded that the exposure of rats to RF energy could be linked to cancer and brain tumors in rats.
(D) The FDA and FCC believe that further cell phone research is unnecessary.
(E) Smaller cell phones have higher SAR ratings.

48. In the context of the passage, the phrase "vague stance" (paragraph 3) means:
(A) obscure opinion
(B) negative perspective
(C) empty promise
(D) odd thought
(E) undefined position

49. It can be inferred from the passage that a phone deemed "safe" (paragraph 2) by the FCC would actually be better described as
(A) probably safe
(B) possibly safe
(C) completely safe
(D) somewhat dangerous
(E) extremely dangerous

50. The author draws a comparison between cigarettes and cell phones in the final sentence of the passage in order to
(A) illustrate a historical precedent
(B) demonstrate how quickly a person becomes hooked on their phone
(C) display her dislike for both
(D) make a point about social etiquette
(E) exaggerate the issue to help her illustrate a point

Answers and Explanations

1. C
Word roots alone could have gotten you to the correct answer. *Bene-* means "good," and *factor* means "doer," so *benefactor* means "someone who does good things." Of the answer choices, (C) makes the most sense. Specifically, a *benefactor* is one who gives aid, usually in the form of money.

2. A
Try to come up with a context clue. Have you ever heard of a "secluded island"? Which of the answer choices best describes such an island? Only (A), *isolate*, makes any sense. *Isolate* and *seclude* both mean "to separate" or "keep away from contact with others."

3. D
Initiative means "resourcefulness," but *ambition* is the closest match here.

4. D
If you have heard that a defendant was "acquitted of all charges," you should know that means the defendant was *cleared* of all charges, so (D) is the correct answer.

5. D
You might have been able to decipher the meaning of *ultimate* if you have studied a foreign language. For instance, the Spanish word for final is *ultimo*. And *ultimate*, in fact, means "final" or "eventual."

6. B
Try to think where you've heard *truncate* before. If that doesn't work, ask yourself whether *truncate* could possibly mean each of the various answer choices. Sometimes, even if you have only the vaguest sense of a word, you will still know what the word cannot mean. *Truncate* does mean *shorten*.

7. C
Erroneous means mistaken. You should have had no problem with this question if you realized *erroneous* has the same root as "error," meaning "mistake."

8. D
Imperative, like *crucial*, means very important or essential.

9. A
Maybe you have heard something like: "The plan is feasible." Which answer

choice best describes a plan? *Feasible* does mean "workable" or "viable."

10. A

Reparations, like *compensation*, means repayment for loss suffered.

11. A

Aptitude is ability; the opposite is inability.

12. D

To *replenish* means to provide more; the opposite is deplete.

13. A

To *disperse* means to scatter; the opposite is gather.

14. A

Abundant means plenty; the opposite is scarce.

15. D

To *polarize* is to cause to concentrate around two conflicting positions. *Unite* means "bring together as one."

16. D

To *mar* is to damage in a way that makes something less attractive or perfect. *Enhance* means "to increase the value or beauty" of something. If you needed to guess, you could eliminate *flatter* and *praise* because they are synonyms.

17. A

In this question, *license* is a verb. It must be, because choice (D), *impress*, can't be a noun, so all the choices in this question must be verbs. As a verb, license means "to allow." The correct answer choice will be a synonym for "prohibit." To *curb* is to restrain.

18. A

The prefix *in-* usually means "not," so something that is interminable is not ter-

minable, that is, never ending. The correct answer choice will be a word that means "short-lived." *Brief* means "short-lived." This is the correct answer.

19. A

Rudimentary means basic; the opposite is advanced.

20. D

To *cede* is to yield, give up, or transfer title to someone else—one country cedes land to another, for instance. If you don't give something up, you hang onto it, so a synonym for "keep" will be the correct answer. *Retain* is the answer choice you are looking for.

21. D

Something *impeccable* is perfect, it doesn't have a *flaw*. *Absurd* means without sense, so this is the correct answer.

22. D

The first pair has a degree bridge where *enunciate*, or articulate, means to pronounce more clearly and precisely. We can eliminate choices (A) and (B), because *recite* and *impress* have no definitive relationship, and *reiterate*, meaning to repeat, has no necessary relationship with *bother*. Next, we can eliminate choice (C) because there is no degree difference between the words. In choice (C), to *inquire* means to *ask*. Choice (D) is the correct answer because to *elaborate*, which means to clarify or to discuss in depth, is, by definition, to *explain* something more clearly and precisely.

23. D

One who *vegetates* is inert or not *active*. If this gave you trouble, think of vegetables, which are markedly inactive living things, or perhaps the expression "veg out" meaning to stagnate, not think or do anything. Similarly, one who *accepts* (D) takes things as they are without doubting, doesn't call things into question; he or she is therefore not *questioning*.

24. A

To *debilitate* means, by definition, to make weak. By definition, to *empower*, choice (A), means to make *strong*. To *countermand*, (B), by definition, does not mean to make something *illegal*; it means to cancel or reverse an order. (A) is the only choice that works, and it's correct.

25. D

By definition, to *exculpate* is to clear from blame. If you weren't sure of the meaning of exculpate, you could try breaking the word apart: *ex-* means remove or undo, *culpa-*, as in *culprit*, means guilt or blame. Likewise, *forgive* (secondary meaning: to grant relief from payment) is to clear from *debt*. (D) is correct.

26. B

Intransigent means unyielding—the opposite of *flexible*. Our bridge is "a person who is intransigent is lacking in flexibility." The only pair that looks good is (B), *disinterested* and *partisanship*. One who's disinterested is unbiased—he doesn't have an interest in either side of a dispute. *Partisan* means partial to a particular party or cause. That's the opposite of disinterested. So partisanship, the quality of being biased, is lacking in a person who could be described as disinterested.

27. D

Quixotic means impractical, after the hero of *Don Quixote*. A *realist* is a person who is especially realistic. *Realistic* is the opposite of *quixotic,* so a realist is never quixotic. In (A), *pedantic* people show off their learning. Many scholars are pedan-

tic, so this won't work. In (B), a *fool* is foolish—a synonym for *idiotic*. The same relationship holds true for (C)—an *idler* is a *lethargic* person. (D) looks good—a *tormentor* is vicious or cruel. The opposite sort of person would be kinder and more *sympathetic*—a tormentor is never sympathetic.

28. B

To *scrutinize* means to *observe* intently, so the relationship is one of degree. In (A), to *pique* interest is to *excite* interest. The words mean the same thing. In (B), to *beseech* means to *request* with great fervor—this is more like it. In (C), to *search* is the process you go through to *discover* something. That's different from the stem pair. In (D) to *grin* is to *smile* broadly—this reverses the original pair.

29. A

Paraphrase means restatement of a text using different words. *Verbatim* means word for word or exact. A paraphrase is not verbatim—the words are near opposites. The only choices opposite in meaning are *approximation* and *precise*, in (A). An approximation is an estimate, while something that's precise is exact, so an approximation is not precise. (A) is correct.

30. A

Castigate means *criticize*. Knowing that, we can build the bridge: people castigate others for their wrongdoings. Try this bridge on the choices. People *congratulate* each other for their *successes*.

31. C

The passage here discusses industrial uses for precious stones, so the correct answer choice (C) should pretty much jump out at you. This passage is not about the "timeless allure" of these stones (A), and gem "hardness" is only mentioned in reference to diamonds, so (D) is out. (B) is incorrect because the passage is not just about diamonds, not to mention that the industrial uses for diamonds that are mentioned are fairly traditional.

32. B

The passage notes parenthetically that a ruby is a sapphire with chromium "impurities," so one can logically infer that both gems come from the same kind of stone, choice (B). All the other answer choices are never mentioned anywhere in the passage.

33. D

The author feels strongly that meals in school cafeterias have become more and more similar to the junk food available at fast food joints. Choice (A) is not applicable, regardless of its validity, because it is not the central point of the passage. Choice (B) is nowhere indicated in the passage, and choice (C) is the opposite of what we are asked in the question. Of the answer choices given, only choice (D) correctly answers the question.

34. C

The very last sentence of the passage states the author's central point: "[The Taj Mahal is] a breathtakingly symmetrical representation of heaven." You may want to mentally rephrase the main idea in your own words, because the correct answer will almost always be a paraphrase of the answer you have found. In this case, answer choice (C) is the close paraphrase we are looking for.

35. A

The sentence tells you that many scientists were trying to suppress or extinguish the "lofty goals" or overly high expectations for the project, suggesting that the scientists thought such goals were unrealistic. Since it was the press that was "dubbing" the project as so exciting, this indicates that the unrealistic expectations were put forth or perpetuated by the media. (B) is out of scope; the passage only discusses the Biosphere 2 project, not projects dealing with aircraft or flight. (C) is a distortion; the passage only suggests that the *press* believed the project was *as* exciting as the moon landing, not that scientists found it more exciting. The author makes no recommendations regarding what the management team (D) should or should not have done, and the passage does not mention whether the management team consulted scientists.

36. A

The meaning of *inception* is origin or commencement. Although choice (D) seems like a good choice, *invention* does not have the give the same meaning to the context. Choices (B) and (C) are not correct.

37. C

The correct answer to this question is (C). In this case, the inference is related to the main point of the paragraph, which is to discuss how great leaders are made. (A) is simply not discussed in the passage. (B) also is not stated in the passage. (D) is a statement that cannot really be judged based on the information available. Only (C) must be true based on the information in the passage.

38. D

The correct answer is (D). Although the other choices might make sense in the context of the sentence, only choice (D) is the correct definition of *backlash*.

39. D

Look for the word that could best be linked to "an upsurge in traffic" and "insufficient." (A) and (B) are both out of scope. *Pollution* is an effect of traffic, but this makes no sense in context, and *resentment* is never alluded to in the passage. (C) is also a distortion. Although exceeding the *capacity* for cars in an area is the cause of traffic, this definition of "volume" does not work in terms of the sentence's structure. (D) is correct.

40. C

Verify each given statement and choose the correct answer. If you didn't read the passage carefully enough, you may have been tempted to choose (D). The passage states, "The group…was allotted thirty years to construct and maintain the bridge…" It does not say that it took thirty years to build. Only choice (C) is correct. The other statements contain details found in the passage but they are not true statements about the bridge.

41. C

This passage describes the fact that elements can be classified into three types based on their likelihood of forming bonds. Although (A) and (B) are both mentioned in the first paragraph, these are simply establishing details. They are not the main ideas of the passage. (D) is not accurate because of the *versus*. This passage discusses elements and bonds, but they are not in a *versus* relationship. Although the periodic table is indeed where the classification of the elements could be found, the table itself is not the main idea of the passage. Thus, (E) is not correct.

42. B

The passage states that there are approximately 90 elements, but most things are made up of combinations of approximately one third of those. That would be approximately 30. Choices (A) and (C) are not correct because most things are not made up of single elements. (D) is not correct because most common things involve only about one third of the 90 elements. (E) is not correct because, whereas the passage does not say it directly, it can be inferred using the evidence from the passage that there are approximately *90 elements* and *most things* are made up of combinations of *one third* of them.

43. C

This is an introductory element to give a simplistic rule that explains a natural occurrence. None of the other answers are correct because this introductory element precedes a statement about elements with full outer shells and the fact that they are not reactive.

44. C

You do not need to know the chemical definition of *inert* to answer this question. You can understand its meaning through context. The passage reads, "they are not looking to find another element to bond with," which implies that they are inactive. Therefore, choice (C) is the correct answer.

45. B

This is a specific detail question answered by the evidence offered in the first two sentences in the last paragraph. Although there are only four inert gases listed, there are actually six inert gases. Thus, choice (A) is not correct. Choice (C) is not correct because it uses the number six, but then only lists four. Choice (D) is not correct because it is not addressed in the passage, and it is not true. Choice (E) is not correct because inert gases, as stated in the final paragraph, do not combine readily with other elements.

46. **E**

The author reveals her primary purpose for writing the passage when she states "There is no doubt that the body absorbs varying levels of radiation emitted by cell phones, but the question is, do these levels pose a health risk?" She then uses the rest of the passage to address this question. Therefore, choice (E) is correct.

47. **C**

This is a detail question that asks you to sift through false distracters to find your answer, which is (C). This question also illustrates why it is very important to read each question carefully. True, paragraph 2 states that Henry Lai's findings could "never be clinically replicated," however, that does not alter the fact that Lai made his conclusions based on them. (A) is incorrect because RF energy is used for the cell phone's communications (paragraph 1), not as a power source for the battery. (B) is incorrect because a SAR level of 1.5 W/kg is below the FCC's "safe" limit of 1.6 W/kg. (D) is contradicted by the text, which says that both organizations "urge further research." (E) is out of scope.

48. **E**

In this sentence, the phrase "vague stance" means that no definite position has been taken by the organizations. Choice (A) is a distracter, but *obscure* does not have the same meaning as *vague* so it is not the correct answer.

Only choice (E) is correct in the context of the passage.

49. **B**

At the end of paragraph 2, the author characterizes the deeming of a cell phone "safe," as misleading because of the FDA's rather vague statement that there is "no hard evidence of adverse health effects [of cell phone use] on the general public." The key here is the phrase "no hard evidence." This could be translated into "so far there is no evidence to prove cell phones are unsafe." That evidence may one day arrive, but it may never arrive. So it is *possible* that they are safe, but it has yet been proven. (B) is your answer. There is no evidence to support (A), (D), and (E), so they are incorrect. (C) is directly contradicted by the author's statement that to deem a cell phone "safe" is misleading.

50. **A**

The comparison between cigarettes and cell phones is a good one because 50 years ago or so, many people smoked cigarettes unaware of how dangerous they were, until it was too late. The author, by making this comparison, is illustrating a historical precedent for what our ignorance of the effects RF radiation may lead to. (B) is incorrect: Like cigarettes, there are many people who seemingly cannot live without cell phones, but this is never discussed. (C) is out of scope. With (D), there is certainly a comparison to make between second-hand smoke and obnoxious cell phone behavior, but that is out of scope. And with (E), the implication of the comparison is not an exaggeration. It is possible that the effects of RF energy upon human health could rival that of smoking.

CHAPTER FIVE

Verbal Ability—Writing

Introduction

You have worked on your reading and vocabulary skills, but for most civil service jobs, writing is equally as important for job success. In some jobs you may have to demonstrate strong writing skills, however, for most jobs it is enough to know how to recognize effective writing. For this reason, most civil service exams will not require you to write an essay or other sample. Instead, various question types will test your knowledge of grammar and the rules of standard written English. This chapter begins with a detailed English grammar lesson. The lesson is followed by samples of different question types that may be included on the civil service exams. Finally, if you still feel unsure about your grasp on the rules of grammar, we provide tips for success to do your best on these questions. At the end of this chapter, test how much you have learned by completing Practice Test 3. You can check the results of this 50-question test with the detailed answer explanations that follow.

Written English Lesson

In this part of the chapter you will find a review of the main topics in written English: punctuation, grammar, and style. There is also a special section on spelling. This lesson will be especially helpful as you review the question types, which are found in the next section.

Punctuation Review

In this section, we will review different forms of punctuation, as well as the rules pertaining to each.

Commas.   Use commas to separate the last two items in a long series.

If more than two items are listed in a series, they should be separated by commas. The final comma—the one that precedes the word *and*—may be omitted. An omitted final comma would not be considered an error on any civil service exam.

> Example: My recipe for cornbread includes cornmeal, butter, eggs, and milk.
> Also Correct: My recipe for cornbread includes cornmeal, butter, eggs and milk.

Look out for commas placed before the first element of a series, or after the last element.

> Incorrect: Jason watches television, morning, noon, and night.
> Incorrect: Action programs, cartoons, and soap operas, are his favorite shows.

Use commas to separate two or more adjectives before a noun, but not after the last adjective in a series.

> Example: It was a long, dull novel.
> Incorrect: The novel was a long, dull, travesty.

If a phrase or clause is not necessary to the main idea expressed by a sentence, it is parenthetical and should be separated by commas.

> Example: Heather, who always attends practice, is the best athlete on the team.

The phrase *who always attends practice* is not necessary information. The main idea here is that Heather is the best player on the team. The clause in the middle merely serves to further describe her; it is therefore set off by commas.

Use commas after introductory phrases.

> Example: Having driven two hundred miles in one day, we were exhausted.

When combining independent clauses with *and*, *but*, *for*, *nor*, *or*, *so*, and *yet*, use a comma before the conjunction.

> Example: Lena tried to make a pot roast, but she burned it.
> Example: The question of who built the pyramids of Egypt has been an ongoing debate, yet one historian believes she has the answer.

Semicolons.   Like commas, semicolons can separate independent clauses where no conjunction is used.

Example: The question of who built the pyramids of Egypt has been an ongoing debate; scholars and Egyptologists continue to argue about the number and identity of the workers.

Colons.   In standard written English, the colon is used only as a means of signaling that what follows is a list, definition, explanation, or restatement of what has gone before. A word or phrase such as *like the following, as follows, namely,* or *this* is often used along with the colon to make it clear that a list, summary, or explanation is coming up.

Example: The rules are as follows: No running, horseplay, or splashing is permitted in the pool area.

The Apostrophe.   The apostrophe has two distinct functions. It is informally used with contractions to indicate that one or more letters have been eliminated, i.e., *he's* (*he is*), *they're* (*they are*), *there's* (*there is*), *let's* (*let us*), etc.

Example: The girl's a member of the varsity basketball team. (The girl is a member of the varsity basketball team.)

The apostrophe is also used to indicate the possessive form of a noun.

Example: The boy's uniform was covered in mud. (The uniform belonging to the boy was covered in mud.)

With plural nouns that end in *s* the apostrophe is placed on the end of the word to indicate possession.

Example: The girls' team sang victory songs all the way home.

Careful: *It's* is the contraction for *it is*. The possessive *its* does not have an apostrophe.

Example: It's getting late. (It is getting late.)
Example: The dog drank all the water in its bowl.

Quotation Marks.   Direct quotes should be placed within quotation marks. If there is an introductory clause, a comma precedes the first quotation mark and the first word of the quotation is capitalized. The ending punctuation goes within the quotation mark. If the quotation is followed by a clause, end it with a comma.

Example: John asked, "How do you do?"
Example: "I'm fine," Sue replied.

If the quotation is broken, punctuate as follows:

Example: "How often," Carlos asked, "do you walk your dog?"

Now that you know about punctuation, let's review a very important topic in written English: grammar.

Grammar Review

English grammar is a topic that could easily fill an entire book. This review covers the main topics of grammar as they pertain to any writing questions on a civil service exam.

Subject-Verb Agreement.   The form of a verb must agree with its subject in person and number.

Agreement of Person.   When we talk about *person*, we are talking about whether the subject and verb of a sentence show that the author is making a statement about him or herself (first person), the person he or she is speaking to (second person), or some other person, place, or thing (third person).

The first person subjects are *I* and *we*.

Example: We are bicycling from New York to Vermont. I am training every other day.

The second person subject is *you*.

Example: Are you sure you wouldn't like to join us?

The third person subjects are *he*, *she*, *they*, *it*, and names of people, places, and things.

Example: The dog yaps day and night.

Agreement of Number.   When we talk about *number*, we are talking about whether the subject and verb show that one thing (singular) or more than one thing (plural) is being discussed.

Incorrect: The children catches the bus to school every morning.
Correct: The children catch the bus to school every morning.

Be especially careful when the subject and verb are separated by a long string of words.

Incorrect: Truth, the ultimate goal of all researchers, are elusive.
Correct: Truth, the ultimate goal of all researchers, is elusive.

Pronouns.   A *pronoun* is a word used in place of a noun. The *antecedent* of a pronoun is the word to which the pronoun refers. A pronoun must clearly refer to and agree with its antecedent.

Example: Research shows that green tea prevents cavities because it reduces bacteria.

Occasionally, the antecedent will appear in a sentence *after* the pronoun.

Example: Because it helps prevent cavities, green tea is a healthy beverage.

	Singular	**Plural**
First Person Pronouns	I, me, my, mine	we, us, our, ours
Second Person Pronouns	you, your, yours	you, your, yours
Third Person Pronouns	he, him, she, her, it, one, his, her, hers, its, one's	their, theirs

Pronouns must agree in number with their antecedents. A singular pronoun should stand for a singular antecedent. A plural pronoun should stand for a plural antecedent. Here is a typical pronoun error.

Incorrect: The school refused to let Ann Marie attend the class field trip because their rules required her to have a permission letter.

What does the plural possessive *their* rules refer to? The singular noun *school.* The singular possessive *its* is what we need here.

Person Agreement.   A first person pronoun should stand for a first-person antecedent, and so on.

Example: Caroline and Joe completed their laboratory report yesterday.

Relative Pronouns.   Never use the relative pronoun *which* to refer to a person. Use *who, whom,* or *that.*

Incorrect: The woman which is waving is my sister.
Correct: The woman who is waving is my sister.

Pronouns and Case.   A more subtle pronoun error is that the pronoun is in the wrong case.

	Subjective Case	Objective Case
First Person Pronouns	I, me, my, mine	me, us
Second Person Pronouns	you	you
Third Person Pronouns	he, she, it, they, one	him, her, it, them, one
Relative Pronouns	who, that, which	whom, that, which

When to Use Subjective Case Pronouns.   As the name implies, use the subjective case for the subject of a sentence or clause.

Example: She is a daring mountain climber.
Incorrect: Danny, Cary, and me are going to the town fair.
Example: Sylvester, who is afraid of the dark, sleeps with a night-light on.

Use the subjective case after a linking verb, such as *to be.*

Example: It is I.

Use the subjective case when making comparisons to the subject of a verb that is not stated but understood.

Example: Wilson is faster than they (are).

When to Use Objective Case Pronouns.   Use the objective case when the pronoun is the object of a verb, of a preposition, or of an infinitive or gerund.

Example: I told him.
Example: I smiled at her.
Example: I sat between Mark and her.
Example: Sylvester, whom I gave a nightlight, thanked me.
Example: To give him a nice gift, we all contributed five dollars.
Example: Writing her was a good idea.

Helpful Hints

Each, every, either, anybody, everybody, or much (or similar forms) requires a singular verb.

EXAMPLE: Everyone admires her extensive vocabulary.

Both, few, several, many, or others require a plural verb.

EXAMPLE: Many comment on her writing ability as well.

All, any, more, most, some, or a part of requires a singular or plural verb depending on the number being referenced.

EXAMPLE: All of the flour needs to be sifted before it is added to the mixture. (singular verb)

EXAMPLE: Only a part of the population votes on election day. (singular verb)

EXAMPLE: When times are difficult, most rise to the challenge. (plural verb)

Myself/Me and Yourself/You.   Use the reflexive pronoun if the subject is acting on his/her/itself or the action was performed *by oneself* (alone).

>   Incorrect: He met with Barbara and myself. (Should be *Barbara and me*)
>   Correct: I discovered the answer myself.

Sentence Structure.   A sentence is a group of words that expresses a complete thought. To express a complete thought, a sentence must contain a subject and a verb.

>   Example: Lions roar.
>   Example: Searching through the cupboards, John found an old can of soup.

Every sentence contains at least one *clause*—a group of words that contains a subject and verb. *Lions roar*, and *John found* are both clauses.

A *phrase* is a group of words that does not have both a subject and a verb. *Searching through the cupboards* is a phrase.

Sentence Fragments.   On writing questions, some of those innocent-looking groups of words beginning with capital letters and ending with periods are only masquerading as sentences. In reality, they are *sentence fragments*: grammatically incomplete because they lack a subject or verb or are not complete thoughts.

>   Incorrect: Arches and vaulted ceilings typical of Romanesque architecture.

This is not a complete sentence because there is no verb.

>   Incorrect: Because we arrived late.

Even though this fragment contains a subject (*we*) and a verb (*arrived*), it is not a complete sentence because it doesn't express a complete thought. We don't know what happened because we arrived late.

Careful: Don't let strings of long difficult words distract you. Read carefully to be sure whether or not there is a verb.

Run-on Sentences.   A *run-on sentence* is actually two (or more) complete sentences stuck together with just a comma or with no punctuation at all.

>   Incorrect: The team practiced diligently, it received a gold ribbon.
>   Incorrect: The team practiced diligently it received a gold ribbon.

There are a number of ways to fix this kind of problem.
Join the clauses with a semicolon.

>   Correct: The team practiced diligently; it received a gold ribbon.

Join the clauses with a coordinating conjunction (*and, but, for, nor, or, so,* or *yet*) and a comma.

>   Correct: The team practiced diligently, and it received a gold ribbon.

Join the clauses with a subordinating conjunction (*after, although, if, since,* or *while*).

Correct: Since the team practiced diligently, it received a gold ribbon.

Finally, the two halves of a run-on sentence can be written as two separate complete sentences.

Correct: The team practiced diligently. It received a gold ribbon.

Verbs.   English has six basic tenses, and each of these has a simple form and a progressive form.

	Simple Form	**Progressive Form**
Present	I walk	I am walking
Past	I walked	I was walking
Future	I will walk	I will be walking
Present Perfect	I have walked	I have been walking
Past Perfect	I had walked	I had been walking
Future Perfect	I will have walked	I will have been walking

Using the Present Tense.   Use the present tense to describe a state or action occurring in the present time.

Example: I am happy.
Example: He works at the municipal building.

Using the Past Tense.   Use the simple past tense to describe an event or state that took place at a specific time in the past and is now finished.

Example: The class dissected a frog in biology class yesterday.

Using the Future Tense.   Use the future tense to describe actions expected to take place in the future.

Example: It will rain tomorrow.
Example: I will call you tonight.

Future actions may also be expressed this way:

Example: I am going to call you tonight.

Using the Present Perfect Tense.   Use the present perfect tense for actions and states of being that start in the past and continue into the present time.

Example: I have been attending Jefferson Junior High for the last two years.

Use the present perfect for actions and states of being that happened a number of times in the past and may happen again in the future.

Example: We have visited the planetarium several times.

Use the present perfect to describe an event that happened at an unspecified time in the past.

Example: Anna has given me her opinion already.

Using the Past Perfect Tense.   The past perfect tense is used for past actions or states that were completed before other past actions or states.

Example: When the alarm clock rang this morning, I noticed that I had set it for eight o'clock.

Using the Future Perfect Tense.   Use the future perfect tense for a future state or event that will take place before another future time or event.

Example: By Saturday, I will have finished the entire novel.

Using the Proper Past Participle Form.   Perfect tenses use a participle form of a base verb.

Example: I have planted tomatoes in the garden.

The past participle is formed by adding *-ed* to the base form, unless it is an irregular verb. Irregular verbs have two different forms for simple past and past participle tenses. If you use the present, past, or future perfect tense, make sure that you use the past participle and not the simple past tense.

Incorrect: I have swam in that lake before.
Correct: I have swum in that lake before.

The following are some of the most common irregular verbs.

Infinitive	Simple Past	Past Participle
break	broke	broken
speak	spoke	spoken
freeze	froze	frozen
forget	forgot	forgotten
get	got	gotten
ride	rode	ridden
rise	rose	risen
arise	arose	arisen
drive	drove	driven
write	wrote	written
eat	ate	eaten
fall	fell	fallen
give	gave	given
take	took	taken
shake	shook	shaken
see	saw	seen
ring	rang	rung
sing	sang	sung
sink	sank	sunk
shrink	shrank	shrunk
drink	drank	drunk
begin	began	begun
swim	swam	swum
run	ran	run
come	came	come
become	became	become
do	did	done
go	went	gone
blow	blew	blown
grow	grew	grown
know	knew	known
throw	threw	thrown
fly	flew	flown
draw	drew	drawn

Note the patterns. Verb forms that end in *-oke, -oze, -ot, -ode, -ose, -ove, -ote, -ang, -ank, -an, -an, -am, -ame, -ew,* or *-ook* are simple past. Verb forms that end in *-en, -wn, -ung, -unk, -un, -um, -ome,* and *-one* are past participles. Train your ear for irregular verb forms that aren't already second nature to you.

Could Have, Should Have, Would Have, Might Have.   The words *could, should, would,* and *might* that express possibility, impossibility, or necessity must be followed by *have.*

Careful: People often incorrectly say *could of.* This is incorrect.

Incorrect: I could of gone if I had enough money.
Correct: I could have gone if I had enough money.

Prepositional Phrases.   The English language has several idioms, expressions that are usually a verb followed by a preposition (*of, at, upon,* etc.). There is no rule to the formation of these idioms, it is simply something you have to become familiar with. Here is a list of several commonly tested idioms.

abide by	contribute to	participate in
accuse of	count (up)on	prevent from
agree to	cover with	prohibit from
agree with	decide (up)on	protect against
agree on	depend (up)on	protect from
apologize for	differ about	provide for
apply to	differ from	provide with
apply for	differ over	recover from
approve of	differ with	rely (up)on
argue with	discriminate against	rescue from
argue about	distinguish from	respond to
arrive at	dream of	stare at
believe in	dream about	stop from
blame for	escape from	subscribe to
care about	excel in	substitute for
care for	excuse for	succeed in
charge for	forget about	thank for
charge with	forgive for	vote for
compare to	hide from	wait for
compare with	hope for	wait on
complain about	insist (up)on	work with
consist of	object to	worry about

Adjectives and Adverbs.   An adjective modifies or describes a noun or pronoun.

Example: A man with a gray beard sat on an old tree stump.

An adverb modifies a verb, an adjective, or another adverb. Most, but not all adverbs end in –*ly*. (Don't forget that some adjectives—*friendly, lovely*—also end in –*ly*.)

Example: The builders finished surprisingly quickly. (*Surprisingly* describes the adverb *quickly*.)

Adverbs such as *almost, nearly, hardly,* and *about* may also modify determiners, numerals, and pronouns.

Example: Hardly anyone has purchased a ticket yet.

Careful: The word *hardly* means *barely*. The adverbial form of the adjective *hard* is *hard*.

Example: We worked hard planting the hedges.

Parallel Structure.   Make sure that when a sentence contains a list or makes a comparison, the items being listed or compared exhibit parallel structure.

Items in a List
Incorrect: I love skipping, jumping, and to play tiddlywinks.
Correct: I love to skip, jump, and play tiddlywinks
Also Correct: I love to skip, to jump, and to play tiddlywinks.
Also Correct: I love skipping, jumping, and playing tiddlywinks.

Logical Comparison.   Comparisons must do more than just exhibit parallel structure; they must make sense. You must compare two like items. If this is unclear, here are some examples:

Incorrect: The rules of chess are more complex than checkers. (incorrectly compares rules to a game)
Correct: The rules of chess are more complex than those of checkers. (compares rules to rules)
Also Correct: Chess is more complex than checkers. (compares game to game)

Comparatives and Superlatives.   Use the comparative form when comparing two items.

Example: They finished more quickly than we. (*Than we did* is understood.)

Careful: Remember to use the correct form of the pronoun.
Careful: Avoid repetitiveness in comparisons.

Incorrect: The oil painting is more prettier than the watercolor is.
Correct: The oil painting is prettier than the watercolor is.

The superlative form of the adjective is used comparing more than two items.

Example: August is the hottest month.

Careful: *Good, better, best* is the correct progression of this adjective. *Bad, worse, worst* is the correct progression of this adjective.

Style Review

Good writing is not only grammatically correct, but also stylistically clear. We will review some problems with style in the following pages and show you how to correct them.

Pronoun Ambiguity.   A problem exists when a pronoun doesn't refer to any antecedent at all or doesn't refer clearly to one, and only one, antecedent.

Unclear: Francesco likes the music they play on this radio station.

Who are *they*? We can't tell because the pronoun has no antecedent.

Correct: Francesco likes the music played on this radio station.

Careful: Sometimes a pronoun seems to have an antecedent until you read more closely and realize that the word it seems to refer to is not a noun, but an adjective, a possessive form, or a verb. Remember, the antecedent of a pronoun should be a noun.

Incorrect: When you are cooking, be careful to watch it.
Correct: When you are cooking dinner, be careful to watch it.
Incorrect: Veronica has always been interested in medicine and has decided to become one.
Correct: Veronica has always been interested in medicine and has decided to become a doctor.
Incorrect: Joe started jogging, and as a result lost a lot of weight. It was very good for his heart. (What does the pronoun *it* refer to? Losing weight or jogging?)
Correct: Joe started jogging because it was very good for his heart, and as a result he lost a lot of weight. (The antecedent of it is clearly *jogging*.)

Misreference.   Remote antecedents can also cause confusion in the following way:

Poor: The president sent a memo to Charlie, and he will address the problem right away. (In this sentence it is unclear what *he* refers to, Charlie or the president.)
Better: The president sent a memo to Charlie, who will address the problem right away.

Dangling Modifiers.   In order to avoid confusion, clauses and phrases should be close to the elements they modify.

Incorrect: <u>To write a clear sentence,</u> <u>subject and verb should agree.</u>
                  phrase   clause

Who is writing the sentence? Certainly not the subject and verb; they can't write.

Correct: To write a clear sentence, you should make sure the subject and verb agree.

Here's another example.

Incorrect: When driving across the bridge, the sun blinded him.
Correct: When driving across the bridge, he was blinded by the sun.

Redundancy.   *Redundancy* means repetitiveness. Words or phrases are redundant when they have basically the same meaning as something already stated. Don't use two words or phrases when one is sufficient.

Incorrect: Blackmore University was established and founded in 1906.
Correct: Blackmore University was established in 1906.

Double Negatives.   In standard written English, double negatives are redundant and wrong.

Incorrect: "I didn't say nothing!" he protested.
Correct: "I didn't say anything!" he protested.

Relevance.   A good sentence contains only related or relevant ideas. Unrelated information, even when set off in parenthesis, should be avoided. If an idea is unrelated to the main point of the sentence, it should be cut.

Irrelevant: Constructing the new baseball field will cost the community over forty thousand dollars (though the entire town loves to watch the Tigers play).
Relevant: Constructing the new baseball field will cost the community over forty thousand dollars. Decision makers feel this investment is worthwhile however, since the entire town loves to watch the Tigers play.

Wordiness.   Wordiness also creates a style and clarity problem.

Wordy: We were in agreement with each other that Max was charitable to a fault.
Concise: We agreed that Max was charitable to a fault.

Commonly Misused or Confused Words.   In Chapter 4 you already read a list of commonly confused vocabulary words. Here is another list of words that are often misused or confused by writers.

accept/except

To *accept* means to receive or agree to something, whereas *except* is usually a preposition meaning excluding, although it can also mean to leave out.

adapt/adopt

To *adapt* is to change (oneself or something) to become suitable for a particular condition or use. To *adopt* is to make something one's own.

affect/effect

To *affect* means to have an *effect* on something. When the word is being used as a verb, the proper word to use is almost always *affect;* when it's being used as a noun, the proper word to use is almost always *effect.*

already/all ready

Already means earlier or previously. *All ready* means all of us are ready.

afflict/inflict

To *afflict* is to torment or distress someone or something. It usually appears as a passive verb. To *inflict* is to impose punishment or suffering on someone or something.

allusion/illusion

An *allusion* is an indirect reference to something, a hint. An *illusion* is a false, misleading, or deceptive appearance.

altogether/all together

Altogether means completely. *All together* means as one group.

among/between

In most cases, use *between* for two items and *among* for more than two.

amount/number

Amount is used to refer to an uncountable quantity, *number* to refer to a countable quantity.

anyway

Anyway means in any way possible, or regardless. *Anyways* is incorrect. Don't use it.

as/like

Like is a preposition; it takes a noun object. *As*, when functioning as a conjunction, introduces a subordinate clause. Remember, a clause is part of a sentence containing a subject and a verb.

as...as...

The idiom is *as*...*as*.... Example: *That dress is <u>as</u> expensive <u>as</u> this one.*

beside/besides

Beside means by the side of or next to. *Besides* means moreover.

emigrate/immigrate

To *emigrate* is to leave one country for another country and is usually used with the preposition *from*. To *immigrate* is to enter a country to take up permanent residence there and is usually used with the preposition *to*.

eminent/imminent

Someone who is *eminent* is prominent or outstanding. Something that is *imminent* is likely to happen soon or is impending.

fewer/less

Use *fewer* before a plural noun; use *less* before a singular one.

leave/let

To *leave* is to depart, to allow something to remain behind after departing, or to allow something to remain as it is. The irregular verb form *left* serves as both the simple past and the past participle. When *leave* is used in the third sense—to allow something to remain as it is—and followed by *alone*, this verb does overlap with *let*. To *let* is to allow or to rent out. These are the verb's core meanings, but it also combines with several different prepositions to produce various specific senses. *Let* is irregular. One form (*let*) serves as present, past, and past participle.

neither...nor...

The correlative conjunction is *neither...nor...*. Example: *We are <u>neither</u> tired <u>nor</u> hungry.*

Avoid the redundancy caused by using *nor* after a negative.

Incorrect: Alice's departure was not noticed by Sue nor Debby.
Correct: Alice's departure was not noticed by Sue or Debby.

its/it's

Many people confuse *its* and *it's*. *Its* is possessive; *it's* is a contraction of *it is*.

lay/lie/laid

Lay means to put or to place. The past tense of *lay* is *laid*, the past participle *has laid*, and the continuous form *is/was laying*. Lie means to recline, to stay, or to rest. The past is *lay*, the past participle *has lain*, the continuous form, *is/was lying*.

Careful: *Lay* is both the present tense of *lay* (as *in put or place*) and the past tense of *lie* (as in *lie down*).

raise/rise

To *raise* is to lift up or to cause to rise or grow, and it usually has a direct object: You raise dumbbells, roof beams, tomato plants, and children. *Raise* is a completely regular verb. To *rise* is to get up, to go up, and to be built up. This verb never takes a direct object: You do not rise something; rather, something rises.

Spelling

Some civil service exams test your spelling skills, while others do not. Here are few spelling rules in English you should be aware of if you have to prepare for a spelling test. Remember: i before e, except after c, except when it sounds like a, as in neighbor and weigh

EXAMPLE: society, transient, receive, beige

A word that ends in a single vowel and a single consonant, and that has the accent on the final syllable, doubles that consonant before a suffix beginning with a vowel. If the final syllable has no accent, do not double the consonant.

EXAMPLE: occur—occurring
EXAMPLE: prefer—preferred
EXAMPLE: benefit + ing = benefiting

If a word ends with a silent e, drop the e before adding a suffix that begins with a vowel.

EXAMPLE: hope—hoping, like—liking

If a word ends in e, drop the final e before a suffix beginning with a vowel.

EXAMPLE: small + er = smaller
EXAMPLE: move + able = movable

Do not drop the e when the suffix begins with a consonant.

EXAMPLE: manage—management, like—likeness, use—useless

When y is the last letter in a word and the y is preceded by a consonant, change the y to i before adding any suffix except those beginning with i.

EXAMPLE: pretty—prettier, hurry—hurried, deny—denied

Knowing your own strengths and weaknesses is important. If you tend to have trouble spelling, you may decide to go against your instinct when selecting an answer choice. In other words, if a word looks right to you, but you know you are a terrible speller, you may guess that the word is actually spelled incorrectly. Finally, if you are not certain whether or not a word is spelled correctly, take your best guess and move on.

The past and past participle forms are irregular; *rose* is the simple past, *risen* the past participle.

set/sit

To *set* is to put or place something, to settle it, or to arrange it. But *set* takes on other specific meanings when it combines with several different prepositions. *Set* is an irregular verb in that one form (*set*) serves as present, past, and past participle. *Set* usually takes a direct object: You set a ladder against the fence, a value on family heirlooms, or a date for the family reunion. To *sit* is to take a seat or to be in a seated position, to rest somewhere, or to occupy a place. This verb does not usually take a direct object. The irregular form *sat* serves as past and past participle. Usually, no direct object follows this verb.

than/then

Use *than* in making comparisons. Use *then* for time.

their/they're/there

Many people confuse *their, there,* and *they're. Their* is possessive; *they're* is a contraction of *they are. There* has two uses: It can indicate place and it can be used as an expletive—a word that doesn't do anything in a sentence except delay the subject.

Use this list, along with the one found in Chapter 4, to make sure that you are not among the many who use the wrong word to say what they mean.

Passive Voice. The passive voice uses the verb *to be* with a past participle. The subject is affected rather than acting. Although passive voice is grammatically correct, excessive or unfounded use of the passive voice is considered poor style. It is often clearer to state the information with an active subject and verb.

Passive: My finger was bitten by the gerbil.
Active: The gerbil bit my finger.

Capitalization. Capitalize proper names.

George lives on Front Street. ("Street" is capitalized because it is part of the proper name.)
The Tigers won five of their last ten games.

Capitalize holidays.

Independence Day is July 4th.
Vincent cooked an enormous turkey for Thanksgiving.

Capitalize the first letter of a person's title when it precedes their proper name.

Principal Young
Dr. McCullough
Aunt Rose

However, when the title is used without the proper name, it remains lower-case. See the following example.

Tim's aunt is the coach of the baseball team. (Because the coach is not mentioned by name, *coach* is not capitalized.)

Capitalize days of the week and months of the year.

We walk to school Mondays, Tuesdays, and Wednesdays.
In July, we often go to the shore.

Capitalize the first word of a direct quotation.

Henry told us, "Sit on the bench outside the office."
"Sit on the bench," Henry told us, "outside the office."

Transitions in Writing.   When you are answering scrambled paragraph questions, transitions are very important. Transitional words and phrases show how sentences or paragraphs are logically linked. A poorly chosen or incorrect transitional word can completely alter the meaning of a sentence or paragraph.

Poor: John is tired, so he will not rest until he finishes the job at hand. (This is not a logical transition.)
Better: Although John is tired, he will not rest until he finishes the job at hand. (The transitional word *although* makes the idea clear.)

Read and study the following transition words as they will come in handy as you answer different types of writing questions.

Transitional Words.
Words that show an idea is moving in the same direction: *and, also, besides, moreover, in addition*
Words that show contrast: *but, meanwhile, on the other hand, yet, however, on the contrary*
Words that show emphasis: *in fact, most of all, in any, even*
Words that illustrate a point: *for example, for instance*
Words of conclusion: *accordingly, so, therefore, consequently*
Words of concession: *of course, naturally, in fact*
Words of time: *formerly, meanwhile, after, later, at the same time, in the first place, first, second, finally*

Words that express a condition: *nevertheless, even though, although*
Words to point out cause/effect: *it follows that, accordingly, for this reason*
Words of comparison: *similarly, in comparison, still*

Now that you have reviewed this lesson on grammar, punctuation, and style, you are ready to review each of the five different question types.

Sample Writing Questions

On different civil service exams, there are several different question types and formats for writing questions. It is impossible to cover every type, but this chapter reviews five of the most common question types. These are:

- scrambled paragraphs
- sentence completions
- identifying errors
- improving sentences
- improving passages

Difficulty Level

Before we explain each of the question types, we have to mention the difficulty level of writing questions. As with vocabulary and reading questions, these questions have a difficulty level that depends on which civil service exam you take. Most entry-level positions expect your skills to be at a high school or college level. This does not mean you have to be a college graduate to answer the most challenging questions; it simply implies that some questions are more difficult than others. Throughout this chapter and on Practice Test 3, you will find questions ranging between these two levels. Again, the job you are applying for determines the skill level you must have. If you struggle with many of the questions in this chapter, spend extra time reviewing the lessons and strategies provided to prepare for test day.

Strategies for Writing Questions

If you want to learn specific tips on how to answer each question type, refer to Tips for Writing Success later in this chapter. Now let's look at each of the question types (scrambled paragraphs, sentence completions, identifying errors, improving sentences, and improving paragraphs) in detail.

Scrambled Paragraphs

The format for this question type can vary, but the questions are generally presented in the following way. You will see six sentences—one topic sentence and five other sentences listed in no particular order. The five sentences will be numbered 1–5. Following the last sentence, you will find four or five answer choices

(the samples in this book use four). Each answer choice lists a different arrangement of the five numbered sentences. You have to select the lettered answer choice
that shows the correct arrangement of the sentences to form a clear and coherent
paragraph.

Here is a sample scrambled paragraph question:

Porpoises and sharks appear to be similar in that they are streamlined, good swimmers, and live in the sea.

(1) For example, the shark has gills, cold blood, and scales, whereas the porpoise
has lungs, warm blood, and hair.

(2) Important differences are apparent, however, to marine biologists who study
these species.

(3) The porpoise, on the other hand, is fundamentally more like man than like the
shark—and it therefore belongs to the order of mammals.

(4) Armed with the knowledge that the porpoise is a mammal, the biologist can
then confidently predict that porpoises have a four-chambered heart and
bones of a particular type.

(5) From this contrast in features, the zoologist knows that the shark has the
physiology of a fish.

   (A) 2, 1, 3, 4, 5
   (B) 1, 3, 4, 5, 2
   (C) 2, 3, 1, 4, 5
   (D) 2, 1, 5, 3, 4

Sentence Completions

Sentence completion questions are basically fill-in-the-blank questions. Some
sentences may have one blank and other questions may have two blanks. When
there are two blanks, you need to make sure that both words make sense in the
sentence. Here is an example of a sentence completion question.

Today's small, portable computers contrast markedly with the earliest
electronic computers, which were _____.

   (A) effective
   (B) invented
   (C) useful
   (D) enormous

Although in one sense, you are being tested on your vocabulary skills, these
questions also test your ability to create a coherent sentence. That is because you
need to determine how the parts of the sentence relate to each other first in order
to figure out how to fill in the blank.

Another Identifying Errors
Question Format

Another format for this question type is one that will present different sentences, which may or may not contain errors as the first few answer choices. The last choice will always read "No mistake." If you spot an error in one of the sentences, that is your answer. If you find that none of the sentences have an error, choose "No mistake." This format is not as common, but you will find some questions like this on the Practice Test at the end of this chapter; be prepared.

Identifying Errors

Another type of question you may encounter on a civil service exam is identifying errors. Identifying error questions typically cover four main areas of written English:

- Basic grammar
- Sentence structure
- Choice of words (diction)
- Idiomatic expressions

That sounds like a lot of ground to cover, but as you will see, most identifying error questions only test a few key grammar and usage concepts. (If you feel unsure of your grammar skills, go back and review the lesson at the beginning of this chapter.)

Essentially, all identifying error questions require you to spot a mistake. You are usually given a sentence with four words or phrases underlined. The underlined parts are labeled (A) through (D). One of the underlined pieces may contain an error. Your task is to spot the error and fill in the corresponding oval on your answer sheet. If the sentence is error-free, the correct answer is (E), "No error." Also, you should assume that the parts of the sentence not underlined are correct. Here's an example.

<u>Although</u> the number of firms declaring
  A
bankruptcy <u>keep</u> growing, the mayor <u>claims that</u> the
            B   C
city <u>is thriving</u>. <u>No error</u>
       C   D

Later in the chapter, we will show you how to use Kaplan's Target Strategy to find the correct answer to this question.

Improving Sentences

Just like identifying errors questions, most improving sentence questions relate to a small number of grammatical issues. Here's the main difference between the two question types: Whereas the errors in the identifying error questions consist of single words or short phrases, the errors in the improving sentence questions generally involve the structure of the whole sentence. As a result, they can be a little harder to identify than the errors in the identifying errors section.

To familiarize yourself with what is expected of you, review the directions for answering improving sentences questions:

Directions: Choose the answer that is grammatically correct and best maintains the meaning of the given sentence. If you think the original is the best choice, select (A); if not, choose among (B), (C), (D), or (E). The result should be a sentence that is clear and precise.

Here's an example of this question type.

The Emancipation Edict freed the Russian serfs <u>in 1861; that being four years</u> before the Thirteenth Amendment abolished slavery in the United States.

    (A) in 1861; that being four years

    (B) in 1861 and is four years

    (C) in 1861 and this amounts to four years

    (D) in 1861, being four years

    (E) in 1861, four years

As the directions instruct, you have to pick the best choice to replace the under-lined portion of the sentence. The correct answer must produce a sentence that's not only grammatically correct, but also effective: It must be clear, precise, and free of awkward verbiage (using more words than necessary to get your point across).

Later in the chapter, you can review Kaplan's Target Strategy for Improving Sentences when it is applied to this sample question.

Improving Passages

Improving passages questions follow short essays. The essays can be about any topic. You do not have to know anything about the topic to answer the questions correctly. The sentences in each passage will be numbered.

Most improving passage questions ask you to clean up awkward and ambiguous sentences.

The most important element to consider in these questions is their *context*. You cannot determine the best way to repair poor or unclear sentences without knowing what comes before and after them.

A few improving passage questions will also ask you about the overall organiza-tion of the essay. Again, context is critical. For example, you can't decide which of five sentences best concludes an essay without knowing what the essay is all about.

Sample improving passage questions are found under the next heading.

Three Kinds of Improving Passage Questions

There are three basic types of improving passage questions:

- General organization questions
- Revising sentences questions
- Combining sentences questions

General Organization Questions.   General organization questions test your grasp of the general organization of the passage. You may be asked to rearrange sentences, or to choose an appropriate paragraph break in the passage. Specific words and sen-tences will not be the focus of these questions; as the name implies, the questions will deal with the overall organization of the passage. Here is one example.

(1) Until recently, I was convinced I had no musical ability whatsoever. **(2)** In grade school, I could hardly keep my voice in tune with other singers around me. **(3)** I thought that I would never play a musical instrument or become a rock star. **(4)** I really enjoyed music, just no one thought I had any talent at all.

(5) When I entered junior high I took music classes with our teacher, Mr. Daniels. **(6)** At first he seemed really stern and strict. **(7)** He gave us lots of warnings that even though he had a reputation for being harsh around school, the reality was ten times worse. **(8)** But after a couple of weeks, he started encouraging us to get into musical ensembles. **(9)** At first I was disinterested, thinking that I would be ridiculed as to my contribution. **(10)** Mr. Daniels insisted that everyone had to play some kind of instrument, so I chose his handbell choir. **(11)** Other kids thought handbells were stupid, but I liked the sound they made—it was so much purer than the electric guitar. **(12)** Mr. Daniels coached us regular after school. **(13)** Not only did the group actually start to sound good, but also I discovered that I had some rhythmic talents that no one had suspected. **(14)** Maybe I will be a rock star yet! **(15)** The whole experience showed me that with encouragement and a sense of adventure you can overcome your limitations. **(16)** As our former First Lady Eleanor Roosevelt once said, sometimes "you must do that which you think you cannot do."

Which of the following sentences, if added after sentence 4, would best link the first paragraph with the rest of the essay?

(A) As a result, I learned that other people's opinions are irrelevant.

(B) However, I soon met an inspiring person who disproved this assumption.

(C) This was why no one thought I would become a rock star.

(D) Nevertheless, I knew all along that I possessed a form of musical genius.

(E) I have held these beliefs about my musical ability for many years.

If you have a firm grasp of the essay after you first read through it, you should jump right to the general organization questions first. Answer these questions while the essay is fresh in your mind.

However, if your grasp of the essay is a bit shaky, work on general organization questions last. Start with questions that ask you to revise or combine sentences: Doing so should improve your grasp of the overall essay, making it easier for you to tackle the general organization questions later.

Revising Sentence Questions.   Revising sentence questions, as the name implies, ask you to choose the best revisions to sentences or parts of sentences. To see how this works, take a look at the following paragraph and question. The question focuses on a single phrase in one sentence, but to answer this typical example of a revision question, you will need to reread the entire paragraph.

(1) The Spanish-American War was one of the shortest and most decisive wars ever fought. **(2)** The postwar settlement, the Treaty of Paris, reflected the results of the fighting. **(3)** Under its terms, Spain was compelled to cede large territories in North America and the Pacific. **(4)** The United States gained control over some of these territories, including Puerto Rico and Guam. **(5)** It was reduced in status from a major to a minor power. **(6)** The United States, in contrast, emerged from the war as a world power, and would soon go on to become a major participant in Asian and European affairs.

In context, which is the best version of the underlined part of sentence 5?
   It was reduced in status from a major to a minor power.
   (A) (As it is now)
   (B) Spain was reduced
   (C) The war caused Spain to be reduced
   (D) As a result of the war, it had been reduced
   (E) It had now been reduced

Sentence 5 refers to Spain's status. That much should have been clear to you by reading sentences 2, 3, 4, and 6. However, the pronoun *it* makes sentence 5 ambiguous. What does *it* refer to? To make this sentence less ambiguous, it should be changed to the noun *Spain*. That leaves (B) and (C) as possible correct answers. Because (B) is a more concise and less awkward construction than (C), (B) is correct.

Combining Sentences Questions.   Again, it should be obvious that this question type asks you to choose the best way to combine two sentences from the passage. Here is a sample paragraph and question.

(6) Albert Einstein was a great physicist. **(7)** He won a Nobel Prize in Physics. **(8)** He got the prize for his research into the photoelectric effect. **(9)** Later physicists demonstrated the validity of Einstein's ideas.

Which of the following is the best way to combine sentences 7 and 8?

He won a Nobel Prize in Physics. He got the prize for his research into the photoelectric effect.

(A) The Nobel Prize in Physics that he won was for his research into the photo-electric effect.

(B) Having researched the photoelectric effect, he won a Nobel Prize in Physics.

(C) He won a Nobel Prize in Physics for his research into the photoelectric effect.

(D) He got the prize in physics, the Noble Prize in Physics, for his research into the photoelectric effect.

(E) Because of his research into the photoelectric effect he got the Nobel Prize in Physics.

Did you choose (C)? It's the best written and most concise of the choices. Whether you are asked to revise or combine sentences, the correct answer will often (but not always) be the shortest answer. Good writing is concise.

The next section, Tips for Writing Success, has Kaplan's Target Strategy for this and other question types. Pay careful attention to each of the strategies as they will be important to getting a high score on the practice test at the end of the chapter.

Tips for Writing Success

With so many question types for writing questions, it's no wonder there are just as many score-raising strategies. This section covers the best tips and strategies for scrambled paragraphs, sentence completions, identifying errors, improving sentences, and improving passages. You can apply the tips you learn here when you complete Practice Test 3 found at the end of this chapter.

Structural Clues to Unscramble Paragraphs

Structural clues are words that authors use to indicate the function of each sentence in relation to other sentences and the author's argument as a whole. They indicate the logical progression of the argument. Fundamental rules of sentence construction and grammar also dictate an argument's progression or "architecture," and hence understanding these rules can also help you identify sentence order. Identifying both these words and grammatical constructions is the key to arranging the sentences. Here are some structural clues.

Sentence Pairs.   As a general rule, it's a good idea to work with sentences in pairs. It is often easier to look for the relationship between two sentences than it is to deal with the paragraph as a whole. For example, if a sentence contains a pronoun, look for the sentence that contains the antecedent.

Nouns and Pronouns.   Paying attention to pronouns and nouns can help you unscramble sentences 1–5. Basically, any time you see an ambiguous pronoun (a pronoun whose antecedent is not found in the same sentence), you know that the previous sentence must define the pronoun. For example, if you come across the sentence, "Rather than finish college, she dropped out to pursue her dream of building the world's largest popsicle stick sculpture," you know that the sentence preceding this one has to tell you who "she" is.

Similarly, if a person is referred to by a last name or nickname (i.e., by something other than a full name), there will be a previous sentence in which the person is mentioned by his or her full name. So if you came across the sentence "The popularity of Michener's Kent State was renewed as the anniversary of the Kent State shootings neared," you would have a previous sentence identifying "Michener" by his full name (James Michener).

Example.   Example clues indicate that the author is providing specific evidence to back up an argument or opinion: *example, for example, for instance, one illustration of this,* etc.

Sequence.   Sequence clues indicate the chronological order of a series of events, or the order in which an author wants to discuss a series of issues: *first…second, until recently…today, in the 1920s…by the 1940s,* etc.

Continuity.   Continuity clues indicate that the author is following up a statement with an additional, consistent statement: *similarly, consequently, therefore, hence,* etc.

Contrast.   Contrast clues indicate that the author is presenting an idea that is inconsistent with the preceding idea: *however, on the other hand, but, nevertheless,* etc.

Kaplan's Target Strategy for Scrambled Paragraphs

The Kaplan Target Strategy for unscrambling scrambled paragraphs has three simple steps:

Step 1. Read through each sentence, circling any important structural clues.
Step 2. Use structural clues to connect the sentences in such a way that they logically follow the topic sentence.
Step 3. Read through your paragraph to make sure it makes sense.

Let's apply this strategy to the sample found earlier in the chapter.

Step 1: Read Through Each Sentence, Circling Any Important Structural Clues.   As you now know, *structural clues* are words that provide information about the relationship between sentences. They are words or phrases that help you predict where the paragraph is going or follow where it has been.

Porpoises and sharks appear to be similar in that they are streamlined, good swimmers, and live in the sea.

(1) For example, the shark has gills, cold blood, and scales, whereas the porpoise has lungs, warm blood, and hair.

(2) Important differences are apparent, however, to marine biologists who study these species.

(3) The porpoise, on the other hand, is fundamentally more like man than like the shark—and it therefore belongs to the order of mammals.

(4) Armed with the knowledge that the porpoise is a mammal, the biologist can then confidently predict that porpoises have a four-chambered heart and bones of a particular type.

(5) From this contrast in features, the zoologist knows that the shark has the physiology of a fish.

    (A) 2, 1, 3, 4, 5

    (B) 1, 3, 4, 5, 2

    (C) 2, 3, 1, 4, 5

    (D) 2, 1, 5, 3, 4

Each of the sentences contains clues that provide information about its relationship to other sentences. Look at sentence (1). It begins with the words "For example." This tells you that sentence (1) must refer back to something specific in a previous sentence.

Step 2: Use Structural Clues to Connect the Sentences in Such a Way That They Logically Follow the Topic Sentence.   The key to connecting the sentences is to keep in mind that endings connect with beginnings. Every sentence has to connect smoothly to the next, without any ambiguity or loose ends. Structural clues are the tools that enable you to make these connections.

Your topic sentence says:

Porpoises and sharks appear to be similar in that they are streamlined, good swimmers, and live in the sea.

The phrase should make you suspicious that despite the fact that porpoises and sharks appear similar, the author is going to tell you how they are not similar. Therefore, it's a good idea to actively look for a sentence that talks about differences. As soon as you do this, sentence (2) leaps out at you:

(2) Important differences are apparent, however, to marine biologists who study these species.

This sentence starts by talking about the important differences that you predicted would be discussed. Furthermore, the sentence uses the big structural clue "however." "However" tells you that there is some type of contrast, i.e., that even though things seem one way, in reality they are another.

Now that you have seen how the second sentence connects with the first, you have to think about how the second sentence will connect with the third. Sentence (2) mentioned differences between porpoises and sharks generally. What do you think the next sentence will address? Here's a hint: Paragraphs tend to move from the general to the specific.

At this point, Sentence (1) should be making more sense:

(1) For example, the shark has gills, cold blood, and scales, whereas the porpoise has lungs, warm blood, and hair.

This sentence begins with the words "For example." This is a pretty big clue that the rest of the sentence is going to present a specific example of something. And this sentence delivers exactly what it promises. It discusses specific differences between porpoises and sharks.

Sentence (5) picks up where sentence (1) ends: "From this contrast in features…" refers specifically to the physiological differences mentioned in sentence (1).

You now have two sentences left. Take a look at them to see which should come first. The things to think about are which of the two better connects to the fourth sentence and which sentence best wraps up the paragraph. In other words, which sentence doesn't leave anything hanging at the end?

(3) The porpoise, on the other hand, is fundamentally more like man than like the shark—and it therefore belongs to the order of mammals.
(4) Armed with the knowledge that the porpoise is a mammal, the biologist can then confidently predict that porpoises have a four-chambered heart and bones of a particular type.

Think about where the paragraph has gone so far. The topic sentence noted similarities between porpoises and sharks. Sentence (2) noted that they were different despite their similarities. Sentence (1) identified some differences. Sentence (5) drew a conclusion about sharks based on these differences. Sentence (3) begins by distinguishing porpoises from something mentioned previously—"The porpoise, on the other hand…." (You know that the porpoise is being distinguished from the shark.) Sentence (4) then picks up on the reference to the porpoises as mammals and finishes the idea, i.e., it mentions how scientists can use this data.

Step 3: Read Through Your Paragraph to Make Sure It Makes Sense.
   Paragraph 1

Porpoises and sharks appear to be similar in that they are streamlined, good swimmers, and live in the sea.
(2) Important differences are apparent, however, to marine biologists who study these species.
(1) For example, the shark has gills, cold blood, and scales, whereas the porpoise has lungs, warm blood, and hair.

Classic Paragraph Structures

The more you practice scrambled paragraphs, the more you will recognize paragraph structures that appear repeatedly. For example, scrambled paragraphs usually start off general and get progressively more specific and detailed. Often, the author will introduce some sort of contrast and counterexample at the end. (Look for clues such as "however" or "nevertheless.") As a general rule, with practice you will find that the basic structure of paragraphs becomes more and more familiar.

(5) From this contrast in features, the zoologist knows that the shark has the physiology of a fish.

(3) The porpoise, on the other hand, is fundamentally more like man than like the shark—and it therefore belongs to the order of mammals.

(4) Armed with the knowledge that the porpoise is a mammal, the biologist can then confidently predict that porpoises have a four-chambered heart and bones of a particular type.

When you put these sentences together in order, they make logical sense. There are no awkward transitions or phrases that seem out of sequence.

Now that you have reviewed the best strategies for scrambled paragraph questions, here are some tips for answering sentence completion questions.

Clue Words for Solving Sentence Completions

Clue words tell you how the parts of a sentence fit together to create meaning. Structural clues help you to get a fix on whether the sentence will continue along in the same line or shift directions and contrast with the rest of the sentence. Be on the lookout for structural clues such as the following:

Continuations	Contrasts
; (a semicolon)	but
and	however
because	although
also	despite
consequently	yet

The more clues you uncover, the clearer the sentence becomes, and the better you can predict what goes in the blanks. Take a look at this example.

Though some have derided it as _____ the search for extraterrestrial intelligence has actually become a respectable scientific endeavor.

Here, *though* is a clue word. *Though* sets up a contrast between the way some have *derided* (belittled or ridiculed) the search for extraterrestrial intelligence and the fact that the scientific endeavor has become respectable. Another important clue is *actually*. *Actually* completes the contrast: Though some think the endeavor ridiculous, the reality is that it has become respectable.

These clues tell you that whatever goes in the blank must complete the contrast implied by the word *though*. Therefore, to fill in the blank, you need a word that would be used to describe the opposite of *a respectable scientific endeavor*. *Foolish* or *trivial* would be good predictions for the blank.

Kaplan's Target Strategy for Sentence Completion Questions

If you can master this strategy, you will be on your way to a higher score on sentence completion questions. Here are the four steps:

Step 1. Read the sentence for clue words.
Step 2. Predict the answer.
Step 3. Select the best match.
Step 4. Plug your answer choice back into the sentence.

Step 1. Read the Sentence for Clue Words.   Read the sentence. Now think about the sentence for five seconds. Take special note of the clue words. A clue word like *but* tells you to expect a CONTRAST in the next part of the sentence; a clue word like *moreover* tells you that what follows is a CONTINUATION of the same idea. Clue words such as *and, but, such as*, *however*, and *although* tell you how the parts of the sentence will relate to each other.

Step 2. Predict the Answer.   Decide what sort of word should fill the blank or blanks. Do this before looking at the answer choices. You don't have to guess the *exact* word; a rough idea of the *kind* of word you will need will do. It's often enough to simply predict whether the missing word is positive or negative. But often you will be able to go further. For example, you may be able to predict whether you need a pair of synonyms to fill in the blanks or two words that contrast.

Step 3. Select the Best Match.   Compare your prediction to each answer choice. Read every answer choice before deciding which answer best completes the sentence.

Step 4. Plug Your Answer Choice Back into the Sentence.   Put your answer choice in the blank (or blanks). Only one choice should really make sense. If you have gone through the four steps and more than one choice still looks good, eliminate the choice(s) that you can, guess from the remaining choices, and move on. If all of the choices look great or all of the choices look terrible, circle the question and come back to it when you have finished the other questions.

When There Are Two Blanks

One approach for two-blank sentence completion questions is to take them one blank at a time. Choose the easier blank, cross out any choices that clearly don't fit, and finish by checking ONLY the remaining choices for the other blank.

Let's use Kaplan's Target Strategy for Sentence Completion Questions on a sample question.

The king's _____ decisions as a diplomat and administrator led to his legendary reputation as a just and _____ ruler.

　　(A) quick . . capricious
　　(B) equitable . . wise
　　(C) immoral . . perceptive
　　(D) generous . . witty

Step 1. Read the Sentence for Clue Words.　The clues here are the phrase *led to* and the word *just.* You know that the kind of decisions the king made *led to* his having a reputation as a just and _____ ruler. So whatever goes in both blanks must be consistent with *just.*

Step 2. Predict the Answer.　Both blanks must contain words that are similar in meaning. Because of his _____ decisions, the king is viewed as a just and _____ ruler. So if the king's decisions were good, he would be remembered as a good ruler, and if his decisions were bad, he would be remembered as a bad ruler.

Just, which means *fair*, is a positive-sounding word; therefore, you can predict that both blanks will be similar in meaning and that both will be positive words. You can write a plus sign in the blanks or over the columns of answer choices to remind you.

Step 3. Select the Best Match.　One effective way to choose the best answer is to determine which answer choices have the kinds of words you predicted—in this case, words that are both positive and synonymous. In (A), *quick* and *capricious* are not necessarily positive, and they are not similar in meaning. (*Capricious* means erratic or fickle.) In (B), *equitable* means fair. *Equitable* and *wise* are similar, and they are both positive. When you plug them in, they make sense, so (B) looks right. But check out the others to be sure. In (C), *immoral* and *perceptive* are not similar at all; moreover, *perceptive* is positive, but *immoral* is not. In (D), *generous* and *witty* are both positive, but they are not very similar, and they don't make sense in the sentence. In (E), *clever* and *uneducated* aren't similar, and *clever* is positive, but *uneducated* isn't. Thus, (B) is the best match.

Step 4. Plug Your Answer Choice Back into the Sentence.　The king's equitable decisions as a diplomat and administrator led to his legendary reputation as a just and wise ruler. Choice (B) is the correct answer.

On the civil service exam, you are also likely to encounter identifying error questions. Keep reading to learn more about the strategies for mastering this question type.

Common Mistakes in Identifying Error Questions

Although you have already reviewed the grammar and style lesson found earlier in this chapter, here is a brief review of the most common mistakes you will find on identifying error questions.

Common Mistake 1: Subject-Verb Agreement—When Subject Follows Verb.   Singular subjects call for singular verbs. Plural subjects call for plural verbs. In certain situations, subject-verb agreement can be tricky because it is not obvious what the subject of the sentence is. Pay close attention if the subject follows the verb.

For example, it's tricky when the subject comes after the verb, as it does in a clause beginning with the word *there*. Take a look at the following:

> Despite an intensive campaign to encourage conservation, there is many Americans who have not accepted recycling as a way of life.

This sentence demonstrates one of the most common of all subject-verb agreement errors. The subject of the sentence is not *there*. The subject is *Americans*, which is plural. Therefore, the singular verb is incorrect; *is* should be replaced by the plural verb *are*.

Common Mistake 2: Subject-Verb Agreement—When Subject and Verb Are Separated.   To make things more complicated, test writers sometimes insert some additional information about the subject before the verb appears. Don't let intervening phrases fool you. Find the subject of the sentence and then determine if the verb agrees with the subject.

> Example: The local congressman, a reliable representative of both community and statewide interests, are among the most respected persons in the public sector.

The way to determine whether the verb agrees with the subject is to identify the subject of the sentence. You see the plural *community and statewide interests* right in front of the verb *are*, but that's not the subject. It's part of the modifying phrase that's inserted between the subject *congressman*, which is singular, and the verb, which should also be singular, *is*.

Again, don't let intervening phrases fool you. In the previous example, the commas were a tip-off that the verb was separated from the subject.

Common Mistake 3: Subject-Verb Agreement—When the Subject Seems Plural.   Sometimes the subject can seem plural. Remember, when the subject of a sentence is in the form neither _____ nor _____ or in the form either _____ or _____ and the nouns in the blanks are singular, the verb should be singular.

Remember Kaplan's Tips for Vocabulary Success

If it's the vocabulary and not the sentence structure that is giving you problems with sentence completion questions, go back and review Tips for Vocabulary Success in Chapter 4. You can use context clues as well as other strategies, such as word charge, to answer questions that challenge your vocabulary skills.

KAPLAN

If the nouns in a *neither-nor* or *either-or* construction are plural, then a plural verb is correct. Some other constructions that seem to make plural (compound) subjects but actually don't are: *along with*, *as well as*, and *in addition to*.

Poor pitching, along with injuries and defensive lapses, are among the problems that plagued last year's championship team.

The phrase *along with injuries and defensive lapses* is a modifying phrase that separates the subject *poor pitching* from the verb *are*. This sentence is tricky because there seem to be three problems that plagued the baseball team. But, in fact, phrases like *along with* or *in addition to* do not work in the same way as the conjunction *and* does. If the previous sentence had begun *Poor pitching, injuries, and defensive lapses*, the plural verb *are* would have been correct. However, as written, the sentence has only one subject, *poor pitching*, and its verb should be *is*.

Beware of fake compound subjects. Check for compound subject constructions and intervening phrases.

Common Mistake 4: Confusion of Simple Past and Past Participle.   A typical error is confusion between the simple past and the past participle forms of a verb. A past participle form may be substituted for the simple past form. For regular verbs, the simple past and past participle are identical, ending in -ed. But irregular verbs like see usually have two different forms for simple past and past participle. Review the list of irregular verbs earlier in this chapter if you are confused.

Several passersby seen the bank robber leaving the scene of his crime.

The verb form *seen* is the past participle and should be used only with a helping verb, such as *have* or *be*. This sentence requires the simple past form *saw*.

Common Mistake 5: Nonidiomatic Preposition after Verb.   Identifying error questions also test your recognition of prepositions that idiomatically combine with certain verbs.

Here's a sentence that uses the wrong preposition.

City Council members frequently meet until the early morning hours in order to work in their stalemates.

It's not always wrong to write *work in*. You might use it to speak about the field one *works in* or the place one *works in*. But this combination does not correspond to the meaning of this sentence. The writer means to say *work through* or *work out*—that is, overcome—the stalemates.

A list of idiomatic prepositional phrases is found in this chapter. Consult the list if you have any doubts.

Common Mistake 6: Wrong Word.   The lesson at the beginning of this chapter included a list of commonly misused and confused words. When you are reading through an identifying error question, be sure that the correct word is used, not just a word that sounds like the correct word.

Common Mistake 7: Wrong Tense.   To make sure the sentence is using the correct tense, pay attention to the time cues in the sentence. If you are confused about the verb tenses, go back to the lesson at the beginning of the chapter.

Here's a sentence with a verb in the wrong tense.

Over the last half-century, the building of passenger airliners had grown into a multibillion-dollar industry.

In a one-verb sentence like this one, time-descriptive phrases help you determine what the time frame of a sentence is. The action being described is a process that began during the last half-century and that is continuing to the present day. Any action starting in the past and continuing today is expressed by a verb in the present perfect tense. The present perfect form of this verb is *has grown*. Using the verb *had* makes it seem that passenger airliners aren't being made anymore. With practice, you will be able to spot mistakes like this with confidence.

Common Mistake 8: Number Agreement Problems.   Identifying error questions may also test number agreement between the singular or plural noun and the phrase or word describing it. For instance, a noun may be plural while a phrase describing the noun belongs with a singular noun. Nouns in a sentence must have logical number relations. Make sure that the nouns in a sentence logically agree in number.

The advertisement in the newspaper requested that only persons with a high school diploma apply for the position.

Nouns in a sentence must have logical number relations. The noun in question, the subject of the second clause of this sentence, is *persons*, a plural noun. However, the noun *diploma* is singular. Because the phrase *with a high school diploma* is singular, it seems to say that *persons* share one diploma, when in fact each person has his own diploma. The phrase should read *with high school diplomas.*

Common Mistake 9: Pronoun in the Wrong Number.   You will be tested on your ability to tell whether or not a noun and the pronoun that refers to that noun agree in number. A singular pronoun should be used to refer to a singular noun; a plural pronoun should be used with a plural noun. Be sure that a pronoun agrees with its antecedent in number.

In the following example, the pronoun does not match the noun to which it refers in number.

The typical college student has difficulty adjusting to academic standards much higher than those of their school.

The pronoun *their* should refer to a plural noun, but in this sentence, it refers back to *student*, a singular noun. Therefore, the pronoun should be the singular form *his* or *hers*, and not the plural form *their*.

Common Mistake 10: Pronoun in the Wrong Case in Compound Noun Phrases. An incorrect pronoun case is an error of the *between you and I* variety. Pronouns can either be *subjects* performing actions (I went, you saw, he ate, they sang, etc.) or objects receiving actions or *objects* (with me, give you, see her, stop them, etc.). Usually the choice of pronoun is obvious, but when pronouns are in a compound noun phrase, it's easier to make a mistake. To identify the error, isolate the pronoun from the compound.

Can you identify the compound phrase in the sentence below and the error in the choice of pronoun?

Him and the rest of the team stopped by the malt shop for milkshakes after the game.

In this sentence, the compound subject is *Him and the rest of the team*. To identify the error, isolate the pronoun from the compound. Take away the second part of the compound subject (*and the rest of the team*), and you are left with *him*. As you can see, *him* is incorrect because *him* wouldn't stop by the malt shop; *he* would. The correct pronoun case for this sentence is *he*, the subject form.

Common Mistake 11: Pronoun Shift.   *Pronoun shift* is a switch in pronoun person or number within a given sentence. In English, singular words like *one*, *someone*, and *a person* can represent people in general. So can plural words like *people* or *they*. Be on the lookout when general statements use pronouns because this is one of the most common mistakes made in the English language; consider whether these pronouns are consistent.

One cannot sleep soundly if you exercise vigorously before retiring to bed.

The subject in the first clause is *one*, and the subject in the second clause is *you*. These two pronouns refer to the same performer of two actions, so they should be consistent in person and number. The sentence should not shift to the second person *you* form.

Common Mistake 12: Pronoun with Ambiguous Reference.   There are two ways questions might test your ability to recognize an ambiguous pronoun reference. First, a sentence may be given in which it is impossible to determine what noun the pronoun refers. Pronoun reference can also be ambiguous if the pronoun's antecedent is not explicitly stated in the sentence. Be sure to locate the antecedent of any pronoun in identifying error questions.

Take a look at this example.

The United States entered into warmer relations with China after its compliance with recent weapons agreements.

To which country does the pronoun *its* refer? Grammatically and logically, either country could be the antecedent of the pronoun. With the limited information provided by this sentence alone, you simply can't determine which country the pronoun stands in for. The reference is ambiguous.

Common Mistake 13: Faulty Comparison.   Most faulty comparisons happen when two things that logically cannot be compared are compared. A comparison can be faulty either logically or grammatically. In every sentence, you should first identify what things or actions are being compared.

Try to identify the faulty comparison in the next sentence.

To lash back at one's adversaries is a less courageous course than attempting to bring about reconciliation with them.

The comparison in this sentence is logically correct in that two actions are compared. But the problem lies in the grammatical form of the words compared. An infinitive verb, *to lash*, expresses the first action, but a gerund, *attempting*, expresses the second action. These verb forms should match to make the comparison parallel. If *lashing* replaced *to lash*, the comparison would be grammatically parallel and logically valid. Check all comparisons for logic and grammatical consistency.

Common Mistake 14: Misuse of Adjective or Adverb.   These questions test your ability to recognize misuses of one-word modifiers. Keep in mind that adjectives modify nouns and adverbs modify verbs, adjectives, and other adverbs. Now ask yourself what the underlined word is intended to modify as you look at the sentence below.

The applicants for low-interest loans hoped to buy <u>decent</u> built houses for their families.

The word *decent* is an adjective. However, this modifier describes an adjective, explaining how the houses were built. A word that modifies an adjective like *built* is an adverb. So the word needed in this sentence is the adverb *decently*. Notice also that this adverb ends in *-ly*, the most common adverbial ending.

Remember, superlative adverbs and adjectives (adverbs and adjectives ending in *-est* (such as biggest, loudest, fastest, etc.) should express comparisons between three or more things or actions. Comparative adverbs and adjectives end in *-er* (bigger, louder, faster, etc.) and express comparisons between two things or actions.

You should also not forget that some adjectives and adverbs, usually those of two or more syllables, form the comparative with *more* instead of the *-er* ending, and *most* instead of the *-est* ending converts some modifiers to superlatives.

Common Mistake 15: Double Negative.   In standard written English, it is incorrect to use two negatives together unless one is intended to cancel out the other. Notice the two negative words in this sentence.

James easily passed the biology exam without hardly studying his lab notes.

Without is a negative, as is any word that indicates absence or lack. *Hardly* is a less familiar negative; it also denotes a scarcity of something, but perhaps not a total absence. With these two negatives, the sentence is incorrect.

In identifying errors questions, be on the lookout for negatives that are not obviously negative, such as *hardly*, *barely*, and *scarcely*.

There are several common mistakes in identifying error questions, but there are also strategies for answering identifying error questions. You should review these strategies closely and remember them as you complete the practice test at the end of this chapter.

Kaplan's Target Strategy for Identifying Errors

To tackle identifying error questions, Kaplan's test experts have devised a Target Strategy that will guide you in answering these types of questions. The four steps are as follows:

Step 1. Read the whole sentence, listening for the mistake.
Step 2. If you clearly hear the mistake, choose it and move on.
Step 3. If not, read each underlined choice, and eliminate choices that contain no errors.
Step 4. Choose from the remaining choices.

Try this out on our earlier example. Start by reading it to yourself.
Although the number of firms declaring
      A
bankruptcy keep growing, the mayor claims that the
          B   C
city is thriving. No error
    D   E

Steps 1 and 2. Read the Whole Sentence, Listening for the Mistake. If You Clearly Hear the Mistake, Choose It and Move On.   Did you hear the mistake? If so, your work is done, and you can move on to the next question. If you didn't hear the mistake on the first reading, go back, read each underlined part, and start eliminating underlined parts that are correct.

Steps 3 and 4. If Not, Read Each Underlined Choice, and Eliminate Choices That Contain No Errors. <u>Choose From the Remaining Choices.</u> The word *although* seems fine in this context. The word *keep* is a plural verb, but its subject is *number*, which is singular. That seems to be a mistake. The phrase *claims that* sounds all right; it has a singular verb for a singular subject, *mayor*. Similarly, *is thriving* sounds all right, and it too provides a singular verb for the singular subject *city*. Choice (B) contains the mistake, so (B) is the correct answer. This is a classic example of subject-verb agreement.

Please keep in mind that not all the identifying errors questions contain errors. When you are reading each sentence just to spot mistakes, you may fall into the trap of spotting mistakes where there are none.

The next question type, improving sentences, also has a list of common mistakes and a corresponding target strategy. They are covered in the following sections.

Common Mistakes in Improving Sentence Questions

Answering improving sentence questions correctly begins with simply reading the sentence carefully. So read carefully. It can't be said enough. The error, if there is one, will often be obvious to you at the first reading.

If it isn't, remember that only a rather limited range of grammar rules is tested. For that reason, we have provided a list of the grammatical problems that occur often on improving sentence questions. Once your ear has become attuned to these grammar mistakes, you will have an easier time identifying them on test day.

Common Mistake 1: Run-On Sentences.   In a typical run-on sentence, two independent clauses, each of which could stand alone as a complete sentence, are erroneously joined together, either with no punctuation or, most often, with just a comma. If both clauses in this sentence are independent; each could stand alone as a sentence. It is therefore incorrect to join them with just a comma between them. There are several ways to correct run-on sentences. One way is simply to change the comma into a period, producing two separate sentences. A second way is to change the comma into a semicolon. A semicolon can be described as a "weak period." It's used to indicate that two clauses are grammatically independent but that the ideas expressed are not so independent as to warrant separate sentences. Substituting a semicolon for the comma would correct the run-on sentence.

But there are other ways to join two independent clauses. In the next example, the two clauses are independent but one is logically subordinate to the other. To make the correction, you can convert the clause expressing the subordinate idea into a grammatically subordinate, or dependent, clause. Sound confusing? It's not. Here is an example.

Identify the two clauses in the following sentence.

Soft drink companies are continually introducing lower-calorie and caffeine-free beverages, negative press against these companies continues to increase year after year.

Although the clauses in this sentence are grammatically independent, they are not unrelated. Logically, the first clause depends on the second one; it seems to express a response to what is described in the second clause. You can logically infer that the soft drink companies are introducing these products because the amount of negative press against them is great. So, a good way to correct the error in this sentence would be to make the first clause grammatically dependent on the second clause, as follows:

> Although soft drink companies are now introducing lower-calorie and caffeine-free beverages, negative press against these companies continues to increase year after year.

A fourth way to correct a run-on sentence is simply to reduce the two independent clauses to one. This can be done in sentences in which the independent clauses have the same subject. You can compress the two clauses into one independent clause with a compound predicate.

> The Humber Bridge in Britain was completed in 1981, it is the longest single-span suspension bridge in the world.

In this sentence, the pronoun *it*, the subject of the second clause, refers to Humber Bridge, the subject of the first clause. To correct this sentence, remove both the comma and the pronoun *it*, and insert the coordinating conjunction *and*. The sentence now reads:

> The Humber Bridge in Britain was completed in 1981 and is the longest single-span suspension bridge in the world.

Now the sentence consists of one independent clause with a compound predicate, and only one subject.

Common Mistake 2: Sentence Fragments.   Sentence fragments are parts of sentences that have no independent clauses. What looks like a sentence may actually be a mere fragment. A sentence fragment has no independent clause. A sentence should always have at least one clause that could stand alone. Sometimes you may have to remove a word to create an independent clause, while other times you may have to insert a word.

Here is an example of a sentence fragment followed by the correction.

> In the summertime, the kindergarten class that plays on the rope swing beneath the crooked oak tree.

Here we have a fragment not because something is missing, but because something is included that makes the clause dependent. The word *that* makes everything after the comma a dependent clause. Simply remove the word *that*, and look at what you get.

In the summertime, the kindergarten class plays on the rope swing beneath the crooked oak tree.

Now you have a grammatically complete sentence that is shorter than the fragment.

Common Mistake 3: Misplaced Modifiers.   A modifier is a word or group of words that gives the reader more information about a noun or verb in the sentence. To be grammatically correct, the modifier must be positioned so that it is clear which word is being modified. A modifying phrase that begins a sentence should relate to the sentence's subject. Usually, this kind of introductory modifier is set off by a comma, and then the subject immediately follows the comma.

Here's an example of a sentence with a misplaced modifying modifier.

An advertisement was withdrawn by the producer of the local news program that was considered offensive by the city's minority communities.

Grammatically, the phrase *that was considered offensive by the city's minority communities* refers to *the local news program*, because this is the nearest noun. Is that what the writer means? Is it the local news program or the advertisement that was offensive to the minority communities? If the writer means to say that the advertisement was deemed offensive, she should rewrite the sentence as follows to make her idea clear.

The producer of the local news program withdrew an advertisement that was considered offensive by the city's minority communities.

Common Mistake 4: Faulty Parallelism.   This class of errors covers a wide range of faulty sentence constructions. A certain set of words in a sentence, or the general design of a sentence, often requires a parallel construction. If this construction is off-balance, then parallelism in the sentence is faulty.

For example, compare these two sentences.

My hobbies include swimming, gardening, and to read science fiction.
My hobbies include swimming, gardening, and reading science fiction.

In the first sentence, two of the hobbies use the *–ing* gerund form, but the third uses a different structure—the infinitive. The sentence is not parallel. In the second version, all three hobbies correctly use the same *–ing* form, creating a balanced sentence.

There are generally two situations in which the questions test your ability to spot errors in parallel construction. The first occurs in sentences with pairs of connective words that require parallelism.

Here is a list of connective words that demand parallel constructions:

neither…nor
either…or
both…and
the better…the better
the more…the more (or less)
not only…but also

For example, the phrases following the words *neither* and *nor* in a sentence must be parallel in grammatical structure. That is, if a noun phrase follows *neither*, then a noun phrase must follow *nor*, too. If the phrase after a first paired connective word is adverbial, the phrase after the second connective word must also be adverbial.

The second common way in which the use of parallel grammatical structure is tested is when a sentence consists of a list of two or more items. That list can comprise two or more nouns or noun phrases, verbs or verb phrases, or dependent clauses. Any kind of list calls for grammatically parallel items. Look for the answer choice that shows a list of grammatically parallel items.

Common Mistake 5: Faulty Coordination/Subordination.   These two kinds of errors occur when sentence clauses are joined incorrectly. Faulty coordination and faulty subordination are closely related, but require separate explanations.

Coordination between two clauses is faulty if it doesn't express the logical relation between the clauses. Often, this error involves a misused conjunction. A conjunction is a connective word joining two clauses or phrases in one sentence. The most common conjunctions are:

- And
- But
- Because
- However

To identify and correct faulty coordination, determine what the relationship between the sentence's two clauses really is.

Identify the conjunction in the following sentence. Why does it fail to connect the clauses logically?

Ben Franklin was a respected and talented statesman, and he was most famous for his discovery of electricity.

To identify and correct the faulty coordination, determine what the relationship between the sentence's two clauses really is. Does the conjunction *and* best express the relationship between the two facts the writer states about Ben Franklin? *And* normally expresses a consistency between two equally emphasized facts. However, the fact that Franklin is best known for his discovery of electricity is presented in contrast to the fact that he was a talented statesman. Thus, the use of *and* is an error in coordination.

A better way to connect these two contrasting ideas would be to use the conjunction *but*, which indicates some contrast between the two clauses. In this sentence, *but* points to a common expectation. An individual usually distinguishes herself or himself in one field of accomplishment—in politics or in science—but not in both. So Franklin's distinction in two diverse fields seems to contradict common expectations and calls for a *but*.

Faulty subordination is most commonly found in a group of words that contains two or more subordinate, or dependent clauses, but no independent clause. There are several connective words that, when introducing a sentence or clause, always indicate that the phrase that follows is dependent or subordinate. They are:

- Since
- Because
- So that
- If

Whenever a dependent clause begins a sentence, an independent clause must follow somewhere in the sentence. Pay careful attention for this kind of error on improving sentence questions.

Look at the group of words below and identify the faulty subordination.

Since the small electronics industry is one of the world's fastest growing sectors, because demand for the computer chip continues to be high.

Since indicates that the first clause in the group of words is subordinate and needs to be followed by an independent clause. But *because* in the second clause indicates that the second clause is also subordinate. The sentence is faulty because there is no independent clause to make the group of words grammatically complete. Result: two sentence fragments. The second connective word *because* should be eliminated to make the group of words a complete and logical sentence. With this revision, the *since* clause expresses a cause, and the independent clause expresses an effect or result.

To learn how to improve sentences, the fourth question type, you should spend time reviewing Kaplan's Target Strategy for Improving Sentences, which follows here.

Kaplan's Target Strategy for Improving Sentences

The Kaplan Target Strategy for improving sentences has four simple steps:

Step 1. Read the sentence carefully, listening for a mistake.
Step 2. Identify the error(s).
Step 3. Predict a correction.
Step 4. Check the choices for a match that doesn't introduce a new error.

Let's use this method on the example given earlier.

The Emancipation Edict freed the Russian serfs <u>in 1861; that being four years</u> before the Thirteenth Amendment abolished slavery in the United States.

    (A) in 1861; that being four years
    (B) in 1861 and is four years
    (C) in 1861 and this amounts to four years
    (D) in 1861, being four years
    (E) in 1861, four years

Step 1. Read the Sentence Carefully, Listening for a Mistake.   The original sentence just doesn't sound right.

Step 2. Identify the Error(s).   The semicolon and phrase *that being* seem like the wrong way of joining the two parts of the sentence.

Step 3. Predict a Correction.   The semicolon and *that being* seem unnecessary. Joining the two sentence fragments with a simple comma would probably work. (Incidentally, answer choices that contain the word *being* are usually wrong.) Plug in your choice to be sure it sounds best. Choice (E) has just a comma. Is that enough?

Step 4. Check the Choices for a Match That Doesn't Introduce a New Error.   All the answer choices begin with *in 1861* and end with *four years*, so you have to look at what's between to see what forms the best link. Scan the choices, and you will find that the *and is* in (B), the *and this amounts to* in (C), and the *being* preceded by a comma in (D) are no better than choice (A)—the original sentence. Choice (E) is the best way to rewrite the underlined portion of the sentence, so (E) is the correct answer.

   Remember: Because you should begin by reading the original sentence carefully, you should never waste time reading choice (A).

   Don't give up yet! The final strategy for improving passages will complete your review of Tips for Writing Success.

Kaplan's Target Strategy for Improving Passages

Kaplan's Target Strategy works for all three kinds of improving passage questions. Here are the five steps.

Step 1. Skim the passage for the overall idea and tone.
Step 2. Read the question.
Step 3. Reread the relevant portion and its context.
Step 4. Predict the correction.
Step 5. Check for a match that doesn't introduce a new error.

Step 1. Skim the Passage for the Overall Idea and Tone.   Read the entire essay quickly. Get a sense of the essay's overall main idea, as well as the main idea of each paragraph. This will come in handy when you are asked to answer questions about the essay as a whole.

Step 2. Read the Question.   Now read the question closely. Make sure that you understand exactly what you are asked to do. Questions that require you to revise or combine sentences will supply you with the sentence numbers. Questions that ask about the entire essay generally won't refer to specific sentences.

Step 3. Reread the Relevant Portion and Its Context.   Go back and reread that sentence or two that the question is about. But don't stop there. This next part is very important! Also *reread the sentences before and after the target sentence(s)*. This will provide you with the context (the surrounding ideas or information) for the sentence(s). Context helps you to choose the best answer from the answer choices.

Note: For those questions about the essay as a whole, skim quickly over the entire essay to refamiliarize yourself with its contents.

Step 4. Predict the Correction.   Say in your head what you think the correct sentence or answer should be.

Step 5. Check for a Match That Doesn't Introduce a New Error.   Go to the answer choices and pick the choice that best matches the sentence or idea in your head. Make sure the one you pick doesn't introduce a new mistake if you are correcting a sentence.

So, to summarize: read the essay quickly; read the question; reread the target sentences and the sentences that surround them; make up a sentence that would eliminate the mistake; and choose the answer choice that best matches your sentence.

Summary

This chapter covered a lot of material. Not only did you review the essentials of standard written English—grammar, punctuation, style—but also you familiarized yourself with some of the most common writing question types found on civil service exams. It's unlikely that you will have absorbed and perfected the many strategies found in this chapter, so continue to review the Tips for Writing Success as you work through this book. If you want to test how much you really know and how much you learned in this chapter, complete Practice Test 3. The 50 multiple-choice questions test your writing skills. If you want to check your results on this test, use the answer key and detailed answer explanations found after the test.

Practice Test 3

1 (A)(B)(C)(D)   11 (A)(B)(C)(D)   21 (A)(B)(C)(D)(E)   36 (A)(B)(C)(D)(E)
2 (A)(B)(C)(D)   12 (A)(B)(C)(D)   22 (A)(B)(C)(D)(E)   37 (A)(B)(C)(D)(E)
3 (A)(B)(C)(D)   13 (A)(B)(C)(D)   23 (A)(B)(C)(D)(E)   38 (A)(B)(C)(D)(E)
4 (A)(B)(C)(D)   14 (A)(B)(C)(D)   24 (A)(B)(C)(D)(E)   39 (A)(B)(C)(D)(E)
5 (A)(B)(C)(D)   15 (A)(B)(C)(D)   25 (A)(B)(C)(D)(E)   40 (A)(B)(C)(D)(E)
6 (A)(B)(C)(D)   16 (A)(B)(C)(D)   26 (A)(B)(C)(D)(E)   41 (A)(B)(C)(D)(E)
7 (A)(B)(C)(D)   17 (A)(B)(C)(D)   27 (A)(B)(C)(D)(E)   42 (A)(B)(C)(D)(E)
8 (A)(B)(C)(D)   18 (A)(B)(C)(D)   28 (A)(B)(C)(D)(E)   43 (A)(B)(C)(D)(E)
9 (A)(B)(C)(D)   19 (A)(B)(C)(D)   29 (A)(B)(C)(D)(E)   44 (A)(B)(C)(D)(E)
10 (A)(B)(C)(D) 20 (A)(B)(C)(D)   30 (A)(B)(C)(D)(E)   45 (A)(B)(C)(D)(E)
                                   31 (A)(B)(C)(D)(E)   46 (A)(B)(C)(D)(E)
                                   32 (A)(B)(C)(D)(E)   47 (A)(B)(C)(D)(E)
                                   33 (A)(B)(C)(D)(E)   48 (A)(B)(C)(D)(E)
                                   34 (A)(B)(C)(D)(E)   49 (A)(B)(C)(D)(E)
                                   35 (A)(B)(C)(D)(E)   50 (A)(B)(C)(D)(E)

What follows are six sentences that form a paragraph. The first sentence is the first sentence of the paragraph. The remaining five sentences are listed in random order. Choose the order for the five sentences that will create the best paragraph, one that is both well-organized and grammatically correct.

1. It is ironic that, despite the many successes of scientific medicine, many afflictions stubbornly resist all attempts to combat them.

   (1) Those affected by this deadly virus and other modern plagues cannot be blamed for suspecting that scientific medicine is somehow missing something important.

   (2) If body and mind are indeed linked, future doctors may be able to manipulate the mind in order to have a healing effect on currently intransigent physical problems.

   (3) This connection would appear to be an obvious factor for examination, since the brain has long been established as the command center of the body.

   (4) Perhaps the gap in understanding stems from the fact that doctors have overlooked a potent connection between body and mind.

   (5) Until recently, for example, science has been largely powerless in the face of HIV, which seems designed by nature to withstand the weapons of immunologists.

   (A) 5, 1, 4, 2, 3
   (B) 5, 1, 3, 2, 4
   (C) 1, 5, 4, 3, 2
   (D) 5, 1, 4, 3, 2

2. Early in the eighteenth century, the astronomer Edmund Halley wondered to himself why it was that the night sky is dark.

(1) This apparently naive question brings to mind another naive question posed by Isaac Newton and which involved a falling apple.

(2) A star's brightness stays the same over any distance, so each of those stars would be visible to us, and the heavens would be filled with light.

(3) The fact that they are not indicates that there is something fundamentally wrong with the popular conception of the universe.

(4) In an infinite universe, after all, there would have to be a star lying in every possible line of sight in the sky.

(5) Halley's question is in fact interesting to consider because if the universe were truly infinite, as most suppose, the entire sky would be ablaze at night.

(A) 1, 5, 4, 2, 3
(B) 1, 4, 5, 2, 3
(C) 1, 5, 3, 4, 2
(D) 1, 5, 2, 3, 4

3. The study of indoor environmental pollution is a controversial new area of scientific research.

(1) For example, inhabitants of houses with statistically "average" levels of radon are exposed to approximately 300 percent more radiation than the average American receives from X-ray medical procedures in a lifetime.

(2) Consequently, it is a serious concern that hundreds of thousands of homes exceed "average" pollution levels.

(3) One area of debate is that the use of the terms "high," "low," and "average" in reports of the concentrations of indoor pollutants can be misleading.

(4) Clearly, more attention needs to be paid to issues such as the labeling of indoor pollutant concentrations.

(5) Such labels do not necessarily imply any correlation with "acceptable" or "unacceptable" health risks.

(A) 3, 5, 1, 2, 4
(B) 3, 5, 2, 1, 4
(C) 5, 3, 2, 1, 4
(D) 3, 5, 4, 2, 1

4. Many people find it puzzling that groups of people sometimes engage in behavior that seems to be clearly dangerous or, at least, ill-conceived.

(1) For that reason, when the leader exhibits a preference for a specific solution to the crisis, the other members may choose to ignore any other alternatives.

(2) The resulting lack of balanced judgment—groupthink—may well cause the group to reach a decision that in retrospect is obviously wrong.

(3) Individual members of the group prize the high morale derived from its cohesion and fear rejection if they break ranks.

(4) Irving Janis developed the "groupthink" hypothesis in 1972 in an attempt to explain how fatal errors can occur in a group's decision making.

(5) According to this hypothesis, groupthink can arise when a highly cohesive group with a strong-willed leader faces a crisis.

(A) 4, 5, 1, 2, 3
(B) 1, 2, 4, 5, 3
(C) 4, 5, 3, 1, 2
(D) 5, 4, 3, 1, 2

5. In spite of a recent revival of interest in nineteenth-century women writers, Lydia Maria Child remains an obscure name.

(1) Child's writing was, by contrast, politically passionate; she devoted her literary energies to vindicating the rights of women, Indians, and African American slaves.

(2) The most likely explanation for this oversight is that she cannot be classified with her female contemporaries, who mainly produced stylized domestic fiction.

(3) Our gain, though, would not compensate for the fact that her voice was not sufficiently heard when it would have been most relevant.

(4) So powerful was her voice, in fact, that the abolitionist William Lloyd Garrison hailed her as "first woman in the Republic."

(5) His endorsement leaves no room for doubt that the modern reader should be made aware of her work.

(A) 2, 1, 5, 4, 3
(B) 2, 1, 4, 5, 3
(C) 1, 2, 4, 5, 3
(D) 4, 5, 3, 2, 1

6. The famous economist Adam Smith was notorious for his absent-mindedness and tendency to enter strange fits of distraction.

(1) When the spell was broken, he stopped and took up the conversation where he had left off, not realizing he had done anything out of the ordinary.

(2) On one occasion, Smith was walking in Edinburgh with a friend when a guard presented his pike in salute.

(3) He returned the honor with his cane and then astonished his friend by following exactly in the guard's footsteps, duplicating with his cane every motion of the pike.

(4) Smith, who had been thus honored on countless occasions, was suddenly hypnotized by the saluting soldier.

(5) Encountering the organized reliability of *The Wealth of Nations*, it is difficult to imagine the spellbound principal of this anecdote as the father of modern economics.

(A) 2, 4, 3, 5, 1
(B) 2, 4, 1, 5, 3
(C) 2, 4, 3, 1, 5
(D) 2, 4, 1, 3, 5

7. When we read newspaper quotations, we assume them to represent exactly what the speaker said.
    (1) People speak with bizarre syntax, hesitations, repetitions, and contradictions, making it necessary for the journalist to translate speech into prose.
    (2) Journalists must contend, however, with the fact that exact quotations of human speech would be virtually unreadable.
    (3) Indeed, the idea of a reporter inventing rather than reporting speech is repugnant because so much of our knowledge comes from what we read in the press.
    (4) When the speaker does not recognize the quote as his or her own, however, the journalist has taken too much license.
    (5) These translations may not be exact quotes, but they are valid as long as they remain faithful to the subject's thought and characteristic way of expression.
    (A) 3, 2, 1, 5, 4
    (B) 2, 3, 1, 5, 4
    (C) 3, 2, 1, 4, 5
    (D) 1, 2, 3, 4, 5

8. The thistle is a type of prickly plant that grows throughout North America.
    (1) His cry awoke the Scots, who fell upon their attackers and saved their nation from conquest.
    (2) In Scotland, however, the thistle has been the cherished national flower for centuries.
    (3) According to legend, as marauding Norsemen crept toward a camp full of sleeping Scottish soldiers, one invader stepped on a thistle and let out a yelp.
    (4) Most thistles are considered wild flowers, with the exception of the artichoke, which is harvested and eaten before it has a chance to bloom.
    (5) Ironically, the thistle's self protective feature protected not only the flower, but the nation.
    (A) 4, 2, 5, 1, 3
    (B) 4, 2, 1, 5, 3
    (C) 2, 4, 3, 1, 5
    (D) 4, 2, 3, 1, 5

Choose the word or words that best complete the following sentences.

9. The school's tennis team is _____
    (A) known for its competitive players.
    (B) known for the competitiveness of its players when they compete.
    (C) known because its players are said to be competitive.
    (D) known to be competitive and have competitive players.

10. We left our house on time, _____ we still arrived late.
    (A) consequently
    (B) therefore
    (C) so
    (D) none of these

11. _____ years of neglect left the house in a terrible state, the silver door handles still looked shiny and new.
    (A) however
    (B) despite
    (C) although
    (D) regardless of

12. The graceful curves of the colonial-era buildings that dominated the old part of the city contrasted sharply with the modern, _____ subway stations and made the latter appear glaringly out of place.
    (A) festive
    (B) grimy
    (C) angular
    (D) gigantic

13. It was difficult to tell what the auditor was thinking, as his expression was _____.
    (A) palpable
    (B) salient
    (C) titular
    (D) impassive

14. If all world leaders were to _____ violent solutions to problems, there would soon be a _____ of war.
    (A) emulate…tutelage
    (B) condole…deluge
    (C) eschew…cessation
    (D) becloud…demagogue

15. The leader of the minority party met with members of the business _____ to devise an economic reform package.
    (A) caucus
    (B) aerie
    (C) milieu
    (D) rostrum

In questions 16–20, look for errors in punctuation, capitalization, or usage. If there is no error, select choice (D).

16. (A) "Is there room for me in the car?" Janet asked.
    (B) The shore is three miles from the center of town.
    (C) The Hawks beat the bluejays two to one.
    (D) No mistake.

17. (A) There's no business like show business.
    (B) Sue's mother warned her to be careful.
    (C) What are the chances of winning?
    (D) No mistake.

18. (A) Who has my briefcase?
    (B) If there ready, let's go.
    (C) Uncle Tito plays the bongo drums.
    (D) No mistake.

19. (A) I have nothing but respect for principal Volken.
    (B) The rainstorm had no effect on the game.
    (C) It's difficult to imagine the struggles he faced.
    (D) No mistake.

20. (A) While making dinner, the hot oil burned the chef's hand.
    (B) It seemed fitting to have the back to school party in September.
    (C) As a writer, I try to follow the rules of grammar and style.
    (D) No mistake.

Each sentence contains exactly one error or no errors. The error, if there is one, is underlined and has a letter below it. If the sentence contains an error, select the underlined part that contains the error. If the sentence is correct, select choice (E).

21. In the wake <u>of</u> recent thefts, the town's

         A

wealthier residents <u>have installed</u> gates, alarm

         B

systems, and even video surveillance

equipment in their neighborhoods, hoping

<u>that it will</u> prevent <u>further burglaries</u>. <u>No error</u>

  C   D   E

22. One reason that a growing number of people

<u>have no</u> family doctor <u>may be that</u> fewer and

  A   B

fewer medical students <u>are choosing to train</u> as

           C

<u>a general practitioner.</u> <u>No error</u>

    D   E

23. <u>Under</u> the proposed law, which many <u>deem</u>

  A   B

too harsh, any motorist <u>convicted of</u> drunk

          C

driving would spend thirty days in prison and

lose <u>their license</u> for five years. <u>No error</u>

    D   E

24. Although <u>they had been</u> political rivals on

        A

<u>more than one</u> occasion, John Quincy Adams

   B

<u>remained</u> one of Thomas Jefferson's closest

  C

friends until <u>his</u> death. <u>No error</u>

      D   E

25. The advisory board <u>cautioned</u> employees that the

        A

<u>existing</u> program of <u>health benefits</u> <u>were</u> likely to

  B   C   D

be eliminated. <u>No error</u>

     E

26. Citizens <u>protesting</u> the planned demolition of
              A

the historic YMCA building claim <u>that without</u>
                             B

the YMCA, many young people in the town

<u>would of</u> grown up <u>with no</u> access to sports
   C   D

facilities and no place for after-school

recreation. <u>No error</u>
          E

27. Even <u>those who</u> profess <u>to care</u> about "green"
        A   B

issues often fail to consider <u>how</u> their daily
                       C

choices <u>effect</u> the environment. <u>No error</u>
      D   E

Choose the answer that is grammatically correct and best maintains the meaning of the given sentence. If you think the original is the best choice, select (A); if not, choose among (B), (C), (D), or (E). The result should be a sentence that is clear and precise.

28. Although the candidate received crucial votes from rural precincts, <u>but he was defeated by</u> his opponent's broad base of political support.
(A) but he was defeated by
(B) defeating him by
(C) and what made his defeat possible
(D) he was defeated by
(E) and he was defeated by

29. Changing over from a military to a peacetime economy means producing tractors rather than tanks, radios rather than rifles, and <u>to producing running shoes rather than combat boots</u>.

(A) to producing running shoes rather than combat boots
(B) to the production of running shoes rather than combat boots
(C) running shoes rather than combat boots
(D) replacing combat boots with running shoes
(E) to running shoes rather combat boots

30. Some of the classes taught in American <u>classrooms are interpretations of lessons used worldwide, particularly those in European history</u>.
(A) classrooms are interpretations of lessons used worldwide, particularly those in European history
(B) classrooms, there are interpretations of lessons used worldwide, particularly European history
(C) classrooms, and in particular European history, is an interpretation of lessons used worldwide

(D) classrooms, particularly in European history, are interpretations of lessons used worldwide

(E) classrooms being interpretations, European history in particular, of those used worldwide

31. Last of the world's leaders to do so, the Prime Minister admits that terrorist threats <u>credible enough to warrant</u> the imposition of stringent security measures.
(A) credible enough to warrant
(B) credible enough warrant
(C) are credible enough to warrant
(D) credible enough, warranting
(E) are credible enough to be warranted

32. The protest movement's impact will depend on both how many people it touches and <u>its durability</u>.
(A) its durability
(B) is it going to endure
(C) if it has durability
(D) how long it endures
(E) the movement's ability to endure

33. <u>Upon entering the jail, the prisoners' personal belongings are surrendered to the guards.</u>
(A) Upon entering the jail, the prisoners' personal belongings are surrendered to the guards.
(B) Upon entering the jail, the prisoners surrender their personal belongings to the guards.
(C) The prisoners' personal belongings having been surrendered to the guards upon entering the jail.

(D) Upon entering the jail, the guards are to whom the prisoners surrender their personal belongings.
(E) Upon entering the jail, the prisoners will have been surrendering their personal belongings to the guards.

34. Exposed to the extremely long and severe cold spell, <u>frost soon killed the buds of the citrus trees and they did not produce fruit that season</u>.
(A) frost soon killed the buds of the citrus trees and they did not produce fruit that season
(B) soon the buds of the citrus trees were killed by frost, and therefore not producing fruit that season
(C) the buds of the citrus trees were soon killed by frost, they did not produce fruit that season
(D) fruit was not produced by the citrus trees that season because their buds had been killed by frost
(E) the buds of the citrus trees were soon killed by frost, and the trees did not produce fruit that season

35. <u>Although its being fictional in form</u>, the new book on America raises many historical questions.
(A) Although its being fictional in form
(B) Despite its fictional form
(C) Whereas it was fictional in form
(D) Its form being fictional
(E) Even though fictional form was there

36. Of all the countries in the UN Security Council, <u>the representative of China was the only one to speak</u> to the General Assembly today.

    (A) the representative of China was the only one to speak

    (B) making the representative from China the only one to speak

    (C) China's representative only spoke

    (D) China's governor spoke only

    (E) China was the only one whose representative spoke

37. Most wholesale dealers are reluctant to reveal either how much they pay for their goods or <u>their profit margin per item sold</u>.

    (A) their profit margin per item sold

    (B) how great a profit margin per item sold

    (C) how great a profit they receive per item sold

    (D) if their profit margin per item sold

    (E) how great the margin of profit

38. According to Aristotle, a catastrophe <u>is when the action of a tragic drama turns toward its disastrous conclusion</u>.

    (A) is when the action of a tragic drama turns towards its disastrous conclusion

    (B) is where a tragic drama turns the action toward its disastrous conclusion

    (C) occurs where, towards its disastrous conclusion, the action of a tragic drama is turning

    (D) approaches when the action of a tragic drama has turned toward its disastrous conclusion

    (E) is the turning point at which the action of a tragic drama approaches its disastrous conclusion

39. <u>Were it not for the warming effects of the Gulf Stream, England's climate would resemble that of Greenland.</u>

    (A) Were it not for the warming effects of the Gulf Stream, England's climate would resemble that of Greenland.

    (B) Had the Gulf Stream not such warming effects, England's climate would resemble Greenland.

    (C) Without the warming effects of the Gulf Stream, England's climate were resembling Greenland's.

    (D) If not for the warming effects of the Gulf Stream, therefore England's climate would have resembled that of Greenland.

    (E) If the Gulf Stream would not have had its warming effects, England's climate would resemble that of Greenland.

Read the passage and select the best answer for each question that follows. Your answers should follow the conventions of standard written English.

The following is a draft of a letter to a local newspaper protesting cuts in funding for after-school sports programs.

(1) I disagree with the editor's view that after-school sports programs should be cut in our city government's search for ways to reduce spending. (2) The editor argues that extracurricular sports play a less important role than academic studies, distracting students from the opportunity to increase their knowledge after school is out. (3) However, I myself believe that playing sports enhances students' academic performance. (4) Why is sports so effective in this regard? (5) The main reason is that sports teaches people to excel. (6) It gives students the chance to strive for greatness. (7) It shows them that it takes courage and discipline to succeed in competition with others. (8) Top athletes such as Michael Jordan become role models for young people everywhere, inspiring them with his brilliant individual performances. (9) In addition to these personal attributes, playing in team sports show young people how to interact with each other, achieving shared goals. (10) Such principles have a direct impact on how students perform in their academic studies. (11) I know that being selected for the school lacrosse team taught me many valuable lessons about working with others. (12) Not only that, friendships that I have made there were carried into the rest of my school life. (13) In summary, I would urge the editor to strongly reconsider his stance on extra curricular sports. (14) There are doubtless other ways of city government saving the money they require.

40. Which of the following is the best way to revise the underlined portion of sentence 3 (reproduced below)?

However, I myself believe that play-ing sports enhances students' academic performance.

(A) However, I myself believe that playing sports should enhance
(B) Playing sports, however, I believe enhances
(C) However, I personally believe that playing sports enhances
(D) I believe, however, that play-ing sports enhances
(E) However, I myself believe that to play sports is to enhance

KAPLAN

41. Which of the following is the best way to revise and combine sentences 6 and 7 (reproduced below)?

It gives students the chance to strive for greatness. It shows them that it takes courage and discipline to succeed in competition with others.

(A) Although it gives students the chance to strive for greatness, it also shows them that it takes courage and discipline to succeed in competition with others.

(B) While it gives students the chance to strive for greatness, also showing them that it takes courage and discipline to succeed in competition with others.

(C) It gives students the chance to strive for greatness, showing them that it takes courage and discipline to succeed in competition with others.

(D) Because it gives students the chance to strive for greatness, they are shown that it takes courage and discipline to succeed in competition with others.

(E) It gives students the chance to strive for greatness and show them that it takes courage and discipline to succeed in competition with others.

42. Which of the following is the best version of the underlined portion of sentence 8 (reproduced below)?

Top athletes such as Michael Jordan become role models for young people everywhere, <u>inspiring them with his</u> brilliant individual performances.

(A) (As it is now)
(B) inspiring him with their
(C) inspiring them with their
(D) to inspire them with his
(E) inspiring him with his

43. Which of the following is the best way to revise the underlined portion of sentence 12 (reproduced below)?

<u>Not only that,</u> friendships that I have made there were carried into the rest of my school life.

(A) And,
(B) Moreover,
(C) Nevertheless,
(D) Sequentially,
(E) Finally,

44. The author could best improve sentence 14 (reproduced below) by

There are doubtless other ways of city government saving the money they require.

(A) making an analogy to historical events
(B) taking alternative points of view into account
(C) including a personal anecdote about her participation in team sports
(D) speculating about the motivations of those advocating cuts
(E) providing examples of other areas in which spending could be reduced

(1) Despite his early death at 35, Austrian composer Wolfgang Amadeus Mozart is one the most famous musicians in history for three reasons. **(2)** He was extraordinarily talented, he was exposed to music at an early age, and his love of it. **(3)** Mozart's talent showed early. **(4)** At age seven, he was already writing sonatas for the harpsichord. **(5)** He could improvise music at the keyboard and played any piece of music in any style—even when blindfolded!

(6) Mozart was always encouraged and even driven by his father. **(7)** Leopold Mozart was a composer, and Wolfgang learned to play and read music when he was a small child. **(8)** To establish his son early and build a path for his future career, he lost no time showing him off to audiences. **(9)** He arranged for six-year-old Wolfgang to play in the palaces of most of the major European cities. **(10)** Leopold Mozart determining that his gifted son should reap the rewards his talent deserved.

(11) And Mozart loved music. **(12)** As a child, Leopold was often surprised with tunes his son had written. **(13)** Some of these little pieces were so technically challenging that although Wolfgang could play them easily, his father's adult friends and colleagues could not play them at all! **(14)** He once wrote that composing music was such a delight to him that he could not describe it in words.

45. In context, what is the best way to revise and combine sentences 1 and 2 (reproduced below)?

Despite his early death at 35, Austrian composer Wolfgang Amadeus Mozart is one the most famous musicians in history for three reasons. He was extraordinarily talented, he was exposed to music at an early age, and his love of it.

(A) Despite his early death at 35, Austrian composer Wolfgang Amadeus Mozart is one the most famous musicians in history for three reasons: he was extraordinarily talented, he was exposed to music at an early age, and he loved it.

(B) Despite his early death at 35, Austrian composer Wolfgang Amadeus Mozart is one the most famous musicians in history for three reasons, this is because he was extraordinarily talented, he was exposed to music at an early age, and his love of it.

(C) Despite his early death at 35 years of age, Austrian composer Wolfgang Amadeus Mozart is one the most famous musicians in history for the following three reasons: he was extraordinarily talented, he was exposed to music at an early age, and he loved it.

(D) Despite his death at 35, which was early, Austrian composer Wolfgang Amadeus Mozart is one the most famous musicians in history for three reasons: that he was extraordinarily talented, that he was exposed to music at an early age, and that he had a love of it.

(E) Despite his early death at 35, Austrian composer Wolfgang Amadeus Mozart is one the most famous musicians in history for three reasons: he was extraordinarily talented, he was exposed to music at an early age, and his love of it.

46. In context, which revision is needed in sentence 5?
(A) No revision is needed
(B) Replace "He" with "Mozart"
(C) Replace "could improvise" with "could have improvised"
(D) Replace "played" with "play"
(E) Eliminate the phrase "in any style"

47. In context, which is the best version of sentence 8 (reproduced below)?

To establish his son early and build a path for his future career, he lost no time showing him off to audiences.

(A) (As it is now)
(B) To establish his son early and build a path for his future career, Leopold Mozart lost no time showing him off to audiences.
(C) To establish Wolfgang early and build a path for his future career, he lost no time showing him off to audiences.
(D) To establish his son early and build a path for his future career, he lost no time showing Wolfgang off to audiences.
(E) To establish his son early and build a path for his future career, Mozart lost no time showing him off to audiences.

48. In context, what revision is necessary in sentence 10?
(A) No revision is necessary
(B) Change "determining" to "determines"
(C) Change "determining" to "was determined"
(D) Change "determining" to "having determined"
(E) Change "should reap" to "should be reaping"

49. In context, what is the best version of sentence 12 (reproduced below)?

As a child, Leopold was often surprised with tunes his son had written

(A) As a child, the tunes his son had written often surprised Leopold.
(B) As a child, his son often surprised Leopold with tunes he had written.

(C) As a child, surprising Leopold with tunes he had written was his son.

(D) Leopold was often surprised with tunes that, as a child, his son had written.

(E) Tunes written by his son as a child often surprised Leopold.

50. Sentence 14 would make the most sense if placed after
(A) sentence 1
(B) sentence 2
(C) sentence 11
(D) sentence 12
(E) sentence 13

Answers and Explanations

1. **D**

5, 1, 4, 3, 2

(5) is the most logical first sentence—it provides an *example* of an affliction or illness resisting doctors' attempts to combat it. (1) must follow, as *this deadly virus* must refer to HIV in sentence (5). In sentence (4), *this gap in understanding* refers to the concept of *missing something important* in (1). *This connection* in (3) refers to the mind/body reference in (4). (2) concludes by suggesting how mind/body medicine might improve the medicine of the future.

2. **A**

1, 5, 4, 2, 3

(1) must come first because *this naive question* can refer to only the question posed in the topic sentence. (4) must follow, as *in an infinite universe* expands on the issue mentioned in (5). In sentence (2), *each of those stars* connects back to *a star lying in every possible line of sight* in (4). Finally, *the fact that they are not* in (3) refers to *the heavens would be filled with light* in (2).

3. **A**

3, 5, 1, 2, 4

(3) logically follows the topic sentence, as *one area of debate* and expands on why the study of indoor pollution is *controversial*. (5) can only come next, as *such labels* must refer to *high, low, etc.*" in (3). (1) follows logically because it explains why such labels might not correlate with *acceptable* health risks. Finally, (2) draws a conclusion from the statement in (1)—that people in *above-average* pollution households deserve wider concern. (4) raises a future policy consideration.

4. **C**

4, 5, 3, 1, 2

(4) provides the beginning of an explanation for the phenomenon described in the topic sentence. (5) logically follows by explaining when "groupthink" typically occurs. The last three sentences are trickier. Why does groupthink occur? (3) tells us why—group members prize the solidarity of the group above all other considerations. What would happen as a result? (1) tells us—whatever the leader says, the group will tend to agree. Finally, (2) spells out the consequence—wrong decisions are often made.

5. **B**

2, 1, 4, 5, 3

(2) logically follows the topic sentence because it begins the explanation of why Child was ignored. (1) expands on the contrast between Child and

other nineteenth-century women writers mentioned in (2). Finally, (4, 5, 3) concludes the paragraph, as *his endorsement* in (5) must refer to *William Lloyd Garrison* in (4). (3) must follow (5) because *our gain* refers to the *modern reader* in (5).

6. C

2, 4, 3, 1, 5

(2) logically follows the topic sentence by providing a specific example of the phenomenon mentioned in the topic sentence. (4, 3, 1) follows in chronological sequence and (5) wraps it up with a mention of how paradoxical this anecdote seems.

7. A

3, 2, 1, 5, 4

(3) logically follows the topic sentence because it explains *why* we assume that newspaper quotes must be direct quotations. (2) introduces the contrasting point in the paragraph—that journalists often find it impossible to directly translate real speech. (1) explains why, and (5) draws a conclusion from (2) and (1)—that approximations of a speaker's actual words are acceptable, so long as they are true to the spirit of the speaker's ideas. (4) follows up with an example of when the journalist has gone too far.

8. D

4, 2, 3, 1, 5

(4) logically follows the topic sentence, as it gives us more detail on the plant. (2) follows (4) as it diverts the discussion to why the thistle is the national flower of Scotland. (3, 1, 5) relate in a chronological sequence a historical myth or legend that explains why the thistle is so important to the Scots.

9. A

The most concise and clearest answer choice is (A). Choices (B), (C), and (D) are unnecessarily wordy.

10. D

The first clause states that *we left on time*, the second clause contradicts this because *we arrived late*. The linking word must show a contrast. There are no contrasting transition words, so (D) is the best answer.

11. C

Choice (A) is obviously incorrect. Choices (B), (C), and (D) are all words that show contrast so they could be correct. However, if you insert choices (B) and (D) into the sentence, they do not make sense grammatically. Only *although* makes sense in the sentence grammatically and contextually.

12. C

You are specifically told that there is a contrast between the buildings and the subway stations. Checking the answer choices for a word that contrasts in meaning with *graceful curves*, you find that the answer is (C), *angular*, which means *jagged* or *angled*.

13. D

The key to this question is the word *as*, which signals a cause and effect relationship. You must look for a word that tells you why "it was difficult to tell what the auditor was thinking." *Impassive* means expressionless, revealing nothing. (A), *palpable*, means obvious or easily perceived. *Salient*, (B), means prominent. Choice (C), *titular*, refers to having a title, often in name only.

14. C

The logical relationship in this sentence is cause and effect, an *if...then* relationship, although in this case the *then* is implied. To *eschew* is to forego or avoid. *Cessation* refers to stopping or ceasing. Avoiding violence, the sentence says, would stop war. (A) is incorrect because to *emulate* is to strive to equal or surpass through imitation, while *tutelage* is instruction or guardianship, from the same root as *tutor*. The words in (B), *condole* and *deluge*, are incorrect because *condole* means to feel or express sympathy for another, while *deluge* means an overwhelming amount or a flood. In (D), *becloud* and *demagogue* mean to obscure or cover, as with clouds (becloud), and a popular leader who appeals to the emotions of the people (demagogue).

15. A

This question must be answered by looking at context. First, note the words that are clues, such as *minority party*, *members*, and *business*, as well as *economic reform package*. You are looking for a term that is used in politics to apply to a group with members. *Caucus* means a group with a special focus within a larger group or party. *Aerie*, (B), is a nest or a house built on a high place. (C), *milieu*, is an environment or setting. *Rostrum*, (D), is an elevated platform for public speaking.

16. C

The word *Bluejays* should be capitalized because it is the name of a team.

17. D

There are no mistakes.

18. B

Look at the use of *there* in choice (B). It should be *they are,* or *they're*. Although you've spotted the error, read the final answer choice just to be sure.

19. A

The rules is that one must capitalize the first letter of a person's title when it precedes their proper name. In the first sentence *principal* should be capitalized.

20. C

This sentence contains a dangling modifier. As written, it seems that the hot oil was making dinner. The correct sentence would read, *While making dinner, the chef burned his hand on hot oil.*

21. C

If you look for the antecedent of the pronoun *it* here, you won't find it—this is a case of ambiguous pronoun reference.

22. D

This sentence has number agreement problems: because *students* is a plural noun, the second part of the sentence should also be plural: *as general practitioners*.

23. D

The pronoun *their* is plural and does not agree in number with its singular antecedent, *motorist*. The sentence should read *his or her license*.

24. D

Another pronoun error: in this sentence, it is not clear whether *his* refers to Adams or to Jefferson; hence this sentence contains a vague pronoun reference.

KAPLAN

25. **D**

Although *benefits* is the closest noun to the verb *were*, the subject of the verb is actually the singular *program*; (D) should be *was*. (A) uses an appropriate verb tense in context. (B) appropriately modifies the noun *program*. (C) is a correctly used prepositional phrase.

26. **C**

This sentence has a nonidiomatic preposition after the verb: *would of* is not standard written English, and it makes no sense. The sentence should read *would have grown up*.

27. **D**

Affect and *effect* are commonly confused words. Here, *affect* (meaning *to influence* or *to have an effect on*) would be the correct word, not *effect*.

28. **D**

The original sentence contains both a dependent and an independent clause, but it uses two connecting words when only one is needed. Choice (D) creates an independent clause with no unnecessary connecting word joining the two clauses.

29. **C**

This sentence presents a list of comparisons. All items in a list must have parallel construction. Only choice (C) gives the last comparison an appearance parallel to the previous two comparisons. The word *producing* could have been repeated in all three comparisons. But because it wasn't repeated in the second comparison, it can't be repeated in the third one either.

30. **D**

As written, it is unclear what noun *particularly those in European history* is intended to modify. (D) corrects this error without adding any other ones. (B) is grammatically incorrect. The singular verb is in (C) does not agree with its subject *Some*, which is grammatically plural. (E) is a sentence fragment.

31. **C**

The second clause of the given sentence lacks a main verb. Choice (C) provides the verb *are* for the subject *threats* so that the second, dependent clause is complete, and the sentence is correct.

32. **D**

This sentence uses a *both…and…* pair, so it requires parallel blocks of words following each half of the pair. Only choice (D) has a second block of words, *how long it endures*, similar to the first block, *how many people it touches*.

33. **B**

Upon entering the jail is an introductory phrase that describes the prisoners (they are the ones entering the jail). As the sentence is worded, it sounds as though the prisoners' personal belongings are entering the jail. (B) and (E) are the only two choices that place *the prisoners* right next to the phrase that describes them. (B) is the best choice; (E) puts the verb in an awkward and incorrect tense.

34. **E**

This sentence contains a misplaced modifier. The introductory phrase should modify the noun immediately following the comma. In choices (E) and (C), the modified noun, the buds, is in the correct position following the introductory modifying phrase. But notice that choice (C) introduces a new error when it links the second clause to the first with only a comma. Only choice (E) corrects the original problem without adding a new one.

35. **B**

The underlined selection here is awkward and wordy. (B) expresses the same idea more clearly and concisely. (C) introduces an inconsistent verb tense. (D) does not express the correct relationship between the clauses. (E) is awkward and unnecessarily wordy.

36. **E**

As written, this sentence calls *the representative of China* one of *the countries on the UN Security Council.* Although it's slightly longer than some of the other choice, only (E) is correct in context. (B), (C), and (D) do not address the error.

37. **C**

The given sentence has faulty parallelism. With coordinating words like *either...or*, word order and sentence structure following the two coordinating words should be parallel. Here, a dependent clause follows the word *either*: *how much they pay for their goods.* Choice (C) contains a dependent clause and makes the wording after *or* parallel to the wording after *either*.

38. **E**

The problem with this sentence is faulty logic, rather than grammatical error. A *catastrophe*, a noun, cannot actually be *when...*, though it could occur *when....* Only choice (E) solves the original

problem without introducing a new one. A *catastrophe can be*, and *is*, a *turning point.*

39. **A**

The sentence contains no error and is not wordy or awkward.

40. **D**

The key to this problem is realizing that *I myself* is redundant—if the author has already used *I*, there's no need to add *myself* to clarify. (D) provides the best fix here—notice that it's also the shortest, most straightforward answer. Choices (A) and (E) still include *myself.* (C) substitutes another redundancy—the word *personally.* (B) is unnecessarily convoluted and is missing a comma following *I believe.*

41. **C**

The context here suggests a strong link between the two sentences—the idea is that sports provide students with the chance to strive for greatness by showing them it takes courage. Choice (C) is the best answer. (A) introduces an illogical contrast. (B) creates a sentence fragment. (D) uses the passive voice unnecessarily. In (E), the verb *show* doesn't agree with the subject *it.*

42. **C**

The key to this sentence is spotting a subject-verb agreement problem—the subject in the sentence is *top athletes*, not *Michael Jordan*—he's only introduced as an example of a top athlete. So the underlined pronouns should be *them* (to agree with *young people*) and *their* (to agree with *top athletes*).

43. B

To fix this ambiguous introductory phrase, you're looking for a conjunction that expresses the idea of listing an *additional benefit* of participation in team sports. (B) *moreover* does this effectively. *And*, (A), is not an idiomatic conjunction with which to begin a sentence. (C) creates an unnecessary contrast. In (D), *sequentially* means in order, not *consequently*. (E), *finally*, is wrong because this sentence describes the second item in a list of two.

44. E

Sentence 14 provides a weak ending to the passage because it refers to o*ther ways of the city government saving money*, without suggesting what these might be. So the best improvement to sentence 14 might be (E) to provide examples of alternative areas for cuts. (A) would be an odd solution—historical events haven't been mentioned thus far in the passage. (B) would weaken the essay just at the point at which the author needs to strengthen it. (C) would be repetitive—the author has already included a personal anecdote. Finally, (D) would simply offer a digression at this point.

45. A

There are two problems here. The sentences are choppy as written, and the items in the second sentence's list are not parallel. (A) does the best job of combining the sentences and corrects the parallelism error. (B) creates a run-on sentence: two independent clauses combined with a comma splice. (C) and (D) address the errors, but unnecessarily add additional words and phrases,

making the sentence wordier than it needs to be. (E) correctly combines the sentences, but fails to address the parallelism problem.

46. D

The conjunction *and* requires that the two verbs in the compound predicate be in parallel form, which they are not here (*He could improvise...and played...*). (D) makes the two verbs parallel. (B) is unnecessary—the pronoun *he* clearly refers to Mozart. (C) introduces an inconsistent verb tense. (E) alters the meaning of the sentence.

47. B

This sentences uses the pronouns *his*, *he*, and *him*. Sometimes the pronoun refers to the elder Mozart, sometimes it refers to Wolfgang, so the reader is likely to lose track of which person is being referred to. (B) is best because none of the pronouns is ambiguous. (C) and (D) still leave some pronoun usage unclear. (E) is confusing because *Mozart* could refer to either of the men.

48. C

As written, this sentence is actually a fragment. (Remember, the *–ing* verb form can never be a predicate verb.) Changing *determining* to *was determined* corrects the problem. (B) and (E) introduce verb tenses that are inappropriate in context. (D) does not correct the error.

49. B

Leopold was not a child when he was surprised by his son's tunes; his son was. (B) corrects the error without introducing any additional issues. In

(A), the phrase *as a child*, is modifying *tunes*. (C) and (E) introduce the passive voice unnecessarily. (D) is awkwardly worded.

50. C

The best choice here is (C), because the pronoun *he* in sentence 14 refers to *Mozart*, and the ideas make sense in sequence. (A) is incorrect because sentence 14 does not give the three reasons referred to in sentence 1. Placing it after sentence 2, as (B) suggests, does not make sense in context. (D) is wrong because sentences 12 and 13 deal with the same specific detail and should not be separated. (E) is incorrect because the pronoun reference would be unclear and the ideas in sentence 14 do not follow as logically from sentence 13 as they do from sentence 11.

CHAPTER SIX

Mathematics Ability

Introduction

Whether you realize it or not, you use math skills all the time in your daily life. Every time you calculate a tip, balance your check book, or even plan the timing of your commute to arrive to work on time, you are using some kind of mathematical skill. As often as you use math, you may still be hesitant to say that you enjoy it or feel that it's one of your strengths. This chapter can change that attitude. We begin with a step-by-step lesson in math, from the basic definition of numbers, all the way up to geometry and algebra. Don't worry if these last two topics make you panic. The lesson covers basic geometry and basic algebra at the same level you will find on a civil service exam. When you have worked through the lesson, you will then review a few of the possible question types you may face on test day. As always, we provide you with the best score-raising strategies so that no question is too difficult for you to answer. Practice Test 4, found at the end of this chapter, covers the skills and question types you will study. Score yourself using the answer key and be sure to review the detailed answer explanations that follow the test to get the most out of your practice.

Mathematics Lesson

Here you will find a review of the main topics in mathematics: arithmetic, algebra, geometry, and data interpretation. You should study each topic carefully because the questions will generally test a combination of skills rather than just one mathematical concept.

Arithmetic

The math skills tested on most civil service exams include basic computation, using integers, fractions, decimals, and percentages. To succeed on your test, you need to have a firm grasp of arithmetic concepts such as number properties, factors, divisibility, units of measure, ratio and proportion, percentages, and averages. These skills may be tested in basic operations questions or in word problems. Even if you feel that you know these concepts, spend time reviewing this section. The more you practice, the more comfortable you will feel working with numbers on your test.

First, take a look at a few definitions.

Number Type	Definition	Examples
Real Numbers	Any number that can name a position on a number line, regardless of whether that position is negative or positive.	-75% $.5$ $\frac{3}{4}$ $-5\ -4\ -3\ -2\ -1\ \ 0\ \ 1\ \ 2\ \ 3\ \ 4\ \ 5$
Rational Numbers	Any number that can be written as a ratio of two integers, including integers, terminating decimals, and repeating decimals.	$5 = \dfrac{5}{1}, \quad 2 = \dfrac{2}{1}, \quad 0 = \dfrac{0}{1}, \quad -6 = \dfrac{-6}{1}$ $2\dfrac{50}{100}, \text{ or } \dfrac{250}{100}$ $\dfrac{1}{3}$ (.33333)
Integers	Any of the positive counting numbers (which are also known as natural numbers), the negative numbers, and zero.	Positive integers: 1, 2, 3… Negative integers: $-1, -2, -3$… Neither negative nor positive: zero

Fractions	A fraction is a number that is written in the form $\frac{A}{B}$ where A is the numerator and B is the denominator. An improper fraction is a number that is greater than 1 (or less than –1) that is written in the form of a fraction. An improper fraction can be converted to a mixed number, which consists of an integer (positive or negative) and a fraction.	$\frac{-5}{6}, \ \frac{3}{17}, \ \frac{1}{2}, \ \frac{899}{901}$ $\frac{-65}{64}, \ \frac{9}{8}, \ \frac{57}{10}$ $-1\frac{1}{64}, \ 1\frac{1}{8}, \ 5\frac{7}{10}$
Positive/Negative	Numbers greater than zero are positive numbers; numbers less than zero are negative; zero is neither positive nor negative.	Positive: 1, 5, 900 Negative: –64, –40, –11, $\frac{-6}{13}$
Even/Odd	An even number is an integer that is a multiple of 2. **Note:** Zero is an even number. An odd number is an integer that is not a multiple of 2.	Even numbers: –6, –2, zero, 4, 12, 190 Odd numbers: –15, –1, 3, 9, 453
Prime Numbers	An integer greater than 1 that has no factors other than 1 and itself; 2 is the only even prime number.	2, 3, 5, 7, 11, 13, 59, 83
Consecutive Numbers	Numbers that follow one after another, in order, without any skipping.	Consecutive integers: 3, 4, 5, 6 Consecutive even integers: 2, 4, 6, 8, 10 Consecutive multiples of 9: 9, 18, 27, 36
Factors	A positive integer that divides evenly into a given number with no remainder.	The complete list of factors of 12: 1, 2, 3, 4, 6, 12
Multiples	A number that a given number will divide into with no remainder.	Some multiples of 12: zero, 12, 24, 60

Odds and Evens

Even ± Even = Even $2 + 2 = 4$
Even ± Odd = Odd $2 + 3 = 5$
Odd ± Odd = Even $3 + 3 = 6$
Even × Even = Even $2 \times 2 = 4$
Even × Odd = Even $2 \times 3 = 6$
Odd × Odd = Odd $3 \times 3 = 9$

Positives and Negatives

There are few things to remember about positives and negatives.

Adding a negative number is basically subtraction.

$6 + (-4)$ is really $6 - 4$ or 2.
$4 + (-6)$ is really $4 - 6$ or –2.

Subtracting a negative number is basically addition.

6 – (–4) is really 6 + 4 or 10.
–6 – (–4) is really –6 + 4 or –2.

Multiplying and dividing positives and negatives is like all other multiplication and division, with one catch. To figure out whether your product is positive or negative, simply count the number of negatives you had to start. If you had an odd number of negatives, the product is negative. If you had an even number of negatives, the product is positive.

6 × (–4) = –24 (1 negative → negative product)
(–6) × (–4) = 24 (2 negatives → positive product)
(–1) × (–6) × (–4) = –24 (3 negatives → negative product)

Similarly,

–24 ÷ 3 = –8 (1 negative → negative quotient)
–24 ÷ (–3) = 8 (2 negatives → positive quotient)

Absolute Value

Absolute value describes how far a number on the number line is from zero. It doesn't matter in which direction the number lies—to the right on the positive side, or to the left on the negative side.

For example, the absolute value of both 3 and –3 is 3.

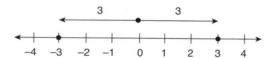

To find the absolute value of a number, simply strip the number within the vertical lines of its sign.

|4| = 4
|–4| = 4

When absolute value expressions contain different arithmetic operations, perform the operation first, and then strip the sign from the result.

|–6 + 4| = |–2| = 2
|(–6) × 4| = |–24| = 24

Factors and Multiples

To find the prime factorization of a number, keep breaking it down until you are left with only prime numbers.

To find the prime factorization of 168:

$$168 = 4 \times 42$$
$$= 4 \times 6 \times 7$$
$$= 2 \times 2 \times 2 \times 3 \times 7$$

To find the greatest common factor (GCF) of two integers, break down both integers into their prime factorizations and multiply all prime factors they have in common. The greatest common factor is the largest factor that goes into each integer.

For example, if you're looking for the greatest common factor of 40 and 140, first identify the prime factors of each integer.

$$40 = 4 \times 10$$
$$= 2 \times 2 \times 2 \times 5$$
$$140 = 10 \times 14$$
$$= 2 \times 5 \times 2 \times 7$$
$$= 2 \times 2 \times 5 \times 7$$

Next, see what prime factors the two numbers have in common and then multiply these common factors.

Both integers share two 2s and one 5, so the GCF is $2 \times 2 \times 5$ or 20.

If you need to find a common multiple of two integers, you can always multiply them. However, you can use prime factors to find the least common multiple (LCM). To do this, multiply all of the prime factors of each integer as many times as they appear. Don't worry if this sounds confusing, it becomes pretty clear once it's demonstrated. Take a look at the example to see how it works.

To find a common multiple of 20 and 16:

$$20 \times 16 = 320$$

320 is a common multiple of 20 and 16, but it is not the least common multiple.

To find the least common multiple of 20 and 16 first find the prime factors of each integer:

$$20 = 2 \times 2 \times 5$$
$$16 = 2 \times 2 \times 2 \times 2$$

Now, multiply each prime integer the greatest number of times it appears in each integer:

$$2 \times 2 \times 2 \times 2 \times 5 = 80$$

The Order of Operations

You need to remember the order in which arithmetic operations must be performed. PEMDAS (or Please Excuse My Dear Aunt Sally) may help you remember the order.

Please = Parentheses
Excuse = Exponents
My Dear = Multiplication and Division (from left to right)
Aunt Sally = Addition and Subtraction (from left to right)

$3^3 - 8(3 - 1) + 12 \div 4$
$= 3^3 - 8(2) + 12 \div 4$
$= 27 - 8(2) + 12 \div 4$
$= 27 - 16 + 3$
$= 11 + 3$
$= 14$

Divisibility Rules

If you've forgotten—or never learned—divisibility rules, spend a little time with this chart. Even if you remember the rules, take a moment to refresh your memory. There are no easy divisibility rules for 7 and 8.

Divisible by	The Rule	Example: 558
2	The last digit is even.	A multiple of 2 because 8 is even.
3	The sum of the digits is a multiple of 3.	A multiple of 3 because $5 + 5 + 8 = 18$, which is a multiple of 3.
4	The last 2 digits comprise a 2-digit multiple of 4.	NOT a multiple of 4 because 58 is not a multiple of 4.
5	The last digit is 5 or zero.	NOT a multiple of 5 because it doesn't end in 5 or zero.
6	The last digit is even AND the sum of the digits is a multiple of 3.	A multiple of 6 because it's a multiple of both 2 and 3.
9	The sum of the digits is a multiple of 9.	A multiple of 9 because $5 + 5 + 8 = 18$, which is a multiple of 9.
10	The last digit is zero.	NOT a multiple of 10 because it doesn't end in zero.

Properties of Numbers

Here are some essential laws or properties of numbers.

Commutative Property for Addition.   When adding two or more terms, the sum is the same regardless of which number is added to which.

$$3 + 2 = 2 + 3$$
$$a + b = b + a$$

Associative Property for Addition.   When adding three terms, the sum is the same, regardless of which two terms are added first.

$$2 + (5 + 3) = (2 + 5) + 3$$
$$a + (b + c) = (a + b) + c$$

Commutative Property for Multiplication.   When multiplying two or more terms, the result is the same regardless of which number is multiplied by which.

$$2 \times 4 = 4 \times 2$$
$$ab = ba$$

Associative Property for Multiplication.   When multiplying three terms, the product is the same regardless of which two terms are multiplied first.

$$2 \times (4 \times 3) = (2 \times 4) \times 3$$
$$a \times (b \times c) = (a \times b) \times c$$

Distributive Property of Multiplication Over Addition.   When multiplying groups, the product of the first number, and the sum of the second and third number, is equal to the sum of the product of the first and second number, as well as the product of the first and third number.

$$a(b + c) = ab + ac$$
$$3 \times (7 + 18) = 3 \times 7 + 3 \times 18$$

Fractions and Decimals

Generally, it's a good idea to reduce fractions when solving math questions. To do this, simply cancel all factors that the numerator and denominator have in common.

$$\frac{28}{36} = \frac{4 \times 7}{4 \times 9} = \frac{7}{9}$$

To add fractions, get a common denominator and then add the numerators.

$$\frac{1}{4} + \frac{1}{3} = \frac{3}{12} + \frac{4}{12} = \frac{3+4}{12} = \frac{7}{12}$$

To subtract fractions, get a common denominator and then subtract the numerators.

$$\frac{1}{4} - \frac{1}{3} = \frac{3}{12} - \frac{4}{12} = \frac{3-4}{12} = \frac{-1}{12}$$

To multiply fractions, multiply the numerators and multiply the denominators.

$$\frac{1}{4} \times \frac{1}{3} = \frac{1 \times 1}{4 \times 3} = \frac{1}{12}$$

To divide fractions, invert the second fraction and multiply. In other words, multiply the first fraction by the reciprocal of the second fraction.

$$\frac{1}{4} \div \frac{1}{3} = \frac{1}{4} \times \frac{3}{1} = \frac{1 \times 3}{4 \times 1} = \frac{3}{4}$$

Comparing Fractions

To compare fractions, multiply the numerator of the first fraction by the denominator of the second fraction to get a product. Then, multiply the numerator of the second fraction by the denominator of the first fraction to get a second product. If the first product is greater, the first fraction is greater. If the second product is greater, the second fraction is greater.

Here's an example:

Compare $\frac{2}{5}$ and $\frac{5}{8}$

1. Multiply the numerator of the first fraction by the denominator of the second.

   $2 \times 8 = 16$

2. Multiply the numerator of the second fraction by the denominator of the first.

   $5 \times 5 = 25$

3. The second product is greater, therefore, $\frac{5}{8}$ (the second fraction), is greater than $\frac{2}{5}$.

To convert a fraction to a decimal, divide the numerator by the denominator. To convert $\frac{8}{25}$ to a decimal, divide 8 by 25.

$$\frac{8}{25} = 0.32$$

To convert a decimal to a fraction, first set the decimal over 1. Then, move the decimal point over as many places as it takes until it is immediately to the right of the digit farthest to the right. Count the number of places that you moved the decimal. Then, add that many zeros to the 1 in the denominator.

$$0.3 = \frac{0.3}{1} = \frac{3.0}{10} \text{ or } \frac{3}{10}$$

$$0.32 = \frac{0.32}{1} = \frac{32.0}{100} \text{ or } \frac{8}{25}$$

Common Percent Equivalencies

Being familiar with the relationships among percents, decimals, and fractions can save you time on test day. Don't worry about memorizing the following chart. Simply use it to review relationships you already know (e.g., $50\% = 0.50 = \frac{1}{2}$) and to familiarize yourself with some that you might not already know. To convert a fraction or decimal to a percent, multiply by 100. To convert a percent to a fraction or decimal, divide by 100.

Fraction	Decimal	Percent
$\frac{1}{20}$	0.05	5%
$\frac{1}{10}$	0.10	10%
$\frac{1}{8}$	0.125	12.5%
$\frac{1}{6}$	$0.16\overline{6}$	$16\frac{2}{3}\%$
$\frac{1}{5}$	0.20	20%
$\frac{1}{4}$	0.25	25%

$\dfrac{1}{3}$	$0.33\overline{3}$	$33\dfrac{1}{3}\%$
$\dfrac{3}{8}$	0.375	37.5%
$\dfrac{2}{5}$	0.40	40%
$\dfrac{1}{2}$	0.50	50%
$\dfrac{3}{5}$	0.60	60%
$\dfrac{2}{3}$	$0.66\overline{6}$	$66\dfrac{2}{3}\%$
$\dfrac{3}{4}$	0.75	75%
$\dfrac{4}{5}$	0.80	80%
$\dfrac{5}{6}$	$0.83\overline{3}$	$83\dfrac{1}{3}\%$
$\dfrac{7}{8}$	0.875	87.5%

Rounding

You might be asked to estimate or round a number on the test. Rounding might also help you determine an answer choice. There are a few simple rules to rounding. Look at the digit to the right of the number in question. If it is a 4 or less, leave the number in question as it is and replace all the digits to the right with zeros.

For example, round off 765,432 to the nearest 100. The 4 is the hundreds digit, but you have to look at the digit to the right of the hundreds digit, which is the tens digit, or 3. Because the tens digit is 3, the hundreds digit remains the same and the tens and ones digits both become zero. Therefore, 765,432 rounded to the nearest 100 is 765,400.

If the digit to the right of the number in question is 5 or greater, increase the number by 1 and replace all the digits to the right with zeros.

For example, 837 rounded to the nearest 10 is 840. If 2,754 is rounded to the nearest 100, it is 2,800.

Place Units

Rounding requires that you know the place unit value of the digits in a number.

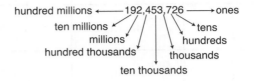

Symbols of Inequality

An inequality is a mathematical sentence in which two expressions are joined by symbols such as $\neq$ (not equal to), $>$ (greater than), $<$ (less than), $\geq$ (greater than or equal to), $\leq$ (less than or equal to). Examples of inequalities are:

$5 + 3 \neq 7$	5 plus 3 is not equal to 7
$6 > 2$	6 is greater than 2
$8 < 8.5$	8 is less than 8 and a half
$x \leq 9 + 6$	x is less than or equal to 9 plus 6
$c \geq 10$	c is greater than or equal to 10. (c is an algebraic variable. That means, it varies, and could be any number greater than or equal to 10.)

Exponents and Roots

An exponent indicates the number of times that a number (or variable) is to be used as a factor. On your civil service exam you will usually deal with numbers or variables that are squares (a variable multiplied by itself) and cubes (a variable multiplied by itself 3 times).

You should remember the squares of 1 through 10.

Square = A number raised to the exponent 2 (also known as the second power)		Cube = A number raised to the exponent 3 (also known as the third power)	
2^2	$2 \times 2 = 4$	2^3	$2 \times 2 \times 2 = 8$
3^2	$3 \times 3 = 9$	3^3	$3 \times 3 \times 3 = 27$
4^2	$4 \times 4 = 16$	4^3	$4 \times 4 \times 4 = 64$
5^2	$5 \times 5 = 25$	5^3	$5 \times 5 \times 5 = 125$
6^2	$6 \times 6 = 36$		
7^2	$7 \times 7 = 49$		
8^2	$8 \times 8 = 64$		
9^2	$9 \times 9 = 81$		
10^2	$10 \times 10 = 100$		

To add or subtract terms consisting of a coefficient (the number in front of the variable) multiplied by a power (a power is a base raised to an exponent), both the base and the exponent must be the same. As long as the bases and the exponents are the same, you can add the coefficients.

$x^2 + x^2 = 2x^2$ can be added. The base (x) and the exponent (2) are the same.
$3x^4 - 2x^4 = x^4$ can be subtracted. The base (x) and the exponent (4) are the same.
$x^2 + x^3$ cannot be combined. The exponents are different (2) and (3).
$x^2 + y^2$ cannot be combined. The bases are different (x) and (y).

To multiply terms consisting of coefficients multiplied by powers having the same base, multiply the coefficients and add the exponents.

$2x^5 \times (8x^7) = (2 \times 8)(x^{5+7}) = 16x^{12}$

To divide terms consisting of coefficients multiplied by powers having the same base, divide the coefficients and subtract the exponents.

$6x^7 \div 2x^5 = (6 \div 2)(x^{7-5}) = 3x^2$

To raise a power to an exponent, multiply the exponents.

$(x^2)^4 = x^{2 \times 4} = x^8$

A square root of a nonnegative number is a number that, when multiplied by itself, produces the given quantity. The radical sign $\sqrt{}$ is used to represent the positive square root of a number, so $\sqrt{25} = 5$, because $5 \times 5 = 25$.

To add or subtract radicals, make sure the numbers under the radical sign are the same. If they are, you can add or subtract the coefficients outside the radical signs.

$$2\sqrt{2} + 3\sqrt{2} = 5\sqrt{2}$$

$\sqrt{2} + \sqrt{3}$ cannot be combined.

To simplify radicals, factor out the perfect squares under the radical, take the square root of the perfect square, and put the result in front of the radical sign.

$$\sqrt{32} = \sqrt{16 \times 2} = 4\sqrt{2}$$

To multiply or divide radicals, multiply (or divide) the coefficients outside the radical. Multiply (or divide) the numbers inside the radicals.

$$\sqrt{x} \times \sqrt{y} = \sqrt{xy}$$

$$3\sqrt{2} \times 4\sqrt{5} = 12\sqrt{10}$$

$$\frac{\sqrt{x}}{\sqrt{y}} = \sqrt{\frac{x}{y}}$$

$$12\sqrt{10} \div 3\sqrt{2} = 4\sqrt{5}$$

To take the square root of a fraction, break the fraction into two separate roots and take the square root of the numerator and the denominator.

$$\sqrt{\frac{16}{25}} = \frac{\sqrt{16}}{\sqrt{25}} = \sqrt{\frac{4}{5}}$$

The Power of 10

When a power of 10 (that is, the base is 10) has an exponent that is a positive integer, the exponent tells you how many zeros to add after the 1. For example, 10 to the 12th power (10^{12}) has 12 zeros.

When the exponent of a power of 10 is positive, the exponent indicates how many zeros the number would contain if it were written out. For example, $10^4 =$ 10,000 (4 zeros) because the product of 4 factors of 10 is equal to 10,000.

When multiplying a number by a power of 10, move the decimal point to the right the same number of places as the number of zeros in that power of 10.

$0.0123 \times 10^4 = 123$

When dividing by a power of 10 with a positive exponent, move the decimal point to the left.

$43.21 \div 10^3 = 0.04321$

Multiplying by a power with a negative exponent is the same as dividing by a power with a positive exponent. Therefore, when you multiply by a number with a positive exponent, move the decimal to the right. When you multiply by a number with a negative exponent, move the decimal to the left.

For example:

$10^3 = 1.000 = 1,000$

Percents

Remember these formulas: $\text{Part} = \text{Percent} \times \text{Whole}$ or $\text{Percent} = \dfrac{\text{Part}}{\text{Whole}}$

From Fraction to Percent.   To find part, percent, or whole, plug the values you have into the equation and solve.

$44\% \text{ of } 25 = 0.44 \times 25 = 11$

42 is what percent of 70?

$42 \div 70 = 0.6$
$0.6 \times 100\% = 60\%$

To increase or decrease a number by a given percent, take that percent of the original number and add it to or subtract it from the original number.

To increase 25 by 60%, first find 60% of 25.

$25 \times 0.6 = 15$

Then, add the result to the original number.

$25 + 15 = 40$

To decrease 25 by the same percent, subtract the 15.

$25 - 15 = 10$

Average, Median, and Mode

$$\text{Average} = \frac{\text{Sum of the Terms}}{\text{Number of the Terms}}$$

The formula to calculate the average of 15, 18, 15, 32, and 20 is:

$$\frac{15 + 18 + 15 + 32 + 20}{5} = \frac{100}{5} = 20.$$

When there are an odd number of terms, the median of a group of terms is the value of the middle term, with the terms arranged in increasing order.

Suppose that you want to find the median of the terms 15, 18, 15, 32, and 20. First, put the terms in order from small to large: 15, 15, 18, 20, 32. Then, identify the middle term. The middle term is 18.

When there is an even number of terms, the median is the average of the two middle terms with the terms arranged in increasing order.

Suppose that you want to find the mode of the terms 15, 18, 15, 32, and 20. The mode is the value of the term that occurs most; 15 occurs twice, so it is the mode.

Ratios, Proportions, and Rates

Ratios can be expressed in different forms.

One form is $\frac{a}{b}$.

If you have 15 dogs and 5 cats, the ratio of dogs to cats is $\frac{15}{5}$. (The ratio of cats to dogs is $\frac{5}{15}$.) Like any other fraction, this ratio can be reduced; $\frac{15}{5}$ can be reduced to $\frac{3}{1}$. In other words, for every three dogs, there's one cat.

Another form of expressing ratios is *a:b*.

The ratio of dogs to cats is 15:5 or 3:1. The ratio of cats to dogs is 5:15 or 1:3.

Pay attention to what ratio is specified in the problem. Remember that the ratio of dogs to cats is different from the ratio of cats to dogs.

To solve a proportion, cross-multiply and solve for the variable.

$$\frac{x}{6} = \frac{2}{3}$$
$$3x = 12$$
$$x = 4$$

A rate is a ratio that compares quantities measured in different units. The most common example is miles per hour. Use the following formula for such problems:

Distance = Rate × Time or $D = R \times T$

Remember, although not all rates are speeds, this formula can be adapted to any rate.

Units of Measurement

You should remember these basic units of measurement. Spend some time reviewing the list that follows.

Distance.
  1 foot = 12 inches
  1 yard = 3 feet = 36 inches

  Metric: 1 kilometer = 1,000 meters
      1 meter = 10 decimeters = 100 centimeters = 1,000 millimeters
      (Remember the root *deci* is 10; the root *centi* is 100, the root *milli* is 1,000)

Weight.
  1 pound = 16 ounces

  Metric: A gram is a unit of mass. A kilogram is 1,000 grams.

Volume.
  1 cup = 8 ounces
  2 cups = 1 pint
  1 quart = 2 pints
  4 cups = 1 quart
  1 gallon = 4 quarts

  Metric: A liter is a unit of volume. A kiloliter is 1,000 liters.

You must be careful when approaching a problem that includes units of measurement. Be sure that the units are given in the same format. You may have to convert pounds to ounces or feet to yards (or vice versa) to arrive at the correct answer choice.

Algebra

Algebra has been called math with letters. Just like arithmetic, the basic operations of algebra are addition, subtraction, multiplication, division, and roots. Instead of numbers though, algebra uses letters to represent unknown or variable numbers. Why would you work with a variable? Let's look at an example.

You buy 2 bananas from the supermarket for 50 cents total. How much does one banana cost?

That's a simple equation, but how would you write it down on paper if you were trying to explain it to a friend?

Perhaps you would write: $2 \times ? = 50$ cents.

Algebra gives you a systematic way to record the question mark.

$2 \times b = 50$ cents or $2b = 50$ cents, where $b =$ the cost of 1 banana in cents.

Algebra is a type of mathematical shorthand. The most commonly used letters in algebra are a, b, c and x, y, z.

The number 2 in the term $2b$ is called a *coefficient*. It is a constant that does not change.

To find out how much you paid for each banana, you could use your equation to solve for the unknown cost.

$$2b = 50$$

$$\frac{2b}{2} = \frac{50}{2}$$

$$b = 25$$

Algebraic Expressions

An expression is a collection of quantities made up of constants and variables linked by operations such as $+$ and $-$.

Let's go back to our fruit example. Let's say you have 2 bananas and you give one to your friend. You could express this in algebraic terms as:

$2b - b$

$2b - b$ is an example of an algebraic expression, where $b = 1$ banana.

In fact, this example is a **binomial** expression. A binomial is an expression that is the sum of two terms. A term is the product of a constant and one or more variables. A **monomial** expression has only one term; a **trinomial** expression is the sum of three terms; a **polynomial** expression is the sum of two or more terms.

$2b$ = monomial
$2b - b$ = binomial
$2(b + x)$ = binomial
$2 + b^2 + y$ = trinomial or polynomial

On the test an algebraic expression is likely to look something like this:

$(11 + 3x) - (5 - 2x) = ?$

In addition to algebra, this problem tests your knowledge of positives and negatives, and the order of operations (PEMDAS).

The main thing you need to remember about **expressions** is that you can only combine like terms.

Let's talk about fruit once more. Let's say in addition to the 2 bananas you purchased you also bought 3 apples and 1 pear. You spent $4.00 total. If b is the cost of a banana, a is the cost of an apple, and p is the cost of a pear, the purchase can be expressed as $2b + 3a + p = 4.00$.

However, let's say that once again you forgot how much each banana cost. You could NOT divide $4.00 by 6 to get the cost of each item. They're different items.

While you cannot solve expressions with unlike terms, you *can* simplify them. For example, to combine monomials or polynomials, simply add or subtract the coefficients of terms that have the exact same variable. When completing the addition or subtraction, do not change the variables.

$6a + 5a = 11a$
$8b - 2b = 6b$
$3a + 2b - 8a = 3a - 8a + 2b = -5a + 2b$ or $2b - 5a$

Coefficient = The number that comes before the variable. In $6x$, 6 is the coefficient.
Variable = The variable is the letter that stands for an unknown. In $6x$, x is the variable.
Term = The product of a constant and one or more variables.
Monomial = One term: $6x$ is a monomial.
Polynomial = Two or more terms: $6x - y$ is a polynomial.
Trinomial = Three terms: $6x - y + z$ is a trinomial.

To review:

$6a + 5a^2$ cannot be combined. Why not? The variables are not exactly alike; that is, they are not raised to the same exponent. (One is a, the other is a^2.)

$3a + 2b$ cannot be combined. Why not? The variables are not the same. (One is a, the other is b.)

Multiplying and dividing monomials is a little different. Unlike addition and subtraction, you can multiply and divide terms that are different. When you multiply monomials, multiply the coefficients of each term. (In other words, multiply the numbers that come before the variables.) Add the exponents of like variables. Multiply different variables together.

$$(6a)(4b) = (6 \times 4)(a \times b)$$
$$= 24ab$$
$$(6a)(4ab) = (6 \times 4)(a \times a \times b)$$
$$= (6 \times 4)(a^{1+1} \times b)$$
$$= 24a^2b$$

Use the FOIL method to multiply and divide binomials. FOIL stands for First Outer Inner Last.

$$(y + 1)(y + 2) = (y \times y) + (y \times 2) + (1 \times y) + (1 \times 2)$$
$$= y^2 + 2y + y + 2$$
$$= y^2 + 3y + 2$$

Equations

The key to solving equations is to do the same thing to both sides of the equation until you have your variable isolated on one side of the equation and all of the numbers on the other side.

$$8a + 4 = 24 - 2a$$

First, subtract 4 from each side so that the left side of the equation has only variables.

$$8a + 4 - 4 = 24 - 2a - 4$$
$$8a = 20 - 2a$$

Then, add 2a to each side so that the right side of the equation has only numbers.

$$8a + 2a = 20 - 2a + 2a$$
$$10a = 20$$

Finally, divide both sides by 10 to isolate the variable.

$$\frac{10a}{10} = \frac{20}{10}$$

$$a = 2$$

Treat Both Sides Equally.   Always perform the same operation to both sides to solve for a variable in an equation.

Sometimes you're given an equation with two variables and asked to solve for one variable in terms of the other. This means that you must isolate the variable for which you are solving on one side of the equation and put everything else on the other side. In other words, when you're done, you'll have x (or whatever the variable you're looking for is) on one side of the equation and an expression on the other side.

Solve $7x + 2y = 3x + 10y - 16$ for x in terms of y.

Because you want to isolate x on one side of the equation, begin by subtracting $2y$ from both sides.

$$7x + 2y - 2y = 3x + 10y - 16 - 2y$$
$$7x = 3x + 8y - 16$$

Then, subtract $3x$ from both sides to get all the xs on one side of the equation.

$$7x - 3x = 3x + 8y - 16 - 3x$$
$$4x = 8y - 16$$

Finally, divide both sides by 4 to isolate x.

$$\frac{4x}{4} = \frac{8y - 16}{4}$$

$$x = 2y - 4$$

Substitution

If a problem gives you the value for a variable, just plug the value into the equation and solve. Make sure that you follow the rules of PEMDAS and are careful with your calculations.

If $x = 15$ and $y = 10$, what is the value of $4x(x - y)$?

Plug 15 in for x and 10 in for y.

$$4(15)(15 - 10) = ?$$

Then, find the value.

$$(60)(5) = 300$$

Inequalities

Solve **inequalities** like you would any other equation. Isolate the variable for which you are solving on one side of the equation and everything else on the other side of the equation.

$$4a + 6 > 2a + 10$$
$$4a - 2a > 10 - 6$$
$$2a > 4$$
$$a > 2$$

The only difference here is that instead of finding a specific value for *a*, you get a range of values for *a*. That is, *a* can be any number greater than 2. The rest of the math is the same.

There is, however, one *crucial* difference between solving equations and inequalities. **When you multiply or divide an inequality by a negative number, you must change the direction of the sign.**

$$-5a > 10$$

$$\frac{-5a}{-5} > \frac{10}{-5}$$

$$a < -2$$

If this seems confusing, think about the logic. You're told that −5 times something is greater than 10. This is where your knowledge of positives and negatives comes into play. You know that negative × positive = negative and negative × negative = positive. Because −5 is negative and 10 is positive, −5 has to be multiplied by something negative to get a positive product. Therefore, *a* has to be less than −2, not greater than it. If $a > -2$, then any value for *a* that is greater than −2 should make −5*a* greater than 10. Say *a* is 20; −5*a* would be −100, which is certainly NOT greater than 10.

Algebra Word Problems

Understanding algebra word problems is probably one of the most useful math skills you can have. The great thing about word problems is that they're not only important on test day, they're also useful in everyday life. Whether you're figuring out how much a piece of clothing will cost you with sales tax, or calculating your earnings, algebraic word problems help you figure out unknown amounts.

Word Problems with Formulas

Some of the more challenging word problems may involve translations with mathematical formulas. For example, you might see questions dealing with averages, rates, or areas of geometric figures. (More about geometry later.) For example:

If a truck driver travels at an average speed of 50 miles per hour for 6.5 hours, how far will the driver travel?

To answer this question, you need the distance formula:

Distance = Rate × Time or $D = R \times T$

Once you know the formula, you can plug in the numbers:

$D = 50 \times 6.5$
$D = 325$ miles

Here's another example:

Thomas took an exam with 60 questions on it. If he finished all the questions in two hours, how many minutes on average did he spend answering each question?

To answer this question, you need the average formula:

$$\text{Average} = \frac{\text{Sum of Terms}}{\text{Number of Terms}}$$

Then plug in the numbers:

$$x = \frac{(2 \text{ hours} \times 60 \text{ minutes})}{60 \text{ questions}} = \frac{120}{60} = 2 \text{ minutes per question}$$

You may have noticed there's a trick in this question as well. Do you see it? The time it took for Thomas to finish the exam is given in *hours*, but the question is asking how many *minutes* each question took. Be sure to read each the question carefully so you don't fall for tricks like this.

Working With a Question

Sometimes you do not need to use a formula to solve a word problem. You need to know how to work with the question. Remember to translate the words into math.

When you see:	Think:
Sum, plus, more than, added to, combined total	$+$
Minus, less than, difference between, decreased by	$-$
Is, was, equals, is equivalent to, is the same as, adds up to	$=$
Times, product, multiplied by, of, twice, double, triple	$\times$
Divided by, over, quotient, per, out of, into	$\div$
What, how much, how many, a number	$x, n, a, b,$ etc.

Geometry

You are likely to see some basic geometry on your civil service exam. These questions test your knowledge of lines and angles, triangles, and circles. You might also see some coordinate geometry questions or word problems that don't include diagrams. If you are concerned about your geometry skills, take some time to review this section, spending more time with the subjects that are less familiar to you.

Lines and Angles

There are 180° in a straight line.

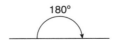

Line Segments

Some of the most basic geometry problems deal with line segments. A **line segment** is a piece of a line, and it has an exact measurable length. A question might give you a segment divided into several pieces, provide the measurements of some of these pieces, and ask you for the measurement of the remaining piece.

      If $PR = 12$ and $QR = 4$, $PQ =$

$PQ = PR - QR$

$PQ = 12 - 4$

$PQ = 8$

The point exactly in the middle of a line segment, halfway between the endpoints, is called the midpoint of the line segment. To bisect means to cut in half, so the **midpoint** of a line segment bisects that line segment.

M is the midpoint of AB, so $AM = MB$.

Angles

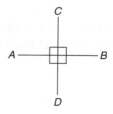

A **right angle** measures 90° and is usually indicated in a diagram by a little box. The figure above is a right angle. Lines that intersect to form right angles are said to be **perpendicular**.

In the figure above, line AB and line CD are perpendicular.

Angles that form a straight line add up to 180°. In the previous figure, $a + b = 180$.

The angle marked b is less than 90°; it is an **acute angle**. The angle marked a is greater than 90°. Angles greater than 90° are called **obtuse**.

Right angle = 90°
Acute angle < 90°
Obtuse angle > 90°

When two lines intersect, adjacent angles are **supplementary**, meaning they add up to 180°. In the figure above $a + b = 180$.

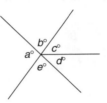

Angles around a point add up to 360°. In the figure above $a + b + c + d + e = 360$.

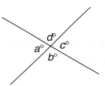

When lines intersect, angles across the vertex (the middle point) from each other are called vertical angles and are equal to each other. Above, $a = c$ and $b = d$.

Parallel Lines

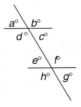

When parallel lines are crossed by a transversal:

- Corresponding angles are equal (for example $a = e$, $d = h$)
- Alternate interior angles are equal ($d = f$)
- Same side interior angles are supplementary ($c + f = 180$)
- All four acute angles are equal, as are all four obtuse angles (a, c, e, g are equal, b, d, f, h are equal)

Triangles

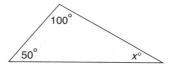

The three interior angles of any triangle add up to 180°. In the figure above $x + 50 + 100 = 180$, so $x = 30$. By finding the sum of the two angles, x can be calculated. The sum of $100 + 50 = 150$, so $x = 180 - 150$.

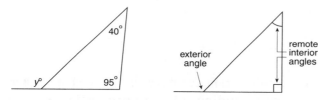

An exterior angle of a triangle is equal to the sum of the remote interior angles. In the figure above, the exterior angle labeled $y°$ is equal to the sum of the remote interior angles so $y = 40 + 95 = 135$.

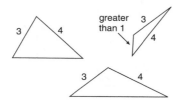

The length of one side of a triangle must be **greater than the positive difference** and **less than the sum** of the lengths of the other two sides. For example, if it is given that the length of one side is 3 and the length of another side is 4, then the length of the third side must be greater than $4 - 3 = 1$ and less than $4 + 3 = 7$.

Triangles—Area and Perimeter.

The **perimeter** of a triangle is the sum of the lengths of its sides. The perimeter of the triangle in the figure above is 3 + 4 + 6 = 13.

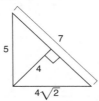

Area of triangle = $\dfrac{1}{2}$ (base)(height) or $A = \dfrac{1}{2}bh$.

The height is the perpendicular distance between the side that is chosen as the base and the opposite vertex. In this triangle, 4 is the height when 7 is chosen as the base.

Area = $\dfrac{1}{2}bh = \dfrac{1}{2}(7)4 = 14$

Similar Triangles.   Similar triangles have the same shape: **corresponding angles are equal** and **corresponding sides are proportional**. The triangles below are similar because they have the same angles. The 3 corresponds (or relates to) the 4 and the 6 corresponds to the unknown *s*. Because the triangles are similar, therefore, you can set up a proportion to solve for *s*.

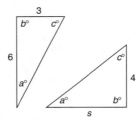

$$\frac{3}{4} = \frac{6}{s}$$
$$3s = 24$$
$$s = 8$$

Special Triangles

Isosceles Triangles.   An isosceles triangle is a triangle that has **two equal sides**. Not only are two sides equal, but the angles opposite the equal sides, called base angles, are also equal to one another.

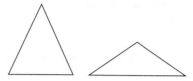

So, if you were asked to determine angle *a* in the isosceles triangle below, you could set up an equation. Because the sum of the degrees in a triangle is 180, and you are given one angle of 40°, then: $2a = 180 - 40$, $2a = 140$, $\dfrac{2a}{2} = \dfrac{140}{2}$, $a = 70°$.

Equilateral Triangles. Equilateral triangles are triangles in which all **three sides are equal**. Because the sides are equal, all the angles are also equal. If all three angles are equal, and the sum of the angles in a triangle is 180°, how many degrees is each angle in an equilateral triangle?

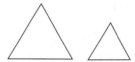

$$\frac{180}{3} = 60$$

The answer is 60°.

Right Triangles.   A right triangle is a triangle with a right angle. (Remember, a right angle equals 90°.) Every right triangle has exactly two acute angles. The sides opposite the acute angles are called the legs. The side opposite the right angle is called the hypotenuse. Because it is opposite the largest angle, the hypotenuse is the longest side of a right triangle.

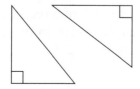

KAPLAN

The Pythagorean Theorem

The Pythagorean theorem states the following:

$\text{leg}1^2 + \text{leg}2^2 = (\text{hypotenuse})^2$

The theorem can also be written out as:

$a^2 + b^2 = c^2$

The following right angle has legs with lengths of 2 and 3:

If one leg is 2 and the other leg is 3, then:

$$2^2 + 3^2 = c^2$$
$$4 + 9 = c^2$$
$$13 = c^2$$
$$c = \sqrt{3}$$

Your knowledge of squares and square roots will really come in handy when using the Pythagorean therorem.

Quadrilaterals

A quadrilateral has 4 sides. The perimeter of a quadrilateral (or any polygon) is the sum of the lengths of its sides.

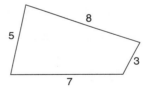

The perimeter of the quadrilateral in the figure above is: $5 + 8 + 3 + 7 = 23$.

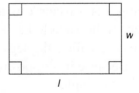

A **rectangle** is a parallelogram containing four right angles. Opposite sides are equal. The formula to find the area of a rectangle is: Area = (length)(width), which is sometimes abbreviated as $A = lw$. In the diagram above, l = length and w = width, so area = lw and perimeter = $2(l + w)$.

A **square** is a rectangle with four equal sides. The formula to calculate the area of a square is: Area = (side)^2. Notice this can also be written as $A = lw$. However, since $l = w$ in a square, you can use the notation s^2 (see notation below).

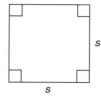

In the diagram above, s = length of a side, so area = s^2 and perimeter = $4s$.

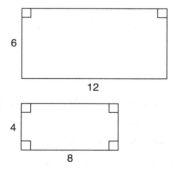

A parallelogram is a quadrilateral with two sets of parallel sides. Opposite sides are equal, as are opposite angles. The formula for the area of a parallelogram is:

Area = (base)(height) or $A = bh$

In the diagram above, h = height and b = base, so you can use the formula: $A = bh$.

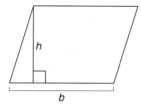

If two rectangles (or squares, because squares are special rectangles) are similar, then the corresponding angles are equal (90°) and corresponding sides are in proportion. In the figures above, the two rectangles are similar because all the angles are right angles, and each side of the larger rectangle is $1\frac{1}{2}$ times the corresponding side of the smaller rectangle.

Circles

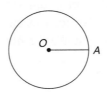

A **circle** is a figure in which each point is an equal distance from its center. In the diagram above, O is the center of the circle.

The **radius** (r) of a circle is the direct distance from its center to any point on the circle. All radii of one circle have equal lengths. In the figure above, OA is the radius of circle O.

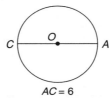

A **chord** is a line segment that connects any two points on a circle. Segments AB and AC are both chords. The largest chord that may be drawn in a circle is the diameter of that circle.

The **diameter** (d) of a circle is a chord that passes through the circle's center. All diameters are the same length and are equal to twice the radius. In the figure above, AC is a diameter of circle O.

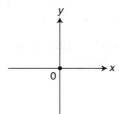

$AC = 6$

The **circumference** of a circle is the distance around it. It is equal to πd, or $2\pi r$. In this example Circumference $= \pi d = 6\pi$.

The **area** of a circle equals π times the square of the radius, or πr^2. In this example, since AC is the diameter, $r = \dfrac{6}{2} = 3$ and area $= \pi r^2 = \pi(3^2) = 9\pi$.

Coordinate Geometry

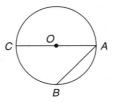

Coordinate geometry has to do with plotting points on a graph. The previous diagram represents the coordinate axes—the perpendicular number lines in the coordinate plane. The horizontal line is called the *x*-axis. The vertical line is called the *y*-axis. In a coordinate plane, the point *O* at which the two axes intersect is called the origin, or (0, 0).

The pair of numbers, written inside parentheses, specifies the location of a point in the coordinate plane. These are called coordinates. The first number is the *x*-coordinate, and the second number is the *y*-coordinate. The origin is the zero point of both axes, with coordinates (0, 0).

Starting at the origin:

- To the right: *x* is positive.
- To the left: *x* is negative.
- Up: *y* is positive.
- Down: *y* is negative.
- The two axes divide the coordinate plane into 4 quadrants. When you know what quadrant a point lies in, you know the signs of its coordinates. A point in the upper left quadrant, for example, has a negative *x*-coordinate and a positive *y*-coordinate.

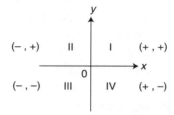

If you were asked the coordinates of a given point, you would start at the origin, count the number of units given to the right or left on the *x*-axis, and then do the same up or down on the *y*-axis.

If you had to plot given points you would start at the origin, count the number of units given on the *x*-axis, and then on the *y*-axis. To plot (2, −3) for example, you would count 2 units to the right along the *x*-axis, then three units down along the *y*-axis.

Data Interpretation

Data interpretation is another name for questions that include graphical information such as tables, charts, and graphs. On your civil service exam, you are likely to see some type of table, chart, or graph. You will have to gather information from these graphics and use them to solve accompanying questions. Keep in mind that no matter which type of graphic representation you see, labels or keys must be given to identify the material. By carefully reading the labels, you can understand what information is contained and in what manner it is organized. Remember, a table, chart, or graph is a visual way of organizing information.

Line Graphs

A line graph presents information by plotting points on an *xy* coordinate system, then connecting them with a line. Because you can plot more than one line, a line graph is widely used to communicate relationships. Also, because the lines clearly indicate rising or decreasing trends, a line graph is a great way to show growth or decline trends.

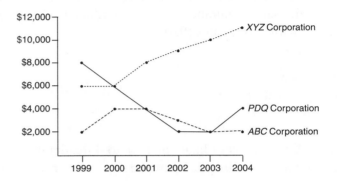

Notice that the previous graph is not titled. Charts, tables, and graphs on the test may not have titles. However, we can use the information found on the *x*- and *y*-axes to decode or make sense of the graph. The *x*-axis is labeled 1999–2004. Therefore, each marking represents one year from 1999 to 2004. The *y*-axis is marked in units of increasing dollar value. Each unit going up the *y*-axis increases $2,000. The lines themselves are labeled *ABC Corporation*, *PDQ Corporation*, and *XYZ Corporation*. Therefore, we can see the dollar amount of each company at a particular point in time during the period of 1999–2004. A line connects these points to show an upward, or downward trend.

Bar Graphs

A bar graph is also called a histogram or histograph. In it, numerical values are shown in bars of varying length. This type of graph is also a good, clear way to show comparisons.

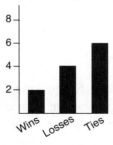

The bar graph below labels the various bars on the horizontal axis "wins," "losses," or "ties." The vertical axis shows units of 2. This bar graph represents the numerical value of a team's wins, losses, and ties. See how far each vertical bar extends on the vertical axis. The bar representing wins of Team 1 is at the 2 unit;

the team has 2 wins. The bar representing Team 1 losses is at 4 units; the team has 4 losses. The bars representing ties are at 6 units; both teams have 6 ties.

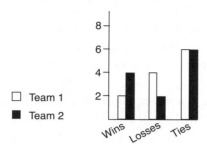

A bar graph has the added benefit of illustrating multiple comparisons in a way that is still visually clear. The previous bar graph includes a second set of bars. These bars, the shaded bars, represent the performance of another team. By placing the two sets of bars side by side, we can easily see that Team 2 won more games than Team 1, it lost fewer, and it tied the same number of games.

A bar graph can be vertical or horizontal. Decode it the same way you would a line graph, by reading the labels on the *x*- and *y*-axes, which tell what the bars represent and the value of the units given.

Tables

Tables compare information in rows and columns. Because information appears side by side, tables are a good way to present detailed information to compare.

	Mon	Tues	Wed	Thurs	Fri
New York	70°	72°	65°	71°	80°
Boston	65°	70°	60°	63°	72°
L.A.	81°	82°	85°	80°	80°
Miami	80°	85°	86°	81°	84°

Labels in the far left column and on the top row will identify the information in the table. The left column in the table above, for example, contains the names of cities. The top row is labeled with days of the week. Let's say you were looking for the temperature in New York on Thursday. You would find the row labeled New York and the column labeled Thursday. The box that aligns with these two axes gives you the temperature in New York on Thursday, 71°.

Tables may also use pictures rather than numbers. Either way, when you are looking for information in a table, find the row corresponding to the information you are looking for. Then, read across and find the vertical column that corresponds to the second detail you are looking for. The box at which these details meet will give you your data.

Pie Charts

A pie chart is a circle cut into parts. You can think of it as showing the pieces of a pie or how the pie is divided. Thus, a pie chart is a good chart to use when showing the distribution of a whole, or into which parts a whole is divided. On a pie chart, the portions or pieces of the pie will be labeled. The labels will explain what the different sections represent and the percentage of the whole each section comprises.

Note: The whole pie always equals 100%. That does not mean that the numbers shown in a pie chart will equal 100. However, you should think of a pie chart as 100% with each section representing a part (percentage) of the whole.

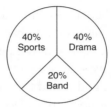

The pie chart above shows the various after-school activities of students in a class. The whole pie represents the whole class. As the labels indicate, 40% of the students participate in sports, 40% participate in the drama club, and 20% participate in the band.

While pie charts are a great way to show how a whole is divided, they can be difficult to use if the pie is divided into sections that are too small.

The following pie chart shows an example of when NOT to use a pie chart. It is meant to show the after-school activities of an entire class, but breaking the sections down into such small pieces makes the chart difficult to use.

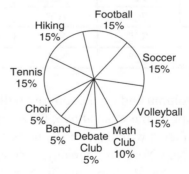

Pictographs

A pictograph uses simple drawings to depict quantities.

Each truck = 1,000 vehicles

Pictographs can make a point vividly, but they work best when a large number of items is being shown. The key at the bottom of the previous figure lets us know that each truck represents 1,000 vehicles. Always look at the key to know exactly what is being shown in any pictograph.

Now that you have completed these math lessons, you are ready to review some of the question types you will face on test day. Review these carefully as you will find similar questions on Practice Test 4 at the end of this chapter.

Sample Mathematics Questions

All of the math questions you will see will generally test some combination of three main math topics: arithmetic, algebra, and geometry. However, the way these questions are presented can vary widely. This section covers some of the most common types of math questions you will see on the civil service exam. These question types are:

- Calculations
- Word Problems
- Data Interpretation
- Quantitative Reasoning

Difficulty Level

Before we start reviewing the question types, let's talk about difficulty levels. Like every other section on a civil service exam, the difficulty level of math questions will vary depending on the exam you take and which type of job it is for. For example, clerical exams are likely to test very basic arithmetic, while an administrative exam might be slightly more challenging because the job requires more math skills. This chapter and its practice test include math questions at both levels so that you are prepared for whatever civil service exam you face.

Calculations

The word *calculations* may sound like something directly out of a math textbook. In terms of civil service exams, calculations are questions that simply provide you with a math problem and ask you to complete a calculation. In other words, there will be no context and no graphical information to interpret. Instead, you will see an equation and you will have to solve it using only your math skills.

Here is a sample calculation question:

$2^3(3 - 1)^2 + (-4)^2 =$

    (A) 48
    (B) 32
    (C) 136
    (D) −48

To answer this question, it is up to you to remember to use PEMDAS (the order of operations reviewed earlier in this chapter) and to apply it when finding the correct answer—which is (C).

Word Problems

Word problems are most like the kinds of math questions you do every day without realizing it. For example, if a bill totals $23.47 and you pay $25.00, how much change should you get back? Word problems on tests can be slightly more complex and usually give you more information than you even need to know to find the answer. Here is one example.

Rene's dress shop is suffering from slow business. Rene decides to mark down all her merchandise. The next day, she sells 33 winter coats. Now, only 30% of the winter coats she had in stock remains. How many winter coats were in stock before the sale?

  (A) 990
  (B) 99
  (C) 110
  (D) 1,110

This question is fairly straightforward and if you solve it correctly, the answer is (C), 110.

Another kind of word problem does not provide a lot of context. It is actually more like a math question written out in words. These questions look like the following example.

What is the least common multiple of 12 and 8?

  (A) 12
  (B) 24
  (C) 18
  (D) 96

This type of question almost seems to be testing math vocabulary because you have to have an understanding of least common multiples to find the correct answer—(B). Not all questions will test your knowledge of terms and concepts, other word problems may just be a math question written out in words. Here is a sample of this question type.

10. If 40% of x is 8, what is x% of 40?

  (A) 80
  (B) 30
  (C) 10
  (D) 8

The correct answer, (D), can be found by simplifying this question into mathematical terms (e.g., $0.4x = 8$; ? $= 40(x\%)$).

By reviewing the Tips for Math Success you will learn how to change word problems from everyday English into mathematical terms.

Data Interpretation

Data interpretation questions test your ability to read and understand graphical elements such as charts, graphs, or other diagrams. If you carefully reviewed the data interpretation section of the lesson, these questions should be straightforward. Here is one example.

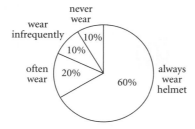

The previous diagram shows the safety habits of a group of 60 skateboarders. How many of the group always wear their helmets?

    (A) 60

    (B) 36

    (C) 12

    (D) 30

If you want to know how best to answer this question, refer to Kaplan's Target Strategy for Data Interpretation Questions found later in this chapter.

Quantitative Reasoning

Quantitative reasoning questions aren't entirely math questions. What makes this question type different is that you have to use reasoning skills along with math skills to find the correct answer. This may sound confusing, but here are two different types of quantitative reasoning questions to help clear things up.

Number Relationships.   The instructions for number relationship questions instruct you to find the relationship between the two numbers in an expression. You will usually see three expressions. Arrows point from a number on the left to a blank box, then to a number on the right. The final set in the column has a blank at the end. You have to decide what number should go in the blank.

3 → ☐ → 7	(A) 5
5 → ☐ → 9	(B) 6
1 → ☐ → __	(C) 10
	(D) 4

If you are still confused about number relationship questions, Kaplan's Tips for Math Success will show you exactly how to answer this question.

Visual Problems.   These problems ask you to look at a shaded shape and determine how much of the whole is shaded. Basically, they are asking you to express a fraction of a whole. The key to doing well on this question type is taking the time to actually count the shaded and unshaded sections that make up the whole.

Look at this example.

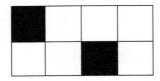

(A) $\dfrac{2}{6}$

(B) $\dfrac{1}{2}$

(C) $\dfrac{1}{4}$

(D) 2

Again, Tips for Math Success will detail the best strategy for answering this question type correctly.

Tips for Math Success

At the beginning of this book, we reviewed two proven score raising strategies for math questions: picking numbers and backsolving. If you need to review them again, here they are in greater detail. But the math strategies don't stop there. We provide you with strategies for other math question types so you can get a top score on your civil service exam.

Picking Numbers

Sometimes you get stuck on a math question because it's too general or abstract. A good solution to this problem is to substitute particular numbers for the equation variables.

This *picking numbers* strategy works especially well with questions dealing with even/odd numbers. Look at the following example.

If *a* is an odd integer and *b* is an even integer, which of the following must be odd?

   (A) $2a + b$
   (B) $a + 2b$
   (C) ab
   (D) a^2b
   (E) ab^2

Rather than trying to wrap your brain around abstract variables, simply pick numbers for a and b. When you are adding, subtracting, or multiplying even and odd numbers, you can generally assume that what happens with one pair of numbers generally happens with similar pairs of numbers. Let's say, for the time being, that $a = 3$ and $b = 2$. Plug those values into the answer choices, and there's a good chance that only one choice will be odd:

(A) $2a + b = 2(3) + 2 = 8$
(B) $a + 2b = 3 + 2(2) = 7$
(C) $ab = (3)(2) = 6$
(D) $a^2b = (3^2)(2) = 18$
(E) $ab^2 = (3)(2^2) = 12$

Choice (B) is the only odd answer for $a = 3$ and $b = 2$; thus, it is fair to assume that it must be the only odd answer choice, no matter what odd numbers you plug in for a and b. The answer is (B).

Another good situation for picking numbers is when the answer choices to percent problems are all percents. Look at the following example.

From 1985 to 1990, the document production of office x increased by 20 percent. From 1990 to 1995, the document production increased by 30 percent. What was the percent increase in the document production in the office over the entire ten-year period from 1985–1995?

(A) 10%
(B) 25%
(C) 50%
(D) 56%
(E) 60%

Rather than attempting to solve this problem in the abstract, choose a number for the document production in 1985 and see what happens. There is no need to pick a realistic number. You are better off picking a number that is easy to work with. In percent problems, the number that is easiest to work with is almost always 100.

Now that you have a number, plug it into the problem. The document production from this office in 1985 was 100. What would the 1990 document production be? Twenty percent more than 100 is 120. Now, if 1990's document production was 120, what would the number of documents in 1995 be? What is 30 percent more than 120?

Be careful. Do not just add 30 to 120. You need to find 30 percent of 120 and add that number on.

Thirty percent of 120 is $(0.30)(120) = 36$. Add 36 to 120, and you get 156 documents in 1995. What percent greater is 156 than 100? It is a 56 percent increase. The answer is (D).

A third problem ideal for picking numbers is when the answer choices to a word problem are algebraic expressions.

If n computers cost p dollars, then how many dollars would q computers cost?

(A) $\dfrac{np}{q}$

(B) $\dfrac{nq}{p}$

(C) $\dfrac{pq}{n}$

(D) $\dfrac{n}{pq}$

(E) $\dfrac{p}{nq}$

The difficult thing about this question is it uses variables instead of numbers. Picking numbers will help make it more real. First, pick numbers that are easy to work with. For example, $n = 2$, $p = 4$, and $q = 3$. The question then becomes: "If two computers cost $4.00, how many dollars would three computers cost?" The answer is $6.00. When $n = 2$, $p = 4$, and $q = 3$, the correct answer should equal 6. Plug those values into the answer choices and see which ones yield 6:

(A) $\dfrac{np}{q} = \dfrac{(2)(4)}{3} = \dfrac{8}{3}$

(B) $\dfrac{nq}{p} = \dfrac{(2)(3)}{4} = \dfrac{6}{4} = \dfrac{3}{2} = 1\dfrac{1}{2}$

(C) $\dfrac{pq}{n} = \dfrac{(4)(3)}{2} = \dfrac{12}{2} = 6$

(D) $\dfrac{n}{pq} = \dfrac{2}{(4)(3)} = \dfrac{2}{12} = \dfrac{1}{6}$

(E) $\dfrac{p}{nq} = \dfrac{4}{(2)(3)} = \dfrac{4}{6} = \dfrac{2}{3}$

Choice (C) is the only one that yields 6, so it must be the correct answer.

When picking numbers for an abstract word problem like this one, try all five answer choices. Sometimes more than one choice will yield the correct result. When that happens, pick another set of numbers to eliminate the coincidences. *Avoid picking 0 and 1.* These often give several *possibly correct* answers.

Backsolving

Sometimes it is not possible simply to pick numbers and solve the problem. In these cases, the answer choices become your tools, and you can work backward to find the right choice. We call this *backsolving*, which essentially means plugging the choices back into the question until you find the one that fits.

Backsolving works best when:

■ The question is a complex word problem, and the answer choices are numbers
■ The alternative is setting up multiple algebraic equations

Backsolving is not ideal:

■ If the answer choices include variables
■ On algebra questions or word problems that have tricky answer choices, such as radicals and fractions (plugging them in takes too much time)

Sometimes backsolving is faster than setting up an equation. For example:

A social welfare program draws 27 members. If there are seven more males than females in the program, how many members are male?

   (A) 8
   (B) 10
   (C) 14
   (D) 17
   (E) 20

The five answer choices represent the possible number of males in the program, so try them in the question stem. The choice that gives a total of 27 members, with seven more males than females, will be the correct answer.

Often, answer choices are arranged in ascending (least to greatest) or descending (greatest to least) order. If this is the case, start with choice (C) when backsolving. For example, plugging in (C) gives you 14 males in the program. Because there are seven more males than females, there are seven females in the club. But $14 + 7 < 27$. The sum is too small, so there must be more than 14 males; thus, you can eliminate answer choices (A), (B), and (C) just like that.

Either (D) or (E) will be correct. Plugging in (D) gives you 17 males in the program; $17 - 7$ equals 10 singers, and $17 + 10 = 27$ members total. Choice (D) is correct.

Backsolving also works well with algebra problems with multiple equations. For example,

If $a + b + c = 110$, $a = 4b$, and $3a = 2c$, then $b =$

   (A) 6
   (B) 8
   (C) 9
   (D) 10
   (E) 14

You are looking for *b*, so plug in the answer choices for *b* in the question and see what happens. The choice that gives us 110 for the sum $a + b + c$ must be correct. Start with the midrange number, 9, choice (C).

If $b = 9$, then $a = 4 \times 9 = 36$
$2c = 3a = 3 \times 36 = 108$
$c = 54$
$a + b + c = 36 + 9 + 54 = 99$

Because this is a smaller sum than 110, the correct value for *b* must be larger. Therefore, eliminate answer choices (A), (B), and (C). Now, plug in either (D) or (E), and see which answer works.

Short on time? Try guessing between (D) and (E). But guess intelligently. Because (C) wasn't that far off the correct answer, you want to choose a number just slightly bigger than 9. That's choice (D).

Kaplan's Target Strategy for Any Math Question

It is not enough to know about the types of math questions on the test. If it were, we could end this section right now. To maximize your score on math questions, you will need to work systematically. Just like with other questions, the key to working systematically on math questions is to think about the question before you look for the answer.

On the more basic questions, you may find that you know the answers right away and are able to work through them quickly. However, when working through the harder problems, a few extra seconds spent thinking about your approach and deciding whether to work on the problem immediately or to come back to it later is very important and will help you earn more points.

Kaplan's Target Strategy is a good system for tackling *all* math problems. If you can quickly conjure up these steps on test day, you will find that the questions will seem manageable and that you are using your time efficiently. The steps are as follows:

Step 1. Estimate the question's difficulty.
Step 2. Read the question.
Step 3. Skip or do.
Step 4. Look for fastest approach.

We will now show you how our Target Strategy works as we use it to answer this sample math question:

At a diner, Joe orders three strips of bacon and a cup of coffee and is charged $2.25. Stella orders two strips of bacon and a cup of coffee and is charged $1.70. What is the price of two strips of bacon?

    (A) $0.55
    (B) $0.60
    (C) $1.10
    (D) $1.30
    (E) $1.80

Step 1. Estimate the Question's Difficulty.   The previous question is a moderately difficult word problem.

Step 2. Read the Question.   Even with easy questions, make sure you always know what is being asked. If you try to start solving the problem before reading the question all the way through, you may end up doing unnecessary work. This question looks straightforward, but read through it carefully, and you will see a slight twist. You are asked to find the cost of two strips of bacon, not one. Many people will find the price of a single bacon strip and forget to double it. Don't make this mistake.

Step 3. Skip or Do.   If a problem renders you clueless, circle it in your test booklet and move on. Spend your time on the problems you can solve; if there's still time at the end of the section, come back to the ones you had trouble with then. It is better to get two points from two less challenging problems than spend the same amount of time on one tricky question you are unsure of.

Step 4. Look for the Fastest Approach.   On an easy question, all the information you need to solve the problem may be provided in the question or in a diagram. Harder questions often hide the information that will help you solve the problem. Also, if you get the answer too easily, you may have missed something. (In this case, you're asked to find the price of two strips of bacon, not one.)

Look for shortcuts. Sometimes the obvious way of doing a problem is the long way. If the method you choose involves lots of calculating, look for another route. There is usually a shortcut you can use that won't involve tons of arithmetic.

Again, in the sample question, the cost of bacon and coffee could be translated into two distinct equations using the variables b and c. You could find c in terms of b, and then plug this into the other equation. But if you think carefully, you will see there's a quicker way. The difference in price between three bacon strips and a cup of coffee and two bacon strips and a cup of coffee is the price of one bacon strip. So one bacon strip costs $2.25 - $1.70 = $0.55.

(Remember, you have to find the price of two strips of bacon. Twice $0.55 is $1.10.) On this question, you can also use alternate techniques, such as picking numbers and backsolving, which were covered earlier in this chapter.

Kaplan's Target Strategies for Educated Guessing

If you are running out of time and need to answer a few questions quickly, you should try to make an educated guess. To make an educated guess, you need to eliminate answer choices that you know are wrong and guess from what is left.

The more answer choices you can eliminate, the better chance you have of guessing the correct answer from what's left over. You do this by:

- Eliminating unreasonable answer choices
- Eliminating the obvious on hard questions
- Eyeballing lengths, angles, and areas on geometry problems

Eliminating Unreasonable Answer Choices.   Before you guess, think about the problem, and decide which answers don't make sense.

The ratio of doctors to patients in a certain hospital is 13:11. If there are 429 doctors in the room, how many patients are there?
    (A) 143
    (B) 363
    (C) 433
    (D) 507
    (E) 792

The ratio of doctors to patients is 13:11, so there are more doctors than not. Because there are 429 doctors, there must be fewer than 429 patients. You can eliminate choices (C), (D), and (E). The answer must be either (A) or (B), so guess. The correct answer is (B).

Eliminating the Obvious on Hard Questions.   On more difficult questions, obvious answers are usually wrong. So eliminate them when you guess. This strategy does not hold true for easier questions, when the obvious answer could be right. In the following difficult problem, which obvious answer would you eliminate?

A number *x* is increased by 30 percent, and then the result is decreased by 20 percent. What is the final result of these changes?
    (A) *x* is increased by 10 percent
    (B) *x* is increased by 6 percent
    (C) *x* is increased by 4 percent
    (D *x* is decreased by 5 percent
    (E) *x* is decreased by 10 percent

If you picked (A) as the obvious choice to eliminate, you would be right. Most people would combine the decrease of 20 percent with the increase of 30 percent, getting a net increase of 10 percent. That's the easy, obvious answer, but not the correct answer. If you must guess, avoid (A). The correct answer is (C).

Eyeballing Lengths, Angles, and Areas on Geometry Problems.   Use diagrams that accompany geometry problems to help you eliminate wrong answer choices. First, double check for specific instructions involving whether or not the diagram is drawn to scale. Diagrams are always drawn to scale unless there's a note like this: Note: Figure not drawn to scale. If it's not drawn to scale, you cannot use this strategy. If it is, estimate quantities or eyeball the diagram, then eliminate answer choices that are way too large or too small.

Length: When a geometry question asks for a length, use the given lengths to estimate the unknown length. Measure off the given length by making a nick in your pencil with your thumbnail. Then hold the pencil against the unknown length on the diagram to see how the lengths compare. Try it.

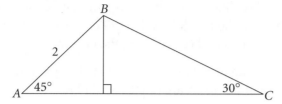

In the figure above, what is the length of *BC*?

(A) $\sqrt{2}$
(B) 2
(C) $2\sqrt{2}$
(D) 4
(E) $4\sqrt{2}$

▥ AB is 2, so measure off this length on your pencil.

▥ Compare BC with this length.

▥ BC appears almost twice as long as AB, so BC is approximately 4.

▥ Because $\sqrt{2}$ is approximately 1.4, and BC is clearly longer than AB, choices (A) and (B) are too small.

▥ Choice (E) is greater than 4, so eliminate that.

▥ Now guess between (C) and (D). The correct answer is (C).

Angles: You can also eyeball angles. To eyeball an angle, compare the angle with a familiar angle, such as a straight angle (180 degrees), a right angle (90 degrees), or half a right angle (45 degrees). The corner of a piece of paper is a right angle, so use that to see if an angle is greater or less than 90 degrees.

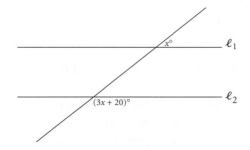

In the previous figure, if $\ell_1 \parallel \ell_2$, what is the value of *x*?
- (A) 40
- (B) 50
- (C) 80
- (D) 100
- (E) 130

■ You see that *x* is less than 90 degrees, so eliminate choices (D) and (E).
■ Because *x* appears to be much less than 90 degrees, eliminate choice (C).
■ Now pick between (A) and (B). In fact, the correct answer is (A).

Areas: Eyeballing an area is similar to eyeballing a length. You compare an unknown area in a diagram to an area that you do know.

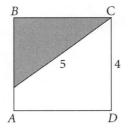

In square *ABCD* above, what is the area of the shaded region?
- (A) 4
- (B) 6
- (C) 8
- (D) 9
- (E) 10

Because *ABCD* is a square, it has the area 4^2, or 16. The shaded area is less than one half the size of the square, so its area must be less than 8. Eliminate answer choices (C), (D), and (E). The correct answer is (B).

Word problems provide their own strategies. Here is Kaplan's Target Strategy for this question type.

Kaplan's Target Strategy for Word Problems

Step 1. Decode the question.
Step 2. Set up an equation.
Step 3. Solve for the unknown.

Let's use these steps to solve a sample word problem.

Step 1. Decode the Question.   As with nonalgebraic word problems, in order to solve a question, any question, you know what it is asking you to do. You need to translate the English into math. Remember this table from the lesson?

When you see:	Think:
Sum, plus, more than, added to, combined total	+
Minus, less than, difference between, decreased by	−
Is, was, equals, is equivalent to, is the same as, adds up to	=
Times, product, multiplied by, of, twice, double, triple	×
Divided by, over, quotient, per, out of, into	÷
What, how much, how many, a number	x, n, a, b, etc.

In the table you see how algebraic variables come into play solving word problems. The letter, or variable, stands for the unknown amount we need to find.

Here's an example.

Amy is 18 months older than her brother Sean and three years older than her sister Katie. If the sum of their ages is 20 years, how old is Amy?

What is the question looking for? Amy's age.

Step 2. Set Up an Equation.   Now that we know what's being asked of us, we have to set up an equation to find Amy's age.

Let x = Amy's age. That means that Sean's age is $x - 18$ (if x = Sean's age, then Amy's age would be $x + 18$) and Katie's age is $x - 3(12)$. The sum of all their ages is 20, so:

$$x + x - 18 + x - (3 \times 12) = 20 \times 12$$

Hopefully you noticed that this is a trick question. Ages are given in months and in years. We have to convert everything to the same measurement in order to solve correctly. That's why we multiplied the 3 and the 20 by 12, because there are 12 months in a year.

Step 3. Solve for the Unknown.   We know what's being asked of us, we set up an equation, the only thing left to do is the math. Make sure you do your calculations in the right order and properly.

$$\begin{aligned} x + x - 18 + x - (3 \times 12) &= 20 \times 12 \\ 3x - 54 &= 240 \\ 3x - 54 + 54 &= 240 + 54 \\ 3x &= 294 \\ x &= 98 \end{aligned}$$

Amy is 98 years old? How could that be?

Remember, we were working with months. Don't forget to translate the number of months back into years when you are finished.

$98 \div 12 \approx 8$ years old.

Data interpretation questions require a similar target strategy.

Kaplan's Target Strategy for Data Interpretation Questions

Step 1. Read the question.
Step 2. Decode the diagram.
Step 3. Find the answer.

Let's apply these three steps to a sample question.
Remember this example from earlier in the chapter?

The previous diagram shows the safety habits of a group of 60 skateboarders. How many of the group always wear their helmets?

(A) 60
(B) 36
(C) 12
(D) 30

Step 1. Read the Question. It may seem obvious, but the point here is not to spend any time examining the chart, graph, or table until you read the question. Think of the information in a diagram as detail questions on the reading comprehension section. It doesn't make sense to spend too much time reviewing all the details until you know what the questions are asking.

An essential element of reading the question includes reading exactly what the diagram illustrates. In this example we are told that the pie chart shows the safety habits of a group of 60 skateboarders. The size of the group is important information that you may chose to circle or underline.

Naturally, the other important part of reading the question is determining what the question asks. This question asks how many of the group (the 60 total) always wear their helmets.

Step 2. Decode the Diagram. Now that you have read the question and know what you are looking for, refer to the diagram. Use the labels provided to decode it.

This pie chart is divided into sections, each labeled with a percent amount and titled *always wear helmet*, *often wear*, *wear infrequently*, *never wear*. Thus, the sections represent how often the group of 60 skateboarders wears their helmets.

Step 3. Find the Answer.   Now that we know what we are looking for and what the diagram means, we can look for the relevant information within the diagram and do any calculations necessary. Remember we want to know how many of the group always wear their helmets. The diagram shows a section labeled 60% as always wearing their helmets. We need a number, so we must convert the 60% into a number of skateboarders. 60% of 60 = 0.60 × 60 = 36. The correct answer is (B).

Now that we have covered the best strategies for word problems it's time to review the best strategies for another math question type: quantitative reasoning.

Quantitative Reasoning Strategies— Number Relationships

Remember the number relationship example from Sample Mathematics Questions? If not, here is the question again, along with a strategy for finding the correct answer.

$$3 \rightarrow \boxed{} \rightarrow 7 \qquad \text{(A)} \quad 5$$

$$5 \rightarrow \boxed{} \rightarrow 9 \qquad \text{(B)} \quad 6$$

$$1 \rightarrow \boxed{} \rightarrow \underline{} \qquad \text{(C)} \quad 10$$

$$\text{(D)} \quad 4$$

To find the answer, look at each expression and think about what operation was performed on the number on the left to arrive at the number on the right. Because it is possible for more than one relationship or operation to fit in the missing box, always be sure to test your assumption on all the examples given.

$$3 + 4 = 7$$
$$5 + 4 = 9$$

The pattern is +4. Therefore, to find the missing number, add 4 to 1; 1 + 4 = 5. The correct answer is choice (A), 5

Whenever you are solving these questions, be sure to work ACROSS from left to right, not up and down when you are looking for the pattern.

Look at the next example:

$$2 \rightarrow \boxed{} \rightarrow 4$$

$$3 \rightarrow \boxed{} \rightarrow 6$$

$$5 \rightarrow \boxed{} \rightarrow \underline{}$$

Look at the first row of numbers: 2 and 4. The operation being performed could be +2 or ×2. Note this, then look at the next row of numbers: 3 and 6; 3 × 2 = 6. The pattern is ×2, rather than +2. The number that belongs in the blank is 5 × 2, or 10. When you approach number relationship questions, work through all the examples and predict the answer before reading the answer choices. This will help keep you from choosing incorrect answers or becoming confused.

Visual problems have their own strategies. We'll review these next.

Quantitative Reasoning Strategies—Visual Problems

Remember this example?

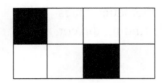

(A) $\dfrac{2}{6}$

(B) $\dfrac{1}{2}$

(C) $\dfrac{1}{4}$

(D) 2

Here is how to answer this question. The rectangle is sectioned into 8 equal squares. Two are shaded and 6 are not. In other words 2 out of 8 are shaded. This can be expressed as a fraction: $\dfrac{2}{8}$. Reduced, $\dfrac{2}{8} = \dfrac{1}{4}$. The correct answer is $\dfrac{1}{4}$, or choice (C).

Notice how the incorrect answers assume that you have made a mistake in counting either the total number of sections or the number of sections that are shaded. Choice (A) puts the shaded portion, 2, over the amount that are not shaded, 6, rather than the whole, which is 8.

You could rule out choice (B) because you can easily see that less than $\dfrac{1}{2}$ of the whole is shaded. Choice (D) is incorrect because it fails to put the number of shaded squares as a numerator above the number of sections in the whole.

Sometimes in visual problems you may find it that you will have to create lines to divide a whole into equal parts so that you can count them. Doing this will help you work quickly and accurately.

In the previous drawing, the square is sectioned into four equal smaller squares. A triangular region of one of these squares is shaded. The triangular region is $\frac{1}{2}$ of one square. Because the other three square regions are not divided in this way, you may be tricked into counting the shaded portion or the whole incorrectly. To avoid this, divide the other three square regions in half as well.

By making all the sections the same, you can more easily count the sections that make up the whole: there are 8. How many are shaded? 1 of 8, or $\frac{1}{8}$.

Summary

A review of math skills and strategies is essential for test preparation. Now that you have reviewed the entire math lesson, read through the sample questions, and worked through the strategies, you are ready to take Practice Test 4, which will help you determine your strengths (what you don't have to review much more) and your weaknesses (topics you need to continue to review until test day). The 50 multiple-choice questions test your math skills and the answer explanations will help you understand any questions that you miss. Remember, if you are certain that your civil service exam does not test your math skills, you can consider proceeding directly to Chapter 7: Following Directions, Coding, and Memory.

Practice Test 4

50 Questions
50 Minutes

1	(A) (B) (C) (D)	14	(A) (B) (C) (D)	27	(A) (B) (C) (D)	40	(A) (B) (C) (D)
2	(A) (B) (C) (D)	15	(A) (B) (C) (D)	28	(A) (B) (C) (D)	41	(A) (B) (C) (D)
3	(A) (B) (C) (D)	16	(A) (B) (C) (D)	29	(A) (B) (C) (D)	42	(A) (B) (C) (D)
4	(A) (B) (C) (D)	17	(A) (B) (C) (D)	30	(A) (B) (C) (D)	43	(A) (B) (C) (D) (E)
5	(A) (B) (C) (D)	18	(A) (B) (C) (D)	31	(A) (B) (C) (D) (E)	44	(A) (B) (C) (D)
6	(A) (B) (C) (D)	19	(A) (B) (C) (D)	32	(A) (B) (C) (D) (E)	45	(A) (B) (C) (D)
7	(A) (B) (C) (D)	20	(A) (B) (C) (D)	33	(A) (B) (C) (D)	46	(A) (B) (C) (D) (E)
8	(A) (B) (C) (D)	21	(A) (B) (C) (D)	34	(A) (B) (C) (D)	47	(A) (B) (C) (D)
9	(A) (B) (C) (D)	22	(A) (B) (C) (D)	35	(A) (B) (C) (D) (E)	48	(A) (B) (C) (D) (E)
10	(A) (B) (C) (D)	23	(A) (B) (C) (D)	36	(A) (B) (C) (D) (E)	49	(A) (B) (C) (D) (E)
11	(A) (B) (C) (D)	24	(A) (B) (C) (D)	37	(A) (B) (C) (D)	50	(A) (B) (C) (D) (E)
12	(A) (B) (C) (D)	25	(A) (B) (C) (D)	38	(A) (B) (C) (D)		
13	(A) (B) (C) (D)	26	(A) (B) (C) (D)	39	(A) (B) (C) (D) (E)		

1. 172 → ☐ → 167

58 → ☐ → 53

47 → ☐ → __

43	42	40	44
(A)	(B)	(C)	(D)

2. 20 → ☐ → 38

10 → ☐ → 18

9 → ☐ → __

22	18	16	20
(A)	(B)	(C)	(D)

3. 99 → ☐ → 91

7 → ☐ → −1

12 → ☐ → __

0	4	5	−2
(A)	(B)	(C)	(D)

4. 4 → ☐ → 12

9 → ☐ → 27

1 → ☐ → __

9	3	42	4
(A)	(B)	(C)	(D)

5.

0.5 → ☐ → 0.05

1.0 → ☐ → 0.1

10.0 → ☐ → ___

| 1.0 | 10 | 100 | 0.01 |
| (A) | (B) | (C) | (D) |

8.

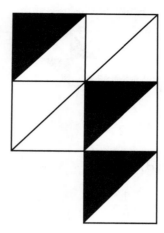

(A) $\dfrac{5}{10}$

(B) $\dfrac{3}{5}$

(C) $\dfrac{3}{10}$

(D) $\dfrac{4}{10}$

6.

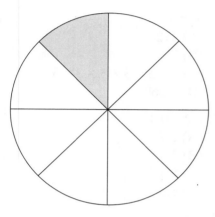

(A) $\dfrac{1}{6}$

(B) $\dfrac{1}{4}$

(C) $\dfrac{1}{8}$

(D) $\dfrac{1}{10}$

9.

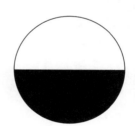

(A) $\dfrac{1}{2}$

(B) $\dfrac{1}{50}$

(C) $\dfrac{10}{100}$

(D) $\dfrac{100}{100}$

7.

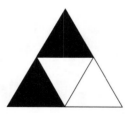

(A) $\dfrac{1}{4}$

(B) $\dfrac{2}{5}$

(C) $\dfrac{2}{3}$

(D) $\dfrac{1}{2}$

KAPLAN

10.

(A) $\dfrac{1}{2}$

(B) $\dfrac{1}{3}$

(C) $\dfrac{1}{4}$

(D) $\dfrac{2}{7}$

11. $52.3 \times 10.4?$
(A) 543.92
(B) 534.92
(C) 5334.92
(D) 5439.2

12. $(3d - 7) - (5 - 2d) =$
(A) $d - 12$
(B) $5d - 2$
(C) $5d + 12$
(D) $5d - 12$

13. $\dfrac{3}{4} + 7.55 =$
(A) 8.3
(B) 8.2
(C) 7.25
(D) 5.6

14. $-6(3 - 4 \times 3) =$
(A) 66
(B) 54
(C) 18
(D) −12

15. $x = \sqrt{3}$, $y = 2$, and $z = \dfrac{1}{2}$
$x^2 - 5yz + y^2 =$
(A) 1
(B) 2
(C) 4
(D) 7

16. $3^3 \times 3^4 =$
(A) 312
(B) 3^7
(C) $3 \times 3 \times 3 \times 3 \times 3 \times 3$
(D) 1,260

17. $6.2 - 0.4 =$
(A) 2.2
(B) 2.8
(C) 5.8
(D) 6.5

18. $0.3 \times 19.95 =$
(A) 5.985
(B) 5.895
(C) 5.85
(D) .5895

19. $\dfrac{16}{35} > ?$

(A) $\dfrac{7}{8}$

(B) $\dfrac{5}{6}$

(C) $\dfrac{12}{61}$

(D) $\dfrac{43}{45}$

20. $1\dfrac{1}{2} \times 2\dfrac{1}{4} \times \dfrac{2}{3} =$

(A) $5\dfrac{2}{8}$

(B) 3

(C) $2\dfrac{1}{2}$

(D) $2\dfrac{1}{4}$

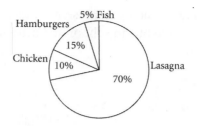

22. The pie chart above shows the lunch orders of a group of 150 junior high school students. How many students ordered lasagna?
(A) 105
(B) 100
(C) 95
(D) 70

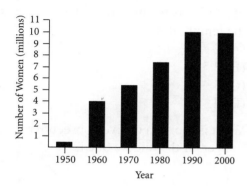

21. The diagram above shows the number of women in the workplace in the years 1950–2000. Which year experienced the greatest increase of women in the workplace?
(A) 1960
(B) 1950
(C) 2000
(D) 2010

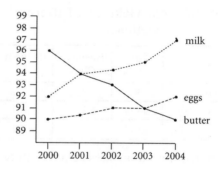

23. What is the difference between the price of milk in 2004 and the price of milk in 2000?
(A) 2 cents
(B) 4 cents
(C) 5 cents
(D) 6 cents

24. The diagram below represents students who take the bus to school in 3 school districts.

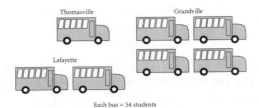

How many students take the bus in Grandville?
(A) 54
(B) 108
(C) 200
(D) 216

Price of Different Tickets on Different Airlines

	First Class	Business Class	Economy Class
Happy Air	$301	$252	$108
Jet Stream Airways	$309	$250	$99
Lucky Travel Airline	$357	$312	$89

25. How much does a business class ticket cost on Lucky Travel Airline?
(A) $357
(B) $312
(C) $108
(D) $99

26. All of the following can be a product of a negative integer and a positive integer EXCEPT
(A) −6
(B) 1
(C) −1
(D) −2

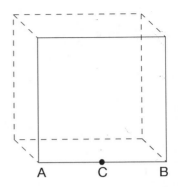

27. If the surface area of the cube above is 96, and C is the midpoint of AB, what is the length of AC?
(A) 2
(B) 2.5
(C) 3
(D) 4

28. What is the sum of five consecutive integers if the middle one is 9?
(A) 55
(B) 50
(C) 45
(D) 30

29. If a man earns $200 for his first 40 hours of work in a week and then is paid one-and one-half times his regular rate for any additional hours, how many hours must he work to make $230 in a week?
(A) 43
(B) 44
(C) 45
(D) 46

30. Which of the following demonstrates the commutative property of addition?

(A) $1 + 3 = 4$

(B) $1 + 3 = 3 + 1$

(C) $1 + 3 = \dfrac{1}{3} \times \dfrac{3}{1}$

(D) $1 + 3 = 1 - (-3)$

31. The price of copper rose by 25 percent and then fell by 20 percent. The price after these changes was

(A) 20 percent greater than the original price
(B) 5 percent greater than the original price
(C) the same as the original price
(D) 5 percent less than the original price
(E) 15 percent less than the original price

32. A number of bricks were purchased to build a fireplace at a cost of 40 cents each, but only $\dfrac{3}{4}$ of them were needed. If the unused 190 bricks were returned and their cost refunded, what was the cost of the bricks used to make the fireplace?

(A) $76
(B) $228
(C) $304
(D) $414
(E) $570

33. Edward has $400 more than Robert. After Edward spends $60 on groceries, he has 3 times more money than Robert. How much money does Robert have?

(A) 90
(B) 120
(C) 140
(D) 170

34. A recent poll showed that 42% of people polled favored a new bill, 28% were opposed to it, 20% were neither for nor against it and the rest did not vote at all. What fractional part of the whole did not vote at all?

(A) $\dfrac{1}{10}$

(B) $\dfrac{1}{9}$

(C) $\dfrac{2}{10}$

(D) $\dfrac{9}{10}$

35. If an "anglet" is defined as 1 percent of 1 degree, then how many anglets are there in a circle?

(A) 0.36
(B) 3.6
(C) 360
(D) 3,600
(E) 36,000

36. To meet a government require- ment, a bottler must test 5 percent of its spring water and 10 percent of its sparkling water for purity. If a customer ordered 120 cases of spring water and 80 cases of spar- kling water, what percent of all the cases must the bottler test before he can send it out?
(A) 6.5%
(B) 7.0%
(C) 7.5%
(D) 8.0%
(E) 8.5%

37. Five less than 3 times a certain number is equal to the original number plus 7. What is the original number?
(A) 2
(B) 6
(C) 11
(D) 12

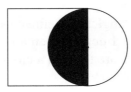

38. A square and a circle are drawn as shown above. The area of the square is 64 in². What is the area of the shaded region?
(A) 4π in²
(B) 8π in²
(C) 16π in²
(D) 32π in²

39. At an international dinner $\frac{1}{5}$ of the people attending were from South America. If the number of North Americans at the dinner was $\frac{2}{3}$ greater than the number of South Americans, what fraction of people at the dinner were from neither South America nor North America?

(A) $\frac{1}{5}$

(B) $\frac{2}{5}$

(C) $\frac{7}{15}$

(D) $\frac{8}{15}$

(E) $\frac{2}{3}$

40. The price of a stock decreased by 20%. By what percent must the price increase to return to its origi- nal value?
(A) 20%
(B) 25%
(C) 50%
(D) 120%

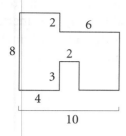

41. What is the area of the polygon above, in square units, if each corner of the polygon is a right angle?
(A) 40
(B) 62
(C) 68
(D) 74

42. If $abc \neq 0$, then $\dfrac{a^2bc + ab^2c + abc^2}{abc} = ?$

(A) $a + b + c$
(B) abc
(C) $a^3b^3c^3$
(D) $a^2 + b^2 + c^2$

43. A clothing supplier stores 800 coats in a warehouse, of which 15 percent are full-length coats. If 500 of the shorter length coats are removed from the warehouse, what percent of the remaining coats are full length?
(A) 5.62%
(B) 9.37%
(C) 35%
(D) 40%
(E) 48%

44. Liza has 40 less than three times the number of books that Janice has. If B is equal to the number of books that Janice has, which of the following expressions shows the total number of books that Liza and Janice have together?
(A) $4B - 40$
(B) $3B - 40$
(C) $4B$
(D) $4B + 40$

45. A 25-ounce solution is 20% alcohol. If 50 ounces of water are added to it, what percent of the new solution is alcohol?

(A) $6\dfrac{2}{3}$ %

(B) $7\dfrac{1}{2}$ %

(C) 10%

(D) $13\dfrac{1}{3}$ %

46. Which of the following is greater than 1,000.01?
(A) 0.00001×10^8
(B) 0.0101×10^4
(C) 1.1×10^2
(D) 1.00001×10^3
(E) 0.00010001×10^7

47. A rectangular picture that is 4 inches wide and 6 inches long is enlarged so that it is 10 inches long without changing the width. What is the perimeter, in inches, of the enlarged picture?
(A) 20
(B) 24
(C) 28
(D) 40

48. An insurance company provides coverage for a certain dental procedure according to the following rules: the policy pays 80% of the first $1,200 of cost, and 50% of the cost above $1,200. If a patient had to pay $490 of the cost for this procedure himself, how much did the procedure cost?
(A) $1,200
(B) $1,300
(C) $1,500
(D) $1,600
(E) $1,700

49. A car rental company charges for mileage as follows: x dollars per mile for the first n miles and $x + 1$ dollars per mile for each mile over n miles. How much will the mileage charge be, in dollars, for a journey of d miles, where $d > n$?
(A) $d(x + 1) - n$
(B) $xn + d$
(C) $xn + d(x + 1)$
(D) $x(n + d) - d$
(E) $(x + 1)(d - n)$

50. If the price of item X increased by 20%, and then by a further 20%, what percent of the original price is the increase in price?
(A) 24%
(B) 40%
(C) 44%
(D) $66\frac{2}{3}\%$
(E) 140%

Answers and Explanations

1. B
The number in the right column is 5 less than the number in the left hand column. The relationship is –5. The missing number = 47 – 5 = 42.

2. C
The number in the right column is 2 less than twice the number in the left hand column. The relationship is to multiply the term by 2, and then subtract 2. The missing number = (9 × 2) – 2 = 18 – 2 = 16.

3. B
The number in the right column is 8 less than the number in the left hand column. The relationship is –8. The missing number = 12 – 8 = 4.

4. B
The number in the right column is 3 times the number in the left column. In the final row, if 1 is the number on the left, then 3 is the number on the right.

5. **A**

Each number on the left is divided by 10 to arrive at the number on the right. Therefore, 0.5 divided by 10 = 0.05; 1.0 divided by 10 = 0.1; 10 divided by 10 = 1.

6. **C**

Count the total pieces of the circle and count the number of pieces shaded. There are 8 pieces and 1 is shaded; 1 part of 8 is shaded, or $\dfrac{1}{8}$.

7. **D**

Count the total pieces of the triangle and count the number of pieces shaded. There are 4 pieces and 2 are shaded; 2 parts of 4 are shaded, or $\dfrac{2}{4}$, which reduces to $\dfrac{1}{2}$.

8. **C**

Count the total pieces of the diagram and count the number of pieces shaded. There are 10 pieces and 3 are shaded; 3 parts of 10 are shaded, or $\dfrac{3}{10}$.

9. **A**

Count the total pieces of the circle and count the number of pieces shaded. There are 2 pieces and 1 is shaded; 1 part of 2 is shaded, or $\dfrac{1}{2}$.

10. **C**

There are 8 sections and 2 are shaded; $\dfrac{2}{8}$ reduces to $\dfrac{1}{4}$.

11. **A**

$52.3 \times 10.4 = 543.92$; be careful when doing the multiplication to know where the decimal place belongs in the product.

12. **D**

Subtract:

$$3d - 7 - 5 - (-2d)$$

Combine like terms:

$$3d - (-2d) - 7 - 5$$
$$5d - 12$$

Note that $3d$ minus $-2d$ equals $+5d$, because subtracting a negative is the same as adding a positive.

13. **A**

First, change the fraction to a decimal; $\dfrac{3}{4} = 0.75$. Now, add the two decimals:

$$0.75 + 7.55 = 8.3.$$

14. **B**

According to the order of operations, start in the parentheses. Perform multiplication before subtraction: $-6(3 - 12)$. After the subtraction: $-6(-9)$. Since a negative times a negative is a positive, the answer is 54.

15. **B**

Remember, $5yz$ means $5 \bullet y \bullet z$. First, we will replace x, y, and z with the values given. Then, we will carry out the indicated operations using the PEMDAS order of operations—Parentheses, Exponents, Multiplication and Division, Addition, and Subtraction.

$$
\begin{aligned}
x^2 5yz + y^2 &= (\sqrt{3})^2 - 5 \bullet 2 \bullet \frac{1}{2} + 2^2 \\
&= 3 - 5 \bullet 2 \bullet \frac{1}{2} + 4 \\
&= 3 - 5 + 4 \\
&= -2 + 4 \\
&= 2
\end{aligned}
$$

16. B

When multiplying numbers to a power, add the powers. Thus, $3^3 \times 3^4 = 3^7$.

17. C

Line up the decimal points and subtract:

$$\begin{array}{r} 6.2 \\ -\ 0.4 \\ \hline 5.8 \end{array}$$

18. A

Be careful when you multiply decimals that you put the decimal in the correct place; $0.3 \times 19.95 = 5.985$.

19. C

Notice that $\dfrac{16}{35}$ is just slightly greater than $\dfrac{16}{32}$, or $\dfrac{1}{2}$. Answers (A) and (B) are (D) are far greater than $\dfrac{1}{2}$.

20. D

$$1\frac{1}{2} = \frac{3}{2}; \quad 2\frac{1}{4} = \frac{9}{4}$$

$$\frac{3}{2} \times \frac{9}{4} \times \frac{2}{3} = \frac{9}{4} = 2\frac{1}{4}$$

21. A

The height at which the vertical bars reach on the y-axis represent the number of women in the workplace at a given year in millions. In order to find the year at which there was the greatest increase of women in the workplace, look for the greatest leap between the previous bar and the next. The bar at 1950 is at less than 1 million, while the bar at 1960 shows a dramatic rise to the 4 million mark. Therefore, the year 1960 experienced the greatest increase of women in the workplace. Choice (A) is the correct answer.

22. A

First, find the percent of students in the pie chart who ordered lasagna: 70%. Since there are 150 students in the whole group, 70% of 150 ordered lasagna; $0.7 \times 150 = 105$.

23. C

Locate the price of milk in 2000 on the y-axis. It is 92 cents. Then locate the price of milk in 2004. It is at 97 cents on the y-axis. The price of milk has gone up 5 cents.

24. D

There are 4 buses under the label Grandville. The key indicates that each bus represents 54 students; 54×4 students take the bus to Grandville = 216 students.

25. B

Find the row labeled "Lucky Travel Airline." Read across until you reach the corresponding column labeled business class. The box that aligns with these two labels will give you the price of a business class ticket on Lucky Airlines. It is $312, choice (B).

26. B

Remember to count the number of negatives to determine whether the product of negative and positive integers is either negative or positive. An odd number of negatives will yield a negative number, while an even number of negatives will yield a positive number. Because choice (B) is a positive integer, it is not the product of a negative and a positive integer.

27. **A**

On this question it is best to use back-solving. If $AC = 2$, the edge length of the cube is 4, so each face of the cube is $4^2 = 16$ square inches. There are 6 faces to a cube, so the entire surface area would be $16 \times 6 = 96$ square inches.

28. **C**

This is an addition problem. If the middle integer is 9, place them in order. You would have: $7 + 8 + 9 + 10 + 11 = 45$.

29. **B**

To learn the man's overtime rate of pay, we have to figure out his regular rate of pay. Divide the amount of money made, $200, by the time it took to make it, 40 hours. $200 ÷ 40 hours = $5 per hour. That is the normal rate. The man is paid $1\frac{1}{2}$ times his regular rate during overtime, so when working more than 40 hours he makes $\frac{3}{2} \times$ $5 per hour = $7.50 per hour. Now we can figure out how long it takes the man to make $230. It takes him 40 hours to make the first $200. The last $30 are made at the overtime rate. Because it takes the man one hour to make $7.50 at this rate, we can figure out the number of extra hours by dividing $30 by $7.50 per hour. $30 ÷ $7.50 per hour = 4 hours. The total time needed is 40 hours plus 4 hours, or 44 hours.

30. **B**

The commutative property of addition states that when adding two or more terms, the sum is the same, no matter the order in which the terms are added.

31. **C**

Here we have a percent problem with no numbers. One thing you know: *You can't simply subtract the percents to get "25% minus 20% equals a 5% increase,"* because the percents are of different wholes. The percent decrease is a percentage of the new, increased amount, not a percentage of the original amount. The best way to solve problems like this is to use a concrete number. *Because we're dealing with percents, the number to start with is 100.* (Don't worry about whether 100 is a "realistic" number in the context of the problem; we just need a convenient number to tell us how big the final amount is relative to the starting amount.) Say the price of copper starts at $100. 25% of $100 is $25, so if the price of copper increases by 25%, it rises by $25 to $125. Now the price decreases by 20%. 20% is just $\frac{1}{5}$, so the price drops by $\frac{125}{5}$ or $25. So the price drops to $100. That's the original price, so the answer is (C).

32. **B**

You are looking for the cost of the bricks that were actually used to make the fireplace. In order to find that, we need to know how many bricks were used, and what each brick costs. Because $\frac{3}{4}$ of the bricks were used, $\frac{1}{4}$ of the bricks weren't used. That unused quarter of the total amounted to 190 bricks. That means that number of bricks that were used, $\frac{3}{4}$ of the total, amounted to 3 × 190, or 570 bricks. Each brick cost 40 cents, so the total cost of the bricks that were used must have been 0.40 × 570 = 228 dollars.

33. D

Translate the words into math and solve for the unknown. Let x = the unknown amount of money Robert has.

"Edward has 400 more than Robert": $x + 400$

"After he spends $60 on groceries": $x + 400 - 60$

"he has 3 times more than Robert": $x + 400 - 60 = 3x$

Now that you've set up an equation, solve for x.

$$x + 400 - 60 = 3x$$
$$x + 340 = 3x$$
$$340 = 2x$$
$$170 = x$$

34. A

$42 + 28 + 20 = 90\%$ voted.

$100 - 90 = 10$, so $\dfrac{10}{100}$ or $\dfrac{1}{10}$ did not vote.

35. E

If an "anglet" is 1 percent of a degree, then there are 100 anglets in each degree. Because there are 360 degrees in a circle, there are 100 × 360, or 36,000, anglets in a circle. Never let the introduction of a new term like "anglet" worry you; you really only have to substitute the word in for values you know.

36. B

For the spring water, the bottler must test 0.05(120) = 6 cases, and for the sparking water, he must test 0.1(80) = 8 cases. The total number of cases to be tested for the spring and sparkling water combined is 6 + 8 = 14, which is $\dfrac{14}{200} = \dfrac{7}{100} = 7\%$ of all cases.

37. B

Translate the English into math bit by bit. "Five less than 3 times a certain number" becomes "$3x - 5$"; "is equal to the original number plus 7" becomes "$= x + 7$." So altogether you have $3x - 5 = x + 7$.

Now solve for x:

$$3x - 5 = x + 7$$
$$3x - x = 7 + 5$$
$$2x = 12$$
$$x = 6$$

38. B

The shaded region represents half the area of the circle. Find the length of the radius to determine this area. Notice that the diameter of the circle is equal to a side of the square. Since the area of the square is 64 in², it has a side length of 8 in. So, the diameter of the circle is 8, and its radius is 4. The area of a circle is πr^2, where r is the radius, so the area of this circle is $\pi(4)^2 = 16\pi$ in². This isn't the answer though; the shaded region is only half the circle, so its area is 8π in².

39. C

You should notice immediately that the problem contains two fractions: $\dfrac{1}{5}$ and $\dfrac{2}{3}$. The least common denominator is 15, so let's say the total number of people at the dinner was 15. That means we have 3 South Americans in the room. We also have North Americans numbering two-thirds more than that, or $3 + \dfrac{2}{3}(3)$, which is 5. So there were 8 people from South America or North America, which means 7 people were not from either place. So $\dfrac{7}{15}$ of the people in the room were from neither South America nor North America. The correct answer, therefore, is (C).

40. **B**

The key here is that while the value of the stock increases and decreases by the same amount, it doesn't increase and decrease by the same percent because the "whole" is different once the stock has lost value.

If it seems confusing, this is a good question to pick numbers for. Let's pick $100 for the price of the stock. If the price decreases by 20%, the price is now $80. For the price to return to its original value of $100, it must be increased by $20. What percent of 80 equals $20?

$$x\%(80) = 20$$
$$x\% = \frac{20}{80}$$
$$x\% = \frac{1}{4}$$

$\dfrac{1}{4}$ is equal to 25%.

41. **B**

Think of the figure as a rectangle with two rectangular bites taken out of it. Sketch in lines to make one large rectangle as shown below.

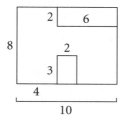

The area of a rectangle is length times width. If we call the length of the large rectangle 10, then its width is 8, so its area is $10 \times 8 = 80$ square units. The rectangle missing from the top right corner has dimensions of 6 and 2, so its area is $6 \times 2 = 12$ square units. The rectangle missing from the bottom has dimensions of 2 and 3, so its area is $2 \times 3 = 6$ square units. To find the area of the polygon, subtract the areas of the two missing shapes from the area of the large rectangle: $80 - (12 + 6) = 80 - 18 = 62$ square units, choice (B).

42. **A**

$$\frac{a^2bc + ab^2c + abc^2}{abc} =$$

$$\frac{a \times a\cancel{bc}}{\cancel{abc}} + \frac{b \times a\cancel{bc}}{\cancel{abc}} + \frac{c \times a\cancel{bc}}{\cancel{abc}} =$$

$$a + b + c$$

43. D

The warehouse has two kinds of coats in it: full-length and shorter coats. Initially 15 percent of the coats are full-length, but then a number of the short coats are removed. You are asked to calculate what percent of the remaining coats are full-length. The key to this question is first to calculate the number of full-length coats. At first, there are 800 coats in the warehouse; if 15 percent of these are full-length, then $\frac{15}{100}$ × 800 = 15 × 8 = 120 coats are full-length.

Then 500 short coats are removed. So that makes 300 coats in total remaining. There are still 120 full-length coats in the warehouse. What percentage of 300 does 120 represent? $\frac{120}{300} = \frac{40}{100} =$ 40 percent.

44. A

This is a translation problem. You're told that Janice has B books. Lisa has 40 less than 3 times the number of books Janice has, which you can translate as $L = 3B - 40$.

The total number they have together equals $B + 3B - 40$ or $4B - 40$ which is choice (A).

45. A

You are asked what percent of the new solution is alcohol. The *part* is the number of ounces of alcohol; the *whole* is the total number of ounces of the new solution. There were 25 ounces originally. Then 50 ounces were added, so there are 75 ounces of new solution. How many ounces are alcohol?

20% of the original 25-ounce solution was alcohol. 20% is $\frac{1}{5}$, so $\frac{1}{5}$ of 25, or 5 ounces are alcohol. Now you can find the percent of alcohol in the new solution:

$$\% \text{ alcohol} = \frac{\text{alcohol}}{\text{total solution}} \times 100\%$$

$$= \frac{5}{75} \times 100\%$$

$$= \frac{20}{3} \% = 6 \frac{2}{3} \%$$

46. E

Solving this is just a matter of restating each answer choice as a simple number by multiplying out the powers of 10. To multiply by a positive power of 10, simply move the decimal point to the right the same number of places as the exponent of 10. So to simplify (A), take 0.00001 and move the decimal point 8 places to the right. After 5 places we have 1.0; 3 more places gives us 1,000. We want a number greater than 1,000.01, so we move on. Moving the decimal 4 places to the right in (B) only gives us 101. (C) becomes 110. (D) converts to 1,000.01 exactly. Therefore we know (E) is right without figuring it out (as a matter of fact it converts to 1,000.1).

47. C

The original rectangle was 4 inches by 6 inches. It was lengthened to 10 inches with the width remaining at 4 inches. The perimeter of a rectangle can be found by adding twice the length to twice the width (or by adding up each of the four sides). So the perimeter would be 4 + 10 + 4 + 10 = 28, choice (C).

48. E

It's a good idea to use backsolving for this question. Because the policy pays

80% of the first $1,200 of cost, the patient must pay 20% of $1,200. One-fifth of $1,200 is $240.

Using backsolving, let's try (B). If the procedure cost $1,300, then the patient pays: $240 + 50% of $100; $240 + $50 = $290, which is too small.

We need a larger number, so try (D). If the procedure cost $1,600, then the patient pays: $240 plus 50% of $400, which is $240 + $200, totaling $440—too small. The answer must be (E).

49. A

This question becomes much simpler when you substitute numbers for the variables. For instance, suppose you pick $x = 4$, $n = 2$, $d = 5$. The problem now reads: 4 dollars per mile for the first 2 miles, and 5 dollars a mile for each mile over 2 miles. How much will the mileage charge be for a journey of 5 miles?

That's easily calculated: the first 2 miles cost 2×4 dollars and the remaining 3 miles cost 3×5 dollars for a total cost of $8 + 15$, or 23 dollars. Of the answer choices, only (A) has value 23 when $x = 4$, $n = 2$, and $d = 5$. Without the picking numbers strategy at their disposal, many test takers might be stumped by a question like this one. With the strategy in mind, however, *you* can answer it fairly quickly.

50. C

Let's say the price was originally $100. It increases by 20% of $100 (which is $20), so now the price is $120. The price then increases by 20% of $120 ($\frac{1}{5} \times \$120 = \$24$), which means an increase of $24. So the price is now $144, or 44% more than its original price of $100. The correct answer, therefore, is (C).

CHAPTER SEVEN

Following Directions, Coding, and Memory

Introduction

Reading the title of this chapter may get your imagination running wild. Unlike more standard topics such as math or reading comprehension, these may seem downright bizarre. However, each of these topics: following directions, coding, and memory are in fact crucial elements to many types of civil service exams. In this chapter, you will first review a lesson about following directions, coding, and memory and how these skills apply to your civil service job. Following the lesson are samples of different question types that may be included on the civil service exam. Finally, if you still feel you need extra help to hone these skills, Kaplan provides target strategies for each question type. At the end of this chapter, test how much you have learned by completing Practice Test 5. You can check the results of this 50-question test with the detailed answer explanations that follow.

Following Directions, Coding, and Memory Lesson

These unique skills need to be in top form in order for you to do your best on the civil service exam. You should spend time reviewing these lessons and then familiarizing yourself with the question types and target strategies.

Do not be concerned that these are such short reviews. Essentially, there's not much you can be taught about following directions, coding, or memorizing. Instead, we'll review how each of these skills is used on the job.

Following Directions Review

Following directions sounds easy, right? You simply need to do what you are told to do. The reason this skill is so important is that civil service organizations employ hundreds and even thousands of people. It would certainly diminish efficiency if each one of those employees did everything their own way. In addition, there simply isn't time for managers and supervisors to needlessly repeat their instructions to employees who just aren't paying attention.

When civil service exams include a section on following directions it's to find out if potential employees are keen listeners and quick learners. Employers are also seeking applicants who can adopt new skills without having to explain them over and over again. Even if your civil service exam does not test your ability to follow directions, remember that once you have the job, you need to stay focused, pay attention to what you are told, and do exactly what is asked of you.

Coding Review

It's true that not every civil service job will require you to code documents, files, cases, and other matters. However, for jobs that do require this skill, you really need to be in top form. Coding is a way of classifying or categorizing something. Codes can be names, numbers, letters, or any combination of these. By giving something a code, you are creating a more efficient way of naming, filing, and locating it. One code you may be familiar with already is the Dewey Decimal System, which is used by libraries to sort and shelve books. Without that system, consider how long it would take to organize every single book available.

On the job, especially if you have a clerical position, coding will be very important. You may be responsible for thousands of files or documents. Whether you are coding them yourself, or only filing them in the correct place according to the code, you must be extremely careful. Take a moment to think of the consequences of a file that is placed in the wrong place or a misnamed file. This is why employers need to know exactly what kind of aptitude applicants have for this skill.

Memory Review

Having a strong memory may seem like an odd skill requirement for a civil service job. However, consider this scenario: an investigator visits a scene and two hours later returns to the office to write a report. Notes taken at the scene are helpful, but memories of observations and details will really make the report complete. Law enforcement agents and firefighters must also have keen memories. Think of a firefighter dashing into a burning building he has never been in before. He has to navigate his way in, and more importantly has to remember exactly how to get back out. This is why memory is tested on some civil service exams.

If you want to know more specifically how your memory will be tested, be sure to review the section of memory questions as well as Kaplan's Target Strategy for Memory Questions.

Speed and Accuracy

As was the case with clerical ability questions that were reviewed in Chapter 3, these three topics and their respective questions sometimes include time limits to test your speed and accuracy. This is especially true of coding and memory questions. Like alphabetizing, coding and memorizing information is easy if you have an unlimited amount of time. However, that is not the case. Just as important as your coding and memorization skills is your ability to be fast and accurate. When you are answering these questions, don't allow yourself to be distracted or you will not have time to answer all the questions.

Scoring on Coding and Memory Questions

Knowing that coding and memory sections are timed closely, it's no wonder that they are scored differently than other questions. First, you may not be expected to answer every question within the given time period. To discourage test takers from guessing randomly so that they can answer every single question in a section, a fraction of a point is deducted for any incorrect answers. If you know that a section has a guessing penalty such as this, focus on answer fewer questions correctly rather than answering every question by whatever means you can.

Now let's review the different kinds of questions.

Sample Following Directions, Coding, and Memory Questions

Because there are several types of civil service exams, you should be aware that there are several different formats these questions can take. This part of the chapter will review the six question types most commonly found on civil service exams. However, you should know that Practice Test 5 as well as any civil service exam you take may present these questions in a slightly different format.

When you are ready, start by reviewing the different types of following directions questions.

Following Directions Questions

The two main types of following directions questions are:

1. Oral directions
2. Written directions

We will review each of these types now.

Type 1: Oral Directions Questions. Following oral directions is another way of saying *listening skills*. This is because no part of the actual question is written in your textbook. Instead, the person administering your exam will read some directions aloud. Only the answer choices, and occasionally some figures, shapes, numbers, or words are found in your test booklet. Even the instructions for answering these questions are read aloud. The instructions for this section are similar to the following:

"I will now read some directions. Follow these directions exactly and do exactly what I say. Directions will only be said once and will not be repeated for any reason. Listen carefully and follow these directions exactly."

When the section begins, you will listen to some information that is read aloud. After reading the directions, speakers will pause briefly and during this time you should mark your answer.

Here is a sample following oral directions question.

In your test booklet, you will see five different digital clocks labeled (A) through (E) showing the time. For question 1, mark which clock shows the latest time of the day.

[PAUSE]

Test Booklet

5:35 P.M.   6:49 P.M.   8:13 P.M.   4:56 P.M.   9:51 A.M.

(A)   (B)   (C)   (D)   (E)

Answer Sheet
(A)
(B)
(C)
(D)
✓(E)

In this case, the answer is (C); 8:13 P.M. is the latest time of day shown on the five clocks. Perhaps you think this question is easy, but remember that you will not be able to read any of the text that is in bold. You also need to pay close attention that choice (E) shows a time of the morning. If it were P.M., then choice (E) would be correct.

These questions are trickier than they seem. To get the most out of this practice you should have a friend or study partner read the directions to you so that you can actually practice listening, not just reading. If you don't practice listening to these directions before test day, you could easily freeze up when you are trying to answer these questions on the official exam.

Be sure to take the time to review Kaplan's Target Strategy for Oral Directions Questions and apply what you learn when you take Practice Test 5 at the end of this chapter.

Type 2: Written Directions Questions.   Following written directions is somewhat similar to reading comprehension questions that were covered in Chapter 4. You will have to read some directions, usually a set of 4 or 5 rules, and you will have to use those rules to answer the questions that follow. Here is an example of a set of rules that is more brief and less detailed than one found on the test, but it will give you an idea of how these questions work.

There are four combinations of numbers used to code files: 001, 004, 066, 003. Here are the rules for determining which set of numbers should be used when coding files.

1. Files that contain time-sensitive documents should be coded 001.
2. Files that are dated prior to 2004 should be coded 004.
3. Files that contain personal information should be coded 066.
4. Files that are dated January 1, 2006 through June 2006 that are not time-sensitive should be coded 003.

What code would be used for a time-sensitive file dated May 31, 2006?

(A) 001
(B) 004
(C) 066
(D) 003

The correct answer is (A). Although the date of the files falls under the one explained in rule 4, it says that rule does not apply to files that are not time sensitive. Time-sensitive documents regardless of date should be coded 001 according to rule 1.

Avoiding Errors on Your Answer Sheet

You need to be careful when you are working that you enter your answer exactly where you are supposed to. This is especially true for following oral directions questions where no question appears in your test booklet. Make whatever marks you are permitted to in the test booklet and then transfer your answers to the answer sheet. Marking answers on the wrong line can ruin your score. Be very careful you are filling in the answer sheet correctly.

Now you can start a review of coding questions.

Coding Questions

There are also two types of coding questions:

1. Postal coding
2. Standard coding

We will review each of these separately.

Type 1: Postal Coding Questions.   Although these particular questions are specific to the Postal Worker Exam, understanding how they work will help you with other coding questions on other civil service exams. Here's how these questions are set up.

First, you are given a coding guide that looks similar to the following:

CODING GUIDE

Address Range	Delivery Route
201–400 Grinnell Drive 11–1000 Sunset Canyon Road 55–99 2nd Ave. North	A
401–600 Grinnell Drive 100–154 2nd Ave. North	B
12000–14000 Sallo Lane 20–70 Rural Route 2	C
Any mail that is not deliverable to one of the above address ranges	D

The instructions tell you to use the Coding Guide to determine the correct Delivery Route code (A, B, C, or D) for each address you are given. Here is what a postal coding question looks like.

499 Grinnell Drive

   (A)
   (B)
   (C)
   (D)

KAPLAN

One of the most difficult things about the coding is the time limit. You will probably only have about 20 seconds total to answer each question so you need to work quickly, but don't sacrifice your accuracy.

By looking at the Coding Guide, you should be able to determine that 499 Grinnell Drive is in Delivery Route B. Therefore, the correct answer is (B).

Don't disregard these question types even if you have no desire to be a postal worker. The way these questions are written is similar to other coding questions that we will review now.

Type 2: Standard Coding Questions.   Because coding can be a vital skill in several civil service professions, it's not just found on the Postal Worker Exam. In fact, many clerical exams have coding questions that do not pertain simply to addresses and delivery routes. They are, in fact, much more detailed and thus, more difficult. On top of this, you should still expect to have strict time limits to complete these questions.

Coding questions begin with a brief paragraph explaining how the code works and what it is meant to show. The explanation is followed by the actual code. This may appear as a table or chart, or it may just be a long list of codes. The questions ask you what the code would be for a specific situation. Let's take a look at a sample coding question.

Your task is to assign codes to currently blank files. Each code is comprised of a two-letter code, followed by a one-number code, followed by a two-letter code. The codes are found in the table below. The first two letters indicate the year the file was created, the one number shows the name of the person who originated the file, and the other two-letter code shows to which department the files belong.

CODES

Year	Originator	Department
AB—2002	1—Mary Wilson	HR—Human Resources
BC—2003	2—Greg Turnbul	FN—Finance
CD—2004	3—Mei Ling	AD—Administration
DE—2005	4—Luis Gomez	MK—Marketing

What code would be used for a Marketing file created by Mei Ling in 2004?
    (A) MK3FN
  ✓(B) MK3CD
    (C) CD3FN
  ✗(D) CD3MK

According to the coding system, the code CD3MK should be used for the file. Therefore, choice (D) is correct. If you found this question easy, that's because the sample system is relatively basic. Don't think that you won't need to do further preparation before test day—these questions actually require a lot of practice. Be sure to review Kaplan's Target Strategy for Standard Coding Questions as well as the coding questions in Practice Test 5.

For now, let's move on to memory questions.

Memory Questions

As the question name implies, these questions test your memory. The type of information may vary, but your task is always to remember as many details as you can.

There are two types of memory questions:

1. Visual questions
2. Textual questions

At the most essential level, these are the same, but we will review some of their differences here.

Type 1: Visual Memory Questions.   Visual memory questions are fairly self-explanatory. Either on its own page in your test booklet or in a separate "memory book" that is handed out during the exam, a graphical element will be presented. This could be a photograph of a scene, a drawing of a scene or of various people, or some other graphical depiction such as a chart or table. For simplicity, we will refer to any of these as a "picture." Typically, you will have five minutes to study the picture and to commit to memory as many details about what you see as possible. You will not be allowed to take notes or do any writing or drawing of any kind. The only help you will have to remember is your own brain. At the end of five minutes—or however long you are given to study—you must turn the page or return your "memory book" to the exam proctors. From this point on, you will not be allowed to look at the picture again. Next, you will be instructed to open your test booklet to the questions pertaining to what you just saw.

Here is a sample picture and question.

CODING GUIDE

Address Range	Delivery Route
779–2214 Lysander Dr 261–785 E 44th St 1100–1990 Finley Ave	A
1630–2301 W Olive 22090–30020 Clinton Pkwy	B
1956–2500 Griffith Park 250–700 E Rockland Hwy 99–215 Rural Route 5	C
Any mail that is not deliverable to one of the above address ranges	D

695 E Rockland Hwy

    (A)

    (B)

    (C)

    (D)

In this case, the correct answer is (C). Rather than worrying about the correct answer, you're probably more focused on the fact that this question looks identical to the postal coding question. It's true, this memory question is a variation on the postal coding question. The biggest, and certainly the most important difference, is that the Coding Guide will not be visible as you answer memory questions. You will instead have to memorize everything from the guide in five minutes and then answer questions. This not only makes these questions different from coding questions, it certainly makes them more difficult.

Type 2: Textual Memory Questions.   The biggest difference between visual and textual memory questions is quite obvious. Instead of studying a picture, you will have to memorize some type of writing. This may be a "story" or this may be a list of rules, or some other type of written report. You need to figure out which details are most important—again, without taking notes of any kind—and commit them to memory usually in about five minutes.

Here's a sample textual memory question. If you really want to start your practice, give yourself only two minutes to memorize as much as you can from this story. Then cover up the story—no cheating—and try to answer the practice question.

When I went to the store last week on Friday, I went to buy eggs, milk, a loaf of bread, bran cereal, and 6 bananas. When I got home I realized that I completely forgot to buy bananas but I had bought apples, which weren't on my shopping list. I decided to wait until Saturday to go back to the store to buy the bananas. That was lucky because when I went back to buy them, the bananas were on sale for 19 cents per pound. I would have paid exactly twice as much if I had bought them on Friday.

How much did bananas cost per pound on Friday?
  (A) 19 cents per pound
  (B) 6 cents per pound
  (C) 29 cents per pound
  (D) 38 cents per pound

If you look back at the story, the last line states that on Friday, bananas cost twice as much as they did on Saturday and on Saturday they were 19 cents per pound. Therefore, on Friday they cost 38 cents per pound and choice (D) is the correct answer.

Maybe you didn't have any trouble answering this question, but remember, on test day you will have absolutely no opportunity to refer back to the text that you must memorize. Also, on the actual exam you typically will have five minutes to memorize, however, the story will be much longer than the one used here.

Time Limits on Memory Questions

When you are given either a picture, chart, or text to memorize, you need to be aware of exactly how much time you have. The memorization time is strictly regulated. For example, even if the information is found in your test booklet, you will still be required to turn the page and not look back once the time is up. This rule is taken very seriously on test day. When time is called DO NOT flip back and steal glances at the information. This is as serious as any other kind of cheating. If you are caught, you will be ejected from the test room and any score you may have earned will be disqualified. It's also possible that the so-called "memory books"—books containing the information to be memorized—will be collected once time is up, preventing everyone from cheating. Either way, know exactly how much time you will have and pace yourself accordingly. To learn strategies for answering this question type, refer to Tips for Following Directions, Coding, and Memory Success.

Difficulty Level

Please note that the difficulty of questions on the civil service exam you take will depend on the type of job you are applying for. The practice test found at the end of this chapter includes following directions, coding, and memory questions at intermediate and more challenging levels so that you are prepared for whatever civil service exam you face on test day.

Tips for Following Directions, Coding, and Memory Success

You may have noticed that these question types are quite specific and are really meant to challenge you. To help you do your best, we have Kaplan Target Strategies for each question type. Review these strategies and be sure to use them when answering the questions on Practice Test 5.

Kaplan's Target Strategy for Oral Directions Questions

Here is Kaplan's Target Strategy for oral directions questions.

Step 1. Listen carefully, but don't close your eyes.
Step 2. Make brief notes while you listen, but don't distract yourself trying to write everything down.
Step 3. Pay careful attention to any graphics in the test booklet.
Step 4. Mark your answer and move on.

Let's review each of these steps in detail while we apply them to the following question.

In your test booklet, you will see five different digital clocks labeled (A) through (E) showing the time. For question 1, mark which clock shows the latest time of the day.

[PAUSE]

Test Booklet

5:35 P.M.	6:49 P.M.	8:13 P.M.	4:56 P.M.	9:51 A.M.
(A)	(B)	(C)	(D)	(E)

Answer Sheet

(A)
(B)
(C)
(D)
√(E)

Step 1. Listen Carefully, but Don't Close Your Eyes.   To keep their minds focused and to try to hear every word that is spoken, many people are tempted to close their eyes while listening to the directions. That would be a grave mistake. In the sample question in which you have to refer to the graphics test booklet, this would be disastrous. Many oral directions questions have you looking at things in your test booklet so listen carefully, but keep your eyes open.

Step 2. Make Brief Notes While You Listen, but Don't Distract Yourself Trying to Write Everything Down.   Unlike memory questions, you can take notes on the information presented to you. In the previous question, the only note you should make is "LATEST." The rest of the instructions is informative, but not crucial to selecting the correct answer. Do not try to write down everything you hear. You will only distract yourself from paying attention to the directions. Remember, you are being tested on how well you can follow directions, *not* on your note-taking skills.

Step 3. Pay Careful Attention to Any Graphics in the Test Booklet.   Test takers who struggle with their listening skills will be eager to have anything in the test booklet to look at. However, don't just jump at the first answer you think *looks* correct. You have to be just as careful reviewing this information as you do listening to the instructions. For example, in this question, you might have seen 9:51 and thought that is definitely later than 4:56, 5:35, 6:49, and 8:13. However, if you failed to notice the A.M. not the P.M. that is written after the number, you would have just missed earning another point to your score.

Step 4. Mark Your Answer and Move On.   Remember that the oral directions will only be read once. Exam administrators will not repeat the directions for any reason. Therefore, there's no reason to delay marking your answer and preparing yourself to listen carefully to the next set of directions.

Now let's see how the strategy changes for written directions.

Kaplan's Target Strategy for Written Directions Questions

There are four steps to this strategy. These are:

Step 1. Read the information carefully, marking important details as you do.
Step 2. Don't look at the questions until you have studied the directions.
Step 3. Check your answer against the information provided.
Step 4. Mark your answer and move on.

Now let's review these steps as we review a written directions question found earlier in this chapter.

There are four combinations of numbers used to code files: 001, 004, 066, 003. Here are the rules for determining which set of numbers should be used when coding files.

1. Files that contain time-sensitive documents should be coded 001.
2. Files that are dated prior to 2004 should be coded 004.
3. Files that contain personal information should be coded 066.
4. Files that are dated January 1, 2006 through June 2006 that are not time-sensitive should be coded 003.

What code would be used for a time-sensitive file dated May 31, 2006?
  (A) 001
  (B) 004
  (C) 066
  ✓(D) 003

Step 1. Read the Information Carefully, Marking Important Details as You Do. As you read the explanatory paragraph and the numbered rules, you should make notes. For example, after reading through the information, you may have made notes such as these:

001 = time-sensitive docs
004 = pre-2004
066 = personal
✓003 = 2006, NOT time sensitive

This means that all the written directions have been simplified—while remaining accurate—into a few brief notes you can use to answer questions.

Step 2. Don't Look at the Questions Until You Have Studied the Directions. You may be tempted to look over the questions even before you have reviewed the directions. Don't. You have to know the directions first before you can start to answer the questions correctly. If you start right in with the questions and attempt to apply them to the directions, you will lose valuable time.

Step 3. Check Your Answer against the Information Provided. In a way, following written directions questions are similar to reading comprehension questions. The answers are right there in the written directions, you just have to find them. Don't make assumptions when you can easily check your answers. In the previous question, if you didn't go back and note that the question says "time sensitive" then you might have incorrectly coded it as 003 based simply on the date. Don't miss out on points by assuming you have the correct answer.

Step 4. Mark Your Answer and Move On.   Although following written directions questions are not tightly timed, you shouldn't slack off. You should be answering at least two questions per minute. When you think or know you have the correct answer, mark it and move on.

Now let's review some strategies for coding questions.

Kaplan's Target Strategy for Postal Coding Questions

This is Kaplan's Target Strategy for postal coding questions.

Step 1. Memorize the answer choices.
Step 2. Take a moment to review the Coding Guide, but ignore Box D.
Step 3. Know the differences that make an address fall into route D.
Step 4. Keep pace and don't spend too much time on any question.

To make sure you know how to put these steps into practice, let's review them along with this question found earlier in the chapter.

CODING GUIDE

Address Range	Delivery Route
201–400 Grinnell Drive 11–1000 Sunset Canyon Road 55–99 2nd Ave. North	A
401–600 Grinnell Drive 100–154 2nd Ave. North	B
12000–14000 Sallo Lane 20–70 Rural Route 2	C
Any mail that is not deliverable to one of the above address ranges	D

The instructions tell you to use the Coding Guide to determine the correct Delivery Route code (A, B, C, or D) for each address you are given. Here is what a postal coding question looks like.

499 Grinnell Drive

(A)
✓(B)
(C)
(D)

Step 1. Memorize the Answer Choices.   For postal coding questions, your first piece of good luck is that the answer choices are always the same. There are four delivery routes: A, B, C, and D. There also are four corresponding answer choices: A, B, C, and D. Don't bother thinking, just know that the answer choices are always the same.

Step 2. Take a Moment to Review the Coding Guide, But Ignore Route D.   Don't spend too much time studying the Coding Guide. Your time is limited so you need to get started on the questions right away. Most importantly, you should completely ignore the left column for Route D. There are no address ranges listed here so you needn't worry about what it does say. Essentially, you need to focus on the address ranges you are given. Also, you shouldn't try to memorize the information in the chart. Remember, you can refer back to it throughout this section of the exam so there's no harm in making sure your answer is correct based on the chart, not just your memory.

Step 3. Know the Differences That Make an Address Fall into Route D.   Fortunately, there's only three elements of the address that can result in a question being coded for delivery route D. Either the address number, the street name, or the street type (e.g., Blvd., Street, Ave., etc.) is different. You don't have to identify which element is different, you only have to know that if one is different, you should mark (D) immediately and turn your attention to the next question.

Step 4. Keep Pace and Don't Spend Too Much Time on Any Question.   On the Postal Worker Exam, you will have only 6 minutes to answer as many of the 36 questions as you can. It's not likely that you will be able to answer 6 questions per minute and complete them all, but you should work quickly and carefully. Try to answer at least 3 questions per minute (that's one every 20 seconds) but do not sacrifice accuracy. You don't want to lose fractions of points for incorrect answers. Once you have determined what you believe to be the correct answer, mark it and move on.

Kaplan's Target Strategy for Standard Coding Questions
This strategy has four steps. These are:

Step 1. Simplify the paragraph and study the code.
Step 2. Mark the order of the information in the question.
Step 3. Apply the corresponding code.
Step 4. Don't waste time second-guessing your answers.

Let's apply these steps to this question found earlier in the chapter.

Your task is to assign codes to currently blank files. Each code is comprised of a two-letter code, followed by a one-number code, followed by a two-letter code. The codes are found in the table below. The first two letters indicate the year the file was created, the one number shows the name of the person who originated the file, and the other two-letter code shows to which department the files belong.

CODES

Year	Originator	Department
AB—2002	1—Mary Wilson	HR—Human Resources
BC—2003	2—Greg Turnbul	FN—Finance
CD—2004	3—Mei Ling	AD—Administration
DE—2005	4—Luis Gomez	MK—Marketing

What code would be used for a Marketing file created by Mei Ling in 2004?

   (A) MK3FN

   (B) MK3CD

   (C) CD3FN

 ✓(D) CD3MK

Step 1. Simplify the Paragraph and Study the Code.   Although the leading paragraph or prompt is important, you might also note that it repeats much of the information found in the table. For example, that the year is a 2-letter code, that the originator is a 1-number code, and that the department is a 2-letter code. You should skim (remember Chapter 4?) the paragraph, but you should really pay attention to the codes in the table. Those are what you will need to answer each question.

Step 2. Mark the Order of the Information in the Question.   Let's take a closer look at the sample question. It reads: What code would be used for a Marketing file created by Mei Ling in 2004? In the question it tells you the department first, the originator second, and the year last. However, the code is always: YEAR; ORIGINATOR; DEPARTMENT. To make sure that you code this information correctly, consider marking up the question like this:

                                 3   2   1

What code would be used for a Marketing file created by Mei Ling in 2004?

This way you know to code the year first, the originator second, and the department last.

Step 3. Apply the Corresponding Code.   Now that you know you have to code the file in question in that order, go through and apply the code. In this case, the correct answer is CD3MK, which is choice (D).

Step 4. Don't Waste Time Second-Guessing Your Answers.   Most coding questions are strictly timed. You may not even have enough time to answer every question. Try to be accurate the first time. When you mark your answer, don't let doubt creep in. Be confident in your answer and move on.

Let's move on to the last question type, memory questions.

Kaplan's Target Strategy for Memory Questions

Since both visual and textual questions ultimately test your memory skills, we've created a single strategy for use with either question.

Step 1. Focus on one element at a time during the study period.
Step 2. Use any memorization techniques you can.
Step 3. Take the questions one at a time.
Step 4. Be confident about your answer and move on to the next.

Let's take another look at the visual and textual memory questions found earlier in the chapter.

Visual Question.

CODING GUIDE

Address Range	Delivery Route
779–2214 Lysander Dr 261–785 E 44th St 1100–1990 Finley Ave	A
1630–2301 W Olive 22090–30020 Clinton Pkwy	B
1956–2500 Griffith Park 250–700 E Rockland Hwy 99–215 Rural Route 5	C
Any mail that is not deliverable to one of the above address ranges	D

695 E Rockland Hwy
   (A)
   (B)
 √(C)
   (D)

Textual Question.

When I went to the store last week on Friday, I went to buy eggs, milk, a loaf of bread, bran cereal, and 6 bananas. When I got home I realized that I completely forgot to buy bananas but I had bought apples, which weren't on my shopping list. I decided to wait until Saturday to go back to the store to buy the bananas. That was lucky because when I went back to buy them, the bananas were on sale for 19 cents per pound. I would have paid exactly twice as much if I had bought them on Friday.

How much did bananas cost per pound on Friday?
   (A) 19 cents per pound
   (B) 6 cents per pound
   (C) 29 cents per pound
   (D) 38 cents per pound

Step 1. Focus on One Element at a Time during the Study Period.   Especially if you are presented with a photograph or drawing, you may be tempted to view the entire thing at once. However, you are not there to judge the quality of the picture, you are there to notice and memorize as many details you can. If it helps mentally divide the picture into 4 parts, like this:

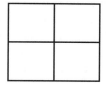

Look at each quarter separately. By breaking down a large element into smaller ones, your task won't be so overwhelming and you can focus on different details as you go. In the case of the sample question, the segments are already divided for you. You can study the information in each box helping you see the big picture.

For textual questions, try to break down the story into paragraphs, events, or even separate sentences. You should read the whole story, but don't try to memorize it from beginning to end right away. Work on it in smaller chunks and you will be much more likely to retain more details.

Step 2. Use Any Memorization Techniques You Can.   Since you can't take notes of any kind while studying the "memory book," you need to do the next best thing—use your brain. Here are a few of the memorization techniques you might want to use.

Visualization.   Ironically, this technique is less effective when your task is to study a picture. With visualization, you apply a mental picture to a word. In the case of the Coding Guide in the sample visual question, the street name "W Olive" may lead you to picture a bowlful of olives—1630–2301 of them to be exact. It may not be the most logical visualization, but anything that helps your mind hold on to facts is helpful.

Mnemonics.   A mnemonic is simply a memory device, but in this case a mnemonic could be a way to shorten the information to make it more memorable. For example, the shopping list in the story is: eggs, milk, bread, cereal, bananas. Maybe you think of a breakfast menu of French toast (eggs, bread) and cereal with fruit (cereal, milk, bananas). Another mnemonic would be to take the first letter of each of the items: e, m, b, c, b. You could come up with the rhyme "ME B.B.C." to remember these five items. The idea is to create something memorable so that when study time is over, you will have no problem answering the questions.

Associations.   Associations work like this: instead of trying to remember everything, you can make associations between the information you see and things relevant to your own life. For example, to remember that Griffith Park is on Route C, you might remember (or can imagine) you had a teacher named Mrs. Griffith who gave you a C on you exam. It doesn't matter how silly or crazy the association is, as long as it helps you remember the information, it's helpful.

Step 3. Take the Questions One at a Time.   When the study time is over and you are allowed to open your test booklet, it can be tempting to start reading through all the questions and to see how much you remember. That would be a mistake. By trying to review even more material, you are likely to confuse the details of what you memorized with what you read in a question. Instead, read one question at a time and don't worry about what the next one will be.

Step 4. Be Confident About Your Answer and Move on to the Next.   Without the picture or story in front of you, it's very easy to second-guess your answers. Resist this temptation. When you have answered a question, be confident that it is correct and move on.

Summary

In this chapter you have learned about three very different skills that are tested on some civil service exams. You know the kinds of skills that are expected of you as well as the different question types you may be facing on test day. Go back and review the lessons and the Kaplan Target Strategies often so that they become second nature to you before test day. To practice answering these question and to improve your skills take the 50-question practice test that follows. Using all the tips and strategies you have just learned, answer these questions. When you have finished, be sure to review the detailed answer explanations for any questions you miss.

Practice Test 5

1 (A) (B) (C) (D) (E)   14 (A) (B) (C) (D)   27 (A) (B) (C) (D)   40 (A) (B) (C) (D)

2 (A) (B) (C) (D) (E)   15 (A) (B) (C) (D)   28 (A) (B) (C) (D)   41 (A) (B) (C) (D)

3 (A) (B) (C) (D) (E)   16 (A) (B) (C) (D)   29 (A) (B) (C) (D)   42 (A) (B) (C) (D)

4 (A) (B) (C) (D) (E)   17 (A) (B) (C) (D)   30 (A) (B) (C) (D)   43 (A) (B) (C) (D)

5 (A) (B) (C) (D) (E)   18 (A) (B) (C) (D)   31 (A) (B) (C) (D) (E)   44 (A) (B) (C) (D)

6 (A) (B) (C) (D)   19 (A) (B) (C) (D)   32 (A) (B) (C) (D) (E)   45 (A) (B) (C) (D)

7 (A) (B) (C) (D)   20 (A) (B) (C) (D)   33 (A) (B) (C) (D) (E)   46 (A) (B) (C) (D)

8 (A) (B) (C) (D)   21 (A) (B) (C) (D)   34 (A) (B) (C) (D) (E)   47 (A) (B) (C) (D)

9 (A) (B) (C) (D)   22 (A) (B) (C) (D)   35 (A) (B) (C) (D) (E)   48 (A) (B) (C) (D)

10 (A) (B) (C) (D)   23 (A) (B) (C) (D)   36 (A) (B) (C) (D)   49 (A) (B) (C) (D)

11 (A) (B) (C) (D)   24 (A) (B) (C) (D)   37 (A) (B) (C) (D)   50 (A) (B) (C) (D)

12 (A) (B) (C) (D)   25 (A) (B) (C) (D)   38 (A) (B) (C) (D)

13 (A) (B) (C) (D)   26 (A) (B) (C) (D)   39 (A) (B) (C) (D)

Directions for questions 1–5: *To simulate the actual test, do not simply read the directions (in bold) for these questions. Have a friend or study partner read them aloud and do your best to answer them just by listening.*

In your test booklet you will see 5 different numbers, marked (A) through (E). For question 1, mark the letter of the corresponding number that is closest to 437, but not greater than 519.

[PAUSE]

1.
     (A) 458
     (B) 519
     (C) 491
     (D) 468
     (E) 453

If 2 dozen is the same as 24, mark (C) for question 2 and (E) for question 3. If 2 dozen is not the same as 24, mark (A) for number 2 and (B) for number 3.

[PAUSE]

2.

   (A)
   (B)
   (C)
   (D)
   (E)

3.

   (A)
   (B)
   (C)
   (D)
   (E)

In your test booklet you will see five different shapes. For question 4, if the square is to the right of the circle, mark (D). If it is not to the right of the circle, mark (A).

[PAUSE]

4.

   (A)
   (B)
   (C)
   (D)
   (E)

Look again at the five different shapes. For question 5, if the larger triangle is to the right of the smaller triangle and the rectangle is to the left of the circle, mark (B). If the larger triangle is to the left of the smaller triangle and the square is in the middle mark (C).

[PAUSE]

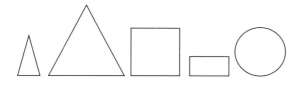

5.

   (A)
   (B)
   (C)
   (D)
   (E)

Directions for questions 6–35: *Choose the best answer to each question.*

There are 4 colors used to code files: red, blue, green, and orange. Here are the rules for determining which color should be used when coding files.

1. Red files should contain only documents relating to financial matters such as receipts and invoices.
2. Blue files should contain only documents that relate to nonfinancial matters from the year 1999 through 2006.
3. Green files should contain only documents that relate to summer session, May through August of 2007.
4. Orange files should contain only documents that relate to nonfinancial matters from the year 1980 through 1998.
5. Red files should contain all bank statements pertaining to the department regardless of date.

COLORS
(A) RED
(B) BLUE
(C) GREEN
(D) ORANGE

6. What color file would be used for a memo dated 1998?
(A) RED
(B) BLUE
(C) GREEN
(D) ORANGE

7. What color file would be used for a document relating to June 2007?
(A) RED
(B) BLUE
(C) GREEN
(D) ORANGE

8. What color file would be used for a signed invoice dated 1984?
(A) RED
(B) BLUE
(C) GREEN
(D) ORANGE

9. What color file would be used for bank statements from 1991?
(A) RED
(B) BLUE
(C) GREEN
(D) ORANGE

10. What color file would be used for a business letter dated 2005?
(A) RED
(B) BLUE
(C) GREEN
(D) ORANGE

There are four locations for storing office documents. Here are the rules for determining where items should be stored.

1. Desktop filing cabinets are only for personal and confidential files.
2. Central filing cabinets are only for general files relating to office business.
3. Off-site storage is for items larger than 1 square foot that are replaceable.
4. Fireproof storage is reserved for irreplaceable items such as original works of art or historical documents.
5. Off-site storage is for general files that are dated prior to but not including 1996.

LOCATIONS
(A) Desktop Filing Cabinets
(B) Central Filing Cabinets
(C) Off-site Storage
(D) Fireproof Storage

11. In what location should an old, unused conference table be stored?
(A) Desktop Filing Cabinets
(B) Central Filing Cabinets
(C) Off-site Storage
(D) Fireproof Storage

12. In what location should a one-of-a-kind painting be stored?
(A) Desktop Filing Cabinets
(B) Central Filing Cabinets
(C) Off-site Storage
(D) Fireproof Storage

13. In what location should a file full of general memos from 1996 be stored?
(A) Desktop Filing Cabinets
(B) Central Filing Cabinets
(C) Off-site Storage
(D) Fireproof Storage

14. In what location should a business letter dated December 31, 1995 be stored?
(A) Desktop Filing Cabinets
(B) Central Filing Cabinets
(C) Off-site Storage
(D) Fireproof Storage

15. In what location should a copy of your birth certificate be stored?
(A) Desktop Filing Cabinets
(B) Central Filing Cabinets
(C) Off-site Storage
(D) Fireproof Storage

CODING GUIDE

Address Range	Delivery Route
200–499 S Bel Air Drive 12–178 N 122nd Street 489–671 Delaware	A
300–601 Walnut Lane 78–120 Chandler Blvd NE	B
78000–80000 Ridge Road 600–629 Fairbanks Ave 221–243 Rural Route 1	C
Any mail that is not deliverable to one of the above address ranges	D

16. 626 Fairbanks Ave
    (A)
    (B)
    (C)
    (D)

17. 77 Chandler Blvd NE
    (A)
    (B)
    (C)
    (D)

18. 601 Walnut Lane
    (A)
    (B)
    (C)
    (D)

19. 119 Chandler Blve NE
    (A)
    (B)
    (C)
    (D)

20. 14 N 122nd Street
    (A)
    (B)
    (C)
    (D)

21. 79010 Ridge Road
    (A)
    (B)
    (C)
    (D)

22. 222 Rural Route 1
    (A)
    (B)
    (C)
    (D)

23. 490 Delaware
    (A)
    (B)
    (C)
    (D)

24. 681 Delaware
    (A)
    (B)
    (C)
    (D)

25. 619 Fairbanks Ave
    (A)
    (B)
    (C)
    (D)

Your task is to assign codes to currently blank files. Each code is comprised of a two-number code, followed by a two-letter code, followed by a two-number code. The codes are found in the table below. The first two numbers indicate the location of the file, the two letters indicate to which department the files belong, and the final two numbers indicate the type of file it is.

CODES

File Location	Department	File Type
18—front office filing cabinets	HR—Human Resources	09—invoices
22—archives	FN—Finance	87—memos
13—central office filing cabinets	AD—Administration	54—applications
05—3rd floor filing cabinets	MK—Marketing	33—brochures

26. What code would be used for a file of invoices belonging to Finance and stored on the 3rd floor?
(A) 09FN05
(B) 05FN09
(C) 18FN54
(D) 13FN09

27. What code would be used for a file belonging to Administration containing memos to be stored in archives?
(A) 22AD87
(B) 22HR87
(C) 22AD54
(D) 22AD33

28. What code would be used for a file to be stored in the front office, used by Marketing, and containing brochures?
(A) 13MK33
(B) 33MK13
(C) 18MK09
(D) 18MK33

29. What code would be used for a file of applications stored in the central office for use by the Human Resources department?
(A) 13HR87
(B) 13AD54
(C) 13HR54
(D) 54HR13

30. What code would be used for a file stored on the 3rd floor, filled with memos for the Marketing department?
(A) 03MK87
(B) 05FN87
(C) 18FN87
(D) 05MK87

Every theft reported to an adjuster needs to be assigned a six-letter code containing the following:

First letter: **Type of Theft**
Second letter: **Location**
Third letter: **Time of Theft**
Fourth letter: **Witnesses**
Fifth letter: **Time Elapsed between Theft and Report**
Sixth letter: **Value of Stolen Item**

Here are the letters associated with each element of the six-letter code:

Type of Theft
A. Breaking and entering
B. Armed robbery
C. Car theft
D. Shoplifting

Location
A. Private home
B. Apartment building/complex
C. Store
D. Office
E. Car
F. Public space (parking garage, park, etc)

Time of Theft
A. 7 A.M.–1 P.M.
B. 1 P.M.–6 P.M.
C. 6 P.M.–11 P.M.
D. 11 P.M.–3 A.M.
E. 3 A.M.–7 A.M.

Witnesses
A. none
B. only one person
C. more than one person
D. security camera

Time Elapsed between Theft and Report
A. 0 and 1 hour
B. 1 and 4 hours
C. 4 and 12 hours
D. 12 and 24 hours
E. More than 24 hours

Value of Stolen Item
A. 0 and 100 dollars
B. 101 and 250 dollars
C. 251 and 500 dollars
D. 500 and 1,000 dollars
E. 1,001 and 5,000 dollars
F. More than 5,000 dollars

31. At 8:35 P.M., approximately 130 dollars worth of clothing was shoplifted from a store. The crime was reported immediately by the lone witness of the crime. The correct code is:
(A) DCCABB
(B) ACCAAB
(C) ACCBAB
(D) DCCBAB
(E) None of the above.

32. A car worth $3,700 dollars was stolen from a parking garage at approximately 4 A.M. last night. It was reported stolen at 10:10 A.M. this morning by the owner. There were no witnesses. The correct code is:
(A) CFEACE
(B) CFECAE
(C) CFDDBE
(D) CFECEA
(E) None of the above.

33. Although it was just reported, the breaking and entering occurred 2 days ago at approximately midnight, according to security cameras that recorded the incident at the attorney's office. Although the doors and locks were damaged, nothing was stolen. The correct code is:
(A) ADDEEA
(B) ADDDAE
(C) ADEADE
(D) AEDACF
(E) None of the above.

34. Mrs. Dubenko was held at gunpoint this morning at 9 A.M. when she was just walking out of her apartment complex. The thief asked for her money and she handed over approximately 75 dollars. She was the only witness and reported the crime immediately. The correct code is:
(A) BBABAB
(B) BBABAA
(C) BBBABB
(D) ABBBAA
(E) None of the above.

35. A painting worth $8,000 was stolen from the home of Judy Chadwick this afternoon while she was out to lunch from 2 P.M. until 4 P.M. When she realized the painting was missing at 6 P.M., she immediately called police. There are no witnesses. The correct code is:
(A) AABBAF
(B) AABFAF
(C) AABABF
(D) AAABCF
(E) None of the above.

Directions for questions 36–40: Study and memorize this chart for five minutes. When five minutes have passed, turn the page and answer the questions. You may NOT take notes on what you read here and you may NOT refer back to the Coding Guide while you are answering the questions.

CODING GUIDE

Address Range	Delivery Route
200–499 S Bel Air Drive 12–178 N 122nd Street 489–671 Delaware	A
300–601 Walnut Lane 78–120 Chandler Blvd NE	B
78000–80000 Ridge Road 600–629 Fairbanks Ave 221–243 Rural Route 1	C
Any mail that is not deliverable to one of the above address ranges	D

Questions on the following page.

36. 599 Walnut Lane

(A)

(B)

(C)

(D)

37. 80 Chandler Blvd NE

(A)

(B)

(C)

(D)

38. 142 N 122nd Street

(A)

(B)

(C)

(D)

39. 691 Delaware

(A)

(B)

(C)

(D)

40. 607 Fairbanks Ave

(A)

(B)

(C)

(D)

Directions for questions 41–45: Study and memorize these rules for five minutes. When five minutes have passed, turn the page and answer the questions. You may NOT take notes on what you read here and you may NOT refer back to these rules while you are answering the questions.

Every employee who is hired between January 1, 2006 and March 15, 2007 will have to understand and implement the following rules pertaining to office administration.

1. All calls received pertaining to accounts payable should be transferred immediately to Don Hillings at extension 2034 by pressing #2304#. If Don is not able to answer, the call will be picked up by voice mail.
2. All filing cabinets found in room 204 must remain locked at all times. This is a secure area. Each employee has his or her own code to enter the room. The code is the same as the last 4 digits of your Social Security number. Keys to the filing cabinets themselves are kept with Gail Bui. If she is unavailable, contact Herman Kingston at extension 2144.
3. When you require an outside extension to dial a number not within the office, you must pick up the receiver, press 9#24, wait for the dial tone, and then enter the ten-digit number you are trying to reach. Any calls made beyond the 619 area code require an additional security code to be entered at the prompt. The security code is 2403.
4. Request for office supplies must be made in writing. Use form number 03-TD6 for this purpose. The form must be filled out completely, including the abbreviation for this department, which is ADMIN-09. Completed forms should be submitted to Lin Chen at office 306.

41. If Gail Bui is not available, what extension should you dial?
(A) 2034
(B) 2403
(C) 2144
(D) 2306

42. Who is in charge of accounts payable?
(A) Don Hillings
(B) Lin Chen
(C) Herman Kingston
(D) Gail Bui

43. What room are the filing cabinets stored in?
(A) 203
(B) 204
(C) 240
(D) 230

44. What is the abbreviation for the administration department?
(A) 03-TD6
(B) #2034#
(C) ADM-09
(D) ASM-08

45. What is the security code for dialing a number that is beyond the 619 area code?
(A) 2034
(B) 2403
(C) 2306
(D) 2144

Directions for questions 46–50: *Study and memorize this story for five minutes. When five minutes have passed, turn the page and answer the questions. You may NOT take notes on what you read here and you may NOT refer back to this story while you are answering the questions.*

Last Monday, June 12, 2006 at approximately 9:17 A.M., Investigator Roberts went to the scene of an automobile accident involving a driver named Sally Hanson, which occurred on Sunday, June 11, 2006 at 11:07 P.M. in the small town of Conyers, Colorado. The investigator reported several pieces of information relating to the case. First, she noticed that the road, which slopes to the left, was covered in loose gravel and other debris not related to the accident. In addition, the current weather conditions were clear and sunny, although on the day of the accident, the weather was wet, cool, and foggy. The temperature on the day of the accident, which was 48 degrees Fahrenheit, was ruled out as a contributing factor to the accident by another expert named Roger Thorne since there could have been no ice on the road. In fact, the temperature the day before the accident was 61 degrees Fahrenheit. Having just turned right from the southbound interstate, the car was headed westbound when the accident occurred and the investigator also noticed on-coming traffic could also not have been a factor because east-bound traffic was shut down on the day of the accident because of road construction. Although the driver's blue convertible with New Mexico license plates registered in 2005 had damage to the front and left side of the car, there was no damage to the right side or the rear of the vehicle.

46. In which direction was the driver headed when the accident occurred?
(A) north
(B) south
(C) east
(D) west

47. What model year was the car involved in the accident?
(A) 2006
(B) 1984
(C) 2005
(D) It doesn't say.

48. What was the name of the investigator who visited the scene?
(A) Thorne
(B) Roberts
(C) Rogers
(D) Hanson

49. At what time did the accident occur?
(A) 9:17 A.M.
(B) 11:07 P.M.
(C) 9:07 A.M.
(D) 11:17 P.M.

50. What were the exact words used to describe the weather on the day of the accident?
(A) wet, cool, and foggy
(B) wet, cold, and foggy
(C) wet, cool, and hazy
(D) wet, cold, and hazy

Answers and Explanations

1. E

The number 453 is only 16 away from 437 and is less than 519.

2. C

Two dozen is the same as 24, therefore you should have marked (C) for question 2.

3. E

Two dozen is the same as 24, therefore you should have marked (E) for question 3.

4. A

The square is to the left of the circle.

5. B

The larger triangle is to the right of the smaller triangle and the rectangle is to the left of the circle.

6. D

According to the rules, orange files should contain only documents that relate to nonfinancial matters from the year 1980 through 1998.

7. C

According to the rules, green files should contain only documents that relate to summer session, May through August of 2007.

8. A

According to the rules, red files should contain only documents relating to financial matters such as receipts and invoices.

9. A

According to the rules, red files should contain all bank statements pertaining to the department regardless of date.

10. B

According to the rules, blue files should contain only documents that relate to nonfinancial matters from the year 1999 through 2006.

11. C

According to the rules, off-site storage is for items larger than 1 square foot that are replaceable.

12. D

According to the rules, fireproof storage is reserved for irreplaceable items such as original works of art or historical documents.

13. B

According to the rules, central filing cabinets are only for general files relating to office business. Don't be confused by the last rule that states that storage is for general files that are dated prior to but not including 1996.

14. C

According to the rules, off-site storage is for general files that are dated prior to but not including 1996.

15. A

According to the rules, desktop filing cabinets are only for personal and confidential files.

For the answers to questions 16 through 25, refer to the Coding Guide for confirmation of the correct answer.

16. C

17. D

18. B

19. B

20. A

21. C

22. C

23. A

24. D

25. C

26. B
The code for 3rd floor is 05, the code for Finance is FN, and the code for invoices is 09. Therefore, 05FN09 is correct.

27. A
The code for archives is 22, the code for Administration is AD, and the code for memos is 87. Therefore, 22AD87 is correct.

28. D
The code for front office is 18, the code for Marketing is MK, and the code for brochures is 33. Therefore, 18MK33 is correct.

29. C
The code for central office is 13, the code for Human Resources is HR, and the code for applications is 54. Therefore, 13HR54 is correct.

30. D
The code for 3rd floor is 05, the code for Marketing is MK, and the code for memos is 87. Therefore, 05MK87 is correct.

31. D
The code for shoplifting is: D
The code for store is: C
The code for 8:35 P.M. is: C
The code for 1 witness is: B
The code for immediate reporting is: A
The code for 130 dollars is: B
Therefore, DCCBAB is correct.

32. A
The code for car theft is: C
The code for parking garage is: F
The code for 4 A.M. is: E
The code for no witness is: A
The code for 6-hour delay to report is: C
The code for 3,700 dollars is: E
Therefore, CFEACE is correct.

33. E
The code for breaking and entering is: A
The code for office is: D
The code for midnight is: D
The code for security camera is: D
The code for 2-day delay to report is: E
The code for no value is: A
Therefore, ADDDEA is correct. Since this is not one of the choices, choice (E) is correct.

34. B
The code for armed robbery is: B
The code for apartment complex is: B
The code for 9 A.M. is: A
The code for 1 witness is: B
The code for immediate reporting is: A
The code for 75 dollars is: A
Therefore, BBABAA is correct.

35. C
The code for breaking and entering is: A
The code for private home is: A
The code for the time between 2 P.M. until 4 P.M. is: B
The code for no witnesses is: A
The code for a 2- to 4-hour delay in reporting is: B
The code for 8,000 dollars is: F
Therefore, AABABF is correct.

For the answers to questions 36 through 40, refer to the Coding Guide for confirmation of the correct answer.

36. **B**

37. **B**

38. **A**

39. **D**

40. **C**

41. **C**

According to rule 1, the extension to call is 2144.

42. **A**

According to rule 1, Don Hillings is in charge of accounts payable.

43. **B**

According to rule 2, filing cabinets are stored in room 204.

44. **C**

According to rule 4, the abbreviation for the administration department is ADM-09.

45. **B**

According to rule 3, the security code for dialing a number that is beyond the 619 area code is 2403.

For the answers to questions 46 through 50, refer to the story for confirmation of the correct answer.

46. **D**

47. **D**

48. **B**

49. **B**

50. **A**

CHAPTER EIGHT

Decision-Making and Reasoning

Introduction

You have made it through a lot of material so far in this book, but it's not over just yet. This chapter covers two more important topics commonly found on civil service exams: decision-making and reasoning. It is not guaranteed that both topics will appear on the test you take, so if you know your exam does not include decision-making, you can study only reasoning or vice versa. If you are unsure at all, take the time to study both.

Each of the two topics has its own lesson, sample questions, and strategies. You should work through each of these in order, then reinforce what you have learned by taking the 40-question practice test at the end of the chapter. If you are unsure of any of the answers, use the detailed explanations to clarify.

Decision-Making Lesson

Unfortunately, there is not a lot to say about decision-making. It's a skill you probably already have, but will need to fine tune both before the exam, and on the job if you are hired. Here are some of the specific skills you should hone, as well as an example of each skill.

■ understanding of correct professional responses

If you are a file clerk and a superior asks you to retrieve some information from your files, you do not first take the time to check your e-mail before gathering the materials requested.

■ differentiating between fact and opinion

If you are a social worker and are presenting a report following a home visit, you should mention exactly what you saw (e.g., floors and sleeping areas were untidy, clothes strewn about), rather than what you felt (e.g., the house was a pigsty).

■ judging something's relevance or importance to a situation

If you are an administrative assistant and you are asked to prepare and ship several different packages, you do worry about having all the correct names and addresses of the recipients but you do not worry about whether all the packing materials are identical.

■ acknowledging appropriate behavior on the job

If you are a call center operator and you are dealing with an irate customer, you should not reply to his anger by shouting back at him.

Three rules you should follow when making a decision are:

1. **Consider the situation carefully.** Don't rush into making a decision.
2. **Avoid absolutes.** If you try to put a situation in terms of *always* or *never*, it can affect your judgment and your perspective.
3. **Don't overthink things and don't second-guess yourself.** Trust that you have made the right decision and move on.

The most important thing to remember is always use common sense. Stop and think through a situation before you react immediately. Don't spend all day worrying over every detail, but don't simply say or do the very first thing that comes to mind. Be mindful of your actions and responses and you will be able to answer these questions with no problems on test day.

Sample Decision-Making Questions

Depending on which civil service exam you take, you will find different question types. Some may be specific to the type of job you are applying to. For example, someone applying for a job as a social worker will include questions pertaining to that field. However, most decision-making questions can be broken down into the following categories:

■ response questions
■ sift and sort questions

If you are confused, don't worry. Each of these question types will be reviewed in detail here.

Response Questions

Response questions test your common sense. With each question you are presented with a situation typical of what different civil service employees might encounter on the job. Your task is to select the best answer from the four choices provided.

Here is a sample response question.

Administrative Assistant Gregory takes a call from a client he knows his manager Sandeep is not fond of. Sandeep is in his office and Gregory thinks Sandeep needs to concentrate because he is always very busy after lunch. What should Gregory do?

(A) say that Sandeep is not in his office and take a message from the client

(B) direct the client's call to another manager who can possibly help the client

(C) let Sandeep know who is on the line and ask how to proceed

(D) forward the call directly to Sandeep's voicemail

What do you think is the appropriate response? You will learn what the answer is in Tips for Decision-Making Success.

Sift and Sort Questions

In any job, but especially in investigative positions, you will be given much more information than you can possibly use to make a decision and plan your next move. Your task will be to go through all the facts and details, determine what is relevant, and then ignore the rest. Then you have to review the relevant information and figure out what is essential to planning the next step.

Sift and sort questions test your ability to recognize a well-written document. You will be presented with a list, table, or other pieces of information, and you will be asked to choose the best answer from among the four choices. The document always contains all the relevant information. In other words, just by reading the document, anyone should be able to understand the situation without any other facts or background information.

Here is a sample question.

Claims Reviewer Meyers is reviewing the information she wrote on a recent house viewing following a tornado:

    Place of Occurrence: 6872 Thompson Lane
    City: Topeka
    State: KS
    Date of Occurrence: August 15, 2006
    Date of Visit: August 17, 2006
    Homeowner: Mrs. Elise Lyons (age 49)
    Other Occupants: N/A
    Pets: 1 dog, 2 parakeets
    Number of Displaced Occupants: 0

Items Damaged: no structural damage other than the missing roof. Loss of personal items and destruction of all soft furnishings in second storey of the house.
Value of Damages: $12,000
Status of Claim: filed and pending

Which of the following expresses the information most clearly and accurately?

(A) Mrs. Elise Lyons, age 49, lives alone with 1 dog and 2 birds (parakeets). In mid-August a tornado damaged her property and displaced all the occupants of the home. A minimum of $15,000 will be needed to repair the damage and her claim should be completed in the next 60 days.

(B) Although Mrs. Lyons does not have to move out of her home, there is significant damage to the house, including a missing roof. A visit to the house 2 days after the incident revealed approximately $12,000 in damage, although pets were unharmed. Claim is pending.

(C) On the 15th of August a tornado ripped through Thompson Lane. The home at number 6872, owned by Mrs. Elise Lyons was left standing but the roof had been ripped off. The damage upstairs was significant, but neither Mrs. Lyons nor her three pets were injured in any way. Her claim for $12,000 in damages is still pending.

(D) On August 15, a tornado damaged the roof and upstairs soft-furnishings at 6872 Thompson Lane, occupied by Elise Lyons. Following a visit to the home on August 17, the damages were estimated to be $12,000 and the claim has been filed and is pending.

To learn the answer to this question, keep reading the Tips for Decision-Making Success.

Tips for Decision-Making Success

You may have noticed that these question types are quite different from the more-common reading, writing, math, and clerical ability questions you have studied so far. Because of these differences, the strategies we provide for you are also quite different. Review the strategies for each question type and be sure to use them when answering these questions on Practice Test 6.

Kaplan's Target Strategy for Response Questions

Here is Kaplan's Target Strategy for Response Questions.

Step 1. Read the question carefully.
Step 2. Beware of absolutes.
Step 3. Don't read between the lines.
Step 4. Pick your answer and move on.

Let's apply these four steps to the previous question.

Step 1. Read the Question Carefully.   Remember the active reading strategies you learned in Chapter 4 (passage maps; circling key words). As you are reading the question, underline the relevant information that will help you decide on your response.

Administrative Assistant Gregory takes a call from a client he knows his manager Sandeep is not fond of. Sandeep is in his office and Gregory thinks Sandeep needs to concentrate because he is always very busy after lunch. What should Gregory do?

    (A) say that Sandeep is not in his office and take a message from the client
    (B) direct the client's call to another manager who can possibly help the client
    (C) let Sandeep know who is on the line and ask how to proceed
    (D) forward the call directly to Sandeep's voicemail

What words did you circle in the question?

Step 2. Beware of Absolutes.   Words that indicate absolutes such as *always, never, first,* and *last* can change how a situation is interpreted. Perhaps in this question the word *always* jumped out at you. You should note it, but remember, if you read the question carefully, you should also have noticed the word *thinks,* which implies an opinion, not a fact.

Step 3. Don't Read between the Lines.   Do not try to assume anything. Read the information as it's written and don't read anything into it. In this case, there is nothing in the question that says what the consequences of Gregory's actions will be. Don't start assuming that you know what the outcome of each response would be. Go with what you think it the most common sense decision.

Step 4. Pick Your Answer and Move On.   In this case, the correct answer is (C). Choices (A), (B), and (D) all require you to take the situation into your own hands (to tell a lie that Sandeep is not there, to presume that another manager can help, to not give Sandeep the opportunity to handle his own calls). You really have no decision to make; common sense should tell you that if you are asked to forward a call that you should do so without assuming you understand the situation better.

    Sift and sort questions have their own strategies. Let's review those now.

Kaplan's Target Strategy for Sift and Sort Questions

There are only three steps to this strategy. These are:

Step 1. Determine if all relevant information is included.
Step 2. Determine if any extra, but irrelevant, information is included.
Step 3. Pick your answer and move on.

    Let's apply these questions to the question we saw earlier.

Claims Reviewer Meyers is reviewing the information she wrote on a recent house viewing following a tornado:

Place of Occurrence: 6872 Thompson Lane

City: Topeka

State: KS

Date of Occurrence: August 15, 2006

Date of Visit: August 17, 2006

Homeowner: Mrs. Elise Lyons (age 49)

Other Occupants: N/A

Pets: 1 dog, 2 parakeets

Number of Displaced Occupants: 0

Items Damaged: no structural damage other than the missing roof. Loss of personal items and destruction of all soft furnishings in second storey of the house.

Value of Damages: $12,000

Status of Claim: filed and pending

Which of the following expresses the information most clearly and accurately?

(A) Mrs. Elise Lyons, age 49, lives alone with 1 dog and 2 birds (parakeets). In mid-August a tornado damaged her property and displaced all the occupants of the home. A minimum of $15,000 will be needed to repair the damage and her claim should be completed in the next 60 days.

(B) Although Mrs. Lyons does not have to move out of her home, there is significant damage to the house, including a missing roof. A visit to the house 2 days after the incident revealed approximately $12,000 in damage, although pets were unharmed. Claim is pending.

(C) On the 15th of August a tornado ripped through Thompson Lane. The home at number 6872, owned by Mrs. Elise Lyons was left standing but the roof had been ripped off. The damage upstairs was significant, but neither Mrs. Lyons nor her three pets were injured in any way. Her claim for $12,000 in damages is still pending.

(D) On August 15, a tornado damaged the roof and upstairs soft-furnishings at 6872 Thompson Lane, occupied by Elise Lyons. Following a visit to the home on August 17, the damages were estimated to be $12,000 and the claim has been filed and is pending.

Step 1. Determine if All Relevant Information Is Included.   Make sure the answer you choose includes all relevant information, in this case, the names, the location, and the details of the incident.

Look at each of the choices and make your own determinations.

(A) Mrs. Elise Lyons, age 49, lives alone with 1 dog and 2 birds (parakeets). In mid-August a tornado damaged her property and displaced all the occupants of the home. A minimum of $15,000 will be needed to repair the damage and her claim should be completed in the next 60 days. **This choice does not include specific details about the dates or the value of the items. It is not correct.**

(B) Although Mrs. Lyons does not have to move out of her home, there is significant damage to the house, including a missing roof. A visit to the house 2 days after the incident revealed approximately $12,000 in damage, although pets were unharmed. Claim is pending. **This choice does not include specific details such as where the house is, but it may be correct as several other details are included. Do not eliminate this choice yet.**

(C) On the 15th of August a tornado ripped through Cherry Hill Lane. The home at number 6872, owned by Mrs. Elise Lyons was left standing but the roof had been ripped off. The damage upstairs was significant, but neither Mrs. Lyons nor her three pets were injured in any way. Her claim for $12,000 in damages is still pending. **This choice does not include specific details about the dates or the value of the items. It is not correct.**

(D) On August 15, a tornado damaged the roof and upstairs soft-furnishings at 6872 Thompson Lane, Topeka, KS, occupied by Elise Lyons. Following a visit to the home on August 17, the damages were estimated to be $12,000 and the claim has been filed and is pending. **It seems that this sums everything up nicely, but you should next determine if any extra, but irrelevant, information is included here.**

Step 2. Determine if Any Extra, but Irrelevant, Information Is Included. If you understand that only the most important points should be included in the report, you would recognize that information about Mrs. Berry's age or her pets is not crucial to understanding the report. This should help you eliminate choices (A) and (C). Now you have to choose between choice (B) and choice (D).

Step 3: Pick Your Answer and Move On. If you read each of these reports, you will see that choice (D) includes all the relevant information. Choice (B) does not include the location of the house, which would be relevant in this type of report.

Now that we have reviewed the different decision-making question types and strategies, let's move on to the next lesson.

Reasoning Lesson

As you will learn later in this chapter, there are actually three different types of reasoning questions: assembling objects; sequences; and logic. The content of this lesson applies entirely to logic questions. If you want to know more about assembling object and sequence questions, you should consult the Sample Reasoning Questions or Tips for Reasoning Success. Otherwise, keep reading to learn the basic principles of reasoning.

To reason is to apply logic to a situation and to make a decision based on logic, rather than emotion. Reasoning involves constructing arguments, evaluating arguments, and formulating or evaluating a plan of action. Here is more information about these topics.

- Argument construction: Recognizing the basic structure of an argument, properly drawn conclusions, underlying assumptions, explanatory hypotheses, or parallels between structurally similar arguments
- Argument evaluation: Analyzing an argument; recognizing elements that would strengthen or weaken it; identifying reasoning errors committed in the argument; or aspects of the argument's development
- Formulating and evaluating a plan of action: Recognizing the relative appropriateness, effectiveness, and efficiency of different plans of action as well as factors that would strengthen or weaken a proposed plan of action

Now that you know the situations to which you can apply reason, you can learn the basics of *how* to reason.

The 7 Basic Principles of Reasoning

1. Understand the Structure of an Argument.   First, you must know how arguments are structured, so that you can know how to break them down into their core components. When we use the word *argument*, we don't mean a conversation where two people are shouting at each other. An argument in reasoning means any piece of text where an author puts forth a set of ideas and/or a point of view, and attempts to support it.

Every argument is made up of two basic parts:

- The *conclusion* (the point that the author is trying to make)
- The *evidence* (the support that the author offers for the conclusion)

There is no general rule about where conclusion and evidence appear in the argument—the conclusion could be the first sentence, followed by the evidence, or it could be the last sentence, with the evidence preceding it.

Consider the following statements:

The Brookdale Public Library will require extensive physical rehabilitation to meet the new building codes passed by the town council. For one thing, the electrical system is inadequate, causing the lights to flicker sporadically. Furthermore, there are too few emergency exits, and even those are poorly marked and sometimes locked.

Suppose that the author of this argument was allowed only one sentence to convey her meaning. Do you think she would waste her time with the following statement? Would she walk away satisfied that her main point was communicated?

The electrical system [at the Brookdale Public Library] is inadequate, causing the lights to flicker sporadically.

Probably not. Given a single opportunity, she would have to state the first sentence to convey her real purpose:

The Brookdale Public Library will require extensive physical rehabilitation....

That is the conclusion. If you pressed the author to state her *reasons* for making that statement, she would then cite the electrical and structural problems with the building. That is the *evidence* for her conclusion.

But does that mean that an evidence statement like, "The electrical system is inadequate" can't be a conclusion? No, we're just saying it's not the conclusion for this particular argument. Every idea, every new statement, must be evaluated in the context of the passage in which it appears.

For the previous statement to serve as the conclusion, the passage would be:

The electrical wiring at the Brookdale Public Library was installed over 40 years ago, and appears to be corroded in some places (evidence). An electrician, upon inspection of the system, found a few frayed wires as well as some blown fuses (evidence). Clearly, the electrical system at the Brookdale Public Library is inadequate (conclusion).

To reason correctly, you have to be able to determine the precise function of every sentence in the passage. Use structural signals when attempting to isolate evidence and conclusion. Key words in the passage—such as *because*, *for*, *since*—usually indicate that *evidence* is about to follow, whereas *therefore*, *hence*, *thus*, and *consequently* usually signal a *conclusion*.

2. Preview the Question.   Before you read the passage, look over the question. This will give you some idea about what you need to look for as you read. It gives you a jump on the question. Suppose the question with the previous library argument asked the following:

The author supports her point about the need for rehabilitation at the Brookdale Library by citing which of the following?

If you were to preview this question before you read the passage, you would know what to look for in advance—namely, evidence, the "support" provided for the conclusion. Or if the question stem asked you to find an assumption on which the author is relying, you would know in advance that a crucial piece of the argument was missing, and you could think about that right away. Previewing the question saves you time in the long run.

3. Paraphrase the Author's Point.   After you read the passage, paraphrase the author's main argument to yourself. That is, restate the author's ideas in your own words. Frequently, authors say pretty simple things in complex ways. So if you mentally translate the text into a simpler form, the whole thing should be more manageable.

In the library argument, for instance, you probably don't want to deal with the full complexity of the author's stated conclusion:

> The Brookdale Public Library will require extensive physical rehabilitation to meet the new building codes just passed by the town council.

Instead, you probably want to paraphrase a much simpler point:

> The library will need fixing-up to meet new codes.

Often, by the time you begin reading through the answer choices, you run the risk of losing sight of the gist of the passage. So restating the argument in your own words will not only help you get the author's point in the first place, it will also help you hold on to it until you have found the correct answer.

4. Judge the Argument's Persuasiveness.   You must read actively, not passively. Active readers are always thinking critically, forming reactions as they go along. They question whether the author's argument seems valid or dubious. Especially when you are asked to find flaws in the author's reasoning, it's imperative to read with a critical eye.

How persuasive is the argument about the library? Well, it's pretty strong, because the evidence certainly seems to indicate that certain aspects of the library's structure need repair. But without more evidence about what the new building codes are like, we can't say for sure that the conclusion of this argument is valid. So this is a strong argument but not an airtight one.

Because part of your task is to evaluate arguments, don't let yourself fall into the bad habits of the passive reader—reading solely for the purpose of getting through the passage. Those who read this way invariably find themselves having to read the passages twice or even three times. Read the passages right the first time—with a critical eye and an active mind.

5. Answer the Question Being Asked.   The question will always ask for something very specific. It's your job to answer exactly what is being asked.

Also, be on the lookout for "reversers," words such as *not* and *except*. These little words are easy to miss, but they change entirely the kind of statement you're looking for among the choices.

6. Try to "Prephrase" an Answer.   This principle, which is really an extension of the last one, is crucial. You must try to approach the answer choices with at least a faint idea of what the answer should look like. That is, "prephrase" the answer in your own mind before looking at the choices. This isn't to say you should ponder the question for minutes—it's still a multiple-choice test, so the right answer is in front of you. Just get in the habit of framing an answer in your head.

Once you have prephrased, scan the choices. Sure, the correct choice on the exam will be worded differently and will be more fleshed out than your vague idea. But if it matches your thought, you will know it in a second.

Continuing with the library situation, suppose you were asked:

> The author's argument depends on which of the following assumptions about the new building codes?

Having thought about the passage argument, you might immediately come up with an answer here—that the argument is based on the assumption that the new codes apply to existing buildings as well as to new buildings under construction. After all, the library will have to be rehabilitated to meet the new codes, according to the author. Clearly, the assumption is that the codes apply to existing buildings. And that's the kind of statement you would look for among the choices.

Don't be discouraged if you can't always prephrase an answer. Some questions just won't have an answer that jumps out at you. But if used correctly, prephrasing works on many questions.

7. Keep the Scope of the Argument in Mind.   When you're at the point of selecting one of the answer choices, focus on the scope of the argument. Most of the choices on this section are wrong because they are "outside the scope." In other words, the wrong answer choices contain elements that don't match the author's ideas or that go beyond the context of the stimulus.

Some answer choices are too narrow, too broad, or have nothing to do with the author's points. Others are too extreme to match the argument's scope—they're usually signaled by such words as *all*, *always*, *never*, *none*, and so on. For arguments that are moderate in tone, correct answers are more qualified and contain such words as *usually*, *sometimes*, *probably*.

To illustrate the scope principle, let's look again at the question previously mentioned:

> The author's argument depends on which of the following assumptions about the new building codes?

Let's say one of the choices read as follows:

> (A) The new building codes are far too stringent.

Knowing the scope of the argument would help you to eliminate this choice very quickly. You know that this argument is just a claim about what the new codes will require: that the library be rehabilitated. It's not an argument about whether the requirements of the new codes are good, or justifiable, or ridiculously strict. That kind of value judgment is outside the scope of this argument.

Now that you have reviewed the 7 basic principles of reasoning, you are ready to learn more about the question types you will see on test day.

Sample Reasoning Questions

What you might find most appealing about reasoning questions is that you do not need any specific knowledge to answer these questions. Instead, you have to reason your way to an answer. But that doesn't mean that you shouldn't familiarize yourself with the question types and study the best methods for answering them.

The three main reasoning question types are:

- assembling objects
- sequence
- logic

Assembling Object Questions

Assembling object questions give you a series of seemingly incongruent shapes and ask you to configure them mentally into a single, unified shape. These are really just glorified puzzles. If you are good at geometry, you'll most likely be good at these questions, too. For some people, spatial questions are quite easy. For these people, shapes and arrangements just appear logically. But not everyone will find these questions quite so easy, especially when they are timed. Let's take a look at an example to get a feel for what assembling object questions are like.

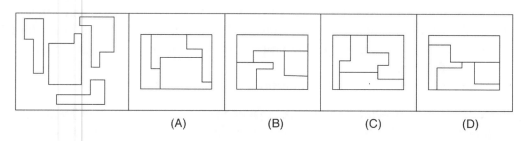

(A)   (B)   (C)   (D)

Sample 1

You will find some tips for finding the correct answer to this and other assembling object questions in Tips for Reasoning Success.

Sequence Questions

A sequence is a logical arrangement of objects, numbers, or letters.

Here are some examples of sequence questions. They are usually either visual (pictures) or alphabetical.

aB bC dE _____
 (A) fG
 (B) FG
 (C) Gh
 (D) eF

Your job is to figure out the logic behind the arrangement of the items and select an answer choice that completes the sequence.

Logic Questions

Logic questions give you three or four carefully worded statements describing a hypothetical situation (similar to what you learned in the Reasoning Lesson). Not all logic questions are exactly alike so we'll review a few of the main question types.

Assumption Questions.   An assumption bridges the gap between an argument's evidence and conclusion. It's a piece of support that isn't explicitly stated, but that is required for the conclusion to remain valid. When a question asks you to find an author's assumption, it's asking you to find the statement without which the argument falls apart.

Here is a sample assumption question:

A study of 20 overweight men revealed that each man experienced significant weight loss after adding SlimDown, an artificial food supplement, to his daily diet. For 3 months, each man consumed one SlimDown portion every morning after exercising, and then followed his normal diet for the rest of the day. Clearly, anyone who consumes one portion of SlimDown every day for at least 3 months will lose weight and will look and feel his best.

Which one of the following is an assumption on which the argument depends?
 (A) The men in the study will gain back the weight if they discontinue the SlimDown program.
 (B) No other dietary supplement will have the same effect on overweight men.

    (C) The daily exercise regimen was not responsible for the effects noted in the study.

    (D) Women won't experience similar weight reductions if they adhere to the SlimDown program for 3 months.

    (E) Overweight men will achieve only partial weight loss if they don't remain on the SlimDown program for a full 3 months.

If you are not sure of the answer, keep reading. This question will be reviewed in detail in Tips for Reasoning Success.

Denial Test.   To test whether a statement is necessarily assumed by an author, we can employ the Denial Test. Here's how it works: Simply deny or negate the statement and see if the argument falls apart. If it does, that choice is a necessary assumption. If, on the other hand, the argument is unaffected, the choice is wrong. Consider these simple statements:

> Allyson plays volleyball for Central High School. Therefore, Allyson must be over 6 feet tall.

You should recognize the second sentence as the conclusion and the first sentence as the evidence for it. But is the argument complete? Obviously not. The piece that's missing—the unstated link between the evidence and conclusion—is the assumption, and you could probably prephrase this one pretty easily:

> All volleyball players for Central High School are over 6 feet tall.

Is this assumption really necessary to the argument? Let's negate it using the Denial Test. What if it's not true that all volleyball players for Central High are taller than 6 feet? Can we still logically conclude that Allyson must be taller than 6 feet? No, we can't. Sure, she might be, but she also might not be. By denying the statement, then, the argument falls to pieces; it is no longer valid. And that's our conclusive proof that the previous statement is a necessary assumption of this argument.

So, we can use the Denial Test to check whether a statement is an assumption, but what if we haven't a clue about what the assumption is? Is there a way to track it down? Fortunately, there is.

Compare the ideas in the evidence with those in the conclusion. If the conclusion has an idea (an important word) but the evidence does not, then you've found an assumption. A new idea cannot occur in the conclusion, so there must be an assumption about this new idea. Every idea in the conclusion needs support— that is, evidence. While it may not be quite clear what the assumption is, knowing something about it allows us to prephrase and eliminate choices.

Luckily, when you read assumption questions you will usually just "feel" as if they are missing something. Often, the answer will jump out at you, but in more difficult assumption questions, it might not be so obvious. Either way, use the Denial Test to quickly check whichever choice seems correct.

Sample Assumption Question Stems. Assumption questions are worded in some of the following ways:

- Which one of the following is assumed by the author?
- Upon which one of the following assumptions does the author rely?
- The argument depends on the assumption that…
- Which one of the following, if added to the passage, will make the conclusion logical?
- The validity of the argument depends on which one of the following?
- The argument presupposes which one of the following?

Strengthen or Weaken Questions. Determining an argument's necessary assumption, as we've just seen, is required to answer an assumption question. But it also is required to answer another common type of question: strengthen or weaken the argument.

Here is a sample strengthen the argument question:

Recent surveys show that many people who have left medical school before graduating suffer from depression. Clearly, depression is likely to cause withdrawal from medical school.

Which of the following, if true, would most strengthen the conclusion above?
- (A) Many medical schools provide psychological counseling for their students.
- (B) About half of those who leave medical school report feeling depressed after they make the decision to leave.
- (C) Depression is very common among management consultants who have a similarly difficult work schedule to those of many young doctors.
- (D) Medical students who have sought depression counseling due to family problems leave at a higher rate than the national average.
- (E) Career change has been shown to be a strong contributing factor in the onset of depression.

The answer here is choice (D). This statement suggests that when some outside event has brought on depression, leaving becomes more likely in the period subsequent to the depression. This confirms that students who are depressed while in school are more likely to drop out. Next we'll review how to weaken an argument.

One way to weaken an argument is to break down a central piece of evidence. Another way is to attack the validity of any assumptions the author has made. The answer to many weaken-the-argument questions is the one that reveals an author's assumption to be unreasonable; conversely, the answer to many strengthen-the-argument questions provides additional support by affirming the truth of an assumption or by presenting more persuasive evidence.

Let's use the same simple statements used in the assumption question but now in the context of strengthen- or weaken-the-argument questions:

Allyson plays volleyball for Central High School. Therefore, Allyson must be over 6 feet tall.

Remember the assumption holding this argument together? It was that all volleyball players for Central High are over 6 feet tall. That's the assumption that makes or breaks the argument. So, if you're asked to weaken the argument, you would want to attack that assumption:

Which one of the following, if true, would most weaken the argument?

Answer: Not all volleyball players at Central High School are over 6 feet tall.

We've called into doubt the author's basic assumption, thus damaging the argument. But what about strengthening the argument? Again, the key is the necessary assumption:

Which one of the following, if true, would most strengthen the argument?

Answer: All volleyball players at Central High School are over 6 feet tall.

Here, by confirming the author's assumption, we've in effect strengthened the argument.

Sample Strengthen/Weaken Question Stems.   The stems associated with these two question types are usually self-explanatory. Here's a list of what you can expect to see on test day:

Weaken:
- Which one of the following, if true, would most weaken the argument above?
- Which one of the following, if true, would most seriously damage the argument above?
- Which one of the following, if true, casts the most doubt on the argument above?
- Which one of the following, if true, is the most serious criticism of the argument above?

Strengthen:
- Which one of the following, if true, would most strengthen the argument?
- Which one of the following, if true, would provide the most support for the conclusion in the argument above?
- The argument above would be more persuasive if which one of the following were found to be true?

Inference Questions.   The third logic question type is the inference question. The process of inferring is a matter of considering one or more statements as evidence and then drawing a conclusion from them. Sometimes the inference is very close to the author's overall main point.

Here is an example where you must make a relatively simple inference:

John's computer suddenly turns off. His lights, television, and radio are still running.
   (A) There is a blackout.
   (B) There is a problem with John's computer.
   (C) John's computer is unplugged.
   (D) John does not know how to use a computer.

In this example, choice (B) is the correct answer. Based on the information given, the only thing we know for sure is that there is a problem with John's computer.

Other times, the question deals with a less central point. The difference between an inference and an assumption is that the conclusion's validity doesn't logically depend on an inference, as it does on a necessary assumption. A valid inference is merely something that must be true if the statements in the passage are true; it's an extension of the argument rather than a necessary part of it.

Let's examine a somewhat expanded version of the volleyball team argument we've used to explain assumption and strengthen/weaken questions:

Allyson plays volleyball for Central High School, despite the team's rule against participation by nonstudents. Therefore, Allyson must be over 6 feet tall.

Inference: Allyson is not a student at Central High School.

Clearly, if Allyson plays volleyball despite the team's rule against participation by nonstudents, she must not be a student. Otherwise, she wouldn't be playing despite the rule; she would be playing in accordance with the rule. But note that this inference is not an essential assumption of the argument because the conclusion about Allyson's height doesn't depend on it.

So be careful: Unlike an assumption, an inference need not have anything to do with the author's conclusion. It may simply be a piece of information derived from one or more pieces of evidence.

Fortunately, the Denial Test works for inferences as well as for assumptions: A valid inference always makes more sense than its opposite. If you deny or negate an answer choice, and the denial has little or no effect on the argument, then chances are that choice cannot be inferred from the passage.

Sample Inference Question Stems.   Inference questions probably have the most varied wording of all the question types. Some questions denote inference fairly obviously. Others are more subtle, and still others may even look like other question types entirely. Here's a quick rundown of the various forms that inference questions may take on your test:

- Which one of the following is inferable from the argument above?
- Which one of the following is implied by the argument above?
- The author suggests that . . .
- If all the statements above are true, which one of the following must also be true on the basis of them?
- The author of the passage would most likely agree with which one of the following?
- The passage provides the most support for which of the following?
- Which one of the following is probably the conclusion toward which the author is moving?
- Which of the following, if true, would best explain . . .

Tips for Reasoning Success

The Reasoning Lesson in this chapter covered the basic principles of reasoning success. However, this lesson did not cover assembling object or sequence questions. In this section, Tips for Reasoning Success, you will learn the best strategies for answering all types of reasoning questions.

Kaplan's Target Strategies for Assembling Object Questions

Do you remember this question from earlier in the chapter?

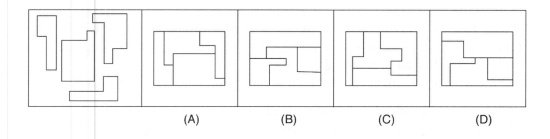

(A)	(B)	(C)	(D)

Not too bad, right?

Or maybe it didn't seem this easy to you. Maybe your brain is wired for different types of questions. So, how should you approach this sort of strange looking question? Try to think of it as a game.

Strategy 1. Change Your Way of Thinking.   First, think about real objects with these shapes and how they fit together. Two halves of a square sandwich cut diagonally make triangles, right? Or think about the way a pizza is cut by straight lines, leaving smaller, individual round-edged triangles. Even a pyramid can be broken up into several smaller triangles. Keep these sorts of real life images in your head because assembling object questions are easily solved if you just think creatively.

For this question, you can see that all four answer choices at first glance look pretty similar. Your best bet is to pick one shape from the initial box and to compare it quickly to the four choices to see if you can quickly eliminate a choice. The shape in the middle, which looks a bit like the state of Utah, is a good one. Quickly scanning all four answer choices, only (A) and (D) have this shape present. Therefore you can easily dismiss two of the choices. Next, just do the same with another shape. Picking the smallest shape at the bottom, you can see that only the shapes in (A) correspond to the original given shapes. Thus, (A) is the correct answer choice.

Strategy 2. Keep Calm.   There is no reason to fear assembling object questions. Just familiarize yourself as much as possible with the way these odd questions look and practice answering them in Practice Test 6. Remember, there is no real way to study for assembling object questions. All you can do is prepare yourself for how the questions look so that you'll never be surprised.

If sequence questions give you a problem, keep reading to learn three easy steps for answering sequence questions.

Kaplan's Target Strategy for Sequence Questions

Step 1. Examine the building blocks and define the sequence.
Step 2. Predict the answer.
Step 3. Select the answer choice that best fits your prediction.

Step 1. Examine the Building Blocks and Define the Sequence.   Stay focused and remember that there always IS a relationship, an arrangement, a movement, or a progression of some sort among the items.

Figure out the progression by adding on one building block at a time.

 1. Examine each building block by itself.
 2. Examine the relationship or movement from one building block to the next.

Don't try to define the progression until you have worked through each of the building blocks given. Look at the first example question to see how this is done.

SEQUENCE TYPE 1—PICTURE SEQUENCE QUESTIONS

Look carefully at the first building block of the sequence:

Your definition doesn't have to be a complete sentence, just something to help you bring the picture into focus. Your definition might be "square with dot in center, line from dot to top corner." Now, look at the next building block of the sequence:

It's a "square with dot in center, line from dot to bottom corner." Now, define this as it relates to the first building block. The building blocks of the sequence are made up of a square with a dot in the center, and a line drawn from that dot to a corner of the square.

But wait! If you try to define your pattern now, you will be in trouble. According to your definition, the third building block should also contain a square with a line drawn from a dot in the center to a corner of the square. However, that is not the case. What happened?

Don't give up on breaking the code, and don't define the code until you have reached the end of the items given. Look carefully at the third square. What can you say about it by itself? In the third building block of the pattern, the line drawn from the dot in the center of the square is drawn to the center of the base, NOT to a corner.

So, you have recognized several important things about the sequence.

- Each item has a square with a dot in the center.
- A line is drawn from the dot in the center to some point of the square's perimeter.
- In each subsequent building block of the pattern, the line is drawn to a different place than in the previous one.

By analyzing each building block of the pattern separately, and then comparing each block to the one that went before it, you defined the pattern.

Marking up the test booklet might help you do this more easily.

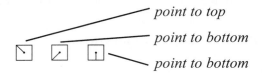

Step 2. Predict the Answer.   If we were to continue the pattern, what would we have next? The next item needs to be a square, with a point in the middle. The line drawn from the point should be in the opposite direction from the previous square. Because in the previous square the line was heading down, in this next one it needs to be heading up. Now that you have a clear idea of what the correct answer should look like, you are ready for Step 3.

Step 3. Select the Answer Choice That Best Fits Your Prediction.   Look at the answer choices again.

    (A)   (B)   (C)   (D)

There it is. Choice (D) matches your prediction. It's the right answer. But… what if no choice exactly matches your prediction? You have got to redefine, refocus, broaden, or narrow your prediction.

What if these were the answer choices?

    (A)   (B)   (C)   (D)

None of these choices has a line drawn from the dot, up. Choice (A) has a dot in the center but no line. In choice (B) the line is too long. Choice (C) has two lines that cross. However, the fourth one still does have a line drawn from the center dot of the square. The line, like those in the rest of the pattern is short. Choice (D) still best fits the prediction you made.

Common Patterns to Look For.   Doing well on picture sequence questions has a lot to do with your powers of observation. Take your time, focus, and look for the details that make one building block different from the next. Some common differences to watch out for are:

Direction of lines: Does one piece of the diagram point up, down, or sideways? Do pieces of the pattern point in opposite directions?

Shapes and size of shapes: Is the pattern made up of squares, circles, or other shapes? Do the shapes increase or decrease in size?

Shading: Are portions of the building blocks shaded? Is the shading increasing or decreasing as you progress through the sequence?

Increasing or decreasing detail: Does each subsequent building block have more or less detail than the one before it?

SEQUENCE TYPE 2—ALPHABET SEQUENCE QUESTIONS

The same techniques you have just learned and practiced for picture sequence questions, also apply to alphabet sequence questions. (We have called this question type *alphabet sequence*, but you might also see letters of the alphabet mixed in with numbers.)

Let's take the example from the beginning of this chapter to work though.

aB bC dE _____
   (A) fG
   (B) FG
   (C) Gh
   (D) eF

Step 1. Examine the Building Blocks and Define the Sequence.   Look carefully at the first building block of the sequence: aB. Define it. Your definition might be "lowercase letter, capital of next letter."

Look at the next building block of the sequence: bC. Again you have "lowercase letter, capital of next letter." Now, define this as it relates to the first building block. The first letter in the pair moved up one letter of the alphabet from a to b. The second letter also moved up a letter in the alphabet from B to C. It seems as though the building blocks of the sequence are made up of two letters, a lowercase letter, followed by a capital letter. And each subsequent pair begins with the second letter of the previous pair.

If you tried to define your pattern now though, you would be wrong. According to our definition, we expect the next pair to be cD. But the third building block is NOT cD, it is dE. Remember, don't define the code until you have reached the end of the three items given.

Okay, we have to look at the third item given, dE. What can we say about it by itself? Well, dE is made up of a lowercase letter followed by a capital of the next letter of the alphabet.

Now that we have defined the pair, see how it relates to the previous item, bC. Instead of the first letter being THE SAME as the second letter of the previous pair, it is the NEXT letter. The first letter doesn't start with a lowercase c, it starts with a d. The pattern then is: firstSECOND secondTHIRD fourthFIFTH or, two alike and one different.

Marking up the test booklet might help you do this more easily.

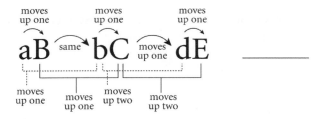

Step 2. Predict the Answer.   If you continue the pattern, what would you have next?

The next pair needs to return to the "move up one" beginning of the pattern. Keep in mind that the pattern just completed itself with dE, so you know you need to return to the beginning of the formula—in which the first letter of the subsequent pair is the same as the second letter of the previous pair. dE should be followed by the next capital letter in the alphabet. So, you move from dE to eF.

Step 3. Select the Answer Choice That Best Fits Your Prediction.   Of the choices provided, choice (D) fits your prediction.

> (A) fG
> (B) FG
> (C) Gh
> (D) eF

This was a not a particularly obvious sequence, but it does illustrate a couple of important points to remember when you approach alphabet sequence problems. Here are some other helpful tips for sequence questions.

Look for Common Patterns

There is only so much the test makers can do with the letters of the alphabet. Look out for the following movements or changes:

- Letters going up or down: Does the pattern move toward Z? As in PQR…or does it move toward A as in LKJIH
- Lowercase vs. capital letters: BdBB, BDbb, BDBb, etc.
- Patterns that skip letters: A C E G (skips 1 letter) or A D G J (skips 2), etc.
- Letters with numbers thrown in: a1 b2 c3 A1B2C3 AB3 BC2 CD1

Analyze these the way you would any other pattern: examine the details in the building block and look for changes as the sequence progresses.

Be Tenacious

Know that there IS a pattern. Analyze one building block at a time. Then, examine the movement from one block to another, trying to see what the difference between them is. Do this for every piece of the pattern. Use all the pieces given to you. Then, define the pattern.

Know Your Alphabet

It may seem obvious, but the only way to find the pattern in an alphabet item is to know the alphabet inside out. If you find yourself getting confused, or just don't see it, write out the alphabet at the top of your test booklet. There is nothing wrong with having a clear list to refer to.

If You Are Stumped, Eliminate Wrong Choices and Guess

Let's say you did your best to define the pattern, and you just aren't clear on what it is. Maybe in the previous example you recognized that each of the first letters of the pair started with a lowercase letter followed by a capital letter. But, the difference between the second and third building block confused you.

Don't give up. Use the information to eliminate clearly incorrect choices. Remember, you know the next pair has to start with a lowercase letter.

aB bC dE _____
    (A) fG
    (B) FG
    (C) Gh
    (D) eF

Right away you can rule out (B) and (C) because they begin with capital letters. Take your best guess from the remaining choices. By eliminating two of the answer choices, you have greatly improved the odds of choosing the correct one.

Kaplan's Target Strategy for Logic Questions

We've developed a method that you can use to attack logic questions. If you read the Reasoning Lesson closely you will see these four steps are similar to some of the basic principles of reasoning. Here are the four steps.

Step 1. Preview the question.
Step 2. Read the passage.
Step 3. Prephrase an answer.
Step 4. Choose an answer.

Step 1. Preview the Question. As we mentioned in the basic principles found in the Reasoning Lesson, previewing the question is a great way to focus your reading of the passage, so that you know exactly what you're looking for.

Step 2. Read the Passage. With the question in mind, read the passage, paraphrasing as you go. Remember to read actively and critically, pinpointing evidence and conclusion. Also get a sense for how strong or weak the argument is.

Step 3. Prephrase an Answer. Sometimes, if you have read the passage critically enough, you will know the answer without even looking at the choices. Other times, you will have only a general idea of what the answer will say. Either way, it will be much easier to find the answer if you have a sense of what you are looking for among the choices.

Step 4. Choose an Answer. If you were able to prephrase an answer, skim the choices for something that sounds like what you have in mind. Take this idea to the choices, aggressively. When you find one that mirrors your idea, disregard the others. If you couldn't think of anything, read and evaluate each choice, throwing out the ones that are outside the scope of the argument. After settling on an answer, you may wish to briefly double-check the question stem to make sure that you are indeed answering the question that was asked.

Now let's apply the Kaplan's Target Strategy to the following question that you read earlier in the chapter.

A study of 20 overweight men revealed that each man experienced significant weight loss after adding SlimDown, an artificial food supplement, to his daily diet. For 3 months, each man consumed one SlimDown portion every morning after exercising, and then followed his normal diet for the rest of the day. Clearly, anyone who consumes one portion of SlimDown every day for at least 3 months will lose weight and will look and feel his best.

Which one of the following is an assumption on which the argument depends?
   (A) The men in the study will gain back the weight if they discontinue the SlimDown program.
   (B) No other dietary supplement will have the same effect on overweight men.
   (C) The daily exercise regimen was not responsible for the effects noted in the study.
   (D) Women won't experience similar weight reductions if they adhere to the SlimDown program for 3 months.
   (E) Overweight men will achieve only partial weight loss if they don't remain on the SlimDown program for a full 3 months.

Step 1. Preview the Question.   We see, quite clearly, that we're dealing with an assumption question. So we can immediately adopt an "assumption mindset," which means that before even reading the passage, we know that the conclusion will be lacking an important piece of supporting evidence. We now turn to the passage, already on the lookout for this missing link.

Step 2. Read the Passage.   Sentence 1 introduces a study of 20 men using a food supplement product, resulting in weight loss for all 20. Sentence 2 describes how they used it: once a day, for 3 months, after morning exercise. So far so good; it feels as if we're building up to something. The key word *clearly* usually indicates that some sort of conclusion follows, and in fact it does: Sentence 3 says that anyone who has one portion of the product daily for 3 months will lose weight, too.

You must read critically! The conclusion doesn't say that anyone who follows the same routine as the 20 men will have the same results; it says that anyone who *simply consumes the product* will have the same results. You should have begun to sense the inevitable lack of crucial information at this point. The evidence in sentence 2 describes a routine that includes taking the supplement after daily exercise, whereas the conclusion focuses primarily on the supplement and entirely ignores the part about the exercise. The conclusion, therefore, doesn't stem logically from the evidence in the first two sentences. This blends seamlessly into Step 3.

Step 3. Prephrase an Answer.   As expected, it's beginning to look like the argument has a serious shortcoming. Of course, we expected this because we previewed the question stem before reading the passage.

In simplistic terms, the argument proceeds like so: "A bunch of guys did A and B for 3 months and had X result. If anyone does A for 3 months, that person will experience X result, too." Sound fishy? You bet. The author must be assuming that A (the product), not B (exercise), must be the cause that leads to the result. If not (here is the Denial Test), the conclusion makes no sense.

So, you might prephrase the answer like this: "Something about the exercise thing needs to be cleared up." That's it. Did you think your prephrasing had to be something fancy and glamorous? Well, it doesn't. So, with our vague idea of a possible assumption, we can turn to Step 4.

Step 4. Choose an Answer.   Because we were able to prephrase something, it's best to skim the choices looking for it. There's our idea, stated in choice (C). Choice (C) clears up the exercise issue. Yes, this author must assume (C) to make the conclusion that eating SlimDown alone will cause people to lose weight.

At this point, if you're stuck for time, pick (C) and move on. If you have more time, check the remaining choices quickly, to double-check that none of them works any better. Be ready to dismiss the other choices unless they make a strong case for themselves.

If these tips aren't enough for you, we also have the following logic traps you should beware of on test day.

Four Logic Traps to Avoid

When you are answering logic questions, do your best to avoid the following traps.

Trap 1—Character Assumption.   Don't select answer choices that make assumptions about a person or group not stated in the question. Here's an example:

Thomas accepted a part-time job as a receptionist in the afternoons. Unfortunately, he lost the first telephone call that he tried to transfer to his boss. When the person called back and Thomas tried to transfer the call again, again he lost it and disconnected the caller.

    (A) Thomas's telephone is broken.
    (B) Thomas's boss will be angry with him.
    (C) Thomas is having trouble connecting calls.
    (D) Thomas should get another job.

The only thing we know for certain is that Thomas is having trouble connecting calls; he lost two of them. Thus, the answer is (C). We cannot speculate on the emotions of his boss, nor do we know whether or not his telephone is broken. Perhaps Thomas's performance will improve in time; he need not get another job yet.

Trap 2—Too Much Information.   Some statements may deliberately try to throw you off the track by including too much information. Look at this example:

The Dixon family eats dinner together three nights a week. On Monday night, Mrs. Dixon has pizza delivered from the Italian restaurant on Main Street. On Tuesday, night Joe Dixon makes hotdogs. On Wednesday night, the Dixons belong to a family bowling team.

    (A) The Dixons eat dinner together Monday, Tuesday, and Wednesday.
    (B) The Dixons are good bowlers.
    (C) Joe Dixon eats alone on Tuesday night.
    (D) There is an Italian restaurant on Main Street.

Despite all the information, we don't know which nights the Dixons eat together. Mrs. Dixon could eat the pizza all by herself. Joe Dixon, likewise could be cooking for one. Do the Dixons eat at the bowling alley together on Wednesday? We don't know. Don't be distracted by the amount of information given. The only thing we know for sure is that (D) there is an Italian Restaurant on Main Street. How do we know? It delivers pizza to Mrs. Dixon on Monday night.

Trap 3—Using Previous Knowledge to Answer a Question.   While it is important to rely on facts, you can rely only on the facts you are given in the question. For example, read the following question:

Sacramento is in California. Albert has been to Sacramento.
  (A) Sacramento is the capital of California.
  (B) Albert has been to California.
  (C) San Francisco is a city in California.
  (D) Albert loved Sacramento.

You might be tempted to choose (A) or (C) because they are facts. However, although these statements are true, they cannot be determined based only on the information given in the first two statements. You should NOT use previous knowledge to answer these questions. Remember, they are testing your ability to reason and make inferences. In this example, the correct answer is (B).

Difficulty Level

As always, the difficulty of questions on the civil service exam you take will depend on the type of job you are applying for. Clerical civil service exams are likely to have very few decision-making or reasoning questions. On the other hand, exams for those entering the investigative fields are likely to have several questions that are also likely to be more challenging. This chapter and its practice test include decision-making and reasoning questions at both levels so that you are prepared for whatever civil service exam you face on test day.

Summary

Whether you are tested on your decision-making or reasoning skills on the civil service exam or not, having both skills will surely help on the job. Because you have reviewed both lessons, all the question types, as well as Kaplan's Target Strategies, you should be well prepared to get a top score on Practice Test 6. Answer these questions carefully and be sure to review any incorrect answers using the detailed explanations that follow the practice test. If you know that your civil service exam does not test your decision-making or reasoning skills, you can choose to skip to Chapter 9: Personal Characteristics and Experience Inventory.

Practice Test 6

40 Questions
40 Minutes

1. (A) (B) (C) (D)   11. (A) (B) (C) (D)   21. (A) (B) (C) (D)   31. (A) (B) (C) (D) (E)
2. (A) (B) (C) (D)   12. (A) (B) (C) (D)   22. (A) (B) (C) (D)   32. (A) (B) (C) (D) (E)
3. (A) (B) (C) (D)   13. (A) (B) (C) (D)   23. (A) (B) (C) (D)   33. (A) (B) (C) (D) (E)
4. (A) (B) (C) (D)   14. (A) (B) (C) (D)   24. (A) (B) (C) (D)   34. (A) (B) (C) (D) (E)
5. (A) (B) (C) (D)   15. (A) (B) (C) (D)   25. (A) (B) (C) (D)   35. (A) (B) (C) (D) (E)
6. (A) (B) (C) (D)   16. (A) (B) (C) (D)   26. (A) (B) (C) (D)   36. (A) (B) (C) (D) (E)
7. (A) (B) (C) (D)   17. (A) (B) (C) (D)   27. (A) (B) (C) (D)   37. (A) (B) (C) (D) (E)
8. (A) (B) (C) (D)   18. (A) (B) (C) (D)   28. (A) (B) (C) (D)   38. (A) (B) (C) (D) (E)
9. (A) (B) (C) (D)   19. (A) (B) (C) (D)   29. (A) (B) (C) (D)   39. (A) (B) (C) (D) (E)
10. (A) (B) (C) (D)   20. (A) (B) (C) (D)   30. (A) (B) (C) (D) (E)   40. (A) (B) (C) (D) (E)

1. You are working in a customer service call center and a client has called up and started yelling at you. How should you handle the situation?
    (A) Hang up the phone; you never have to respond to someone yelling.
    (B) In a loud voice, yell back at him or her.
    (C) Politely ask him or her to calm down and explain the situation.
    (D) Transfer the call directly to your manager.

2. There are have been several thefts of personal items in the office where you work as an administrative manager. Other administrative assistants are looking to you to come up with a plan of action against the thefts. You should:
    (A) offer to promote anyone who catches the thief
    (B) conduct a lengthy investigation into every person who works in the office

    (C) warn all employees to keep a close eye on personal belongings at all times, especially when away from their desks
    (D) suggest installing security cameras at every desk

3. At work, you are asked to help update a database, which was previously sorted alphabetically by last name. The new database will be sorted alphabetically by first name. About which of the following should you be most concerned while you are updating the database?
    (A) Exactly how the new database software was designed before you get started.
    (B) That both first and last names are current and spelled correctly.
    (C) That all the information pertaining to each person is accurate.
    (D) That the old database was correctly alphabetized by last name.

4. A social services department employs several bilingual employees. Which is the most reasonable explanation for this practice?
   (A) It is a state law.
   (B) Social workers that speak more than one language are better able to communicate with citizens who are not native-English speakers.
   (C) In every state there are more people who are bilingual than monolingual.
   (D) All clients prefer to speak in their native language.

5. In which of the following situations would it be acceptable to cancel a planned appointment just minutes before the scheduled meeting?
   (A) You should never cancel an appointment.
   (B) If the person you are meeting with had previously cancelled appointments with you last-minute.
   (C) If there is an emergency situation or unexpected obstacle such as a flat tire.
   (D) If you know the person you are meeting with very well and you know he or she won't mind rescheduling.

6. The following is an employee checklist.

   __ arrive on time, work begins at 9am
   __ dress appropriately (no jeans, no t-shirts, no athletic shoes, no sleeveless shirts)
   __ show your employee identification card to gain entry to the office
   __ please make sure your computer is off when you leave work at 5pm
   __ eating is only permitted in the office dining room
   __ the conference room is off limits
   __ keep personal phone calls to a minimum

   The office manager is asked to turn this checklist into an employee handbook. Which of the following is a good example of an employee handbook entry?
   (A) No matter what, you cannot wear jeans, t-shirts, athletic shoes, or sleeveless shirts. Make sure you are dressed appropriately when you show up for work and show your identification card. Please don't eat in the conference room. You can only eat in the office dining room. Don't make lots of personal calls and when you leave, turn your computer off.
   (B) When you arrive for work before 9am and show your identification card, please make sure that you are dressed appropriately. This means no jeans and t-shirts! You can eat in the office dining room, but stay out of the conference room. If you don't waste too much time you can make some personal calls at work. Don't forget to turn your computer off when you leave!

(C) Work hours begin at 9am. You must dress appropriately for work. This means you are not allowed to wear jeans, t-shirts, athletic shoes, or sleeveless shirts. When you arrive for work have your employee identification ready so that you can enter the office. Throughout the day, please keep your personal phone calls to a minimum. If you want to eat, please eat only in the dining room. The conference room is off limits at all times. The work day ends at 5pm. Before you leave the office, please make sure that your computer is turned off.

(D) When you arrive to work, before sure that you are dressed appropriately. You may not wear jeans, t-shirts, athletic shirts, or sleeveless shirts. Be sure to have your employee identification card with you. During the day, you should only eat in the dining room and you cannot go into the conference room. Keep your personal calls to a minimum and always shut off your computer when you leave.

7. The following is a list of supplies and their cost. These are all supplies that are needed by a department in the county clerks office.

Item	Quantity	Unit price	Total	Notes
Legal pads	40 boxes	$13.00/box	$520	
Toner for copier	2	$78.00	$156	Not required until June 2007
Pens	100 boxes at 20 pens each	$3.43/box	$343	(black, red, and blue)
Desktop computer	1	$876	$876	For new hire in June 2007
Label maker	2	$66	$132	

If an administrative assistant must submit a request in writing for these supplies, which of the following best conveys the office's needs?

(A) To keep the office stocked, the employees will require five items: legal pads (40 boxes), pens (100 boxes), a desktop computer (1), and toner (2 packages). The total amount of these items is $2,027. If this amount exceeds the current 2006 budget, the toner and computer ($1,032) are not required until 2007, and the cost of the remaining items is only $995.

(B) This office really needs some pens (of all colors: blue, black, and red), more paper (legal size—which costs $520), a new computer for the new employee (this is the most expensive item), and 2 label makers for the filing. Toner is also needed because the copier will run out next June.

(C) The employees require the following items for office use: a computer—but not until January 2007, some legal pads (at least 40 boxes), a label maker, and finally some pens (valued at $343).

(D) What we really need in 2006 are: legal pads ($13.00 per box but we only need 40 boxes), pens (especially red because we are out, but also blue and black; these are all the same price and the total will be $343) and 2 label makers for $132. In 2007 we will also need a computer and 2 packagers of toner for the copy machine.

8. The following instructions are provided to new employees learning how to use the filing system.

1. The color of the folder must match the color of the filing cabinet. (Example: Only red files in red cabinets.)

2. Folders are filed in reverse alphabetical order by last name.

3. When replacing a file, please put it exactly where you found it.

4. When creating a new folder, write the last name at the top of the folder.

5. Before leaving the filing room, ensure that all drawers you opened are once again securely locked!

The office manager thought the numbered instructions looked like step-by-step instructions. She decided to rewrite these rules. Which of the following most clearly indicates the rules for new employees?

(A) The most important thing is to make sure that filing drawers are always locked. Otherwise, you have to make sure that the color of the folder matches the cabinet and that the folders are filed in reverse alphabetical order. Don't put files in the wrong place and if you take a file out, be sure to replace it where you found it.

(B) Folders belong in the filing cabinet of the same color. For example, red files belong in red filing cabinets. When creating a new file, write the last name at the top of the folder. When replacing files make sure you put it back in its correct place. Remember, folders are filed in reverse alphabetical order by last name. Finally, when leaving the filing room, please make sure that all drawers are securely locked.

KAPLAN

(C) If you've got a green folder, make sure it goes in a green cabinet. Always put folders back where you found them—they go in reverse alphabetical order by last name. If you need to create a new folder, write the last name at the top. Always make sure drawers are locked.

(D) All the folders in the filing room are found in reverse alphabetical order by last name. Red folders go in red cabinets and so on. When you make a new folder, write the last name at the top and put all folders back where they belong. Do not forget to lock drawers before you leave.

9. You have been asked to take notes on a meeting. This is what you wrote:
    Who: All administrative support staff
    What: meeting to discuss summer vacation scheduling
    Where: Conference Room B
    When: Thursday, April 27 at 3pm
    Why: to avoid overlapping vacation time during the busy summer travel months
    Background: Last summer vacation time was not planned properly and a support staff of 2 remained the majority of August. A minimum support staff of 4 employees is needed at all times, even during slow summer months. With only 6 people on staff, it means only 2 employees can be away on vacation at one time.

Proposed schedule: June: Marjory and Patil have their choice of vacation days
July: Caroline and Rosario will have their choice of vacation days
August: Jordan and Ian will have their choice of vacation days.
NOTE: Employees may trade if they wish to take their vacations in a different month.

Which of the following is the best summary of why the meeting occurred and what was the result?

(A) We had a meeting last week in Conference Room B and this is what happened. This summer, the support staff of Marjory, Patil, Caroline, Rosario, Jordan, and Ian will take turns taking vacation so that there will always be 4 support staff members in the office. This did not happen last year, which is why this is being scheduled now.

(B) Summer vacation scheduling is very important. If people don't properly schedule their vacation, there may not be enough employees in the office to keep things running. So, this year, Marjory and Patil will be away in June, Caroline and Rosario will be away in July, and Jordan and Ian will be away in August. They might trade with each other so this is not concrete information.

(C) A meeting took place on April 27 at 3pm in Conference Room B. During this meeting of the support staff, we planned our summer holidays for this year. Only 2 people may take vacation at one time. Each employee got to choose a month and there were no scheduling conflicts so the problems we had last summer are resolved.

(D) Although there are 6 support staff employees, a minimum of 4 employees is required at all times. Last year, due to improper scheduling, there were only 2 support staff employees in the office during the month of August. To prevent this from occurring again, a meeting of all administrative support staff took place last week to create a proposed schedule for vacations this summer. It was agreed that each month of June, July, and August 2 staff members can schedule holidays. Employees may trade their vacation month with another employee if he or she wishes.

10. Responding to the report of an incident at a local public school, Social Worker Shawn gathers the following information:
Location: Burberry Public School
Time: 1:45 P.M.
Incident: assault
Victim: Mr. Mower, a teacher
Person in question: Ryan Callahan, a fourth-grade student
Injury: Mr. Mower has a slight cut above his eye.
Item used in incident: a wooden ruler

Care given: Mr. Mower was seen by the school nurse.
Status of situation with student: Ryan Callahan confessed and is now speaking with the principal and school counselor.

Social Worker Shawn is filling out a report on the incident. Which of the following expresses the information most clearly and accurately?

(A) Mr. Mower, a teacher at Burberry Elementary School, stated that he was assaulted by Ryan Callahan, a student at the school, at 1:45 P.M. at Burberry Elementary School and suffered a cut above his eye. Ryan Callahan confessed and is waiting until his parents arrive.

(B) Ryan Callahan, a student at Burberry Elementary School, assaulted Mr. Mower, a teacher, at Burberry Elementary School with a wooden ruler. He has a cut above his eye and may need to go to the hospital. Ryan Callahan admitted assaulting Mr. Mower at 1:45 P.M., at which time the incident took place on school grounds.

(C) Mr. Mower, a teacher at Burberry Elementary School, reported that at 1:45 P.M. at the school a student named Ryan Callahan assaulted him with a wooden ruler. Mr. Mower suffered a small cut above his eye, but he is being seen by the school nurse. Ryan Callahan admitted to assaulting Mr. Mower and is at the principal's office, where the school counselor is also in attendance.

(D) Mr. Mower was assaulted with a wooden ruler by a student, Ryan Callahan, who assaulted Mr. Mower at the school where he went and he worked, Burberry Elementary School. Ryan Callahan admitted he did it and Mr. Mower was taken to the school nurse, where he being treated for his injuries. Ryan Callahan is still at school.

11.

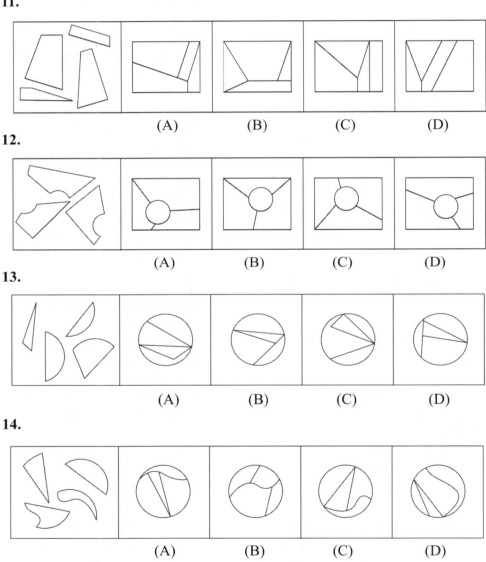

(A)   (B)   (C)   (D)

12.

(A)   (B)   (C)   (D)

13.

(A)   (B)   (C)   (D)

14.

(A)   (B)   (C)   (D)

15.

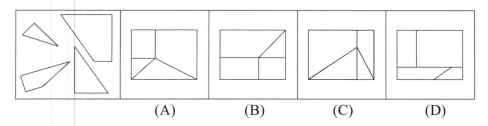

(A)   (B)   (C)   (D)

16.

17.

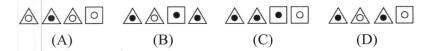

18.

19.   ☆★☆★   ★★★☆   ★★★☆   ☆★★__

       ☆   ★   ★   ☆

    (A)   (B)   (C)   (D)

20.

    (A)   (B)   (C)   (D)

21. ZAB   XCD   VEF   _____
    (A) UGH
    (B) WFG
    (C) YHI
    (D) TGH

22. lfg   mgh   _____   oij
    (A) hgm
    (B) nhi
    (C) ngh
    (D) mhi

23. BxY   cXy   DxY   _____
    (A) ExY
    (B) eXy
    (C) exy
    (D) Dxy

24. ZAB   YBC   _____   WDE
    (A) WDC
    (B) XCD
    (C) XAE
    (D) XCF

25. ABE   BCF   CDG   _____
    (A) DFG
    (B) DEF
    (C) DFH
    (D) DEH

26. Mount Everest is the highest mountain in the world. Mount Everest is in Nepal.
    (A) Mount Everest is in the Himalayas.
    (B) The highest mountain in the world is in Nepal.
    (C) The Rocky Mountains are the highest mountain range in the United States.
    (D) Mount Everest is hard to climb.

27. The bus costs $1.50 for adults and is free for students traveling to school in the morning and returning home from school in the afternoon until 4 P.M. It is now 4:30 P.M. and Karen does not have enough money to take the bus.
    (A) Karen usually gets home before 3 P.M.
    (B) Karen is coming home late from school.
    (C) Karen is a student.
    (D) Karen has less than $1.50.

28. On its way uptown, the local train stops every ten blocks, starting at 10th Street. The express train also starts at 10th Street, but after that it stops only at every other station. The #6 train is an express train.
    (A) The local train is very slow.
    (B) The #6 train does not stop at 40th Street.
    (C) The #6 train stops at 20th Street.
    (D) The #6 train is faster than the #5 train.

29. Brandon was looking for his car keys all morning. He looked under the bed, in the kitchen cabinet, and in his coat pocket. Finally, he looked in the ignition of the car and shouted "Aha!"
    (A) Brandon is always absentminded.
    (B) The lost keys were in the car.
    (C) Brandon left the car running.
    (D) Brandon was late to work.

30. A jury reaches a verdict when all of its members have come to a unanimous agreement. In one recent well-publicized trial, the judge thought that the jury had reached a verdict. Eventually, it was learned that one juror had never been able to agree with the others. The proceeding was ultimately declared a mistrial by the judge.

Based only on the information above, which of the following statements is a valid conclusion?

(A) The jury never actually reached a verdict.

(B) The jury had reached a verdict but had been disrupted by a single juror.

(C) There have been other trials in which the jury failed to reach a verdict.

(D) Only trials in which the jury fails to reach a verdict are declared mistrials.

(E) The judge's role is not as important as that of the individual jurors.

31. In a foreign language class for students who know nothing of the language being taught, those who have already studied another foreign language do much better at first than those who have had no previous foreign language training. After about three months, both groups perform at the same level.

Which of the following conclusions is best supported by the information above?

(A) Students with previous foreign language training studied more at the beginning of the course.

(B) Many foreign languages are very similar to one another.

(C) Students who like learning foreign languages learn better than those who do not.

(D) The ability to learn a new language is initially increased by previous experience in learning a new language.

(E) Advanced knowledge of one subject can interfere with an attempt to learn a new subject.

32. A woman has exactly four daughters: Carla, Deirdre, Edith, and Flora. Carla is older than Edith, but younger than Deirdre. If Flora is Carla's only twin, then we know that

(A) Deirdre is the youngest of the daughters.

(B) Edith is the youngest of the daughters.

(C) Edith is older than both Carla and Flora.

(D) Edith is older than both Carla and Deirdre.

(E) Carla and Deirdre are both younger than Flora.

33. If Carlos follows the safety precautions, then his experiment will go according to plan.

According to the statement above, which of the following must be true?

(A) If Carlos's experiment goes according to plan, then he followed the safety precautions.

(B) If Carlos does not follow the safety precautions, his experiment is potentially dangerous.

(C) If Carlos's experiment does not go according to plan, then he did not follow the safety precautions.

(D) Carlos's experiment will only go according to plan if he follows the safety precautions.

(E) If Carlos does not follow the safety precautions, then his experiment will not go according to plan.

34. Time and time again, it has been shown that students who attend colleges with low faculty/student ratios get the most well-rounded education. As a result, when my children are ready for college, I'll be sure they attend a school with a very small student population.

Which of the following, if true, identifies the greatest flaw in the reasoning above?

(A) A low faculty/student ratio is the effect of a well-rounded education, not its source.

(B) Intelligence should be considered the result of childhood environment, not advanced education.

(C) A very small student population does not, by itself, ensure a low faculty/student ratio.

(D) Parental desires and preferences rarely determine a child's choice of a college or university.

(E) Students must take advantage of the low faculty/student ratio by intentionally choosing small classes.

35. The local high school students have been clamoring for the freedom to design their own curricula. Allowing this would be as disastrous as allowing 3-year-olds to choose their own diets. These students have neither the maturity nor the experience to equal that of the professional educators now doing the job.

Which of the following statements, if true, would most strengthen the above argument?

(A) High school students have less formal education than those who currently design the curricula.

(B) 3-year-olds do not, if left to their own devices, choose healthful diets.

(C) The local high school students are less intelligent than the average teenager.

(D) Individualized curricula are more beneficial to high school students than are the standard curricula, which are rigid and unresponsive to their particular strengths and weaknesses.

(E) The ability to design good curricula develops only after years of familiarity with educational life.

36. If a poor harvest season in a major corn-producing state results in higher prices for a bushel of corn, corn prices in other states will rise as well, whether or not those states are net importers of corn.

Which of the following conclusions is best supported by the statement above?

(A) Agricultural commodities companies in states that are not net importers of corn are excluded from the national corn market when there is a disruption in the national corn supply.

(B) National corn supply disruptions have little, if any, effect on the price of local corn as long as the locality is in a state that is not a net importer of corn.

(C) The corn market in any state is part of the national corn market even if most of the corn consumed in the state is produced in the state.

(D) Poor harvesting seasons come at predictable regular intervals.

(E) Higher prices for corn tend to lead to increased prices for livestock, which rely on corn feed.

37. All German philosophers, except for Marx, are idealists.

From which of the following can the statement above be most properly inferred?

(A) Except for Marx, if someone is an idealist philosopher, then he or she is German.

(B) Marx is the only non-German philosopher who is an idealist.

(C) If a German is an idealist, then he or she is a philosopher, as long as he or she is not Marx.

(D) Marx is not an idealist German philosopher.

(E) Aside from the philosopher Marx, if someone is a German philosopher, then he or she is an idealist.

38. Our architecture schools must be doing something wrong. Almost monthly we hear of domes and walkways collapsing in public places, causing great harm to human life. In their pursuit of some dubious aesthetic, architects design buildings that sway, crumble, and even shed windows into our cities' streets. This kind of incompetence will disappear only when the curricula of our architecture schools devote less time to so-called artistic considerations and more time to the basics of good design.

Which of the following, if true, would most seriously weaken the argument above?

(A) All architecture students are given training in basic physics and mechanics.
(B) Most of the problems with modern buildings stem from poor construction rather than poor design.
(C) Less than 50 percent of the curriculum at most architecture schools is devoted to aesthetics.
(D) Most buildings manage to stay in place well past their projected life expectancies.
(E) Architects study as long and as intensively as most other professionals.

39. A researcher has discovered that steel containing Element X is stronger and more flexible than ordinary steel because Element X reduces the occurrence of microscopic fractures. The level of Element X in much of the steel produced in Canada is naturally high because the ore deposits from which the steel is produced also contain Element X.

Which of the following can be correctly inferred from the statements above?
(A) Steel from Canada is stronger and more flexible than steel from any other country.
(B) Steel that is not from Canada is highly likely to develop microscopic fractures after years of use.
(C) Producing steel from ore deposits containing Element X is the best way to make steel that is stronger and more flexible.
(D) Some steel produced in Canada is less likely to develop microscopic fractures than other steel.
(E) Steel produced from Canadian ore deposits contains the highest levels of Element X found in any steel.

40. Electrical engineers have developed an energy-efficient type of light bulb that can replace the traditional incandescent bulb. The new bulb, known as the electronic lamp, operates by using a high-frequency radio signal rather than the filament featured in incandescent bulbs. Although the electronic lamp currently costs 20 times as much as its traditional counterpart, its use will prove more cost effective in the long run. While a 100-watt incandescent bulb lasts 6 months if burned for 4 hours daily, a 25-watt electronic lamp used for the same amount of time each day lasts up to 14 years.

The argument above assumes that
(A) the typical household use of a light bulb is approximately 4 hours a day
(B) aside from its greater efficiency, the electronic lamp resembles the incandescent light bulb in most aspects

(C) the type of light cast by
the electronic lamp is
different from that cast by an
incandescent bulb

(D) the price of electronic lamps
will decrease as they are
produced in increasingly
greater quantities

(E) a 100-watt incandescent
light bulb does not provide
significantly more light than a
25-watt electronic lamp

Answers and Explanations

1. C

You may be tempted to hang up the phone or to yell back, but these are not appropriate professional responses. The best solution is to remain polite and try to calm the caller down so you can handle the call appropriately. Handling the call may eventually lead to transferring the call to the manager, but you should first try to assess the situation.

2. C

Choices (A), (B), and (D) are not reasonable responses to the thefts. The most reasonable response to prevent further thefts is for employees to guard their belongings more closely.

3. B

Although choices (A) and (D) might seem logical, based on the passage you can assume that because you are there to help update the database, you are not responsible for exactly how the database was designed and whether the old database functioned well. Choice (C) contains an absolute. Remember, absolutes are rarely correct. Although ideally all the information in the database should be correct, it is mostly the first names that will affect the efficiency of the new database. Therefore, choice (B) is correct.

4. B

Watch for the word *always,* as in (C). This is often an indication that a statement is exaggerated or incorrect.

5. C

Remember to beware of absolutes. The word *never* in choice (A) should have alerted you that this is not the correct answer. Of course there will be situations where you will have to cancel at the last minute due to unforeseen situations such as described in choice (C)— the correct answer. Choices (B) and (D) are not professional excuses for a last-minute cancellation.

6. C

Only choice (C) includes all the information from the checklist in a clear and concise manner.

7. A

There is a lot of information in the table. Only choice (A) includes all the most important information without going into too much detail or without omitting any items.

8. B

Although choice (D) seems like a good summary, it is vague on some details. Choice (B) is the most clear and accurate.

9. D

Although choice (D) is the longest, it presents only the most important information and in the most clear and accurate way.

10. C

This information is stated most clearly. The other reports leave out details or oversimplify the details from the report.

11. A

12. C

13. B

14. C

15. C

16. A

Examine the building blocks of each section that makes up the sequence. The first shape has a hole in the middle of it, and the second one is whole. Notice that the second shape is always different from the first. The shapes are either circles, squares, or triangles. Therefore, the next element in the pattern has to begin with a shape with a hole in it, followed by a circle, triangle, or square. Only choice (A) fits this pattern.

17. D

Each set is made up of four arrows. The first, second, and fourth arrow alternate between pointing up or down. The third arrow always points up. The next set should start with an arrow pointing down, followed by one pointing up, the third arrow always points up, and the fourth should point up.

18. D

The pattern is made up of three triangles and a square. The first triangle always has a solid dot in the center, though the second and third triangle alternate between having a solid or an empty dot in the middle. The square also alternates between having a solid or empty dot in the center. Therefore, the next set should include a triangle with a solid dot, a triangle with an open dot, a triangle with a solid dot, and a square with an open dot.

19. D

The sets are made up of four stars; two are filled in and two are not. The missing star in the last set should be empty so that the balance of two filled in and two empty remains the same. There is no reason to believe the star would be only partially filled in.

20. C

Each set is made up of two "houses." One points up, the next points down. In each subsequent set, the second house gains a detail that was present previously in the first house. Therefore, the missing house should point down (as the second one always does) and it should gain the shading in the top triangle that the first house had in the preceding set.

21. D

The first letter of each sequence moves toward A, skipping a letter of the alphabet. Notice that we move from Z to X, having skipped Y. We move from X to V having skipped W. The second and third letters of each sequence move toward Z: AB, CD, EF. The next part of the sequence should move from V to T, skipping U and followed by GH. Writing down the alphabet somewhere in the blank margins of your test booklet would help you map out the sequence and see the skipped letters on a question like this one.

22. **B**

The first letter of each set goes up by one letter: l, m, n, o. The last two letters are also increased by one letter, but the last letter is repeated: fg, gh, hi, ij. So the missing set is nhi.

23. **B**

Notice that in the first and third sets, the first letter is capitalized, the second letter is lowercase, and the last letter is capitalized. In the second set, the first letter is lowercase, the second letter is capitalized, and the last letter is also lowercase. The last 2 letters are always x and y, and the first letter increases by one letter: b, c, d. So, to follow the pattern, you are looking for a set beginning with a lowercase e, followed by a capital X, followed by a lowercase y. The correct answer is choice (B).

24. **B**

As we move from left to right, the first letters are arranged in decreasing alphabetical order, and the second letters and third letters are arranged in increasing alphabetical order: ZAB YBC XCD WDE.

25. **D**

Note the pattern of the first and second letter of each group: AB, BC, CD, DE. Also note the pattern of the third letter of each group: E, F, G, H. The answer is DEH.

26. **B**

If Mount Everest is the highest mountain in the world and it is in Nepal, the highest mountain in the world is in Nepal. Though (A) and (C) and (D) are true, remember that you are supposed to draw a conclusion based *only* on the information given.

27. **D**

Although we are told the price of riding the bus for adults and for students traveling to and from school, no mention is made of Karen's age. Even if Karen is a student, it is after 4 P.M., so she would have to pay $1.50 to ride the bus. All we can tell for certain is that Karen has less that $1.50.

28. **B**

Express trains skip every other station. That is, they start at 10th Street, skip 20th Street, go to 30th Street, skip 40th Street, etc. The #6 train is an express, so it follows this pattern. That makes choice (B) correct, but choice (C) incorrect. We do not know the relative speed of the local train because it is not mentioned, nor do we know how slow the #5 train is.

29. **B**

The car keys must have been in the ignition, because when Brandon finally looked there he shouted "Aha!" Keys can be in an ignition while the car is off; therefore, we cannot assume that the car was running. We do not know if Brandon is always absentminded or if he was late to work that morning.

30. **A**

If one juror had never been able to agree with the others, then the members of the jury never came to a unanimous agreement; they never reached a verdict (A). Choice (B) is incorrect because it contradicts this idea. (C), (D), and (E) may all be true statements, but we have no way of knowing for sure from the information in the passage.

31. **D**

Choice (D)'s conclusion is based solidly on (and is really not much more than a restatement of) the information we have, that students who have already studied one foreign language initially learn a second language faster than do students with no prior foreign-language learning experience.

Choices (A), (B), and (C) base their conclusions on unwarranted assumptions as well as the information in the passage, so they are wrong. Choice (E) contradicts the information in the passage.

32. **B**

It helps to draw a diagram when you are answering this question. According to the question, Carla is older than Edith but younger than Deirdre:

Deirdre
Carla
Edith

If the fourth daughter Flora is Carla's only twin, then we know that Flora and Carla are the same age:

Deirdre
Carla and Flora
Edith

Based on this information, the only conclusion that is true is that Edith must be the youngest daughter, choice (B).

33. **C**

Here, you are told that if Carlos follows the safety precautions, his experiment will go according to plan. Thus, if Carlos' experiment did not go according to plan, then he did not follow the safety precautions. You should see that this is choice (C).

Choices (A) and (B) *might* be true. They do seem logical. However, we don't know that they *might* be true. The fact that his experiment will go according to plan if he follows the safety precautions does not mean that it could not go according to plan if he didn't follow them. That's too big a leap to make. The issue of danger is beyond the scope of the argument. You might assume that the experiment is potentially dangerous but you do not *know* this. Choice (D) is too extreme and is kind of like choice (A)—just because following the safety precautions will lead to a successful experiment does not mean that this is the only thing that will work. This is the same reasoning that eliminates choice (E)—you simply do not know what will happen if Carlos fails to follow safety precautions. You know what happens only if he follows them.

34. **C**

The evidence says that students who attend colleges with low faculty/student ratios get well-rounded educations, but the conclusion is that the author will send his kids to colleges with small student populations. Because colleges can have the second without necessarily having the first, choice (C) is correct.

Choice (A) claims that the author confuses cause and effect, but how could getting a well-rounded education cause a low faculty/student ratio?

Anyway, the real problem is the scope shift from faculty/student ratios to student populations. As for choice (B), the author never mentions intelligence at all. Choice (D) fails because it doesn't point to a problem in the reasoning, just in implementing it. And choice (E) claims students must do something extra to take advantage of the low faculty/student ratio. Because the author never claimed the benefits would be conferred automatically, this isn't a flaw; more importantly, choice (E) misses the real flaw, which we find in choice (C).

35. **E**

First, we need to understand the structure of the argument. Here the statement, "Allowing this would be as disastrous as…" clues us into the author's opinion. Assumption: One needs maturity and experience to design curricula. If the assumption were true, the argument would be strengthened. Check the answer choices, and look for one that affirms the assumption. Choice (A) is just a restatement of the evidence; this choice adds no new information.

In (B) the argument made an analogy: "Allowing students to make their own curricula is as disastrous as letting 3-year olds choose their own diets." If an argument uses an analogy to make a point, it had better do so effectively. The better the analogy, the stronger the argument. This choice does strengthen the argument by showing the analogy to be true. But the question asks for the best strengthener and a more relevant strengthener may be present.

Choice (C) is a classic faulty comparison choice; it is also out of scope. The author doesn't distinguish between local high school students and average teenagers. Moreover, the focus is on experience and maturity, not intelligence. Choice (D) shifts the focus of the argument from "who should or should not design curricula" to "what kind of curricula is best." Notice the scope change in this choice. It's tempting, especially because it brings up an intelligent point about tailoring to individuals, but that's a topic for a different discussion. The best strengthener is choice (E), citing the experience needed to design curricula.

36. **C**

The passages says that if the price of corn rises in a major corn-producing state because of a poor harvest, the price of corn will increase in other states, whether those states import or grow most of their corn. In other words, the price of corn must somehow be standardized. This implies that all states are part of a national corn market, as in (C).

Choice (A) turns the statement 180 degrees; if states that are not importers of corn are not part of the national corn market, their prices won't be affected by a bad harvest in another state, which contradicts the argument. The same is true for choice (B): The argument states that the price of all corn—local and imported—is affected by a bad harvest in one state. Choice (D) is out of scope; the passage focuses on corn prices, not bad harvests. Choice (E), too, is out of scope, because livestock isn't part of the argument, but it might be tempting; it certainly could be true, but it is incorrect because it is out of scope and doesn't have to be true based on the stimulus. Choice (C) is within the scope and must be true.

37. **E**

Read carefully. You are asked to pick the choice from which the statement can be derived, and that's (E): If, as (E) says, anyone who is a German philosopher is an idealist except for the philosopher Marx, then all German philosophers except for Marx are idealists. That being the case, it would certainly be true that, as the statement says, with the exception of Marx, all German philosophers—these folks being a subset of all Germans—are idealists. Now while choice (E)'s claim that all German philosophers are idealists may sound a bit absurd to you (perhaps you know some German philosophers who aren't idealists), we're concerned with strict logic here, not content.

Choice (A) tells us that except for Marx, if someone's an idealist philosopher, then he or she is German, which is precisely the opposite of what we need. Knowing that all idealist philosophers (except Marx) are German doesn't prove that all German philosophers are idealists, because there could be other kinds of German philosophers. Because the statement tells us that Marx is a German philosopher who's not an idealist, choice (B), which contradicts this, is wrong. Choice (C) lets us conclude that German idealists who aren't Marx are philosophers, but we need to conclude that German philosophers (except Marx) are idealists. As for choice (D), like the statement, it tells us that Marx isn't an idealist German philosopher, but we need a statement that ensures that every other German philosopher besides Marx is an idealist.

38. **B**

Because the author concludes from evidence of collapsing buildings that architecture schools should spend more time teaching "the basics of good design," she obviously assumes that the buildings are falling down because of poor design, not poor construction. Choice (B) destroys the argument by demolishing this assumption.

The author claims architecture schools don't focus enough on basic design, not basic physics and mechanics, so choice (A) is not weakening the argument. As for choice (C), the author never spells out how much of the curriculum should be spent on design, so more than half may not be enough for her. Choice (D) distorts the argument—the author never claimed that most buildings are falling down, so the fact that most of them stay up doesn't matter. As for choice (E), other professionals are beyond the scope—the issue is how much architecture schools focus on basic design rather than on more lofty artistic concerns.

39. **D**

We need to find the choice that must logically follow if the passage is true. If making steel with Element X reduces the level of microscopic fractures, and if some Canadian steel contains Element X, it follows that some Canadian steel will be less likely to develop such fractures. So choice (D) can be inferred.

Choice (A) is out of scope and uses extreme language; we can't compare all Canadian steel to all the steel from all other countries. Choice (B) wrongly introduces the idea of "years of use" and "not from Canada," which are outside the scope of the stimulus; we only know specifics about some, not all, Canadian steel and nothing about when fractures might develop. Choices (C) and (E) are too extreme—the passage never says steel from ore deposits rich in Element X is the "best," or that it contains more Element X than any other steel.

40. E

Here we need to identify an assumption. The author attempts to demonstrate that the "electronic lamp" can replace the incandescent bulb (that's the conclusion) because although the electronic lamp now costs much more, it will prove more cost effective *in the long run* (that's a summary of the evidence). He backs up this claim with numbers: A 25-watt electronic lamp can last 28 times longer than a 100-watt incandescent bulb while costing only 20 times as much as the bulb (that's the hard evidence). There's one factor missing from the equation, though, and that's the amount of light the electronic lamp supplies. For the numbers given to support the author's conclusion, the electronic lamp and the normal bulb must each throw about the same amount of light. Otherwise, we might need 15

lamps for every bulb; and if this were the case, the argument would be wrong. Unless we assume, as choice (E) says, that the light produced by the lamp and the bulb is approximately equal, the evidence is meaningless.

Choice (A) isn't assumed because the figure *4 hours a day* doesn't have to represent typical household use; it need only provide a standard by which the lights can be compared. Choice (B) is contradicted by the author. Because the electronic lamp operates by radio waves instead of a filament, it's clear that there are important structural aspects in which it differs from incandescent bulbs. Choice (C) would actually make us doubt the reasonableness of the author's conclusion, so clearly it isn't assumed. If the electronic lamp is supposed to be a replacement for the incandescent bulb, its light should be similar to that produced by the bulb. Choice (D) misconstrues why the electronic lamp is claimed to be cost effective in the long run—the point is that it lasts longer, not that it will become cheaper. The author is arguing that current electronic lamps are more cost effective, not that future lamps will be.

CHAPTER NINE

Personal Characteristics and Experience Inventory

Introduction

There are plenty of things a multiple-choice test cannot tell about you, for example, whether you have the experience to succeed on the job, whether you have the personality to handle your new job environment, or whether you have the desire to make the most of your new career in civil service. However, these *are* things that potential employers want to know about you. To meet the demand for more information about job candidates, government agencies have created question sets that are increasingly more often included in civil service exams. This chapter discusses this unusual question type and lets you know exactly what to expect. You can learn even more about yourself and these questions by completing Practice Test 7 at the end of the chapter.

Personal Characteristics and Experience Inventory Lesson

"Personal characteristics and experience inventory" is quite a mouthful. But then again, it states exactly what it is. This "test" contains items that you must react to while carefully considering your experiences at work, school, or volunteering. Some items are statements and some are questions, but all refer to *your* personal characteristics and *your* personal experiences.

The best news is that there are no correct or incorrect answers. Your only task is to pick the responses that are *most true about you.*

For some questions on this test, more than one response may describe you or your feelings. Try to respond with the answer that *most fits you when you are working.* If you cannot relate the question to any experiences in the workforce, consider another experience that may approximate a job, for example, working:

- in a volunteer position
- within a club or organization
- on a neighborhood project
- in a school theatrical production
- on a political campaign

How Are Personal Characteristics and Experience Inventory Questions Scored?

Your score on this "test" is based on an analysis of your responses to the questions. Test developers do not explain how this section is scored or how that score affects your overall exam score. However, all responses are considered in determining your results, so *do not skip any of these questions.*

Remember, there is no right or wrong way to react to any of these questions. You might be tempted to select only the responses that you feel will make you look your best. However, you must try *not* to manipulate the answers for this section. Test writers have incorporated checks and balances into this section to identify a test taker who might be trying to manipulate or "out-think" the test. Therefore, you must answer as honestly and consistently as possible. Don't waste your time or energy trying to cheat the results of this test—rather, try to relax, be honest, and be yourself. After all, if you get the job using false answers, the person you *really* are will be uncomfortable at work.

Jobs Requiring Personal Characteristics and Experience Inventory Tests

One civil service exam that has been quick to incorporate these questions is the Postal Worker Exam, also known as Test 473. On this exam there are a total of 236 Personal Characteristics and Experience Inventory questions to be completed in 90 minutes. It is the longest section of Test 473, so clearly it is a very important part of this civil service exam.

Psychological Testing

Some civil service jobs, such as police, highway patrol, and firefighters, serve the important purpose of promoting and maintaining public safety. This is quite a serious responsibility. As a result, employees for these positions may be required to take another kind of personal characteristic test. It is usually completely separate to the civil service exam. One common exam that government agencies use is the Minnesota Multiphasic Psychological Inventory, or MMPI. This exam, which can have from 300 up to 500 questions, is designed to assess any psychological issues that could prevent someone from performing their job duties to the standards of the profession.

There are some similarities between Psychological Testing and the Personal Characteristics and Experience Inventory test. First, these questions have no correct answers. Test takers must answer questions honestly, without considering how they should respond to get a better "score." Secondly, these questions must be completed in a relatively short amount of time. This prevents test takers from overthinking their responses.

If you are not sure which type of test you are taking, you can consult the job announcement for the position you want. This announcement should include more detailed information. However, regardless of which type of personal characteristic or psychological test you take, it's not something you can prepare for in advance. The best you can do on these tests is to be completely honest in your responses.

Similar Personal Characteristics and Experience Inventory tests are becoming increasingly common on other civil service exams. Your responses to the questions in these sections can tell potential employers a lot about your previous work and personal experiences and your preferences, which in turn help them determine if you are right for the job. This is especially true for entry-level positions. People who have years of work experience on their resume may not have to complete these kinds of tests. However, if you are applying for an entry-level position, you should anticipate that your civil service exam will include a personal characteristics and experience inventory test.

If you are wondering exactly what kinds of questions make up these tests, the next section details the three most common Personal Characteristics and Experience Inventory questions.

Sample Personal Characteristics and Experience Inventory Questions

A Personal Characteristics and Experience Inventory test usually has three sections. Each section contains a different question type. As mentioned before, the questions present a statement or a question that you should consider in terms of your work, school, or volunteer experiences. The first section, Agree/Disagree, has the same four answer choices for every question. These choices are: Strongly Agree, Agree, Disagree, and Strongly Disagree. The second section, Frequency, also has four choices: Very Often, Often, Sometimes, and Rarely. The third section, Experience, includes questions that have anywhere from four to nine possible responses, all of which are different for every question.

Here is more information about—and sample questions for—each question type.

Agree/Disagree Questions

The first section is the Agree/Disagree section. There are only four answer choices for this question type and the answer choices are always the same for Agree/Disagree questions.

Here is an example.

You prefer to work alone.
- (A) Strongly Agree
- (B) Agree
- (C) Disagree
- (D) Strongly Disagree

Frequency Questions

The next section is the Frequency section. There are also only four answer choices for this question type. Again, answer choices are always the same for Frequency questions.

Here is an example.

You like to set goals to accomplish a work objective.
- (A) Very Often
- (B) Often
- (C) Sometimes
- (D) Rarely

Experience Questions

The final section is the Experience section. Unlike the previous two sections, these questions are followed by anywhere from four to nine answer choices. Also, the answer choices are different for every question so you will need to spend more time reviewing the answer choices.

Here is an example.

What kind of work do you like the least?
- (A) doing the same tasks every day
- (B) standing or sitting in one place for hours at a time
- (C) moving from task to task quickly
- (D) making a lot of decisions
- (E) all of these
- (F) would not mind any of these

Now that you have reviewed all the question types, you can learn some helpful tips for completing this part of your civil service exam.

Tips for Personal Characteristics and Experience Inventory Success

When you take the Personal Characteristics and Experience Inventory test, you have a lot of questions to answer in a short amount of time—you will only have about 20 to 30 seconds to answer each question. Because you are expected to answer all of the questions, increase your chances of finishing the test on time by trying out the following strategies:

- ■ Memorize the answer choices for the Agree/Disagree and the Frequency questions in advance.
- ■ Read the Experience options carefully.
- ■ Mark one and only one response for each item.
- ■ Work at a good pace.

Memorize the Response Choices for the Agree/Disagree and the Frequency Questions in Advance

While you cannot really "learn" the answers to these questions, you can at least become comfortable with the kinds of questions asked and the answer choices for the first two question types. Before you walk into the exam, know both the Agree/Disagree and the Frequency answer choices by heart. They are easy enough to memorize, and then re-reading them won't hold you up. You will just have to scan the now-familiar responses.

Agree/Disagree.
    (A) Strongly Agree
    (B) Agree
    (C) Disagree
    (D) Strongly Disagree

Frequency.
    (A) Very Often
    (B) Often
    (C) Sometimes
    (D) Rarely

Read the Experience Options Carefully

A number of questions in the third section—the Experience section—will offer you answer choices such as these:

All of these
Two of the above
Two or more of the above
None of these
Not sure

These kinds of answer choices can be confusing! Be cautious in choosing the *most appropriate* of the responses, the one that best fits your experience.

Mark One and Only One Response for Each Item

You should evaluate and respond to each question, even if you are not completely sure which choice is best. It is vital to your success that you mark only one answer for each item. There will be some statements or questions where more than one answer choice seems appropriate. Nevertheless, choose only one—the one that applies most closely to your work experiences. Please remember, do not attempt to distort or shape your self-descriptions on this test—just be honest and consistent in marking the *one* answer that best describes your personal opinion.

Work at a Good Pace

If your civil service exam includes as many Personal Characteristics and Experience Inventory questions as the Postal Worker Exam has (236, in all), you will have to work at a fairly rapid pace. Your natural tendency may be to over-evaluate each statement or to reconsider your feelings and reactions once you have answered a question. Don't be tempted to spend a few minutes evaluating your responses; just react.

No matter how many questions there are, you will not have an unlimited amount of time to answer the questions. You should average between two to three questions a minute. However, note that you will move through the Agree/Disagree and the Frequency segments much more quickly than the Experience segment, because those first two sections have only four set answer choices for each item—and you will have memorized those choices by the exam date. The Experience segment will naturally take longer because there are four to nine original answer choices for each item—none of which can be memorized in advance.

Now that you have reviewed these tips, you are one step closer to being prepared for Practice Test 7 and for test day.

Summary

In this chapter you learned about a unique part of civil service exams, the Personal Characteristics and Experience Inventory test. Because these questions are so different than the types of questions you have studied so far in this book, you should have spent a fair amount of time familiarizing yourself with them. If you only learned one thing in this chapter, though, it should be that when you answer these questions, you must be honest. Choosing the answer you *think* is "correct" will only lower your score in the long run. Don't worry about studying this chapter repeatedly, because other than knowing what to expect, you cannot study for these questions.

When you are ready to answer a few questions about yourself, use the 20-question practice test to further familiarize yourself with the Personal Characteristics and Experience Inventory test.

Practice Test 7

20 Questions
10 Minutes

1 Ⓐ Ⓑ Ⓒ Ⓓ   6 Ⓐ Ⓑ Ⓒ Ⓓ   11 Ⓐ Ⓑ Ⓒ Ⓓ   15 Ⓐ Ⓑ Ⓒ Ⓓ Ⓔ Ⓕ
2 Ⓐ Ⓑ Ⓒ Ⓓ   7 Ⓐ Ⓑ Ⓒ Ⓓ   12 Ⓐ Ⓑ Ⓒ Ⓓ   16 Ⓐ Ⓑ Ⓒ Ⓓ Ⓔ
3 Ⓐ Ⓑ Ⓒ Ⓓ   8 Ⓐ Ⓑ Ⓒ Ⓓ   13 Ⓐ Ⓑ Ⓒ Ⓓ   17 Ⓐ Ⓑ Ⓒ Ⓓ
4 Ⓐ Ⓑ Ⓒ Ⓓ   9 Ⓐ Ⓑ Ⓒ Ⓓ   14 Ⓐ Ⓑ Ⓒ Ⓓ   18 Ⓐ Ⓑ Ⓒ Ⓓ Ⓔ Ⓕ Ⓖ Ⓗ
5 Ⓐ Ⓑ Ⓒ Ⓓ   10 Ⓐ Ⓑ Ⓒ Ⓓ   19 Ⓐ Ⓑ Ⓒ Ⓓ
                                              20 Ⓐ Ⓑ Ⓒ Ⓓ Ⓔ Ⓕ Ⓖ

Answer the following questions honestly and accurately.

Agree/Disagree

1. You prefer to work alone.
(A) Strongly Agree
(B) Agree
(C) Disagree
(D) Strongly Disagree

2. You prefer to work unsupervised.
(A) Strongly Agree
(B) Agree
(C) Disagree
(D) Strongly Disagree

3. You dislike short-term deadlines.
(A) Strongly Agree
(B) Agree
(C) Disagree
(D) Strongly Disagree

4. You would rather have a flexible work schedule.
(A) Strongly Agree
(B) Agree
(C) Disagree
(D) Strongly Disagree

5. You prefer to work closely with others.
(A) Strongly Agree
(B) Agree
(C) Disagree
(D) Strongly Disagree

6. You prefer to avoid conflict with coworkers.
(A) Strongly Agree
(B) Agree
(C) Disagree
(D) Strongly Disagree

7. You think it is important to be part of a team.
(A) Strongly Agree
(B) Agree
(C) Disagree
(D) Strongly Disagree

Frequency

8. You will work until a project is finished, even if it's after normal work hours.
(A) Very Often
(B) Often
(C) Sometimes
(D) Rarely

9. You like to set goals to accomplish a work objective.
(A) Very Often
(B) Often
(C) Sometimes
(D) Rarely

10. You often fall behind schedule.
    (A) Very Often
    (B) Often
    (C) Sometimes
    (D) Rarely

11. You have personal conflicts with coworkers.
    (A) Very Often
    (B) Often
    (C) Sometimes
    (D) Rarely

12. You are not productive in the early morning.
    (A) Very Often
    (B) Often
    (C) Sometimes
    (D) Rarely

13. You have trouble managing your time effectively.
    (A) Very Often
    (B) Often
    (C) Sometimes
    (D) Rarely

14. You take breaks during work.
    (A) Very Often
    (B) Often
    (C) Sometimes
    (D) Rarely

Experience

15. What kind of work do you like the least?
    (A) doing the same tasks every day
    (B) standing or sitting in one place for hours at a time
    (C) moving from task to task quickly
    (D) making a lot of decisions
    (E) all of these
    (F) would not mind any of these

16. What motivates you to stay on task?
    (A) myself
    (B) coworkers
    (C) my supervisor reminding me
    (D) none of the above
    (E) all of the above

17. What kind of decisions do you want to be responsible for?
    (A) none
    (B) as few as possible
    (C) only what pertains exactly to my job
    (D) as many as I can

18. What best describes your current job?
    (A) boring
    (B) mentally challenging
    (C) repetitive
    (D) physically challenging
    (E) stressful
    (F) creative
    (G) easy
    (H) none of these

19. What kind of work situation would you like the best?
    (A) working alone
    (B) working as a team
    (C) physically demanding
    (D) repetitive

20. You are often acknowledged for
    (A) my good attitude
    (B) my attention to detail
    (C) my ability to work with others
    (D) meeting my deadlines
    (E) being a leader
    (F) all of the above
    (G) I am not acknowledged

KAPLAN

Answers

Remember, there are no correct answers to these questions. As long as you have answered each question honestly, you will not have to worry about your score on this test.

CONGRATULATIONS!

You have completed all the chapters in *Kaplan's Civil Service Exams*! Hopefully, you have learned a lot about the different exams and the different question types. Be sure to go back often to review any lessons or strategies that will be especially helpful to you as you continue to prepare for test day.

If you want to know more about different civil service jobs, refer to the Resources section that follows.

Good luck in your new civil service career!

PART THREE

Resources

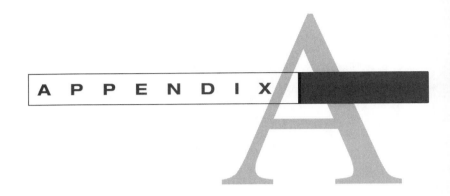

A P P E N D I X

Federal Civil Service Jobs and Job Categories

The following is a sampling of some of the most common federal jobs in several job categories. You will find this and other job information, including salary ranges, on the USAJOBS website: http://www.usajobs.opm.gov/. USAJOBS is the official job site of the U.S. federal government.

Accountant

Department(s): Judicial Branch, Office of Finance and Budget, Accounting and Financial Systems Division

Description/Duties: Duties of the incumbent include the following:

At the entry level, the incumbent performs as an entry-level trainee working under direct supervision to perform the work assignments. As competency increases, the incumbent will work under less direct supervision performing more complex work assignments. At the full-performance level, the incumbent will be responsible for:

Applying knowledge of specialized areas of accounting to solve problems in financial reporting; performing cash and other account reconciliations; reviewing and analyzing data recorded in the AO's accounting system and working with program offices and courts to ensure data integrity; participating in the reconciliation of treasury accounts to the AO accounting system; and Providing ongoing support to district and bankruptcy courts to resolve accounting issues and problems.

Administrative Assistant

Department(s): Agriculture, Forest Service, Homeland Security, Federal Emergency Management Agency (FEMA), Agriculture, Animal and Plant Health Inspection Service, Justice, U.S. Marshals Service, Army Materiel Command, Headquarters

Agency: Social Security Administration

Description/Duties: The Administrative Assistant serves as the District Manager's confidential assistant for labor relations and personnel matters as well as aspects of budget execution, personnel administration, procurement and supply, contract administration, travel, payroll services, reports management, facility management, etc. Provides administrative support for the staff and routinely trains other employees and subordinate office employees in administrative and other assigned (e.g., LAN) systems. Provides technical, operational, or systems administration support to the office.

Agricultural Specialist
Agricultural Marketing Specialist (General)

Department(s): Farm Service Agency, Grain Inspection, Packers and Stockyards Administration, Agricultural Research Service, Foreign Agricultural Service

Description/Duties: The U.S. Department(s) of Agriculture's (USDA) Marketing and Regulatory Programs (MRP) needs bright, energetic, and committed professionals to facilitate the domestic and international marketing of U.S. agricultural products and to protect the health and care of animals and plants in the United States. MRP offers an array of occupations and is committed to diversity in the workplace. We operate in domestic and global markets. Be part of an organization that protects the health and agriculture of the American people. Join our team!

Attorney

Department(s): Homeland Security, Customs and Border Protection

Description/Duties: As an attorney in the Office of Associate Chief Counsel—U.S. Customs and Border Protection (CBP), the selectee performs legal research into the laws, regulations, decisions, and other precedents bearing on the legal issues involving CBP. The selectee represents CBP in various third party administrative hearings on matters such as employee discipline, contract arbitration, broker license revocation, and adverse actions; prepares litigation reports, affidavits, and other documents to assist the Department(s) of Justice in civil actions involving CBP; prepares legal memoranda and proposed legislation for CBP; examines petitions related to civil penalties and forfeiture of assets; provides current information to the field concerning significant changes occurring in law and procedure which may affect the operations of CBP; and formulates decisions and judgments with reference to resolving claims for and against the government arising out of operations of CBP.

Qualifications: To qualify based on education, submit a copy of law school transcript and grade point average or class ranking with your application materials. Application materials will not be returned. Applicant must be a graduate from a full course of study in a School of Law accredited by the American Bar Association and be an active member in good standing of the bar of a state, territory of the United States, the District of Columbia, or the Commonwealth of Puerto Rico.

Other Employment Opportunities:

Army Corps of Engineers

Army, Military District of Washington

Office of the Secretary of the Army

Department(s) of Energy

Homeland Security, Federal Emergency Management Agency (FEMA)

Housing and Urban Development, Office of the General Counsel

Auditor

Department(s): Interior, Office of the Secretary of the Interior

Description/Duties: This position is located in the Administrative Operations Directorate, Indirect Cost Services, Sacramento, California. The incumbent serves as an Auditor/Negotiator and performs a variety of accounting and costs related reviews, such as indirect cost rates, cost allocation plans, direct contract support costs, and contract pricing reviews of external customers. The position is developmental in nature and is an intervening grade leading to the full performance level of GS-12. Assignments at these grade levels are designed to support career progression with increasing difficulty and complexity to develop and test the auditor's ability to perform higher-grade work. Specifically, the incumbent performs analysis of indirect cost rates, cost allocation plan, and direct contract support cost proposals, including financial statements, budget, and general ledger documents, submitted by customers to ensure consistency, mathematical accuracy, reasonableness, and compliance with federal regulations. With guidance from a senior staff member, completes initial reviews and resolves differences between the customer's proposal and federal guidelines. Develops work papers and summaries that result in accurate, logical, clear, and coherent negotiation agreements and plan approvals. As a member of a team, assists in developing contract review programs and carries out specific program steps, such as examining specific cost representations, accounting systems, internal controls, policies and procedures, and other management functions pertinent to the review. The incumbent assists in developing draft advisory reports of review findings, conclusions, and recommendations.

Other Job Opportunities:

Energy, Federal Energy Regulatory Commission

Federal Communications Commission

Veterans Affairs, Inspector General

Treasury, Alcohol and Tobacco Tax and Trade Bureau

Homeland Security, Immigration, and Customs Enforcement Bureau

Bank Examiner

Department(s): Treasury, Office of the Comptroller of the Currency

Description/Duties: Bank information technology (BIT) examiners evaluate technology and bank information systems related functions at national banks. Typical assignments include evaluating the information systems management structure and effectiveness; the adequacy of audit management, development, and acquisitions the organization's ability to identify, acquire, install, and maintain appropriate information technology solutions; and the organization's ability to provide technology services in a secure environment. Candidates for BIT examiner positions need an understanding of bank operations, technology planning, telecommunications, LANs, database, software development, and computer operations. Knowledge of the banking business is essential.

Biologist

Department(s): Army, Field Operating Office of Office of Secretary

Description/Duties: This vacancy announcement is soliciting resumes and transcripts from individuals who seek civilian employment with the Department(s) of Army as an entry level Biologist. All positions are part of a formalized management development program and are civilian positions with the Department(s) of Army. Appointments made from this vacancy announcement may be from a variety of excepted appointing authorities.

Other Employment Opportunities:

Health and Human Services, Centers for Disease Control and Prevention (CDC)

Interior, U.S. Geological Survey

National Science Foundation

Interior, National Park Service

Agriculture, Forest Service

Health and Human Services, National Institutes of Health (NIH)

Border Patrol Agent

Department(s): Homeland Security, Customs and Border Protection

Description/Duties: One of the most important duties performed by a Border Patrol Agent is known as "line-watch." This involves the detection and apprehension of undocumented aliens and their smugglers by maintaining surveillance from a covert position, pursuing leads, responding to electronic sensor alarms, utilizing infrared scopes during night operations, using low-light level television systems, sighting aircraft, and interpreting and following tracks, marks, and other physical evidence. In addition, Border Patrol Agents perform traffic checks, traffic observation, city patrol transportation checks, and other administrative, intelligence, and antismuggling activities.

Computer Clerk and Assistant

Department(s): Navy, Assistant for Administration, Under Secretary of the Navy

Who May Be Considered: You must be enrolled or accepted for enrollment as a degree-seeking student (diploma, certificate, etc.), taking at least half-time academic or vocational and technical course load in an accredited high school, technical, or vocational school, 2-year or 4-year college or university, graduate or professional school. You must be at least 16 years of age at the time of employment.

Description/Duties: Positions will be mainly clerical in nature. Duties may include typing (forms, memos, letters, etc.), data entry and word processing using various office automation software (Word, Excel, Access, etc.), filing, answering telephones, researching, sorting/routine mail, ordering/maintaining supplies and operating fax and copy machines.

Contract Specialist

Department(s): U.S. National Aeronautics and Space Administration, John F. Kennedy Space Center

Office: OP, Procurement Office

Description/Duties: Serves as Contract Specialist responsible for preaward and postaward functions for contracts and orders for various commodities. Preaward functions include (1) review of purchase requests, (2) preparation of various types of solicitations, such as requests for quotations, invitations for bids, and requests for proposals, (3) review of contractor's bid or proposal, including cost/price analysis to determine fair and reasonable price, (4) negotiations, and (5) preparation of award documents, such as, purchase orders, contracts, task orders, and delivery orders resulting in fixed price or cost reimbursement type contracts. Postaward functions include such contract administration activities as monitoring contractor performance, negotiating changes, ensuring compliance with contract terms and conditions, and closing out contracts and orders.

Similar Employment Opportunities:

District of Columbia Government

Health and Human Services, Food and Drug Administration (FDA)

General Services Admin, Public Buildings Service

Defense Intelligence Agency

Agriculture, Rural Housing Service

Corporate Examiner

Agency: National Credit Union Administration

Description/Duties: Serves as examiner-in-charge of examination and supervision of assigned corporate credit unions. These corporate credit unions generally have less than $1 billion in assets, have expanded authorities at the Base Plus level or lower, are basically "Pass-through" corporates (those which primarily rely on another corporate for investment placement and product offerings), and are generally less diverse and complex than those which deal directly in the financial marketplace.

Serves as an investment analyst during examinations or reviews of assigned corporate credit unions. This will generally involve the review of investments in other corporates or wholesale corporate credit unions, and in some cases the review of agency securities, asset backed securities, and other noncomplex investments.

Maintains a corporate examiner district consisting of assigned corporate credit unions. Monitors activity and overall financial condition of assigned corporate credit unions, including monthly supervision and review of internal and external reports. Detects adverse trends and monitors progress being made to correct identified problems.

Corrections Officers

Corrections Officer

Correctional Officers are the largest part of the workforce. All BOP institutions routinely have vacancies for this position. Correctional Officers enforce the regulations governing the operation of a correctional institution, serving as both a supervisor and a counselor of inmates.

Probation Officer

Department(s): Judicial Branch

Agency: U.S. Courts

Sub Agency: U.S. Probation

Description/Duties: Conduct investigations and prepare reports for the United States District Court, the United States Parole Commission, and the Federal Prison System, regarding the background and activities of offenders charged with, or having been found guilty of Federal offenses; provide field supervision and counseling services to offenders in the community.

Probation Officer Assistant

Department(s): Judicial Branch

Agency: U.S. Courts

Sub Agency: U.S. District Court, District of Arizona

Description/Duties: The incumbent provides technical support and services to probation officers and assists officers in the performance of all investigations (i.e., collateral investigations, presentence reports, and postsentence reports). They also assist officers in performing offender supervision functions and providing other technical assistance and services.

Prison Chaplain

Department(s): Department(s) of Justice

Agency: Bureau of Prisons/Federal Prison System

Description/Duties: Staff Chaplains are expected to deliver pastoral care, manage religious programs, and administer resources. Chaplains are expected to provide a pastoral presence throughout the institution through regular visits to the housing units, visiting room, and work sites. Chaplains will set up a schedule of religious activities providing equitable and reasonable opportunities for worship, study, and religious programs. Chaplains will also communicate the mission and goal of the department by being a ready source for expert information to staff and communicating clearly and in a timely manner the variety of activities of the department.

Other Employment Opportunities:

Army, National Guard Units

Veterans Affairs, Veterans Health Administration

Medical Officer

Medical Officers provide direct service to inmates in federal prisons involving the performance of diagnostic, preventive, or therapeutic services.

Dental Assistant

Department(s): Veterans Affairs, Veterans Health Administration

Description/Duties: Performs chair-side assistance in all areas of restorative, prosthodontic, surgical, endodontic, and periodontal treatment as well as general dentistry. Receives and schedules patients for treatment in the dental clinic and dental operating room suites. Maintains dental equipment in a clean and operative manner. Orders and stores dental supplies. Cleans and sterilizes materials, instruments, and equipment. Makes preparations for oral surgery performed in dental service surgical suites. Sets up instruments, equipment, materials, and assures that they are present and properly arranged.

Similar Employment Opportunities:

Armed Forces Retirement Homes

General Engineer

Department(s): Nuclear Regulatory Commission

Description/Duties: Incumbent serves as a technical advisor to the Office of the Inspector General by providing expert analysis and advice regarding emerging and ongoing regulatory issues confronting the NRC. Assists investigators by providing technical and regulatory expertise on a variety of subjects examined during Inspector General event inquiries and investigations. These investigative efforts are typically conducted to assess the adequacy of NRC's oversight of regulatory programs or certain aspects of nuclear power plant operations that have experienced an event or problem. During the conduct of inquiries and investigations, the incumbent may be called upon to provide technical support during interviews of NRC or licensee staff or during reviews of NRC or licensee documents.

Required Qualifications: Candidates must have at least one year of specialized experience at the next lower grade or equivalent.

Other Employment Opportunities:

Health and Human Services, Indian Health Service (IHS)

Transportation, Pipeline and Hazardous Materials Safety AdminArmy Research, Development and Engineering Command

Army Corps of Engineers

Transportation, Research and Innovative Technology Administration

Department of Energy

FBI Special Agent

Department(s): Justice, Federal Bureau of Investigation (FBI)

Description/Duties: As the primary investigative arm of the federal government, the FBI is responsible for protecting the United States by preventing future terrorist attacks, conducting sensitive national security investigations, and enforcing over 260 federal statutes.

The FBI's ten top investigative priorities are:

Protect the United States from terrorist attack.

Protect the United States against foreign intelligence operations and espionage.

Protect the United States against cyber-based attacks and high-technology crimes.

Combat public corruption at all levels.

Protect civil rights.

Combat transnational and national criminal organizations and enterprises.

Combat major white-collar crime.

Combat significant violent crime.

Support federal, state, county, municipal, and international partners.

Upgrade technology to successfully perform the FBI's mission.

While the FBI remains committed to other important national security and law enforcement responsibilities, the prevention of terrorism takes precedence in investigations. The FBI also works with other federal, state, and local law enforcement agencies in investigating matters of joint interest and in training law enforcement officers from around the world.

Foreign Relations and Defense Policy Specialist

Department(s): Defense, Office of the Secretary of Defense, Foreign Relations and Defense Policy Manager

Description/Duties: As a Foreign Relations and Defense Policy Manager, the incumbent makes recommendations by using independent judgment on highly complex and abstract issues of Department of Defense strategy and policy. The incumbent represents the Under Secretary of Defense (Policy) in sensitive presentations and negotiations, and provides recommendations to senior defense officials on overall U.S. foreign policy and national security goals and objectives.

The incumbent uses experience and judgment to prepare senior officials for the Congress, and drafts testimony and other presentations to the Congress; and for public and press contacts of the USD(p). The incumbent maintains expertise by remaining knowledgeable of current developments in the broad area of foreign affairs and foreign policy.

Required Qualifications:

1. Ability to support senior defense officials in internal decision-making, interagency deliberations, dealings with international counterparts, and testifying before Congress regarding policy ramifications of current foreign affairs issues.
2. Demonstrated experience in developing both regional security policy and national security policy related to a specific functional area.
3. Extensive knowledge of U.S. foreign policy and national security decision-making procedures.
4. Demonstrated oral and written skills in integrating complex issues into a unified policy framework assessing the implications of various courses of action for U.S. national security interests.
5. Demonstrated skill in dealing with senior officials in the executive and legislative branches of government, and the private, nonprofit, and international arenas.

Similar Employment Opportunities:

Department of State

Army, Office of the Chief of Staff of Army

Forestry Specialist

Department(s): Agriculture, Forest Service

Description/Duties: Provides support in the management of wildland fires as a Hotshot Superintendent. Operates communications and computer equipment to exchange information for fire weather and other fire management activities. Provides incident response with a crew of highly trained firefighters, operating under the pressure of unpredictable, changing conditions. Ensures that tools and equipment are available. Performs the administrative and human resource management functions relative to the staff supervised. Plans and schedules on-going workload assignments. Sets and adjusts work to be accomplished by subordinates; adjusts program and project priorities; and prepares schedules for work completion. Assigns work to subordinate staff based on priorities, with consideration of the difficulty and requirements of assignments, and the capabilities of employees. Establishes guidelines and performance expectations for staff members, which are communicated through the formal employee performance management system. Provides informal feedback and periodically evaluates employee performance. Provides advice, counsel, and/or instruction to staff members on both work and administrative matters. Interviews candidates for positions to be filled in the organization; recommends or approves appointments, selections, or reassignments to positions appropriate to the selection authority delegated. Effects disciplinary measures as appropriate to the authority delegated in this area. Carries out Equal Employment Opportunity (EEO) policies and program activities.

Minimum Federal Qualification Requirements: Qualifying experience for the GS-9 level includes one year of specialized experience equivalent to GS-8. Specialized experience is experience which is in or directly related to the line of work of the position to be filled and which has equipped the applicant with the particular knowledge, skills, and abilities to successfully perform the duties of the position.

Other Employment Opportunities:

Agriculture, Forest Service

Interior, National Park Service

Geologist

Department(s): Interior, Bureau of Land Management

Description/Duties: The Bureau of Land Management (BLM), an agency within the U.S. Department(s) of the Interior, administers 264 million acres of America's public lands located primarily in 12 western states. BLM manages wildlife, recreation, timber harvest, livestock grazing, mineral extraction, and other public uses. It is our friendly and supportive culture that separates us from other federal agencies. BLM is focused on supporting your career objectives and professional growth, while encouraging a balance between your work life and personal life. For additional information about the BLM, please visit our website.

Other Employment Opportunities:

Army Corps of Engineers

Army, Field Operating Office of Office of Secretary

Agriculture, Forest Service

Interior, U.S. Geological Survey

Agriculture, Natural Resources Conservation Service

IRS Agent

Department(s): Treasury, Internal Revenue Service

Description/Duties: The IRS Internal Revenue Agent is a professional accountant who examines and audits individual, business, and corporate tax returns to determine correct federal tax liabilities and conduct examinations relating to compliance with technical requirements imposed by the Internal Revenue Code. Internal Revenue Agents are challenged every day. Challenges come in the form of research and developing issues and during communications with taxpayers.

Medical Officer

Department(s): Health and Human Services, Centers for Disease Control and Prevention

Description/Duties: The position is responsible for developing overall policy and technical guidance, in collaboration with senior experts in other U.S. Government (USG) implementing Agencies, relative to any of the major HIV/AIDS program areas, including prevention, care and treatment, and capacity development. Develops goals and objectives for Global AIDS Program (GAP) initiatives. Reviews and clears all technical policy documents. Provides assistance to medical professionals and others involved in the development and implementation of the President's Emergency Plan for AIDS Relief (PEPFAR) initiative. Provides support to field programs by bringing together expertise from USG agencies. Develops, markets, and advances state of the art models of prevention or care and treatment strategies, such as the identification and development of new prevention plans for targeted groups. Provides oversight on complex multi-country, multi-agency funded programs, and in collaboration with the senior technical officer in each country monitors the program performance against the goals and objectives in annual work plans. Represents GAP, NCHSTP, CDC and the U.S. Government at a variety of international forums and with key U.S. constituencies, including other donors, UN Agencies, and Congress. Develops and delivers presentations covering the full scope of current and planned GAP activities for seminars, conferences, meetings and other public forums. Develops and delivers scientific papers and other technical documents related to any aspect of the GAP mission.

Similar Employment Opportunities:

Health and Human Services, National Institutes of Health (NIH)

Health and Human Services, Indian Health Service (IHS)

Army Medical Command

Health and Human Services, Food and Drug Administration (FDA)

Navy, Naval Medical Command

Park Ranger

Department(s): Interior, National Park Service

Description/Duties: The incumbent serves as a Law Enforcement Commissioned Ranger responsible for performing law enforcement duties including detection, investigation, apprehension, detention, and prosecution to ensure the protection and safe and appropriate use of National Park resources. Conducts patrols primarily by boat (power and kayak) on marine waters, but also includes patrols by motor vehicle, air, and/or foot. Educates users about the park's resources and requirements pertaining to their use, ensures the safety and security of park visitors, employees, and others working or recreating in the park, and provides for protection of resources, and public and private property. Serves as a provider of emergency services (medical, structure fire, search and rescue, hazardous material spills) within the Incident Command system. Assists with the training and leadership of seasonal and volunteer staff. Shall be assigned to committees and work groups as needed to provide input on day-to-day and future management of the Park.

Similar Employment Opportunities:

Interior, Bureau of Land Management

Army Corps of Engineers

Physician

Department(s): Veterans Affairs, Veterans Health Administration, South Texas Veterans Health Care System

Description/Duties: The incumbent will function as a Staff Physician, and provide primary care and preventive care services to an assigned panel of veteran patients. Physician must be a U.S. citizen and board certified/eligible in Internal Medicine or Family Practice. This position is located at the Frank Tejeda Outpatient Clinic, South Texas Veterans Health Care System, San Antonio, TX.

Physician Assistant

Department(s): Veterans Affairs, Veterans Health Administration

Description/Duties: Standard assignment for the physician assistant is described under the headage of Clinical Practice, which includes routine, nonroutine, nonemergency, and emergency duties and other miscellaneous assignments as appropriate. Also included are any appropriate administrative, educational, or research assignments that are currently assigned. The physician assistant may be assigned utilized at 1 or more CBOC's as well as assignments in the Medical Center MH OP clinic and the Day Treatment Program. The physician assistant exercises as an agent for the staff psychiatrist doing those things that the physician assistant has proved ability to do with competency, education, and experience. Functions listed are performed on a regular and repetitive basis and the maintenance of effectiveness, accuracy, and competency is expected. All work is reviewed, corrected as necessary, and approved by a staff psychiatrist.

Similar Employment Opportunities:

Justice, Bureau of Prisons/Federal Prison System

Navy, Naval Medical Command

Health and Human Services, Indian Health Service (IHS)

Army Medical Command

Physicist

Department(s): Navy, Naval Sea Systems Command

Description/Duties: Incumbent serves as a senior Physicist on major research and development projects that address the broad range of technical areas involved in countering ordnance threat problems, including the development and use of such sophisticated equipment as robotic vehicles of various sizes, for use both on the surface and underwater. Develops and analyzes acoustic, magnetic, or chemical detection based sensor concepts for EOD applications in detection of unexploded ordnance (UXO) and improvised explosive devices (IED). Uses knowledge of explosives and materials properties, detonation, and deflagaration physics to understand explosive phenomenology. Uses models to conduct analyses in EOD technology areas (i.e., impact modeling) and document analyses in written reports. Applies knowledge of physical principles and models to develop concepts for IED disruption and UXO neutralization tools. Develops test methodologies and conducts experimental efforts to assess performance of potential EOD systems and verify models. Writes test reports setting forth results, methods utilized, conclusions, and recommendations. Writes proposals for new work efforts. Functions as a project manager in areas such as mechanics, heat, light, sound, electricity, pneumatics, magnetism, and radiation to test conceptual ideas. Participates in the planning, formulation, and submission of inputs for budgets, developing and providing feedback on the performance of individual tasks and sub-tasks, acting as focal point for communications with customers including development, review and submission of proposals, obtaining personnel and facilities and taking steps necessary to ensure that technical performance, supportability, budget, and schedule goals are met. Presents periodic review of work, findings, and recommendations orally and in written form to customers, management, and task personnel.

Similar Employment Opportunities:

Air Force Materiel Command

Army, Field Operating Office of Office of Secretary

Veterans Affairs, Veterans Health Administration

Nuclear Regulatory Commission

Navy, Naval Sea Systems Command

Commerce, National Institute of Standards and Technology

Program Analyst (EPA)

Agency: Environmental Protection Agency

Description/Duties: The incumbent will serve as Associate Director for the Office of Congressional Affairs (OCA) and reports to the Deputy Associate Administrator for OCA and provides technical expertise for program planning and advice and assistance to managers regarding policy interpretations as it affects the office. OCA serves as the Administrator's principal point of contact for Congress on all Agency matters. The office serves as a liaison for these parties to the Office of the Administrator and senior Agency officials and facilitates communications between EPA Headquarters and Regions and elected officials in coordination with Intergovernmental Relations and Regional Operations Offices in OCIR. The incumbent acts in the absence of the Deputy Associate Administrator (DAA), and in that capacity, implicitly takes on supervisory responsibilities; serves as the principal advisor to the DAA on all congressional affairs and policies of the Agency; provides advice and counsel to the DAA on policy development, planning, coordination, and legislative matters; identifies problem areas, develops and recommends solutions, and specific policies in relation to urgent and often sensitive operational and legislative matter; prepares reports and maintains records of work accomplishments and administrative information, as required, and coordinates the preparation, presentation, and communication of work-related information to the supervisor; proactively provides assistance to the Congressional team leaders on operational issues and ensures timely resolution of problems; performs technical direction and workflow management for priority OCA projects; coordinates as assigned, OCA's strategic planning, budgeting, administrative system work projects, and other internal activities necessary for coordinating implementation of OCIR's priority programs and projects.

Safety Inspector

Department(s): Labor, Mine Safety and Health Administration

Description/Duties: MSHA Inspector job responsibilities include conducting on-site inspections or investigations of underground and surface mines, mills, and quarries in order to: Identify potential hazardous conditions to the safety and health of workers; ensure proper mining equipment maintenance and use; check mining practices for conformance with safety and health laws and regulations; Issue citations when violations and hazards are identified; determine how accidents and disasters are caused and prevented; help direct rescue and fire fighting operations after fires or explosions; investigate safety and health complaints from mine personnel; and discuss inspection/investigation findings and provide technical advice and assistance to mine management and personnel. Locality pay will be added as appropriate. Candidates with surface only experience will be considered for surface positions at the GS-7/9 level only. The full promotion potential for Surface Inspectors is the GS-11 level. Candidates applying for Underground and/or Electrical positions at the GS-9/11 level must have underground experience. The full promotion potential for Underground and Electrical Inspectors is the GS-12 level.

Similar Employment Opportunities:

Transportation, Federal Aviation Administration

State and Local Civil Service Jobs and Job Categories

The following is a sampling of some of the most common state and local jobs in several job categories. You will find this and other job information, including salary ranges, on the state and local websites such as: http://www.mass.gov (for civil service jobs in the state of Massachusetts).

Accountant I (Specialist)

State: California

Agency: California Student Aid Commission

Description/Duties: Under the direction of the Fiscal Manager and the lead Senior Accounting Officer (Spec), the Accountant I performs the more difficult semiprofessional accounting work in the establishment and maintenance of fiscal records, including reconciling accounts, auditing travel expense claims, and responding to inquires.

Account Clerk II

State: California

Agency: Department of Corrections and Rehabilitation

Division: San Quentin State Prison

Description/Duties: Under the general direction of the Accountant I (Supervisor), the Account Clerk II will be responsible for the following: Batch and post to inmate trust accounts the following: cash receipts, inmate payrolls, canteen ducats, deceased inmate payments, transfer of inmate funds, returned canteen cards and canceled checks. Process/audit hobby (Gift Shop Sales) deposits by comparing trust withdrawal orders to sales receipts/tickets. Balancing total sales tape to IWF tax, use tax and total to inmate. Process trust withdrawals, check request, newspaper subscriptions, special commissary and hobby craft request by checking account balances, reviewing forms for accuracy, totaling charges and balancing tapes. Process checks working from departed and discharged list. Process release statements by checking account balances, reviewing negative balances, and listing personal and state funds on form. Responsible for processing all informal inmate appeals in a timely manner and assisting with formal inmate appeals. Assist the preparation of inmate payroll sheets for batching. Perform payroll certification by auditing, listing, and balancing payroll slips.

Administrative Secretary I

State: Arizona

Agency: Department of Corrections

Description/Duties: Performs secretarial and administrative duties of average difficulty; composes correspondence; takes and transcribes written dictation; gathers and summarizes data for reports; maintains the unit's supplies; screens visitors/calls and refers to appropriate staff; schedules appointments and coordinates arrangements for meetings/conferences; assists as the timekeeper; maintains files; and performs other duties appropriate to the assignment.

Agriculture and Consumer Protection Inspector

State: Florida

Agency: Department of Agriculture and Consumer Service, Division of Animal Industry

Description/Duties: The primary duties and responsibilities of an Agriculture and Consumer Protection Inspector are to enforce the provisions of state and federal law regarding animal disease control for the protection of Florida's agricultural industry and public safety. Additional duties include emergency preparedness (ESF-17) and assuring the quality of agricultural products prior to their entrance into the marketing channels. In accomplishing these duties, the employee must cooperate fully with USDA personnel and others engaged in related activities. The incumbent is expected to demonstrate, model, and reinforce the Department(s)'s fundamental values of fairness, cooperation, respect, commitment, excellence, honesty and teamwork in all interactions with coworkers and the public. The following duties and responsibilities are assigned to this position:

Conducts program activities relating to the testing of livestock for disease including collecting samples, vaccinations, issuing permits and quarantines, and assisting Veterinary Medical Officers. Conducts activities relating to emergency preparedness related to livestock and other animals including collection of information for all animal premises and recording this information on emergency management database.

Auditor—Report Editor

State: Texas

Agency: Texas State Auditor's Office

Description/Duties: The State Auditor's Office, a legislative agency that serves as the independent auditor for Texas state government, is seeking qualified individuals to perform moderately-complex to complex content editing and copy editing of audit reports and other agency documents. Work involves coordinating with all levels of agency staff and management and directing the writing, editing, and production and distribution of material that conveys information to the Legislature, state agencies, and the public. Trains others on effective business writing and agency expectations. Works under limited supervision with considerable latitude for the use of initiative and independent judgment.

Biomedical Engineer

State: Illinois

Description/Duties: Apply knowledge of engineering, biology, and biomechanical principles to the design, development, and evaluation of biological and health systems and products, such as artificial organs, prostheses, instrumentation, medical information systems, and heath management and care delivery systems.

Budget Analyst

State: Oklahoma

Description/Duties: Positions in this job family perform analytical work involving the collection and evaluation of agency financial data, budgetary control records and other information concerning agency expenditures and revenues to determine budget requirements, develop budget work programs, prepare proposed legislation, and develop justification for requested funding levels. This includes the analysis of financial information concerning expenditures for payroll, capital projects, operating expenses, supplies and equipment, professional services contracts, and other costs, and of projected revenues from various fees, taxes, tolls, investments, appropriations and other sources and developing recommendations or proposals concerning appropriate changes. It also includes the allocation of projected revenues to various functions and activities, continuing review and evaluation of actual expenditures and revenue against budget projections and making adjustments or corrections as needed.

Civil Engineer

State: Illinois

Agency: Department of the Navy

Description/Duties: Perform engineering duties in planning, designing, and overseeing construction and maintenance of building structures, and facilities, such as roads, railroads, airports, bridges, harbors, channels, dams, irrigation projects, pipelines, power plants, water and sewage systems, and waste disposal units. Includes architectural, structural, traffic, ocean, and geo-technical engineers. Plan and design transportation or water systems or structures, research and analyze data regarding project sites, use computers heavily. Serves as an Office Engineer. As such, is responsible for being a principal source of technical and engineering expertise with regards to office engineering. Performs duties associated with the full scope of the administrative and office engineering functions for all projects under the jurisdiction of the Area/Resident Office. Performs or directs work pertaining to budget reporting, preparation and processing of contract payment estimates, preparation of government estimates for funding purposes, and construction progress reports. Prepares contract modifications initiated in the field.

Computer Systems Analyst

State: Florida

Agency: Lottery

Description/Duties: This is an application software and database development position involving the analysis, design, development, and implementation of client server based solutions in an environment consisting of AIX 5.L, Oracle 9i database, IBM Websphere Suite, Oracle developer suite, Business Objects. 6.0. This position will have primary responsibility of developing and maintaining Oracle applications and repositories using Oracle forms and reports, Kornshell, PL/SQL, ETL, materialized views. Analyzes business needs to develop specific functional requirements for applications software. Develops detailed application systems design documents to direct the implementation phase of software development. Develops system test plans to ensure that software meets design criteria. Diagnoses software problems to determine cause and develops and implements appropriate solutions. Develops acceptance test plans to ensure that software meets functional requirements. Develops sufficient system and user documentation to ensure proper operation and maintainability of application software. Designs and coordinates upgrades to relational databases.

Corrections Officer

State: New York

Description/Duties: As a Corrections Officer, under the direct supervision of a higher-ranking officer, you would be responsible for the custody and security, as well as the safety and well-being of criminal offenders in State Correctional Facilities and Correctional Camps. You would supervise the movement and activities of inmates; make periodic rounds of assigned areas; conduct searches for contraband; maintain order within the facility; and prepare reports as necessary. You would advise inmates on the rules and regulations governing the operation of the facility and assist them in resolving problems. You would have a high degree of responsibility for your actions and decisions. You may also be required to carry firearms in the performance of certain duties and to perform other related work as required.

Custodian

State: Colorado

Agency: Department of Human Services, Division of Facilities Management

Description/Duties: This position exists to perform custodial work that relates to the general upkeep and sanitation of buildings. Perform daily cleaning, sanitizing, and servicing of assigned work area as scheduled. Follows appropriate procedures in the use of disinfectant cleaners, chemicals, and equipment operation and maintenance. Performs work consisting of sweeping, dust mopping, wet mopping, vacuuming, rest room cleaning, washing walls, doors, frames, sills, windows, baseboards, fixtures, furnishings, ceilings, vents, and light fixtures. Performs project floor work consisting of buffing, scrubbing, stripping, waxing and sealing of hard floor surfaces and bonnet cleaning, spot cleaning, shampooing and extracting of carpeted floors by use of appropriate cleaning chemicals and equipment. Collects and disposes of trash and biohazard waste by properly containing and transporting to proper disposal locations. Participates in moving furniture, appliances, equipment, etc. Replaces light bulbs, assists with minor building repairs and snow removal when needed. Performs other duties as assigned.

Minimum Requirements: Six months of custodial experience which must have included prior experience with commercial cleaning equipment floor scrubbers, carpet extractors, and floor buffers; and have good oral and written communication skills. Must be 21 years of age or older.

Economist

State: Massachusetts

Agency: Department of Revenue

Description/Duties: The incumbent of this position prepares and analyzes the Department(s) of Revenue's budget documents; reviews and analyzes financial data; confers with agency staff to identify problems and needs; ability to perform mathematical calculations using formulas in determining the need for spending projections. Compiles information for management uses; and performs related work as required. Prepare financial reports to document transactions and make spending projections. Reconcile appropriation accounts on a periodic basis. Work with Budget Manager to identify and implement strategies for improving reporting and forecasting process. Work with Budget Manager to create and update summary level management reports providing analysis of trends and changes. Conduct variance analyses and produce summary memoranda of results.

Fire/Crash Rescue Specialist

State: Wisconsin

Agency: Department of Military Affairs

Description/Duties: Prevent, control, and extinguish all types of structural, aircraft, missile, separate or component weapons, vehicle, ground, and other miscellaneous fires or potential fires; perform related rescue, first aid and property preservation; operate and maintain all types of fire fighting and related rescue vehicles, equipment systems, devices and apparatuses; perform fire prevention inspections; operate emergency communication systems; and perform administrative duties.

Financial Analyst

State: Michigan

Agency: Department of Management and Budget

Description/Duties: The State Budget Office is filling an analyst position responsible for developing budget and policy recommendations that impact important public policy decisions. The analyst will serve as budget liaison between the Office of the State Budget and the Department(s) of Transportation. Among various responsibilities, the analyst provides fiscal advice to the State Budget Director and the Governor for the development and presentation of the annual Executive Budget related to transportation issues, participates in legislative deliberations, and monitors state-level spending and revenue patterns. The position also conducts efficiency and effectiveness reviews of transportation-related programs and legislation; monitors compliance with legislative intent; and tracks new legislation for fiscal and policy effects.

Forensic Scientist II

State: Virginia

Agency: Department of Forensic Science

Description/Duties: Perform forensic chemical analyses of suspected controlled substances. Incumbents will: 1) use current state-of-the-art methodologies and instrumentation to analyze controlled substances; 2) prepare Certificates of Analyses on findings for use by the criminal justice system; and 3) testify in court as a qualified expert for the Commonwealth at criminal proceedings as to the results of laboratory findings. Position requires occasional overnight travel. Employee will provide own transportation as required. Qualifications: Knowledge of theory and application of organic, inorganic, analytical and physical chemistry; laboratory safety; quality assurance/quality control and lab practices; instrumental analysis (GC, GC/MS, FTIR, UV) and experience in forensic drug analysis required. Successful completion of a documented training program and/or demonstration of competency is required. Experience presenting testimony in a court of law, as an expert witness is preferred. Must be able to analyze data, develop sound conclusions, maintain accurate records, and analyze and solve technical problems. Ability to communicate effectively orally and in writing required. A baccalaureate degree in chemistry or other related science with sufficient chemistry courses is required; graduate degree is preferred.

Human Resource Specialist

State: Colorado

Agency: Department of Transportation

Description/Duties: Human Resource Specialist positions are responsible for job classification, compensation and employment selection activities, data analysis, training, and management consultation. Conduct job analyses, design and develop the employment examinations and hiring processes that minimize delay between recruitment and hiring of outstanding candidates to fill CDOT's critical positions. This includes writing job announcements and advertisements, participating in job fairs, reviewing applications, corresponding with applicants, developing, scheduling, administering and scoring examinations using SPSS, Excel, the State's application system or other software.

Collect and analyze data from the State's Applicant Data System and CDOT databases, using Microsoft Excel, Access, and statistical software such as SPSS. Data are used to score examinations, measure the effectiveness and validity of recruitment and selection efforts, and complete assigned HR research projects. Writes reports for management explaining the results of the statistical analysis. Applies the State's job evaluation system by reviewing job descriptions for accuracy and completeness, advising managers in the use of the classification system, determining correct classification, FLSA status, and pay for positions. Use SAP, Human Resources system, to update and manage personnel data and organizational structure for assigned organizations. Provide training to others on selection and classification theory, practices and techniques. Consult with CDOT supervisors and managers on efficient and effective organization structures and use of the state's classification system, personnel rules and procedures, emerging human resource issues and management techniques. Defends all decisions through the appeals process.

Information Technology Programmer/Analyst

State: Michigan

Agency: Department of Information Technology

Description/Duties: In this position an employee will provide application development and SQL database administration services to the Department(s) of Civil Service. This position will be responsible for the creation, maintenance, and enhancement of client server applications accomplished by using the following tools: Microsoft Access Visual Basic for Applications, Visual Basic, Visual Basic Scripting, SQL, ASP, Net, JavaScript, JAVA, XML, HTML, and other tools as necessary. This position is also responsible for providing technical support for COTS (Custom Off The Shelf) packages implemented for the Department(s) of Civil Service. This position is a backup to the primary SQL database administrator for Civil Service.

Maintenance Mechanic

State: Maryland

Agency: Maryland Military Department

Description/Duties: Maintenance Mechanic is the intermediate level of work in the building and grounds maintenance trades. Responsibilities include the ability to work independently on moderately complex tasks in maintenance, including minor repairs or improvements to buildings, fixtures, mechanical equipment, grounds and roadways, routine construction work, and rendering routine preventative maintenance. Grounds maintenance includes grass cutting, trimming, and snow removal. Employees appointed to these positions will be on call and may be required to report during emergencies.

Nurse Clinician

State: Wisconsin

Agency: Department of Corrections

Description/Duties: This position is responsible for providing skilled nursing care to offenders in both ambulatory and infirmary settings; providing patient assessment and treatment; assisting physicians in providing medical services; managing medications; providing emergency care; and maintaining medical records. In addition, the Nurse Clinician 2 is expected to participate in educational programs for staff and offenders and participate in activities to maintain her/his nursing skill level.

Nurse (RN) Lead

State: North Carolina

Agency: Department of Health and Human Services, OES—Western NC School for the Deaf

Description/Duties: This position will serve as NCSD lead nurse for the student health center (SHC) and supervise four nurses. This position is responsible for organizing and maintaining effective functioning of the SHC in compliance with all state and federal mandates.

Park Manager

State: Colorado

Agency: Department of Natural Resources, Division of Parks and Outdoor Recreation

Description/Duties: Performs as a state peace officer providing public safety by patrolling land and water areas, enforces Colorado Revised Statutes and park rules and regulations; contacts violators and issues warning or citations; checks for appropriate fishing, hunting, and park permits; conducts investigations. Positions will be assigned responsibility for the development, implementation, and operation of visitor/user programs, providing interpretive services; and/or other natural resources management work. Positions will supervise seasonal workers, assigning and overseeing work projects, training and evaluating workers; prepare and maintain records pertaining to park activities and enforcement proceedings. NOTE: Upon successful completion of training at a Colorado Peace Officer Standards and Training (POST) law enforcement academy, and completion of the probationary period, a Park Manager I is eligible to advance to the Park Manager II level, as described by the duties above.

Pharmacist

State: Maryland

Agency: Department of Health and Mental Hygiene

Description/Duties: This is the entry level of professional work in the field of pharmacy at a state facility. Employees in this classification compounds and dispenses needed drugs and pharmaceutical supplies for the patient population. The employee is responsible for the accuracy and proper accounting for drugs; for inspection of drug storage centers in order to assure proper storage of all pharmaceuticals; for withdrawal of outdated preparations; and for the maintenance of adequate, but not excessive, supplies. In a facility with only one pharmacist, this employee will be responsible for the operation of the pharmacy. This employee is responsible to either a higher-level pharmacist or to an administrative supervisor. The employee may supervise any subordinate personnel responsible for requisitioning and storing of drugs.

Psychiatrist

State: Arizona

Agency: Department of Health Services

Description/Duties: Under general direction, is responsible to provide sub-specialty expert psychiatric services in adult/forensic psychiatry for the care and treatment of mentally ill individuals and the forensic treatment programs for a hospital ward, unit or section. Conducts expert sub-specialty professional medical/psychiatric diagnostic examinations. Examines, diagnoses and prescribes psychiatric treatment for sub-specialty mentally ill patients. Develops and reviews clinical treatment plans and completes medical records adhering to hospital policies and procedures. Examines and evaluates patients for admission or discharge. Participates as the treatment team leader for a multi-disciplinary treatment team, coordinating and overseeing the work of the team for the sub-specialty patient population. Prepares records, reports and correspondence on treatment programs and patient progress in treatment. Completes required reports for legal and administrative purposes. Participates in meetings on clinical and administrative issues to facilitate sub-specialty patient care. Participates in education and training programs. Provides psychiatric consultation for local mental health agencies, psychiatrists and community groups to provide assistance in developing and administering psychiatric care at the community level. Participates in the development of policies, procedures, and standards for mental health program services or other professional or sub-professional medical personnel providing medical/psychiatric services.

Public Health Nurse

State: Vermont

Agency: Department of Health

Description/Duties: Nursing Administrator for the Vermont Department of Health Refugee Health Program; oversees the work of the Town Health Officer and the Immunization Programs. Works closely with clinical aspects of Emergency

Preparedness. Responsible for program and policy development program and policy development in support of specific Public Health Priorities with an emphasis on: multigrant management; supervision of other level II PH Nurses; serving as a key member of CPH senior policy team and public health to a variety of stakeholders.

Public Health Scientist II

State: Arizona

Agency: Department of Health Services

Description/Duties: Conducts testing to both identify and quantify chemical agents and poisons deemed to be important by law enforcement and public health agencies. Maintains the laboratory procedures and supplies necessary for the Chemical Emergency Response section. Plays a supportive role in the laboratory in the event of an environmental or other public health emergency. Trains other laboratory staff in new techniques adopted at the ADHS Public Health Laboratory. Provides capacity for the identification of chemical unknowns deemed to be important by law enforcement and public health agencies within Arizona. Provides training to the first responder community throughout Arizona on proper training and shipping protocols of specimens to the CDC in the event of a chemical terrorism or other public health emergencies. Performs other duties as assigned.

Secretary/Receptionist

State: Massachusetts

Agency: Department of Housing and Community Development

Description/Duties: Types letters, memos, budget modifications. Logs and tracks incoming and outgoing mail. Maintains Bureau files. Answers and screens telephone calls, writes concise messages, schedules meetings, maintains Bureau Director's computerized calendar, and performs other related duties as required. Uses computer using Microsoft Access, Excel, FoxPro, Access, Word, also uses Protype, telephone, intercom, Executive Director mailing list, Board Member listing. Provide back-up telephone coverage to other work units as required.

Special Education Consultant

State: Nevada

Agency: Department of Education

Description/Duties: Under the direction of the Director of Special Education, Elementary and Secondary Education, and School Improvement Programs, the special education consultant: Provides leadership in the development of effective programs for students with disabilities, provides leadership in the area of statewide assessment issues regarding students with disabilities, provides leadership for school, district and state improvement planning, provides oversight to ensure that students with disabilities receive special education in accordance with state and federal statues/regulations. As part of this oversight, the education consultant provides training assistance, training and support to and responds to educators, family members, students, policy makers, and others regarding proven practices for effective special education programs, data based decision-making relative to improving performance results of students with disabilities at the school, district and state level, compliance with special education laws and regulations. The education consultant will also facilitate work groups and task forces to ensure appropriate implementation of special education services in individual districts and across the state; coordinate district compliance monitoring efforts; investigate allegations of noncompliance in district special education programs; and collaborate with department staff, district and school based educators, parents, students, university faculty, and other partners.

Social Worker

State: Wisconsin

Agency: Department of Health and Family Services, Division of Children and Family Services

Description/Duties: This position provides consultation to county human services staff, tribal staff, and the court regarding permanency options for children in substitute care. Assess the adoptability of children referred for concurrent planning by county and tribal departments of human/social services to the special needs adoption program; represent the Department(s) in testifying at court hearings as an adoption and permanency planning expert; counsel and educate birth parents, foster parents, and children in the substitute care system regarding permanency alternatives and objectives; participate in mediation where appropriate; provide technical assistance to county staff in preparing for termination of parental rights; provide pre-adoptive intake services and post-placement services to children with special needs whose guardianship has been transferred to the state.

Staff Assistant

State: Nebraska

Agency: Nebraska Information System

Description/Duties: Perform word processing and data entry into spreadsheets. Develop and maintain filing systems and project accounting records. Issue plans and specifications to construction contractors. Prepare standard and customized contracts and enter data into the Nebraska Information System. Provide routine information to telephone callers. Process contractor payments. Prepare time sheets and serve as training coordinator.

Requirements: Typing ability of 40 wpm net; experience/training or education with IBM compatible PC with MS Word, Excel, Access, and Lotus Notes; strong organizational skills; experience working with technical documents; excellent communication skills. DESIRED: Experience with spreadsheet and database software; performing engineering/construction clerical and accounting clerk duties; knowledge and experience working on the Nebraska Information System.

Transportation Engineer

State: Virginia

Agency: Virginia Department of Transportation

Description/Duties: Will review engineering plans for land development activities to determine acceptability for issuance of VDOT permits and for future transportation impacts of the proposed work. Will meet with local government officials/staff, developers, consulting engineers, land use attorneys, and VDOT personnel to discuss and resolve issues concerning transportation planning, traffic engineering, and roadway and hydraulic designs and their impact upon existing and proposed transportation network. Knowledge of roadway design, traffic engineering, and hydraulics as well as the principles, practices, and procedures of engineering. Ability to plan, coordinate, and prioritize multiple assignments within scheduled timeframes. Ability to read and interpret engineering drawings, negotiate in conflicting situations, and to learn and use the details and procedures which apply to geometric design, drainage, traffic and safety, and transportation planning. Ability to communicate clearly and effectively both orally and in writing.

University Police Officer

State: Wisconsin

Agency: University of Wisconsin—Green Bay

Description/Duties: Police officers will enforce laws, investigate calls, complaints, and suspicious things and incidents which may have an impact of the University, maintain order, assist people, identify criminal activity, apprehend offenders, identify the source of problems in the community and work with the community to resolve issues. The police officer will support the department's mission by providing essential functions while respecting the rights and dignity of all individuals and taking pride in all we do.

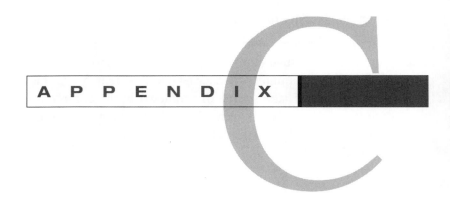

Summary of Benefits

The federal government offers a selection of benefits alongside standard compensation, including:

- Health insurance
- 10 paid holidays per year
- 13 sick days per year
- 13–26 vacation days per year, depending on years of service
- Flex time
- Child care
- Elder care
- Employee assistance programs
- 3-part retirement program includes a Social Security benefit, a 401(k) type plan
- Medicare eligibility
- Life insurance
- Long-term care insurance

With some jobs, you may be eligible for some special bonuses such as a recruitment bonus or a relocation bonus. Other programs they offer on a job-by-job basis include: incentive awards; employee development programs; student loan repayment programs; retention allowances; and interagency transfers. For more information on federal benefits, visit http://www.usajobs.opm.gov/.

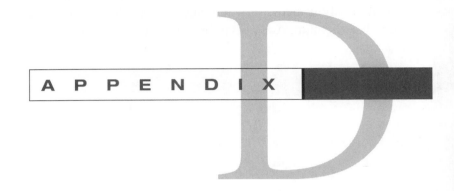

Information for Veterans

The federal government offers preference to veterans in their hiring practices. If you served on active duty in the U.S. military and were separated under honorable conditions, you may be eligible for veterans' preference. If your service began after October 15, 1976, you must have a Campaign Badge, Expeditionary Medal, or a service-connected disability.

Veterans' preference is not a factor for Senior Executive Service jobs or when competition is limited to status candidates (current or former federal career or career-conditional employees).

Some positions in the competitive service such as guard, messenger, elevator operator, and custodian, have been restricted by law to persons entitled to preference under the veteran preference laws. Generally, a nonveteran employee cannot be transferred to such positions if there are veterans available for appointment to them. This restriction does not apply to the filling of such positions by the transfer of a nonveteran already serving in a federal agency in a position covered by the same generic title. For example, a nonveteran who is serving in the position of guard may be considered for transfer to the position of patrolman, guard, fireman, guard-laborer, etc.

For more information on veterans' preference, call the United States Office of Personnel Management at (912) 757-3000 (select "Federal Employment Topics," then "Veterans"). Or, dial (912) 757-3100 for access to an electronic bulletin board.